BOYD'S BIBLE DICTIONARY

JAMES P. BOYD

Self-Pronouncing, Concise Definitions with Textual References and Curious Facts and Information about the Bible.

HOLMAN BIBLE PUBLISHERS
NASHVILLE

KEY TO PRONUNCIATION

The hyphen (-) separates unaccented syllables. The double hyphen (=) separates compound words. (') marks the primary accent and (") the secondary accent.

ā as in fāte; ă in courăge; ā̇ in hāt; â in câre; ä in fär; à in làst; a̟ in fa̟ll; a̱ obscure as in lia̱r.

ē as in mēte; ĕ in rĕdeem; ē̇ in mēt; ē̱ obtuse as in tĕrm; e̱ obscure as in fue̱l.

ī as in pīne; ĭ in cĭtation; ī̇ in pĭn; ī obtuse in fĭrm; i̟ in familia̟r; i̱ obscure in rui̱n.

ō as in nōte; ŏ in annŏtate; ō̇ in nŏt; ô in fôr: o̱ obscure as in valo̱r.

ū as in mūte; ū̇ in tŭb; û obtuse as in hûrl; u̟ in ru̟de; u̱ in pu̱sh.

ȳ as in stȳle; y̆ in nўmph.

ç soft as in çent; c hard not marked; ġ soft as in ġender; ḡ hard before e, i, and y, as ḡet, Ḡideon; g hard otherwise not marked; ş as z in muşe; x̱ as gs in ex̱ample.

Printed in U.S.A. ISBN–0–87981–020–3

THE SELF-PRONOUNCING BIBLE DICTIONARY.

A

Ā. See ALPHA.

Aâr′on (*mountaineer or enlightener*). Son of Amram and Jochebed, and elder brother of Moses and Miriam, Num. xxvi. 59. Direct descendant of Levi by both parents. Called "the Levite," Ex. iv. 14, when chosen as the "spokesman" of Moses. Married Elisheba, daughter of the prince of Judah, and had four sons, Nadab, Abihu, Eleazar, and Ithamar, Ex. vi. 23. Eighty-three years old when introduced in the Bible. Mouthpiece and encourager of Moses before the Lord and the people of Israel, and in the Court of the Pharaoh, Ex. iv. 30; vii. 2. Miracle worker of the Exodus, Ex. vii. 19. Helped Hur to stay the weary hands of Moses in the battle with Amalek, Ex. xvii. 9-12. In a weak moment yielded to idolatry among his people and incurred the wrath of Moses, Ex. xxxii. Consecrated to the priesthood by Moses, Ex. xxix. Anointed and sanctified, with his sons, to minister in the priest's office, Ex. xl. Murmured against Moses at the instance of Miriam, but repented and joined Moses in prayer for Miriam's recovery, Num. xii. His authority in Israel vindicated by the miracle of the rod, Num. xvii. Died on Mt. Hor, at age of one hundred and twenty-three years, and was succeeded in the priesthood by his son Eleazar, Num. xx. 22-29. Office continued in his line till time of Eli. Restored to house of Eleazar by Solomon, 1 Kgs. ii. 27.

Aâr′on-ītes. Priests of the line of Aaron, 1 Chr. xii. 27, of whom Jehoiada was "chief," or "leader," in the time of King Saul, 1 Chr. xxvii. 5.

Ăb (*father*). (1) A syllable of frequent occurrence in the composition of Hebrew proper names, and signifies possession or endowment. Appears in **Chaldaic** form of Abba in N. T., Mark xiv. 36; Rom. viii. 15; Gal. iv. 6. (2) Eleventh month of the Jewish civil, and fifth of the sacred, year; corresponding to parts of July and August. [MONTH.]

Ăb′ă-cŭc, 2 Esdr. i. 40. [HABAKKUK.]

Ā-băd′don (*destroyer*). King of the locusts, and angel of the bottomless pit. The Greek equivalent is Apollyon, Rev. ix. 11.

Ăb′′ă-dī′as, 1 Esdr. viii. 35. [OBADIAH.]

Ā-băg′thà (*God-given*). One of the seven chamberlains in the court of King Ahasuerus, Esth. i. 10.

Ăb′ă-nà (*stony*). A river of Damascus, preferred by Naaman to the Jordan for healing purposes, 2 Kgs. v. 12. Believed to be identical with the present Barada, which rises in the Anti-Libanus range, twenty-three miles N. W. of Damascus, runs by several streams through the city, and thence across a plain into the "Meadow Lakes," where it is comparatively lost.

Ăb′ă-rim (*mountains beyond*). A range of mountains or highlands of Moab, east of and facing Jordan opposite Jericho, Num. xxvii. 12; xxxiii. 47; Deut. xxxii. 49. Ije-abarim, in Num. xxi. 11, heaps or ruins of Abarim. Nebo, Peor, and Pisgah belong to this range. "Passages," in Jer. xxii. 20.

Ăb′bà (*father*). Chaldaic form of Hebrew Ab. Applied to God in Mark xiv. 36; Rom. viii. 15; Gal. iv. 6.

Ăb′dà (*servant*). (1) Father of Adoniram, 1 Kgs. iv. 6. (2) Son of Shammua, Neh. xi. 17. Called Obadiah in 1 Chr. ix. 16.

Ăb′de̲-el (*servant of God*). Father of Shelemiah, Jer. xxxvi. 26.

Ăb′dī (*my servant*). (1) A Merarite, grandfather of Ethan the Singer, and father of Kishi, 1 Chr. vi. 44. (2) Father of Kish, of Levitical descent, 2 Chr. xxix. 12. (3) Son of Elam, who had married a foreign wife, in time of Ezra, Ez. x. 26.

Ăb′dī-as, 2 Esdr. i. 39. [OBADIAH.]

Ăb′dī-ĕl (*servant of God*). Father of Ahi and son of Guni. A Gadite chief of Bashan in the time of King Jotham of Judah, 1 Chr. v. 15. Milton uses the name as that of a fallen angel.

Ăb′dŏn (*servile*). (1) An Ephraimite judge of Israel for eight years, Judg. xii. 13-15. Supposed to be same as Bedan in 1 Sam. xii. 11. (2) Son of Shashak, 1 Chr. viii. 23. (3) A Benjamite, son of Jehiel, of Gibeon, 1 Chr. viii. 30; ix. 36. (4) Son of Micah in Josiah's time, 2 Chr. xxxiv. 20; supposably Achbor in 2 Kgs. xxii. 12. (5) A city in tribe of Asher, assigned to the Levites, Josh. xxi. 30; 1 Chr. vi. 74; associated with modern Abdeh, 10 miles N. E. of Accho, or Acre, the Ptolemais of N. T.

Ā-bĕd′=nĕ-gō (*servant of Nego, or Nebo, name of planet Mercury worshipped as scribe and interpreter*). Name given by the prince of Chaldean eunuchs to Azariah, one of the three friends and fellow-captives at Babylon of Daniel, Dan. i. 7. He refused to bow to the golden image of Nebuchadnezzar, and was condemned to the fiery furnace, from which he miraculously escaped, Dan. iii.

Ā′bĕl (*breath, vapor*). Second son of Adam and Eve. A keeper of sheep, and murdered by his brother Cain through jealousy, Gen. iv. 2-8. *See* also Heb. xi. 4; 1 John iii. 12; Matt. xxiii. 35.

Ā′bĕl (*meadow*). A prefix for several names of towns and places. (1) The "plain of the vineyards" in Judg. xi. 33; *see* marg. (2) A city in the north of Palestine, attacked by Joab, 2 Sam. xx. 14, 15. Probably same as Abel-Beth-Maachah. "Plain of the vineyard," Judg. xi. 33, marg. note. "Great stone of," 1 Sam. vi. 18.

Ā′bĕl=bĕth=mā′a̭-chah (*meadow of house of oppression*). A town in N. Palestine, near Damascus, doubtless the same as attacked by Joab, 2 Sam. xx. 14, 15; and attacked by Benhadad, 1 Kgs. xv. 20, and by Tiglath-pileser, 2 Kgs. xv. 29.

Ā′bĕl=mā′im (*meadow of waters*). Another name for Abel-beth-maachah, 2 Chr. xvi. 4.

Ā′bĕl=mē-hō′lah (*meadow of the dance*). A place in the Jordan valley, 1 Kgs. iv. 12, whither fled the enemy routed by Gideon, Judg. vii. 22. Home of Elisha, 1 Kgs. xix. 16.

Ā′bĕl=mĭz′ră-im (*meadow, or mourning, of Egypt*). A name given by the Canaanites to the threshing floor of Atad, where Joseph and his brethren mourned for Jacob, Gen. l. 11. Probably near Hebron.

Ā′bĕl=shĭt′tim (*meadow of the acacias*). A spot

near Jordan, in Moabite plain, and last halting place of the wandering Israelites, Num. xxxiii. 49. Called Shittim in Num. xxv. 1 ; Josh. ii. 1.

Ā'bĕl, Stone of. Place in the field of Joshua, the Bethshemite, where the ark of the Lord was set down, 1 Sam. vi. 18.

Ā'bĕz (*lofty*). A town in the section allotted to the tribe of Issachar, Josh. xix. 20.

Ā'bī (*progenitor*). Mother of King Hezekiah and daughter of Zachariah, 2 Kgs. xviii. 2 ; Isa. viii. 2. Abijah in 2 Chr. xxix. 1.

Ă-bī'ā, Ă-bī'ah, and **Ă-bī'jah** (*the Lord is my father*), are variants of the same word. Abia in 1 Chr. iii. 10, and Matt. i. 7, is the son of Rehoboam ; and in Luke i. 5, is the eighth of the twenty-four courses of priests. For division of priests *see* 1 Chr. xxiv. and particularly vs. 10.

Ă-bī'ah. (1) A son of Becher, 1 Chr. vii. 8. (2) Wife of Hezron, 1 Chr. ii. 24. (3) Second son of Samuel and associate judge with Joel in Beersheba, 1 Sam. viii. 2 ; 1 Chr. vi. 28.

Ā''bī=ăl'bŏn (*father of strength*). One of David's warriors, 2 Sam. xxiii. 31. Spelled Abiel in other places.

Ă-bī'ă-săph (*father of gathering*). A Levite, one of the sons of Korah, and head of a Korhite family, Ex. vi. 24. Written Ebiasaph in 1 Chr. vi. 23, 37.

Ă-bī'a-thär (*father of abundance*). Son of Ahimelech, and fourth high priest in descent from Eli, of the line of Ithamar, younger son of Aaron, 1 Sam. xxiii. 9, only one of Ahimelech's sons who escaped the vengeance of Saul in the slaughter at Nob, 1 Sam. xxii. 19, 20. Fled to David at Keilah, and became a high priest. Deprived of the high priesthood by Solomon. For fuller history read 1 Sam. xxii. to 1 Kgs. iii.

Ā'bīb (*green fruits*), called also Nisan. Seventh month of Jewish civil, and first of the sacred year, Ex. xii. 2. [MONTH.]

Ă-bī'dä and **Ă-bī'dah** (*father of knowledge*). One of the sons of Midian, 1 Chr. i. 33 ; Gen. xxv. 4.

Ăb'i-dăn (*father of judgment*). Chief of the tribe of Benjamin at exode, Num. i. 11 ; ii. 22 ; vii. 60 ; x. 24.

Ă-bī'el (*father of strength*). (1) Father of Kish

and grandfather of Saul and Abner, 1 Sam. ix. 1. (2) One of David's generals, 1 Chr. xi. 32, called Abialbon in 2 Sam. xxiii. 31.

Ā''bĭ-ē'zer (*father of help*). (1) Eldest son of Gilead and head of a family in tribe of Manasseh, Josh. xvii. 2; 1 Chr. vii. 18. (2) One of David's mighty men, 2 Sam. xxiii. 27; 1 Chr. xi. 28; xxvii. 12.

Ā''bĭ-ĕz'rīte (*father of help*). A family descended from Abiezer, Judg. vi. 11; viii. 32.

Ăb'ĭ-gāil (*father of joy*). (1) Wife of Nabal of Carmel, and afterwards of David. Noted for her beauty and wisdom, 1 Sam. xxv. 3, 14-44. (2) A sister of David, married to Jether the Ishmaelite, and mother of Amasa, 2 Sam. xvii. 25; 1 Chr. ii. 17.

Ăb''i-hā'il (*father of strength*). (1) Father of Zuriel, chief of the house of the families of Marari, Num. iii. 35. (2) Wife of Abishur, 1 Chr. ii. 29. (3) Son of Huri of the tribe of Gad, 1 Chr. v. 14. (4) Wife of Rehoboam, 2 Chr. xi. 18. (5) Father of Esther and uncle of Mordecai, Esth. ii. 15; ix. 29.

Ă-bī'hū (*God is father*). Second son of Aaron and Elisheba, Num. iii. 2; Ex. vi. 23. Ascended Sinai with Moses and the elders, Ex. xxviii. 1. Set apart with his brothers for the priesthood. Consumed, with his brother Nadab, for offering strange fire before the Lord, Lev. x. 1, 2.

Ă-bī'hŭd (*father of praise*). Son of Bela and grandson of Benjamin, 1 Chr. viii. 3.

A-bī'jah and Ā-bī'jam (*whose father is Jehovah*). (1) A son of King Jeroboam I.; died in early life, 1 Kgs. xiv. (2) Son of Rehoboam, and his successor to the throne. A wicked king. Reign, 959-956 B. C., 2 Chr. xii. 16; xiii. Written Abijam in 1 Kgs. xv. 1. (3) A descendant of the high priest Eleazar, 1 Chr. xxiv. 10; Neh. xii. 17. The priestly course *Abia*, Luke i. 5, belonged to Zacharias, father of John the Baptist. (4) A priest who entered the covenant with Nehemiah, Neh. x. 7.

Ā-bī'jam. *See* ABIJAH (2).

Ăb-ĭ-le'nĕ (from Abila, *land of meadows*). A Syrian tetrarchy whose capital was Abila, situated on the eastern slopes of the Anti-Libanus range. The district was watered by the Abana River. Governed by Lysanias in the time of John the Baptist, Luke iii. 1.

Ă-bĭm′ă-el (*father of Mael*). A descendant of Joktan, and supposable father of the Arabic tribe of Mali, Gen. x. 28.

Ă-bĭm′ĕ-lech (*father of a king*). (1) A line of Philistine kings, like the Pharaohs and Cæsars. Kings of Gerar, Gen. xx., xxi., xxvi. 1. (2) Son of Gideon by his concubine of Shechem, Judg. viii. 31; 2 Sam. xi. 21. (3) Son of Abiathar, in David's time, 1 Chr. xviii. 16. (4) Written for the Achish of 1 Sam. xxi. 10, in title to Ps. 34.

Ă-bĭn′ă-dăb (*father of nobility*). (1) A Levite of Kirjath-jearim to whose house the ark was brought, and where it stayed for twenty years, 1 Sam. vii. 1, 2; 1 Chr. xiii. 7. (2) Second son of Jesse, and one of the three who followed Saul to battle, 1 Sam. xvi. 8; xvii. 13. (3) Son of Saul slain at Gilboa, 1 Sam. xxxi. 2. (4) Father of one of the twelve chief officers of Solomon, 1 Kgs. iv. 11.

Ăb′ĭ-nẽr, Hebrew form of Abner, 1 Sam. xiv. 50, marg.

Ă-bĭn′ŏ-ăm (*gracious father*). Father of Barak, Judg. iv. 6, 12; v. 1, 12.

Ă-bī′răm (*high father*). (1) A Reubenite conspirator with Korah, Num. xvi. (2) Eldest son of Hiel, 1 Kgs. xvi. 34; written Abiron in Ecclus. xlv. 18.

Ăb-ĭ-sē′i, or Ăb′ĭ-shū, son of Phinehas, 2 Esdr. i. 2. Abisum in 1 Esdr. viii. 2.

Ăb′ĭ-shag (*ignorance of the father*). The fair Shunamite, of tribe of Issachar, whom David, in his old age, introduced into his harem, 1 Kgs. i. 1–4. After David's death, Adonijah desired to marry her, but Solomon put him to death, 1 Kgs. ii. 13, etc.

Ă-bĭsh′ă-ī (*father of gift*). (1) Eldest son of David's sister Zeruiah and brother of Joab, 1 Chr. ii. 16; one of the chiefs of David's mighty men, 2 Sam. ii. 18. Counselled David to take Saul's life, 1 Sam. xxvi. 5–12. Associated with Joab in assassination of Abner, 2 Sam. iii. 30. A co-general of David's army, 2 Sam. x. 14; xviii. 2. Rescued David from the giant Ishbi-benob, 2 Sam. xxi. 16, 17.

Ă-bĭsh′a-lŏm (*father of peace*). Father-in-law of King Jeroboam, 1 Kgs. xv. 2, 10. Called Absalom in 2 Chr. xi. 20, 21.

Ă-bĭsh′ū-ă (*father of deliverance*). (1) Son of

Bela, 1 Chr. viii. 4. (2) Son of Phinehas, 1 Chr. vi. 4, 5, 50; Ez. vii. 5.

Ăb'ĭ-shur (*father of the wall*). Son of Shammai, 1 Chr. ii. 28, 29.

Ăb'ĭ-tal (*father of dew*). One of David's wives, 2 Sam. iii. 4; 1 Chr. iii. 3.

Ăb'ĭ-tŭb (*father of goodness*). A Benjamite, 1 Chr. viii. 11.

A-bi'ud (*father of praise*). An ancestor of Christ, Matt. i. 13.

Ăb-lū'tion. [PURIFICATION.]

Ăb'nĕr (*father of light*). (1) Son of Ner, and commander-in-chief of Saul's armies, 1 Sam. xiv. 50, 51; xvii. 57; xxvi. 5-14. Proclaimed Ishbosheth King of Israel, and went to war with David, by whom he was defeated, 2 Sam. ii. Quarrelled with Ishbosheth and espoused the cause of David, 2 Sam. iii. 7, etc. Murdered by Joab, 2 Sam. iii. 27-39. (2) Father of a Benjamite chief, 1 Chr. xxvii. 21.

Ȧ-bŏm-ĭ-nā'tion (*bad omen*). A hateful or detestable thing, Gen. xlvi. 34. Used as to animals and acts in Lev. xi. 13; Deut. xxiii. 18. As to idolatry in 2 Kgs. xxiii. 13; Jer. xliv. 4. As to sins in general, Isa. lxvi. 3. The "abomination of desolation" in Dan. ix. 27; xii. 11; Matt. xxiv. 15, doubtless refers to the standards and banners of the conquering Roman armies with their idolatrous images and legends.

Ā'brȧ-hăm and Ā'brăm (*father of a multitude*). Son of Terah, a dweller in Ur of the Chaldees, Gen. xi. 25-31. Founder of the Jewish nation. Migrated from Chaldea to Haran. Moved thence to Canaan, to Egypt and back to Canaan, where he settled amid the oak-groves of Mamre. There confirmed in the thrice repeated promise that his seed should become a mighty nation, and his name changed from Abram to Abraham. Died, aged 175 years, and was buried in the tomb of Machpelah, Gen. xii.-xxvi.

Ăb'sa-lŏm (*father of peace*). (1) A son of David, 2 Sam. iii. 3. Killed his brother Amnon, 2 Sam. xiii. Fled to Geshur, 2 Sam. xiii. 37, 38. Returned and conspired to usurp his father's throne, 2 Sam. xiv.-xvii. Defeated at Gilead and slain by Joab, 2 Sam. xviii. (2) Father of Mattathias, 1 Macc. xi. 70.

Ăb'sạ-lŏm's Pil'lar, built by Absalom in the "King's dale," or valley of Kedron, 2 Sam. xviii. 18.

Ăb'sạ-lŏn. An ambassador of John to Lysias, 2 Macc. xi. 17.

Ȧ-bū'bŭs. Son-in-law of Simon, 1 Macc. xvi. 11-15.

Ȧ-cā'çĭ-ȧ (point). The Acacia seyal of Arabia, a large tree, highly prized for its wood, is supposed to be the Shittim wood of the Bible. A smaller species (Acacia Arabica) yielded an aromatic gum.

Ăc'ȧ-tăn. 1 Esdr. viii. 38. [HAKKATAN.]

Ăc'căd (fortress). A city built by Nimrod in Shinar, Gen. x. 10.

Ăc'cạ-rŏn. [EKRON.]

Ăc'chō (heated sand). The Ptolemais of N. T.; now Acre, on Mediterranean coast, Judg. i. 31; Acts xxi. 7.

Ăc'cŏs. Grandfather of Eupolemus, 1 Macc. viii. 17.

Ȧ-çĕl'dạ-mȧ (field of blood). A field near Jerusalem purchased with Judas' betrayal money, and in which he violently died, Acts i. 19. But bought by the priests as a potters' field in Matt. xxvii. 7.

Ȧ-chā'ĭȧ (trouble). Originally a narrow strip of country on north coast of Peloponnesus, but Achaia and Macedonia came to designate all Greece, Acts xviii. 12, 27; xix. 21; Rom. xv. 26; 2 Cor. i. 1; ix. 2; xi. 10; 1 Thess. i. 7, 8.

Ȧ-chā'ĭ-cus (of Achaia). An Achaian friend of Paul, 1 Cor. xvi. 17.

Ā'chăn and Ā'char (troubler). The Judahite who was stoned to death for concealing the spoils of Jericho, Josh. vii. 16-26. Written ACHAR in 1 Chr. ii. 7.

Ā'chăz (one that takes). In Matt. i. 9 for AHAZ, King of Judah.

Ăch'bôr (mouse). (1) Father of Baal-hanan king of Edom, Gen. xxxvi. 38, 39. (2) A contemporary of Josiah, 2 Kgs. xxii. 12-14; Jer. xxvi. 22; xxxvi. 12. Written ABDON in 2 Chr. xxxiv. 20.

Ā''chĭ-ăch'ȧ-rŭs. Chief minister of Esarhaddon in Nineveh, Tobit i. 21.

Ā-chī'ăs. A progenitor of Esdras, 2 Esdr. i. 2.

Ā'chĭm. Son of Sadoc, in Christ's genealogy, Matt. i. 14.

Ā'chĭ-ôr. A general in army of Holofernes, Judith v., vii., xiii., xiv.

Ā'chĭsh (ā'kĭsh) (*serpent-charmer*). A Philistine king of Gath to whom David twice fled for safety, 1 Sam. xxi. 10–13; xxvii.–xxix.; 1 Kgs. ii. 39, 40. Called Abimelech in title to Ps. xxxiv.

Ăch'ĭ-tôb and Ăch'ĭ-tŭb. A priest in genealogy of Esdras, 1 Esdr. viii. 2.

Ăch'me-thá. The Median city of Ecbatana, Ez. vi. 2.

Ā'chôr, valley of. [ACHAN.]

Ăch'sá and Ăch'sah (*anklet*). Daughter of Caleb. Given in marriage to her uncle Othniel. Josh. xv. 15–18; Judg. i. 12–15. Achsa in 1 Chr. ii. 49.

Ăch'shăph (*fascination*). A city of Asher, Josh. xi. 1; xii. 20; xix. 25.

Ăch'zĭb (*false*). (1) A town of Judah, Josh. xv. 44. (2) A town of Asher, Josh. xix. 29.

Ăc'ĭ-phă. [HAKUPHA.] 1 Esdr. v. 31.

Ăc'ĭ-thō. A progenitor of Judith, Judith viii. 1.

Ă-crăb'bim. [MAALEH-ACRABBIM.] Josh. xv. 3.

Acts of the Apostles. Fifth Book of N. T. Supposably compiled by Luke, shortly after A. D. 63. It carries on the Christian narrative from the ascension of Christ to first imprisonment of Paul, a period of about thirty-three years.

Ā-cū'ă. [AKKUB.] 1 Esdr. v. 30.

Ā'cŭb. [BAKBUK.] 1 Esdr. v. 31.

Ăd'ă-dah (*boundary*). A town in southern Judah, Josh. xv. 22.

Ā'dah (*beauty*). (1) One of Lamech's wives, Gen. iv. 19. (2) One of Esau's wives, Gen. xxxvi. 2, 4. Called Bashemath in Gen. xxvi. 34.

Ăd''a-ī'ah (*adorned by Jehovah*). (1) Maternal grandfather of King Josiah, 2 Kgs. xxii. 1. (2) A Levite, 1 Chr. vi. 41; called Iddo in vs. 21. (3) A Benjamite, 1 Chr. viii. 21. (4) A son of Jehoram, 1 Chr. ix. 12; Neh. xi. 12. (5) Ancestor of Maaseiah, 2 Chr. xxiii. 1. (6) A descendant of Bani, Ez. x. 29, 39. (7) A Judahite, Neh. xi. 5.

Ăd″a̤-lī′ă (*fire-god*). Fifth son of Haman, Esth. ix. 8.

Ăd′ăm (*red earth*). A city of Reuben, on Jordan, Josh. iii. 16.

Ăd′ăm (*red earth*). Used generically for man and woman, and translated *man* in Gen. i. 26,27; v. 1; Job xx. 29; xxi. 33; Ps. lxviii. 18; lxxvi. 10.

Ăd′ăm (*red earth*). The first man. Creative work of the sixth day. Placed in the "Garden of Eden." Tempted to eat of the forbidden fruit, fell under God's disfavor, and driven out of the Garden subject to the curse of sorrow and toil. Died at age of 930 years. Gen. i. 26, etc.; ii.-v.

Ăd′a̤-mah (*earth*). A fenced city of Naphtali, Josh. xix. 36.

Ăd′a̤-mănt (*diamond*). The original is translated "adamant" in Ezek. iii. 9; Zech. vii. 12; and "diamond" in Jer. xvii. 1. Used metaphorically. [DIAMOND.]

Ăd′a̤-mī (*earth*). A place on the border of Naphtali, Josh. xix. 33.

Ā′där (*height*). A boundary town of Edom and Judah, Josh. xv. 3.

Ā′där. Sixth month of Jewish civil, and twelfth of sacred, year; corresponding to parts of February and March, Esth. iii. 7.

Ăd′a̤-să. A place in Judea, 1 Macc. vii. 40, 45.

Ăd′bĕ-ĕl (*breath of God*). A son of Ishmael, Gen. xxv. 13; 1 Chr. i. 29.

Ăd′dăn (*stony*). One of the places from which Jewish captives returned, Ez. ii. 59. Addon in Neh. vii. 61.

Ăd′där (*mighty*). Son of Bela, 1 Chron. viii. 3.

Ăd′dĕr (*viper*). Used in the Bible for any poisonous snake known to the Jews, of which there were several species in Palestine. In Gen. xlix. 17, the cerastes, or horned snake, is, from its habits, supposed to be alluded to. The cockatrice of Isa. xi. 8; xiv. 29; lix. 5; Jer. viii. 17, is adder and asp in Prov. xxiii. 32; Ps. lviii. 4. In Ps. cxl. 3 and Prov. xxiii. 32, a species of viper is thought to be meant.

Ăd′dī (*adorned*). Son of Cosam in Christ's genealogy, Luke iii. 28.

Ăd′dŏn. [ADDAN.]

Ăd′dŭs. (1) Son of the servant of Solomon, 1 Esdr. v. 34. (2) A priest in time of Ezra, 1 Esdr. v. 38.

Ā′der (*flock*). A Benjamite, 1 Chr. viii. 15. Properly EDER.

Ăd′ĭ-dá. A town of lower Judah, 1 Macc. xii. 38.

Ă-dī′el (*ornament of God*). (1) A prince of Simeon, 1 Chr. iv. 36. (2) A priest, 1 Chr. ix. 12. (3) An ancestor of David's treasurer, Azmaveth, 1 Chr. xxvii. 25.

Ā-dĭn (*dainty*). Head of a returned family, Ez. ii. 15; viii. 6; Neh. vii. 20; x. 16.

Ăd′ĭ-ná (*slender*). One of David's captains, 1 Chr. xi. 42.

Ăd′ĭ-nō. One of David's mighty men, 2 Sam. xxiii. 8. [JASHOBEAM.]

Ăd′ĭ-nŭs, 1 Esdr. ix. 48. [JAMIN.]

Ăd″ĭ-thā′im (*double ornament*). A town of Judah, Josh. xv. 36.

Ăd-jūre′. To bind under a curse, Josh. vi. 26; 1 Sam. xiv. 24. To require a declaration of truth at the peril of God's displeasure, Matt. xxvi. 63.

Ăd′la-ī (*Jehovah's justice*). Ancestor of Shaphat, 1 Chr. xxvii. 29.

Ăd′mah (*fort*). One of the cities of the plain of Siddim, Gen. x. 19; xiv. 2. Destroyed with Sodom, Deut. xxix. 23; Hos. xi. 8.

Ăd′mă-thă (*earthy*). One of the seven Persian princes, in Esth. i. 14.

Ăd′ná (*pleasure*). (1) Father of a returned family, Ez. x. 30. (2) A priest in days of Joiakim, Neh. xii. 15.

Ăd′nah (*pleasure*). (1) One of Saul's captains who deserted to David, 1 Chr. xii. 20. (2) A captain in Jehoshaphat's army, 2 Chr. xvii. 14.

Ăd″ō-nā′ī (*Lord*). The Hebrews spoke this word where the word Jehovah occurred.

Ā-dŏn′ī=bē′zek (*lord of Bezek*). King of Bezek, vanquished by Judah, Judg. i. 3–7.

Ăd″ŏ-nī′jah (*the Lord is Jehovah*). (1) Fourth son of David, by Haggith, and rival of Solomon for the throne. Afterwards put to death by Solomon, 2

Sam. iii. 4; 1 Kgs. i., ii. (2) A Levite, 2 Chr. xvii. 8. (3) Same as Adonikam, Neh. x. 16.

Ă-dŏn'ī-kăm (*the Lord is raised*). He returned from captivity with Zerubbabel, Ezr. ii. 13; Neh. vii. 18; 1 Esdr. v. 14. Called Adonijah in Neh. x. 16.

Ăd''ŏ-nī'ram (*lord of heights*). Chief receiver of tribute under David, Solomon, and Rehoboam, 1 Kgs. iv. 6. Written Adoram in 2 Sam. xx. 24; 1 Kgs. xii. 18; and Hadoram in 2 Chr. x. 18.

Ă-dŏn'ī=zē'dec (*lord of justice*). The Amorite king of Jerusalem who formed a league against Joshua, and was slain, Josh. x. 1–27.

Ă-dŏp'tion (*a choosing to*). Receiving a stranger into one's family as an own child thereof, Ex. ii. 10; Esth. ii. 7. Figuratively, reception into the family of God, Rom. viii. 15–17; Gal. iv. 5; Eph. i. 5.

Ă-dō'rȧ, or **Ā'dŏr**, 1 Macc. xiii. 20. [ADORAIM.]

Ăd''ŏ-rā'ĭm (*double mound*). A city of Judah, 2 Chr. xi. 9.

Ă-dō'răm. [ADONIRAM and HADORAM.]

Ăd''ŏ-rā'tion (*address*). The act of paying homage to God; as in bending the knee, raising hands, inclining head, prostrating the body, etc., Gen. xvii. 3; Ps. xcv. 6; Matt. xxviii. 9.

Ă-drăm'mė-lech (*fire king*). (1) An idol introduced into Samaria and worshipped with the cruel rites of Molech, 2 Kgs. xvii. 31. (2) Son and murderer of Sennacherib, king of Assyria, 2 Kgs. xix. 37; 2 Chr. xxxii. 21; Isa. xxxvii. 38.

Ăd''ra-mȳt'tĭ-ûm (*from Adramys, brother of Crœsus*). A seaport town of Mysia in Asia, Acts xvi. 7; xxvii. 2. Now Adramyti.

Ā'drĭ-ȧ. The Adriatic Sea, Acts xxvii. 27.

Ā'drĭ-el (*flock of God*). Son-in-law of Saul, 1 Sam. xviii. 19; 2 Sam. xxi. 8.

Ă-dū'el. An ancestor of Tobit, Tob. i. 1.

Ă-dŭl'lăm (*justice of the people*). (1) A city of Canaan allotted to Judah, Gen. xxxviii. 1; Josh. xii. 15; xv. 35; 2 Chr. xi. 7. Repeopled after the captivity, Neh. xi. 30; Mich. i. 15. (2) The cave Adullam was David's hiding-place, where his friends gathered, 1 Sam. xxii. 1; 2 Sam. xxiii. 13; 1 Chr. xi. 15.

Ă-dŭl'lăm-īte. A native of Adullam.

Ă-dŭl'tẽr-y (*ad*=to and *alter*, other). Under Hebrew law the crime of unchastity, wherein a man, married or single, had illicit intercourse with a married or betrothed woman, not his wife. Punished with fire, Gen. xxxviii. 24; by stoning, Deut. xxii. 22–24. In a spiritual sense, apostasy.

Ă-dŭm'mĭm (*a going up*). A steep pass on the road from Jericho to Jerusalem, Josh. xv. 7; xviii. 17; Luke x. 30–37.

Ăd'vō-cāte (*calling to*). In N. T., helper, intercessor, or comforter. Jews did not have advocates, or attorneys, till after the Roman conquest, John xiv. 16; xv. 26; xvi. 17; Acts xxiv. 1.

Æ-dī'as, Probably Eliah, 1 Esdr. ix. 27.

Æ'ne̳-ăs, or Æ-nē'ăs (*laudable*). The paralytic at Lydda, healed by Peter, Acts ix. 33, 34.

Æ'nŏn (*springs*). A place, west of Jordan, where John baptized, John iii. 23.

Ăf-fĭn'ĭ-ty. Relation by marriage and not by blood or birth, 1 Kgs. iii. 1. For preventive degrees *see* Lev. xviii. 6–17, and MARRIAGE.

Ăg'ă-bă, 1 Esdr. v. 30. [HAGAB.]

Ăg'ă-bŭs (*locust*). A prophet of Antioch, Acts xi. 28; xxi. 10.

Ā'găg (*flame*). General title of the kings of Amelek, Ex. xvii. 14; Num. xxiv. 7; Deut. xxv. 17; 1 Sam. xv. 8–32.

Ā-găg'īte. Subject of Agag, Esth. iii. 1–10.

Ā-găr. [HAGAR, HAGARENES, HAGARITES.]

Ăg'ȧte (from *river Achates*). A species of precious quartz. Second stone in third row of high-priest's breastplate, Ex. xxviii. 19; xxxix. 12; Isa. liv. 12; Ezek. xxvii. 16. Original sometimes translated amethyst.

Ăḡ'ĕ-ē (*fugitive*). Father of one of David's mighty men, 2 Sam. xxiii. 11.

Ăḡ'rĭ-cul''ture (*field culture*). Patriarchal life was pastoral. After the conquest of Canaan, lands were meted and bounded, and landmarks held sacred, Deut. xix. 14. The valley soils of Palestine were fertile; natural waters abundant, Deut. viii. 7; rain plentiful, Deut. xi. 14; Jer. v. 24; James v. 7. The grains grown were wheat, barley, rye, and millet. Orchards produced the vine, olive, and fig.

Gardens grew beans, fitches, pease, lettuce, endive, leeks, garlic, onions, melons, cucumbers, cabbage, etc. The implements were the plough, harrow, and hoe, but these were crude. Grains were cut with the sickle, and the sheaves were threshed by treading with oxen, usually drawing sleds; while winnowing was done in sheets before the wind. Lands rested once in seven years, Lev. xxv. 1-7. The poor were allowed to glean, Lev. xix. 9, 10; Deut. xxiv. 19.

Ă-grĭp′pà. [HEROD.]

Ā′gûr (*gatherer of wisdom*). An unknown sage who compiled Prov. xxx.

Ā′hăb (*uncle*). (1) Seventh king of Israel. Reigned B. C. 919-896, 1 Kgs. xvi. 29. Married Jezebel of Tyre, who introduced the worship of Baal and Astarte. One of the most notorious of O. T. characters. Slain by a chance arrow, and the "dogs licked his blood" according to prophecy, 1 Kgs. xviii.-xxii.; 2 Chr. xviii. (2) A false prophet at Babylon, Jer. xxix. 22.

Ă-hăr′ah (*after the brother*). Third son of Benjamin, 1 Chr. viii. 1. [AHER and AHIRAM.]

Ă-här′hĕl (*behind the fort*). A name in the genealogy of Judah, 1 Chr. iv. 8.

Ă-hăs′ă-ī (*whom Jehovah upholds*). A priest, Neh. xi. 13. Called Jahzerah in 1 Chr. ix. 12.

Ă-hăs′ba-ī (*trusting*). Father of one of David's thirty-seven captains, 2 Sam. xxiii. 34.

Ă-hăs″ū-ē′rus (*prince*). (1) King of Media, supposably Cyaxares, whose son Astyages was Darius, Dan. ix. 1. (2) A Persian king, supposed to be Cambyses, Ez. iv. 6. (3) Another Persian king, probably Xerxes. History in Esther.

Ă-hā′vå (*water*). The place on the Euphrates whence the captives started, on their second return, Ez. viii. 15-21.

Ā′hăz (*who takes*). (1) Son of Jotham, whom he succeeded, and eleventh king of Israel. Reign 742-726 B. C. Weak-minded and idolatrous, 2 Kgs. xvi.; 2 Chr. xxviii. Literally sold out his kingdom. Died dishonored, 2 Kgs. xxiii. 12; 2 Chr. xxviii. 16-27. (2) A son of Micah, 1 Chr. viii. 35, 36; ix. 42.

Ā″ha-zī′ah (*Jehovah sustains*). Son of Ahab, and his successor on the throne of Israel, as the eighth king. Reign 896-895 B. C. A weak and foolish idolater, 1 Kgs. xxii. 49-53. (2) Fifth king of Judah. Reign, B. C. 884, 2 Kgs. viii. 25-29. Killed in the rebellion of Jehu, 2 Kgs. ix. Called Azariah in 2 Chr. xxii. 6; and Jehoahaz in 2 Chr. xxi. 17.

Ah'băn (*discreet*). Son of Abishur, 1 Chr. ii. 29.

Ā'hĕr (*follower*). A title in genealogy of Benjamin, 1 Chr. vii. 12.

Ā'hī (*my brother*). (1) A Gadite chief, 1 Chr. v. 15. (2) An Asherite, 1 Chr. vii. 34.

Ā-hī'ah and **Ā-hī'jah** (*Jehovah's friend*). (1) A priest in Shiloh, 1 Sam. xiv. 3-18. (2) One of Solomon's princes, 1 Kgs. iv. 3. (3) A prophet of Shiloh, 1 Kgs. xiv. 2. His prophecies are in 1 Kgs. xi. 30-39 and 1 Kgs. xiv. 6-16. (4) Father of Baasha, 1 Kgs. xv. 27-34. (5) Name of several other Bible characters, 1 Chr. ii. 25; viii. 7; xi. 36; xxvi. 20; Neh. x. 26.

Ā-hī'am (*uncle*). One of David's thirty captains, 2 Sam. xxiii. 33; 1 Chr. xi. 35.

Ā-hī'an (*brotherly*). A Manassite, 1 Chr. vii. 19.

Ā''hĭ-ē'zĕr (*brother of help*). (1) A chieftain of Dan, Num. i. 12. (2) A chief of archers under David, 1 Chr. xii. 3.

Ā-hī'hud (*renown*). (1) A prince of Asher, Num. xxxiv. 27. (2) A chieftain of Benjamin, 1 Chr. viii. 7.

Ā-hī'jah. [AHIAH.]

Ā-hī'kam (*brother who raises*). An important court officer in reigns of Josiah and Jehoiakim, 2 Kgs. xxii. 12-14; Jer. xxvi. 24.

Ā-hī'lud (*brother born*). (1) Father of Jehoshaphat, the recorder of David's and Solomon's reigns, 2 Sam. viii. 16. (2) Father of Baana, 1 Kgs. iv. 12.

Ā-hĭm'a-ăz (*brother of wrath*). (1) Father-in-law of Saul, 1 Sam. xiv. 50. (2) Son of Zadok the high priest. Played a conspicuous part in the rebellion of Absalom, 2 Sam. xv. 24-37; xvii. 15-22; xviii. 19-33. (3) Solomon's son-in-law, 1 Kgs. iv. 15.

Ā-hī'măn (*brother of the right hand*). (1) One of the giant Anakim of Hebron, Num. xiii. 22, 23;

Josh. xi. 21 ; Judg. i. 10. (2) A gate-keeper of Levi, 1 Chr. ix. 17.

Ă-hĭm′e-lech (*my brother is king*). (1) High priest at Nob, 1 Sam. xxi. 1. Priests of Nob slain by order of Saul, 1 Sam. xxii. 11–20. (2) A Hittite friend of David, 1 Sam. xxvi. 6.

Ă-hī′mŏth (*brother of death*). A Levite, 1 Chr. vi. 25. Mahath in vs. 35, and Maath in Luke iii. 26.

Ă′hĭn-a-dăb (*noble brother*). Royal purveyor to Solomon, 1 Kgs. iv. 14.

Ă-hĭn′ŏ-am (*gracious*). (1) Wife of Saul, 1 Sam. xiv. 50. (2) A wife of David, 1 Sam. xxv. 43 ; xxvii. 3 ; xxx. 5, 18.

Ă-hī′ŏ (*brotherly*). (1) He accompanied the Ark when taken from his father's house, 2 Sam. vi. 3, 4. (2) A Benjamite, 1 Chr. viii. 14. (3) Son of Jehiel, 1 Chr. viii. 31 ; ix. 37.

Ă-hī′rå (*unlucky*). A chief of Naphtali, Num. i. 15.

Ă-hī′ram (*lofty*). Founder of the Ahiramites, Num. xxvi. 38.

Ă-hĭs′a-mach (*helper*). One of the Tabernacle architects, Ex. xxxi. 6 ; xxxv. 34 ; xxxviii. 23.

Ă-hĭsh′a-här (*brother of dawn*). A grandson of Benjamin, 1 Chr. vii. 10.

Ă-hī′shär (*singer's brother*). A controller of Solomon's household, 1 Kgs. iv. 6.

Ă-hĭth′o-phel (*brother of folly*). A privy councillor of David, 2 Sam. xv. 12 ; xvi. 23 ; xxiii. 34. Joined Absalom's conspiracy, 2 Sam. xvii. Hanged himself in despair, 2 Sam. xvii. 23.

Ă-hī′tub (*brother of goodness*). (1) Grandson of Eli, 1 Sam. xiv. 3 ; xxii. 9–11. (2) Father of Zadok the high priest, 1 Chr. vi. 7, 8, 11, 12 ; 2 Sam. viii. 17.

Ah′lăb (*fertile*). A city of Canaan, Judg. i. 31.

Ah′lāi (*ornamental*). Daughter of Sheshan, and wife of his slave, Jarha, 1 Chr. ii. 31–35.

Ă-hō′ah (*brotherly*). Grandson of Benjamin, 1 Chr. viii. 4. Called Ahiah in 1 Chr. viii. 7.

Ă-hō′hīte. From Ahoah, a patronymic of some of David's mighty men, 2 Sam. xxiii. 9, 28 ; 1 Chr. xi. 12 ; xxvii. 4.

Ă-hō'lah (*her tent*). The harlot used by Ezekiel to type Samaria, Ezek. xxiii. 4, 5, 36, 44.

Ă-hō'lĭ-ab (*tent of the father*). One of the Tabernacle architects, Ex. xxxv. 31-35.

Ă-hŏl'ĭ-bah (*my tent*). The harlot used by Ezekiel to type Jerusalem, Ezek. xxiii. 4, 11, 22, 36, 44.

Ă''hō-lĭb'a-mah (*tent of the height*). (1) Wife of Esau, Gen. xxxvi. 2, 25. Called Judith in Gen. xxvi. 34. (2) A title or district in Arabia Petrea, Gen. xxxvi. 41 ; 1 Chr. i. 52.

Ă-hū'mă-ī (*cowardly*). A descendant of Judah, 1 Chr. iv. 2.

Ă-hū'zam or **Ă-hŭz'zam** (*possession*). A son of Asher, 1 Chr. iv. 6.

Ă-hŭz'zath (*possessions*). A friend of King Abimelech, Gen. xxvi. 26.

Ā'ī (*heap of ruins*). (1) An ancient city of Canaan, Gen. xii. 8, where it is spelled HA'I. Captured and destroyed by Joshua, Josh. vii. 3-5 ; ix. 3 ; x. 1 ; xii. 9. Written Aiath in Isa. x. 28 ; and Aija in Neh. xi. 31 ; Ez. ii. 28. (2) A city of Heshbon, Jer. xlix. 3.

Ă-ī'ah (*vulture*). (1) Father of Saul's concubine, 2 Sam. iii. 7 ; xxi. 8-11. (2) Father of one of Esau's wives, 1 Chr. i. 40. Written Ajah in Gen. xxxvi. 24.

Ă-ī'ath. [AI.]

Ă-ī'jȧ. [AI.]

Ăij'a-lŏn. [AJALON.]

Ăij'e-lĕth Shā'här (*hind of the dawn*). In title to Ps. xxii. May mean a musical instrument, the argument of the Psalm, the melody, or tune name.

Ā'in (*eye*). (1) A landmark on eastern boundary of Canaan, Num. xxxiv. 11. (2) A Levitical city in south Judah and then in Simeon, Josh. xv. 32 ; xix. 7 ; xxi. 16. Ashan in 1 Chr. vi. 59.

Ă-ī'rus. A temple servant, 1 Esdr. v. 31.

Ā'jah. [AIAH.]

Ăj'a-lŏn (*place of gazelles*). (1) A Levitical city of Dan, Josh. xix. 42. Became a city of refuge, Josh. xxi. 24, where it is written Aijalon ; also in 1 Sam. xiv. 31. Prominent in Philistine wars, 2 Chr. xxviii. 18. Fortified as Aijalon by Rehoboam, 2 Chr. xi. 10. Now

Yalo, 14 miles west of Jerusalem. (2) **The valley in** which Joshua commanded the moon to stand still, Josh. x. 12. (3) Burial place of the Judge, Elon, Judg. xii. 12.

Ā′kan (*keen of vision*). A Horite chieftain, **Gen.** xxxvi. 27. Jakan in 1 Chr. i. 42.

Ā-kĕl′da-mā. Spelling of Aceldama in Revised Version, Acts i. 19.

Ăk′kŭb (*insidious*). (1) A descendant of Zerubbabel, 1 Chr. iii. 24. (2) A gate-keeper of the temple, 1 Chr. ix. 17. (3) A Levite who assisted Ezra, Neh. viii. 7.

Ā-krăb′bim (*scorpion*). A range forming a south boundary of Judah, Num. xxxiv. 4. Maalehacrabbim in Josh. xv. 3. An Amorite boundary in Judg. i. 36.

Ăl′a-băs′′tẽr (*white stone*). A whitish mineral susceptible of easy carving and fine polish, much used by ancients for vases, ointment boxes, sculptures, etc., Matt. xxvi. 7 ; Mark xiv. 3 ; Luke vii. 37.

Ā-lăm′ĕ-lech (*king's oak*). A border place of Asher, Josh. xix. 26.

Ăl′a-mĕth (*covering*). A grandson of Benjamin, 1 Chr. vii. 8.

Ăl′a-mŏth. Perhaps a musical instrument or melody, 1 Chr. xv. 20 ; Ps. xlvi. title.

Ăl′çĭ-mŭs (*valiant*). A high priest, 1 Macc. vii. 9–25.

Ăl′e-mā. A city of Gilead, 1 Macc. v. 26.

Ăl′e-mĕth (*covering*). (1) A city of the priests in Benjamin, 1 Chr. vi. 60. Written Almon in Josh. xxi. 18. (2) A descendant of Jonathan, 1 Chr. viii. 36 ; ix. 42.

Ăl′′ĕx-ăn′dẽr (*defender of men*). (1) King of Macedon ; surnamed "The Great." Born B. C. 356. Succeeded his father Philip, B. c. 336. Subjugated Asia Minor, Syria, and Palestine. Overthrew the Persian Empire, B. c. 333. Conquered Egypt, B. c. 332. Founded Alexandria, B. c. 332. Consolidated his Persian conquests, with Babylon as capital, B. c. 324. Died, perhaps in Babylon, B. c. 323. Prefigured in Dan. ii. 39; vii. 6; viii. 5–7 ; xi. 3. (2) **Alex-** ander Balas, son of Antiochus IV. Usurped Syrian throne, B. c. 152. His coins are still preserved.

1 Macc. x., xi. (3) Son of Simon, Mark xv. 21. (4) A kinsman of Annas the high priest, Acts iv. 6. (5) A Jewish convert at Ephesus, Acts xix. 33. (6) An Ephesian Christian reprobated by Paul, 1 Tim. i. 20, and perhaps the coppersmith in 2 Tim. iv. 14.

Ăl″ĕx-ăn′drĭ-à (*from Alexander*). The Grecian, Roman, and Christian capital of Egypt. Founded by Alexander the Great, B. C. 332. Situated on the Mediterranean Sea, 12 miles W. of Canopic mouth of the Nile. Noted for its libraries, architecture, and commerce. Conspicuous in early church history as a Christian centre, Acts xviii. 24; xxvii. 6; xxviii. 11.

Ăl″ĕx-ăn′drĭ-anṣ. Inhabitants of Alexandria; but in Acts vi. 9, Jewish colonists from Alexandria, admitted to the privilege of citizenship and worship at Jerusalem.

Ăl′gŭm or **Ăl′mŭg.** Former in 2 Chr. ii. 8; ix. 10, 11; latter in 1 Kgs. x. 11, 12. Supposed to be the red sandal-wood of India. Used in temple furniture.

Ă-lī′ah. [ALVAH.]

Ă-lī′an. [ALVAN.]

Ăl′lĕ-gō″ry (*other speech*). That figure of speech by which a subject is set forth under the guise of some other subject, Gal. iv. 24.

Ăl″le-lū′ĭà (*Praise ye Jehovah*). Written thus in Rev. xix. 1; but HALLELUJAH, in margin of Ps. cvi., cxi., cxii., cxiii., cxvii., cxviii., cxxxv., etc. A common exclamation of joy and praise in Jewish worship.

Ăl-lī′ance (*ans*) (*binding to*). Hebrews forbidden to make alliances with surrounding nations but finally driven to them. Alliances solemnized by presents, oaths, feasts, monuments, offerings, and other pious ceremonies, Gen. xv. 10; xxvi. 30; xxxi. 51–53; Josh. ix. 15; 1 Kgs. xv. 18; v. 2–12; ix. 27. Breach of covenant severely punished, 2 Sam. xxi. 1; Ezek. xvii. 16.

Ăl′lŏm, 1 Esdr. v. 34. [AMI and AMON.]

Ăl′lŏn (*oak*). (1) Ancestor of Ziza, 1 Chr. iv. 37. (2) A boundary place of Naphtali, Josh. xix. 33.

Ăl′lŏn=băch′uth (*oak of weeping*). The tree under which Deborah was buried, Gen. xxxv. 8.

Ăl-mō′dăd (*immeasurable*). Progenitor of an Arab tribe, Gen. x. 26; 1 Chr. i. 20.

Ăl'mŏn, Josh. xxi. 18. [ALEMETH.]

Ălm'ond (*hasten*). Tree resembles the peach in form, height, blossom, and fruit. Covering of fruit downy and succulent. Chiefly valuable for its nut. Gen. xliii. 11; Ex. xxv. 33, 34; xxxvii. 19, 20; Num. xvii. 8; Eccles. xii. 5; Jer. i. 11.

Ăl'mŏn=dĭb''la-thā'ĭm (*hiding of two fig cakes*). One of the last stopping places of the wandering Israelites, Num. xxxiii. 46.

Ălms (*pity*). Almsgiving enjoined by Mosaic law, Lev. xix. 9; Ruth ii. 2. Every third year the tithes of increase were shared with the Levite, the stranger, the fatherless and widow, Deut. xiv. 28. Receptacles for taking of alms placed in the Temple, Mark xii. 41. Almsgiving exhorted, Acts xi. 30; Rom. xv. 25-27; 1 Cor. xvi. 1-4.

Ăl'mŭg. [ALGUM.]

Ăl'oes (*ōz*). Written "Lign (*wood*) Aloes" in Num. xxiv. 6. A costly and sweet smelling wood of India, much prized in the East. Ps. xlv. 8; Prov. vii. 17; S. of Sol. iv. 14; John xix. 39.

Ā'lŏth. Solomon's ninth commissary district, 1 Kgs. iv. 16.

Ăl'phȧ. First letter of the Greek alphabet. Used with omega, the last letter, to express beginning and end, Isa. xli. 4; xliv. 6; Rev. i. 8, 11; xxi. 6; xxii. 13.

Ăl'pha-bĕt. *Alpha* and *beta*, first and second letters of Greek alphabet. Hebrew alphabet comprised twenty-two letters.

Ăl-phæ'us (*changing*). (1) Father of the apostle James the Less, Matt. x. 3; Mark iii. 18; Luke vi. 15; Acts i. 13. Called Clopas or Cleophas, in John xix. 25. (2) Father of Levi or Matthew, Mark ii. 14.

Ăl''-ta-nē'us, 1 Esdr. ix. 33. [MATTENAI.]

Ăl'tar (*high*). First altars were simple memorial piles, Gen. viii. 20; xii. 7; xxvi. 25; xxxv. 1. Afterwards to lay sacrifices upon, Ex. xvii. 15, 16, xxvii. 1-8. Usually built of earth or stone, Ex. xx. 24-26; but sacrificial altars quite elaborate, Ex. xl. 26-33. Still more elaborate in Solomon's Temple, 1 Kgs. viii. 64; 2 Chr. vii. 7. Altar fires to burn perpetually, Lev. vi. 12, 13. *Altar of Incense*, called "golden" to distinguish it from *Altar of Sacrifice*, called "brazen," Ex. xxx. 1-10; xl. 5, 1 Kgs. vii. 48; 1 Chr. xxviii. 18.

Ăl-tăs'chith (*destroy not*). In title to Ps. lvii., lviii., lix., and lxxv. Probably the tune is meant.

Ā'lush (*crowd*). Last halting-place of Israelite before Rephidim, Num. xxxiii. 13, 14.

Ăl'vah (*wickedness*). A duke of Edom, Gen. xxxvi. 40. Called Aliah in 1 Chr. i. 51.

Ăl'văn (*tall*). A Horite, Gen. xxxvi. 23. Alian in 1 Chr. i. 40.

Ā'măd (*enduring*). An unknown place in Asher, Josh. xix. 26.

Ā-măd'a-thă, Esth. xvi. 10, and Amadathus, Esth. xii. 7; Apoch. [HAMMEDATHA.]

Ā'măl (*labor*). An Asherite, 1 Chr. vii. 35.

Ăm'a-lĕk (*valley dweller*). An Edomite chieftain, Gen. xxxvi. 12; 1 Chr. i. 36.

Ăm'a-lĕk-ītes''. A nomad tribe of the Sinai wilderness, Gen. xiv. 7. Called the first of all nations in Num. xxiv. 20. Dwelt to the South, Num. xiii. 29. Smitten by Gideon, Judg. vii. 12–23; by Saul, 1 Sam. xv. 3–9; and David, 1 Sam. xxx. 18; 1 Chr. iv. 43. " Mount of Amalekites " was in Ephraim, Judg. xii. 15.

Ā'măm (*gathering place*). A city in south Judah, Josh. xv. 26.

Ā'măn (*mother*), Esther x. 7; Apoch. [HAMAN.]

Ăm'a-nă (*covenant*). Probably a mount of Anti-Libanus range, S. of Sol. iv. 8.

Ăm''a-rī'ah (*the Lord says*). (1) Father of Ahitub, 1 Chr. vi. 7. (2) A high priest, 2 Chr. xix. 11. (3) Head of a Kohathite family, 1 Chron. xxiii. 19; xxiv. 23. (4) Head of one of the twenty-four courses of priests, 2 Chr. xxxi. 15; Neh. x. 3. (5) A priest in Ezra's time, Ez. x. 42. (6) A priest who returned with Zerubbabel, Neh. x. 3; xii. 2, 13. (1) An ancestor of Zephaniah the prophet, Zeph. i. 1.

Ăm'-a-să (*burden*). (1) Nephew of David, 2 Sam. xvii. 25. Rebelled with Absalom, and defeated by Joab, 2 Sam. xviii. 6. Reconciled to David, 2 Sam. xix. 13, and killed by Joab, 2 Sam. xx. 10. (2) A prince of Ephraim, 2 Chr. xxviii. 12.

Ā-măs'a-ī (*burdensome*). (1) A Levite, 1 Chr. vi. 25, 35. (2) A chief of captains who deserted to David, 1 Chr. xii. 18. (3) A priest who blew the

trumpet before the Ark, 1 Chr. xv. 24. (4) A **Ko-**
hathite, 2 Chr. xxix. 12.

Ă-măsh′ạ-ī (*burdensome*). A priest, Neh. xi. 13.

Ăm-a-sī′ äh (*whom Jehovah bears*). Captain of
200,000 men in Judah, 2 Chr. xvii. 16.

Ăm″ạ-the̅′ĭs, 1 Esdr. ix. 29. [ATHLAI.]

Ăm′ạ-this. A country north of Palestine, 1
Macc. xii. 25.

Ăm″a-zī′ah (*strength of Jehovah*). (1) Eighth
king of Judah. Reign B. C. 837–809, 2 Kgs. xiv. 1–
20. Rebuked by God for idolatry, 2 Chr. xxv. 1–16.
Defeated by Joash and murdered at Lachish, 2 Chr.
xxv. 17–28. (2) A descendant of Simeon, 1 Chr. iv.
34. (3) A Levite, 1 Chr. vi. 45. (4) An idolatrous
priest of Bethel, Amos vii. 10–17.

Ăm-băs′sạ-dŏr (*servant*). A person chosen by
one government to represent it at the seat of another.
Earliest mention in Num. xx. 14 ; Josh. ix. 4 ; Judg.
xi. 17–19. Injury to them an insult to their king, 2
Sam. x. 3–6. The term includes both messenger and
message, Luke xiv. 32. Ministers called ambassadors
of Christ, 2 Cor. v. 20.

Ăm′bĕr. Hardly the fossil vegetable gum of commerce, Ezek. i. 4, 27 ; viii. 2 ; but rather the yellow
composition of gold and silver known as *electrum*.

Ā-mĕn′ (*true*). A final word used to fix the stamp
of truth upon an assertion, Num. v. 22 ; Deut. xxvii.
15 ; Matt. vi. 13 ; 1 Cor. xiv. 16. Promises of God are
amen, 2 Cor. i. 20. A title of Christ, Rev. iii. 14.

Ăm′ė-thyst (*not wine*). A purplish quartz, rank-
ing among the precious stones, and forming the third
stone in the third row of the high priest's breastplate, Ex. xxviii. 19 ; xxxix. 12. A stone in the foun-
dations of the New Jerusalem, Rev. xxi. 20.

Ā′mī (*builder*). A returned captive, Ez. ii. 57.
Amon in Neh. vii. 59.

Ă-mĭn′ạ-dab, Matt. i. 4 ; Luke iii. 33 ; for AM-
MINADAB.

Ă-mĭt′tạ-ī (*true*). The father of Jonah, 2 Kgs.
xiv. 25 ; Jon. i. 1.

Ăm′mah (*head*). A hill near Gibeon to which
Joab pursued Abner, 2 Sam. ii. 24.

Ăm′mī (*my people*). Applied figuratively to the
Israelites, Hos. ii. i. marg.

Ăm-mĭd'ĭ-oi. A family of returned captives, 1 Esdr. v. 20.

Ăm'mĭ-el (*people of God*). (1) The spy of Dan who perished for his evil report, Num. xiii. 12. (2) Father of Machir, 2 Sam. ix. 4, 5. (3) Father of Bath-sheba, 1 Chr. iii. 5; called Eliam in 2 Sam. xi. 3. (4) A door-keeper of the Temple, 1 Chr. xxvi. 5.

Ăm-mĭ'hŭd (*people of praise*). (1) Father of the chief of Ephraim at time of Exode, Num. i. 10; ii. 18; vii. 48, 53; x. 22; 1 Chr. vii. 26. (2) A Simeon-ite, Num. xxxiv. 20. (3) A Naphtalite, Num. xxxiv. 28. (4) Father of Talmai, king of Geshur, 2 Sam. xiii. 37. (5) A descendant of Pharez, 1 Chr. ix. 4.

Ăm-mĭn'a-dăb (*one of the prince's people*). (1) A prince of Judah, Num. i. 7; ii. 3; Ruth iv. 19, 20; 1 Chr. ii. 10. (2) Chief of the sons of Uzziel, 1 Chr. xv. 10–12. (3) Written Amminadib in S. of Sol. vi. 12.

Ăm''mĭ=shăd'da-ī'' (*people of the Almighty*). Father of the prince of Dan at time of the Exode, Num. i. 12; ii. 25; vii. 66; x. 25.

Ăm-mĭz'a-băd (*people of the giver*). Com-mander in David's army, 1 Chr. xxvii. 6.

Ăm'mŏn, Ăm'mŏn-ītes'', Chĭl'drĕn of Ăm'mŏn. Land of the Ammonites was east of the Dead Sea between the Arnon on the south to the Jabbok on the north, Num. xxi. 24; Deut. ii. 19, 20. People called Ammonites from their ancestor Ben-Ammi; Gen. xix. 38. Nomadic, idolatrous, incursive and cruel, 1 Sam. xi. 1–3; Amos i. 13; Judg. x. 6. Reduced to servitude by David, 2 Sam. xii. 26–31. Denounced by Jeremiah and Ezekiel, Jer. xlix. 1–6; Ezek. xxv. 2–10.

Ăm''mŏn-īt'ess. A woman of Ammon.

Ăm'mŏn=nō'. [No.]

Ăm'nŏn (*faithful*). (1) Eldest son of David, killed by his brother Absalom, 2 Sam. xiii. 1–29. (2) Son of Shimon, 1 Chr. iv. 20.

Ā'mok (*deep*). A returned priest, Neh. xii. 7, 20.

Ā'mon or **Ā'mĕn** (*mystery*). An Egyptian god worshipped at Thebes as "Amen the Sun." Written No, in Nah. iii. 8.

Ā'mon (*builder*). (1) A governor of Samaria under Ahab, 1 Kgs. xxii. 26; 2 Chr. xviii. 25. (2)

Fourteenth king of Judah, B. C. 642-640. A shameless idolater, and killed in a conspiracy, 2 Kgs. xxi. 19-26. Reign pictured in Zeph. i. 4; iii. 3, 4, 11.

Ăm'ôr-ītes (*highlanders*). One of the nations of Canaan before the Hebrew conquest, Gen. x. 16; xiv. 7; Num. xiii. 29; Deut. i. 20; Josh. v. 1; x. 6; xi. 3; 1 Sam. xxiii. 29. Occupied both sides of the Jordan, Josh. xiii. 15-27; Num. xxi. 21.

Ā'mos (*weighty*). One of the lesser prophets. Lived during reigns of Uzziah and Jeroboam II., Amos i. 1-7; vii. 14-15. His book is 30th of O. T. It rebukes the sins of Israel and closes with God's promise. Book abounds in rural allusions.

Ā'moz (*strong*). Father of Isaiah, Isa. i. 1; 2 Kgs. xix. 2.

Ăm-phĭp'o-lis (*surrounded city*). A city of Macedonia, 33 miles S. W. of Philippi, Acts xvii. 1.

Ăm'plī-as (*large*). A Roman friend of Paul, Rom. xvi. 8.

Ăm'răm (*exalted*). (1) Father of Moses and Aaron, Ex. vi. 18-20. (2) A descendant of Seir, 1 Chr. i. 41; Hemdan in Gen. xxxvi. 26. (3) A son of Bani, Ez. x. 34.

Ăm'răm-ītes. Descendants of Amram, Num. iii. 27; 1 Chr. xxvi. 23.

Ăm'ra-phel (*keeper of gods*). A Hamite king who joined the expedition against Sodom, Gen. xiv.

Ăm'ŭ-lĕts (*charms*). Belts, rings, necklaces, ornaments, mystically inscribed or not, worn for protection against evil enchantment. Referred to in Gen. xxxv. 4; Judg. viii. 24; Isa. iii. 20; Hos. ii. 13.

Ăm'zī (*strong*). (1) A Levite, 1 Chr. vi. 46. (2) A priest, Neh. xi. 12.

Ā'nab (*grape*). Place in south Judah, Josh. xi. 21.

Ăn'a-ĕl. Tobit's brother, Tob. i. 21.

Ā'nah (*answering*). Father-in-law of Esau, Gen. xxxvi. 2-25.

Ăn''ă-hā'rath (*gorge*). A border place of Issachar and Manasseh, Josh. xix. 19.

Ăn''a-ī'ah (*whom God answers*). (1) A priest who assisted Ezra, Neh. viii. 4. (2) A co-covenanter with Nehemiah, Neh. x. 22.

Ā'năk (*collar*), Children of, Num. xiii. 22. [ANAKIM.]

Ăn'a̱-kĭm or **-kĭms̱.** A race of giants in south-ern Canaan, Deut. i. 28. Defeated by Joshua, and land given to Caleb, Josh. xi. 21–22; xiv. 12–15.

Ăn'a̱-mĭm. A Mizraite people, not located, Gen. x. 13.

Ă-năm'mĕ-lech (*kingly image*). Companion god of Adrammelech, worshipped in Samaria, and representing the female power of the sun, 2 Kgs. xvii. 31.

Ā'nan (*cloud*). A co-covenanter with Nehemiah, Neh. x. 26.

Ăn-ā'nī (*covered by Jehovah*). A descendant of Judah, 1 Chr. iii. 24.

Ăn-a̱-nī'ah (*covered by Jehovah*). (1) A priestly assistant of Nehemiah, Neh. iii. 23. (2) A city of Benjamin, Neh. xi. 32.

Ăn''a̱-nī'as (*whom Jehovah has given*). (1) Five persons mentioned in 1 Esdr. ix. (2) The doubtful convert, whose tragic ending is narrated in Acts v. 1–11. (3) A Jewish disciple at Damascus, Acts ix. 10–27; xxii. 12. (4) A high priest, A. D. 48, Acts xxiii. 2–5; xxiv. 1.

Ă-năn'ḭ-ĕl. A progenitor of Tobit, Tob. i. 1.

Ā'năth (*answer*). Father of Shamgar, Judg. iii. 31.

Ăn-ăth'e-mȧ (*devoted*). The devoted thing, if inanimate, fell to the priests, Num. xviii. 18; if ani-mate, it was to be slain, Lev. xxvii. 28, 29. In N. T. a curse, Rom. ix. 3; 1 Cor. xii. 3; xvi. 22. In the latter instance Maranatha is added, the meaning being "Let him be accursed."

Ăn'a̱-thŏth (*answers*). (1) A descendant of Benjamin, 1 Chr. vii. 8. (2) A co-covenanter with Nehemiah, Neh. x. 19. (3) A Levitical city of Ben-jamin, Josh. xxi. 18; 1 Chr. vi. 60; Isa. x. 30.

Ăn'chŏr (*hook*). Anchors for holding ships to one spot were formerly cast from the stern. Acts xxvii. 29.

Ăn'drew (*manly*). An Apostle of Christ, John i. 35–40; Matt. iv. 18. Brother of Simon Peter, native of Bethsaida, and fisherman. Original disciple of John the Baptist, Mark iii. 3; John vi. 6–13; xii. 22.

Ăn''drŏ-nī'cus (*man conqueror*). (1) A viceroy of Antiochus at Antioch, 2 Macc. iv. 31–38. (2) An-

other officer of Antiochus at Garizim, 2 Macc. v. 23.
(3) A Christian friend of Paul's at Rome, Rom. xvi. 7.

Ā′nem (*two springs*). A Levitical city of Issachar, 1 Chr. vi. 73.

Ā′nĕr (*boy*). (1) A Levitical city in Manasseh, 1 Chr. vi. 70. (2) An Amorite chief of Hebron, Gen. xiv. 13-24.

Ăn′ĕ-thŏth-īte″, 2 Sam. xxiii. 27; **Ăn′tŏth-īte**, 1 Chr. xi. 28; xii. 3; **Ăn″ĕ-tŏth′īte**, 1 Chr. xxvii. 12. An inhabitant of Anathoth.

Ān′gĕl (*messenger*). A messenger, 2 Sam. ii. 5; Luke vii. 24. In a spiritual sense, a messenger of God, Gen. xxiv. 7; Heb. i. 14. Nature, Matt. xviii. 10. Number, 1 Kgs. xxii. 19; Matt. xxvi. 53; Heb. xii. 22. Strength, Ps. ciii. 20; Rev. v. 2. Activity, Isa. vi. 2-6. Appearance, Matt. xxviii. 2-4; Rev. x. 1, 2. Office, Isa. vi. 1-3; Rev. vi. 11; Matt. xiii. 49; xvi. 27; xxiv. 31.

Ā′nĭ-am (*sighing of the people*). A Manassite, 1 Chr. vii. 19.

Ā′nĭm (*fountains*). A city in mountains of Judah, Josh. xv. 50.

Ăn′īse. A plant of the parsley family, producing aromatic seeds used in medicine and cookery, and with which tithes were paid, Matt. xxiii. 23.

Ănk′lĕt. Much worn in the East as ornaments for the ankles, sometimes with bells, Isa. iii. 16-20. [BELLS.]

Ăn′nà (*gracious*). (1) Wife of Tobit, Tob. i. 9. (2) A prophetess at Jerusalem, Luke ii. 36.

Ăn′na-as, 1 Esdr. v. 23. [SENAAH.]

Ăn′nas (*humble*). (1) 1 Esdr. ix. 32. Same as Harim in Ez. x. 31. (2) A Jewish high priest, A. D. 7-23. Succeeded by his son-in-law, Caiaphas, A. D. 25, John xviii. 13; Luke iii. 2.

Ȧ-noint′ (*to smear on*). Anointing with oil or ointment, a common practice in East, Gen. xxviii. 18; xxxi. 13; Deut. xxviii. 40; Ruth iii. 3. A mark of respect, Luke vii. 46, Ps. xxiii. 5; or of induction to priestly office, Ex. xl. 15; Num. iii. 3; or to kingly office, 1 Sam. ix. 16; x. 1; or as an act of consecration, Ex. xxviii. 41; or as an act of healing, Mark vi. 13. Christ was anointed with the Holy Ghost, Luke iv. 18; Acts iv. 27; x. 38; Isa. lxi. 1; Ps. xlv. 7.

Ănt (*emmet*). Twice referred to in O. T. ; first as to its diligence, and second as to its wisdom. Prov. vi. 6 ; xxx. 25.

Ăn'te̤-lōpe (*animal*). The word translated "fallow deer" in Deut. xiv. 5, as well as "pygarg," implies a species of antelope.

Ăn'tĭ-chrīst (*against Christ*). In 1 John ii. 18, 22 ; iv. 3 ; 2 John 7, applied to those who hold heretical opinions of the incarnation.

Ăn'tĭ-ŏch (*after Antiochus*). (1) Capital of the Greek kings of Syria, on the Orontes. First Gentile church founded there, and disciples first called Christians there; Acts xi. 19-21, 26. (2) A city of Pisidia, Acts xiii. 14. Starting point of the persecutions which followed Paul all through Asia Minor, Acts xiv.

Ăn-tī'o-chŭs (*opponent*). (1) A messenger of Jonathan to the Romans, 1 Macc. xii. 16. (2) King of Syria, B. C. 261. Prefigured as "King of the North" in Dan. xi. 6, etc. (3) Antiochus III., called "The Great," B. C. 223, Dan. xi. 14–19. (4) Antiochus IV., called Epiphanes, 1 Macc. i. (5) Antiochus V., Eupator, B. C. 164 ; 1 Macc. vi. 10. (6) Antiochus VI. and VII., 1 Macc. xii.–xvi.

Ăn'tĭ-păs (*like the father*). A martyr of Pergamos, Rev. ii. 13.

Ăn-tĭp'a̤-tĕr (*for the father*). An ambassador to Lacedemon, 1 Macc. xii. 16.

Ăn-tĭp'a̤-trĭs (*for his father*). Ancient Capharsaba, rebuilt and renamed by Herod ; 34 miles N. W. of Jerusalem, Acts xxiii. 31.

Ăn-tō'nĭ-a̤. A fortress on N. W. side of Temple at Jerusalem, Acts xxi. 31–40.

Ăn''to̤-thī'jah (*answers of Jehovah*). A son of Jehoram, 1 Chr. viii. 24.

Ăn'tŏth-īte. A native of Anathoth, 1 Chr. xi. 28 ; xii. 3.

Ā'nub (*confederate*). A descendant of Judah, 1 Chr. iv. 8.

Ā'nus, 1 Esdr. ix. 48. [Bani.]

Ăp-ā'me. Daughter of Bartacus, 1 Esdr. iv. 29.

A̤-pĕl'lĕs (*called*). Friend of Paul, Rom. xvi. 10.

Āpes. Were brought from the same countries

which supplied ivory and peacocks, 1 Kgs. x. 22; 2 Chr. ix. 21.

Ȧ-phär′săch-ītes, Ȧ-phär′săth-chītes, Ȧ-phär′sītes (*rending*). Assyrian nomads settled in Samaria, Ez. iv. 9; v. 6.

Ā′phĕk (*strength*). (1) A royal city of the Canaanites, near Hebron, Josh. xii. 18. Probably Aphekah, Josh. xv. 53. (2) A city in the extreme north of Asher, Josh. xix. 30. Probably Aphik, Judg. i. 31. (3) A place N. W. of Jerusalem, 1 Sam. iv. 1. (4) A Philistine encampment near Jezreel, 1 Sam. xxix. 1. (5) A walled city of Syria, 1 Kgs. xx. 26.

Ȧ-phē′kah, Josh. xv. 53. [APHEK.]

Ȧ-phĕr′e̥-ma. Governor of Judea, 1 Macc. xi. 34.

Ȧ-phĕr′ra. Son of one of Solomon's servants, 1 Esdr. v. 34.

Ȧ-phī′ah (*refreshed*). A progenitor of Saul. 1 Sam. ix. i.

Ā′phĭk, Judg. i. 31. [APHEK.]

Ăph′rah (*dust.*) An uncertain place, Micah i. 10.

Ăph′sēs (*dispersion*). Chief of the 18th course of the temple service, 1 Chr. xxiv. 15.

Ȧ-pŏc′ȧ-lypse (*uncovered*). The Greek name for Revelation.

Ȧ-pŏc′rў-pha (*hidden*). That collection of 14 O. T. books not regarded as canonical. Also the rejected N. T. books.

Ăp′′ŏl-lō′nĭ-ȧ (*belonging to Apollo*). A city of Macedonia, Acts xvii. 1.

Ăp′′ŏl-lō′nĭ-us. (1) A governor of Celo-Syria, 2 Macc. iv. 4. (2) A general under Antiochus, 1 Macc. iii. 10–12. (2) Several other Syrian generals of same name, 1 and 2 Macc.

Ăp′′ŏl-lŏph′ḁ-nēs̥. A Syrian general, 2 Macc. x. 37.

Ȧ-pŏl′lŏs (*belonging to Apollo*). A learned Jew and Christian convert of Alexandria, who became a preacher and friend of Paul, Acts xviii. 24–28; 1 Cor. iii. 6–9; Tit. iii. 13.

Ȧ-pŏll′yon (*destroyer*). Greek name of Abaddon, "angel of the bottomless pit," Rev. ix. 11. [ABADDON.]

Ăp′pḁ-im (*nostrils*). Son of Nadab. 1 Chr. ii. 30, 31.

Ȧ-pŏth'ē-cā''ry (*to place away*). The apothecary's art was called for in the mixing of perfume. Ex. xxx. 35.

Ȧ-pŏs'tle (*one sent forth*). Official name of the twelve disciples. As to power and names *see* Matt. x. 1–42 ; John xvi. 13 ; Mark xvi. 20. In a broad sense, any one commissioned to preach the gospel, 2 Cor. viii. 23 ; Phil. ii. 25. Term applied to Christ, Heb. iii. 1.

Ăp-păr'ĕl. [CLOTHES.]

Ăp-peal' (*drive to*). This right acknowledged by Jewish law, Deut. xvii. 8, 9. It lay to the judges, Judg. iv. 5 ; then to the kings ; later to a special tribunal, 2 Chr. xix. 8–10 ; Ez. vii. 25 ; finally to the Sanhedrim. Paul appealed to the Roman Emperor, Acts xxv. 11.

Ăp'phĭ-à (*productive*). A Christian woman addressed by Paul, Phile. 2.

Ăp'phŭs (*wary*). Surname of Jonathan Maccabeus, 1 Macc. ii. 5.

Ăp''pĭ-ī fō'rŭm (*market-place of Appius*). A town, 43 miles S. E. of Rome, on the Appian Way, Acts xxviii. 15.

Ăp'ple, Ăp'ple=tree (*bursting forth, in Hebrew*). The fruit is alluded to in Prov. xxv. 11 ; S. of Sol. ii. 5 ; vii. 8. Tree mentioned in S. of Sol. ii. 3 ; viii. 5 ; Joel i. 12. For figurative use *see* Prov. vii. 2 ; Zech. ii. 8 ; Ps. xvii. 8 ; Lam. ii. 18.

Ȧq'uĭ-là (*eagle*). A Jewish convert of Pontus, and valuable assistant of Paul, Acts xviii. 2 ; 1 Cor. xvi. 19 ; Rom. xvi. 3, etc.

Är, Är of Mō'ab (*city*). A chief place of Moab, Num. xxi. 28 ; Isa. xv. 1. Aroer in Deut. ii. 36. Used to type the Moabite people or land, Deut. ii. 9, 18, 29.

Ā'rà (*lion*). Head of a family of Asher, 1 Chr. vii. 38.

Ā'rab (*ambush*). A city of Hebron, Josh. xv. 52.

Är'a-bah (*burnt up*). A Hebrew word, Josh. xviii. 18, designating the valley of Jordan and the Dead Sea, and the depression through Arabia to the Gulf of Akabah.

Ȧ-rā'bĭ-à (*desert*). Known in O. T. as " East Country," Gen. x. 30 ; xxv. 6 ; and " Land of the Sons of the East," Gen. xxix.; Judg. vi. 3; vii. 12. Arabia, from *Arâb* the people, in 2 Chr. ix. 14; Isa. xxi. 13; Jer. xxv. 24; Ezek. xxvii. 21. That extensive peninsula lying south of Palestine and between the Red Sea, Indian Ocean, and Persian Gulf. Home of many nomadic races, and in close commerce and even kinship, through Ishmael, with the Hebrews, 1 Kgs. x. 15; 2 Chr. ix. 14. Paul visited it, Gal. i. 17. Often referred to by prophets, Isa. xlii. 11; Jer. xxv. 24.

Ā'răd (*wild ass*). (1) A valorous Benjamite, 1 Chr. viii. 15. (2) A royal city of the Canaanites, Num. xxi. 1; Josh. xii. 14.

Ăr'a̧-dus, 1 Macc. xv. 23. [ARVAD.]

Ā'rah (*wandering*). (1) An Asherite, 1 Chr. vii. 39. (2) Head of a returned family, Ez. ii. 5; Neh. vii. 10.

Ā'ram (*high*). (1) Translated Mesopotamia in Gen. xxiv. 10. The high part of Syria to the N. E. of Palestine. Absorbed by Syria, with capital at Damascus, 1 Kgs. xx. 1; Isa. vii. 8; 1 Kgs. xi. 24. (2) A descendant of Nahor, Gen. xxii. 21. (3) An Asherite, 1 Chr. vii. 34. (4) An ancestor of Christ, Matt. i. 4; Luke iii. 33.

Ā'ram=nā-ha̧-rā'im (*highlands of two rivers*), Ps. lx. title.

Ā'ram=zō'bah [Ā'ram]. Ps. xl. title.

Ā'ram-īt''ess. A female inhabitant of Aram, 1 Chr. vii. 14.

Ā'răn (*wild goat*). A Horite, Gen. xxxvi. 28.

Âr'ă-rat (*high land*). A high mountain of Armenia, and resting place of Noah's ark, Gen. viii. 4.

Ā-ra̧u'nah (*ark*). A Jebusite prince who sold his threshing-floor to David, 2 Sam. xxiv. 18–24; 1 Chr. xxi. 25.

Ăr'bà (*one of four*). A forefather of Anak, Josh. xiv. 15; xv. 13; xxi. 11.

Ăr'bah. Hebron, or Kirjath-arba, Gen. xxxv. 27.

Ăr'băth-īte. An inhabitant of the Arabah, 2 Sam. xxiii. 31; 1 Chr. xi. 32.

Ăr-băt'tĭs. A district in Palestine, 1 Macc. v. 23.

Ȧr'bel. Hos. x. 14. [BETH-ARBEL.]

Ȧr-bē'la. A town in Galilee, 1 Macc. ix. 2.

Ȧr'bīte. A native of Arab, 2 Sam. xxiii. 35.

Ȧrch-an'gel (ărk-ān'jel) (*chief angel*). 1 Thess. iv. 16 ; Jude 9.

Ȧr''chĕ-lā'us (*prince of the people*). A son of Herod the Great, and ethnarch (B. C. 4-A. D. 9) of Idumea, Judea, and Samaria, Matt. ii. 22.

Ȧrch'e-ry (*use of the arcus, or bow*). Use of the bow and arrow, an important art in Biblical times, Gen. xxvii. 3 ; Isa. xxii. 6 ; xlix. ; 2 Ps. cxxvii. 4, 5. Benjamites noted archers, Judg. xix.-xxi.

Ȧr'chĕ-vītes. Probably inhabitants of Erech, Ez. iv. 9.

Ȧr'chī. A place or clan in Joseph, Josh. xvi. 2. [ARCHITE.]

Ȧr'chĭp'pus (*chief of stables*). A Christian teacher at Colossæ, Col. iv. 17 ; Phil. 2.

Ȧr'chīte. Supposed to refer to a clan of Erech, 2 Sam. xv. 32 ; xvi. 16 ; xvii. 5-14. 1 Chr. xxvii. 33.

Ȧr'chĭ-tec''ture (*builder's art*). Descendants of Shem were city builders, Gen. iv. 17 ; x. 11, 12. Hebrew ideas of architecture ripened in Egypt, and by contact with Tyre. David enlarged Jerusalem. Solomon built a palace and temple, 2 Sam. v. 11 ; 1 Kgs. vii. The returned captives were great builders, Ez. iii. 8-10 ; Neh. iii. ; vi. 15.

Ȧrc-tū'rus (*the bear*). The constellation Ursa Major, commonly called the "Great Bear" or "Charles's Wain," Job ix. 9 ; xxxviii. 32.

Ȧrd (*fugitive*). A grandson of Benjamin, Gen. xlvi. 21 ; Num. xxvi. 40.

Ȧr'dăth. A field, 2 Esdr. ix. 26.

Ȧrd'ītes. Descendants of Ard or Addar, Num. xxvi. 40.

Ȧr'dŏn (*fugitive*). A son of Caleb, 1 Chr. ii. 18.

Ȧ-rē'lī (*heroic*). A son of Gad. Children called Arelites, Num. xxvi. 17 ; Gen. xlvi. 16.

Ȧr''ĕ-op'a̤-ḡīte. A member of the court of Areopagus, Acts xvii. 34.

Ȧr''ĕ-op'a̤-gus (*hill of Mars*). A rocky hill near the centre of Athens, where the court of justice sat, Acts xvii. 19-34.

Ā'rēs, 1 Esdr. v. 10. [ARAH 2.]

Ăr'e-tas (*excellence*). (1) An Arab chief, 2 Macc. v. 8. (2) Father-in-law of Herod Antipas, 2 Cor. xi. 32.

Ă-rē'us. A Lacedæmonian king, 1 Macc. xii. 20-23.

Ăr'gŏb (*stony*). A country of Bashan, and one of Solomon's commissary districts, Deut. iii. 4; 1 Kgs. iv. 13.

Ā''rĭ-ă-rā'theṣ. Mithridates IV., king of Cappadocia, B. C. 163-130, 1 Macc. xv. 22.

Ă-rĭd'ạ-ī (*strong*). Ninth son of Haman, Esth. ix. 9.

Ă-rĭd'ạ-thå. Sixth son of Haman, Esth. ix. 8.

Ă-rī'eh (*lion*). A prince of Israel, killed by Pekah, 2 Kgs. xv. 25.

Ā'rĭ-el (*lion of God*). (1) A leader of returning captives, Ez. viii. 16. (2) The city of Jebus-Salem, Jerusalem, Isa. xxix. 1, 2.

Ăr''ĭ-mă-thæ'å (*heights*). Home of Joseph in Judea, Matt. xxvii. 57; Mark xv. 43; Luke xxiii. 51; John xix. 38.

Ā'rĭ-ŏch (*venerable*). (1) A King of Elassar, Gen. xiv. 1-9. (2) Captain under Nebuchadnezzar, Dan. ii. 14, etc. (3) A king of the Elymeans, Judith i. 6.

Ă-rĭs'ạ-ī (*lion like*). Eighth son of Haman, Esth. ix. 9.

Ăr''ĭs-tär'chus (*best ruler*). A Thessalonian companion of Paul on his third missionary tour, Acts xix. 29; xx. 4; xxvii. 2; Col. iv. 10; Phil. 24.

Ăr-ĭs''tŏ-bū'lus (*best counselor*). (1) A Christian and resident at Rome, Rom. xvi. 10. (2) A priest of the Egyptian Jews, 2 Macc. i. 10.

Ärk (*chest*). The vessel in which Noah and his family were saved, Gen. vi., vii., viii. Also a little boat of rushes, Ex. ii. 3.

Ärk of the Cŏv'ĕ-nănt. Built by direction, Ex. xxv. A chest of Shittim wood for tabernacle use, 3 ft. 9 in. long, by 2 ft. 3 in. wide and high, lined and covered with gold, whose lid was the mercy-seat, on either end of which were cherubs. Golden rings were on the sides, through which poles passed for carrying. Captured by Philistines, 1 Sam. iv. 10, 11; returned to Kirjath-Jearim; brought thence by David to Jerusalem, 2 Sam. vi. 1; 1 Chr. xv. 25, 28, etc.; placed in temple by Solomon, 2 Chr. v. 2–10.

Ärk′īte. A descendant of Arka, Gen. x. 17; 1 Chr. i. 15.

** Är-ma-ḡĕd′don** (*hill of Megiddo*). A typical battlefield between the hosts of good and evil, Rev. xvi. 16.

Är-mē′nĭ-à (*Land of Aram*). The plateau of Western Asia, whence flow its great rivers Euphrates, Tigris, Araxes, etc., 2 Kgs. xix. 37; Isa. xxxvii. 38.

Ärm′-let (*for the arms*). An arm ornament in general use in the East. "Bracelet," 2 Sam. i. 10.

Är-mō′nī. A son of Saul, 2 Sam. xxi. 8.

Ärms, Är′mor. Hebrew offensive weapons were the sword, 1 Sam. xvii. 51; xxv. 13; 2 Sam. xx. 8; Judg. iii. 16; spear, 1 Sam. xvii. 7; 2 Sam. ii. 23; xxiii. 8; bow and arrow [ARCHERY]; sling, 2 Kgs. iii. 25; battle-axe, Jer. li. 20. Among defensive armor were breastplates, cuirasses, coats of mail, helmets, greaves, habergeons, shields, bucklers, 1 Sam. xvii. 5–7; 2 Chr. xxvi. 14.

Är′my. Hebrew males twenty years old and upward subject to military duty, Num. i. 2, 3. Tribes formed army divisions. Numerated by hundreds and thousands, each with captains, Num. xxxi. 14. Kings had body-guards, 1 Sam. xiii. 2; xxv. 13. Later, a standing army formed, 2 Chr. xxv. 6. No cavalry till Solomon's time. War declared and exempts used as in Deut. xx. 1–14; xxiv. 5. In N. T. Roman army composed of legions, with chief captains, Acts xxi. 31; tents of legions, or cohorts, and bands, Acts x. 1; mæniples, or thirds of legions; centuries, 100 men each and two to a maniple. Captain of a 100 called a Centurion, Matt. viii. 5; xxvii. 54.

Är′na. A forefather of Ezra, 2 Esdr. i. 2.

Är′nan. Head of a returned family, 1 Chr. iii. 21.

Är′nŏn (*noisy*). A stream emptying into Dead Sea from the East, and boundary between the Amorites and Moabites, Num. xxi. 13; Judg. xi. 18. Afterwards between Moab and Israel, Deut. ii. 24; Josh. xii. 1; xiii. 9; Judg. xi. 13.

Ā′rŏd (*wild ass*). Gadite founder of the Ā′rŏd-ītes, Num. xxvi. 17. Called Ăr′ŏ-dī in Gen. xlvi. 16.

Ā′rŏd-ītes. [AROD.]

Ăr′ŏ-ẽr (*ruins*). (1) A Reubenite city on the Arnon, Deut. ii. 36; Josh. xii. 1, 2; Judg. xi. 26. Later fell back to Moab, Jer. xlviii. 19, 20. (2) A town of Gad, Num. xxxii. 34; Josh. xiii. 25; 2 Sam. xxiv. 5. (3) An unidentified place, Isa. xvii. 2. (4) A town in South Judah, 1 Sam. xxx. 28.

Ăr′ŏ-ẽr-īte″. Designation of Hothan, 1 Chr. xi. 44.

A′rom. A returned family, 1 Esdr. v. 16.

Ăr′pad or Ăr′phad (*strong*). A city, or district, in Syria, dependent on Damascus, Isa. xxxvi. 19; xxxvii. 13; Jer. xlix. 23; 2 Kgs. xviii. 34; xix. 13.

Ăr-phax′ăd (*Chaldean fortress*). (1) A son of Shem, Gen. x. 22, 24; xi. 10-13; 1 Chr. i. 17, 18, 24. (2) A king of the Medes, Judith i. 1-4.

Ăr′rows. [ARMS.]

Ăr″tăx-ẽrx′eṣ (*brave warrior*). (1) A Persian king who stopped the rebuilding of the temple at Jerusalem, Ez. iv. 7, 23, 24. (2) Another Persian king, friendly to Nehemiah, Neh. ii. 1.

Ăr′tẹ-măs (*gift of Artemis*). A friend of Paul, Tit. iii. 12.

Ăr-tĭl′lẽ-ry. The missile equipment of a Jewish soldier, lance, arrows, etc., 1 Sam. xx. 40. [ARMS.]

Ärts. The tricks of magic and astrology, Acts xix. 19. [ASTROLOGERS.]

Ăr′ụ-bŏth (*windows*). The third commissary district of King Solomon, 1 Kgs. iv. 10.

Ā-rụ′-mah (*height*). Residence of Abimelech, near Shechem, Judg. ix. 41.

Ăr′văd (*wandering*). An island, now Ruad, lying three miles off Tyre, Ezek. xxvii. 8-11.

Ăr′vad-īte. A native of Arvad, Gen. x. 18; 1 Chr. i. 16.

Ăr′ză. Keeper of King Elah's palace at Tirzah, 1 Kgs. xvi. 9.

Ā′să (*physician*). (1) Third king of Judah, 1 Kgs. xv. 8-34; reigned B. C. 955-914; abolished idolatry; battled victoriously with Ethiopia, 2 **Chr. xiv.**; involved with Israel; buried with pomp, 2 Chr. xvi. (2) A Levite, 1 Chr. ix. 16.

Ăs″ā-dī′as. An ancestor of Baruch, Bar. **i. 1.**

Ăs′ā-el. An ancestor of Tobit, Tob. i. 1.

Ā′sa-hĕl (*creature of God*). (1) The fleet-footed nephew of David, killed by Abner, 2 Sam. ii. 18–23. (2) A Levitical legal instructor, 2 Chr. xvii. 8. (3) A Levite and tithing-man, 2 Chr. xxxi. 13. (4) A priest, Ez. x. 15.

Ā″sa-hī′ah (*the Lord made*). A learned servant of King Josiah, 2 Kgs. xxii. 12–14. Asaiah in 2 Chr. xxxiv. 20.

Ā″sa-ī′ah (*whom the Lord made*). (1) Prince of a Simeonite family, 1 Chr. iv. 36. (2) A Levite chief, 1 Chr. vi. 30; xv. 6–11. (3) A Shilonite, 1 Chr. ix. 5. Maaseiah in Neh. xi. 5. (4) Asaiah, 2 Chr. xxxiv. 20.

Ăs′a-nă, 1 Esdr. v. 31. [ASNAH].

Ā′saph (*gatherer*). (1) Levitical leader of David's choir, 1 Chr. vi. 39; 2 Chr. xxix. 30; Neh. xii. 46. Twelve of the Psalms are attributed to him, to wit, Ps. l. and lxxiii. to lxxxiii. (2) Ancestor of Joah the chronicler, 2 Kgs. xviii. 18; Isa. xxxvi. 3, 22. (3) Keeper of royal forests under Artaxerxes, Neh. ii. 8. (4) Another conductor of the Temple choir, 1 Chr. ix. 15; Neh. xi. 17.

Ā′saph, SONS OF. A school of poets and musicians founded by Asaph.

Ă-sā′rĕ-el (*oath bound*). A descendant of Judah, 1 Chr. iv. 16.

Ăs″ă-rē′lah (*upright*). A minstrel prophet under David, 1 Chr. xxv. 2. Jesharelah in vs. 14.

Ăs′ca-lŏn. [ASHKELON.]

Ăs-çen′sion, *see* CHRIST.

Ăs′e-năth (*devotee of Neith*, the Egyptian Minerva), Egyptian wife of Joseph, Gen. xli. 45–50; xlvi. 20.

Ā′sẽr, Luke ii. 36; Rev. vii. 6. [ASHER.]

Ăsh. Ash was not indigenous to Palestine; perhaps pine or cedar is meant, Isa. xliv. 14.

Ā′shan (*smoke*). A city in Judah, Josh. xv. 42; and Simeon, Josh. xix. 7; 1 Chr. iv. 32.

Ăsh-bē'à (*I adjure*). A doubtful genealogical name, 1 Chr. iv. 21.

Ăsh'bel (*reproof*). Second son of Benjamin, Gen. xlvi. 21; Num. xxvi. 38; 1 Chr. viii. 1.

Ăsh'chĕ-naz. 1 Chr. i. 6; Jer. li. 27. [ASH-KENAZ.]

Ăsh'dŏd or **Ăz-ō'tus** (*stronghold*). A Philistine city between Gaza and Joppa; assigned to Judah, Josh. xv. 47; 1 Sam. v. 1. Azotus, Acts viii. 40.

Ăsh'dŏd-ītes''. Dwellers in Ashdod, Neh. iv. 7.

Ăsh'dŏth-ītes. Dwellers in Ashdod, Josh. xiii. 3.

Ăsh'dŏth=pĭṣ'gah (*Springs of Pisgah*). Probably the "slopes of Pisgah," to the east, Deut. iii. 17; iv. 49; Josh. xii. 3; xiii. 20.

Ăsh'ĕr (*happiness*). (1) Eighth son of Jacob., Gen. xxx. 13. Aser in Apochrypha and N. T. For boundaries of his allotment *see* Josh. xix. 24-31; xvii. 10, 11; Judg. i. 31, 32. (2) A boundary town of Manasseh, Josh. xvii. 7.

Ăsh'ĕ-rah (*straight*). [ASHTAROTH.]

Ăsh'ĕr-ītes. Members of the tribe of Asher. Judg. i. 32.

Ăsh'es. To sprinkle with or sit in ashes, marked humiliation, grief, and penitence, Gen. xviii. 27; 2 Sam. xiii. 19; Esth. iv. 3; Job ii. 8; Jer. vi. 26; Lam. iii. 16; Matt. xi. 21. The altar ashes, when a red heifer was sacrificed, were watered and used for purifying the unclean, Num. xix. 17-22.

Ăsh'ī-mà (*offence*). A Syrian god worshipped in Samaria, 2 Kgs. xvii. 30.

Ăsh'kĕ-lŏn, Ăs'kĕ-lŏn (*migration*). A Philistine city and seaport on the Mediterranean, 10 miles N. of Gaza, Josh. (Eshkalon) xiii. 3; Judg. (Askelon) i. 18; Judg. (Ashkelon) xiv. 19; 1 Sam. vi. 17. Its destruction predicted in Jer. xlvii. 5-7; Am. i. 8; Zech. ix. 5; Zeph. ii. 7.

Ăsh'kĕ-năz (*fire that spreads*). A grandson of Japhet, Gen. x. 3. Ashchenaz in 1 Chr. i. 6; Jer. li. 27.

Ăsh'nah (*change*). Two towns of Judah, one N. W. the other S. W. of Jerusalem, 16 miles distant, Josh. xv. 33, 43.

Ăsh′pe-naz (*horse-nose*). Master of eunuchs under Nebuchadnezzar, Dan. i. 3.

Ăsh′rĭ-el, 1 Chr. vii. 14. [ASRIEL.]

Ăsh′ta-rŏth and **Ăs′ta-rŏth** (*star*). A city of Bashan, noted for its worship of Ashtoreth, Deut. i. 4; Josh. ix. 10; xii. 4; xiii. 12.

Ăsh′tĕ-răth-īte″. An inhabitant of Ashtaroth, 1 Chr. xi. 44.

Ăsh′tĕ-rŏth Kär-nā′im (*Ashteroth of two peaks*). A city of the giant Rephaim in Bashan, Gen. xiv. 5.

Ăsh′tŏ-rĕth (*star*). The principal female deity of the Phœnicians ; the Ishtar of the Assyrians, and Astarte of the Greeks and Romans. Solomon introduced her worship into his kingdom, Judg. ii. 13 ; 1 Kgs. xi. 5, 33 ; 2 Kgs. xxiii. 13.

Ăsh′ŭr (*black*). Founder of Tekoa, 1 Chr. ii. 24; iv. 5.

Ăsh′ŭr-ītes. Asherites, 2 Sam. ii. 9.

Ăsh′vath. A son of Japhlet, 1 Chr. vii. 33.

Ā′şĭà (*eastern*). Only in N. T., and then with reference to Asia Minor, or even to western Asia Minor, with the capital at Ephesus, Acts ii. 9; vi. 9; xvi. 6; 1 Cor. xvi. 19.

Ā′şĭà-arch (-*ark*). Chief of the religious rites and public games of the Roman province of Asia, Acts xix. 31.

Ăs″ĭ-bī′as, 1 Esdr. ix. 26. [MALCHIJAH.]

Ā-sĭ-el (*made by God*). (1) A progenitor of Jehu, 1 Chr. iv. 35. (2) A scribe under Esdras, 2 Esdr. xiv. 24.

Ăs′ke-lŏn. [ASHKELON.]

Ăs″mō-dē′us. An evil spirit, classed with Abaddon and Apollyon, Tob. iii. 8–17.

Ăs′nah (*thorn-bush*). Father of a returned family, Ez. ii. 50.

Ăs-năp′pẽr (*swift*). Leader of Cuthæan colonists into Samaria, Ez. iv. 10.

Ăsp (*viper*). The hooded venomous serpent known as the African cobra. Adder in Ps. lviii. 4 ; xci. 13, answers the description of asp, Deut. xxxii. 33; Job xx. 14–16; Isa. xi. 8; Rom. iii. 13.

Ăs-pal'ā-thus. A perfume, or ointment, product of Rhodian wood, Ecclus. xxiv. 15.

Ăs'pă-thă. Third son of Haman, Esth. ix. 7.

Ăs'phar. A pool in the wilderness of Thecoe, 1 Macc. ix. 33.

Ăs'rĭ-el (*help of God*). Founder of the Asrielites, Num. xxvi. 31; Josh. xvii. 2; Ashriel, 1 Chr. vii. 14.

Ăss. Five different Hebrew words give it name in the Bible. A patient beast of burden, and palfrey for even kings, Gen. xxii. 3; xii. 16; xxxvi. 24; 1 Chr. xxvii. 30; Job i. 3; Zech. ix. 9, which last is the prophecy of Christ's entry into Jerusalem, Matt. xxi. 1–9.

Ăs'shur. Second son of Shem, Gen. x. 22. Also Hebrew form for Assyria, Ezek. xxvii. 23.

Ăs-shu'rim (*steps*). A tribe descended from Abraham, Gen. xxv. 3.

Ăs''sĭ-dē'ans (*pious*). A sect of orthodox Jews, bound to the external observance of the law, 1 Macc. ii 42.

Ăs'sĭr (*prisoner*). (1) A Levite, Ex. vi. 24; 1 Chr. vi. 22. (2) A forefather of Samuel, 1 Chr. vi. 23, 37. (3) Son of Jeconiah, 1 Chr. iii. 17.

Ăs'sŏs or **Ăs'sus** (*approaching*). A Roman seaport on northern shore of Gulf of Adramyttium, Acts xx. 13, 14.

Ăs'sur, Ez. iv. 2; Ps. lxxxiii. 8. [ASSHUR; ASSYRIA.]

Ăs-sўr'ĭ-ă (*country of Asshur*). That ancient empire on the Tigris whose capital was Nineveh, Gen. ii. 14; x. 11–22. In its splendor it embraced Susiana, Chaldea, Babylon, Media, Armenia, Assyria proper, Mesopotamia, Syria, Phœnicia, Palestine, and Idumea. Assyrian kings frequently invaded Israel, 2 Kgs. xv. 19; xvi. 7–9; xv. 29; 2 Chr. xxviii. 20. Shalmaneser destroyed Samaria, B. C. 721, and carried the people captive. Assyria was overthrown by the Medes and Babylonians, 625 B. C., after an existence of 1200 years.

Ăs'ta-rŏth, Deut. i. 4. [ASHTAROTH.]

Ăs-tär'te. [ASHTORETH.]

Ă-stў'ă-gēs. Last king of the Medes, B. C. 500. Bel and Drag. 1.

Ă-sŭp'pim, HOUSE OF (*gatherings*). Probably store-rooms in the Temple, 1 Chr. xxvi. 15, 17. "Thresholds" in Neh. xii. 25.

Ă-sўn′crĭ-tus (*incomparable*). A Christian friend of Paul, at Rome, Rom. xvi. 14.

Ā′tad, THRESHING FLOOR OF. Name changed to Abel-mizraim, which *see*, Gen. l. 10, 11.

Ăt′a-rah (*crown*). Mother of Onam, 1 Chr. ii. 26.

Ă-tăr′ga-tis (*opening*). A Syrian goddess with a woman's body and fish's tail, 2 Macc. xii. 26.

Ăt′a-rŏth (*crowns*). (1) A town of Gilead, Num. xxxii. 3, 34. (2) A place on the southern boundary of Ephraim, Josh. xvi. 2, 7. (3) Perhaps same as above, 1 Chr. ii. 54.

Ā′tĕr (*shut up*). Heads of two different returned families, Ez. ii. 42; Neh. vii. 21.

Ā′thăch (*stopping place*). A town in southern Judah, 1 Sam. xxx. 30.

Ăth′′a-ī′ah (*whom God made*). A descendant of Pharez, Neh. xi. 4. Uthai in 1 Chr. ix. 4.

Ăth′′a-lī′ah (*afflicted by God*). (1) Wicked wife of Jehoram, king of Judah, who introduced the worship of Baal and was slain by her own guards, 2 Kgs. xi.; 2 Chr. xxii.–xxiv. (2) A Benjamite, 1 Chr. viii. 26. (3) Head of a returned Jewish family, Ez. viii. 7.

Ă-thē′nĭ-anṣ. Inhabitants of Athens, Acts xvii. 21.

Ăth′′ĕ-nō′bĭ-us. An envoy of King Antiochus, 1 Macc. xv. 28.

Ăth′ĕnṣ (*city of Athena, or Minerva*). Capital of Attica and chief seat of Grecian learning and civilization. Situate in S. E. part of the Grecian Peninsula, five miles from its seaport, the Piræus. Paul preached on its Areopagus or Mars' Hill, Acts xvii. 19–22, and founded a church there.

Ăth′lāī (*whom God afflicts*). A son of Bebai, Ez. x. 28.

Ă-tōne′mĕnt (*reconciliation*). The expiation of sin and propitiation of God by the incarnation, life, suffering, and death of Christ. Day of Atonement, an annual day of Hebrew fasting and humiliation, Ex. xxx. 16; Lev. xvi.; xxiii. 27–32.

Ăt′rŏth (*crowns*). A city of Gad, Num. xxxii. 35.

Ăt'tāi (*ready*). (1) A grandson of Sheshan, 1 Chr. ii. 35, 36. (2) A lion-faced warrior of Gad, 1 Chr. xii. 11. (3) A son of King Rehoboam, 2 Chr. xi. 20.

Ăt-tā'lĭ-à. A coast town of Pamphylia, Acts xiv. 25.

Ăt'tă-lus (*increased*). Names of three kings of Pergamos, 1 Macc. xv. 22.

Au-gŭs'tus (*venerable*). Caius Julius Cæsar Octavianus, grand-nephew of, and heir to, Julius Cæsar. Made first emperor of Rome B. C. 27, with title of Augustus. During his reign Christ was born, Luke ii. 1. Died A. D. 14, aged 76 years.

Au-gŭs'tus' Band, Acts xxvii. 1. [ARMY.]

Au-rā'nus. A riotous fellow at Jerusalem, 2 Macc. iv. 40.

Ā'và (*ruin*). A place in Assyria, 2 Kgs. xvii. 24.

Ăv'ă-răn. Surname of Eleazer, 1 Macc. ii. 5.

Ā'ven (*nothingness*). (1) An unidentified plain, Amos i. 5. (2) Beth-aven, or Bethel, Hosea x. 8. (3) Heliopolis or city of On, Ezek. xxx. 17.

Ā-vĕnge', Ā-vĕn'ger. Exaction of just satisfaction, Luke xviii. 8; 1 Thess. iv. 6. "Avenger of Blood" was the pursuer of a slayer to avenge the blood of the slain. He must be a relative of the dead one, Deut. xix. 6.

Ā'vĭm, Ā'vĭms, Ā'vĭtes (*ruins*). (1) A primitive people who pushed into Palestine from the desert of Arabia, Deut. ii. 23. (2) Colonists from Ava sent to people Israel, 2 Kgs. xvii. 31.

Ā'vĭth (*ruins*). The king's city of Edom, Gen. xxxvi. 35; 1 Chr. i. 46.

Awl. Shape not known, but use expressed in Ex. xxi. 6; Deut. xv. 17.

Axe. Seven Hebrew words so translated. It was of stone or iron, crudely fastened to a handle of wood, Deut. xix. 5; 2 Kgs. vi. 5-7.

Ā'zăl. Probably a common noun, Zech. xiv. 5.

Ăz''a-lī'ah (*near Jehovah*). Father of Shaphan the scribe, 2 Kgs. xxii. 3.

Ăz''a-nī'ah (*whom God hears*). Father of Jeshua, Neh. x. 9.

Ă-zā'phĭ-on. Probably Sophereth, 1 Esdr. v. 33.

Ăz'ạ-rȧ. A servant of the temple, 1 Esdr. v. 35.

Ȧ-zăr'ạ-el (*whom God helps*). A Levite musician, Neh. xii. 36.

Ȧ-zăr'ẹ-el (*whom God helps*). (1) A companion of David at Ziklag, 1 Chr. xii. 6. (2) A Levite musician, 1 Chr. xxv. 18. (3) A prince of Dan, 1 Chr. xxvii. 22. (4) Son of Bani, Ezra x. 41. (5) A priest, Neh. xi. 13.

Ăz''ạ-rī'ah (*whom God helps*). (1) Grandson of Zadok, 1 Kgs. iv. 2 ; 1 Chr. vi. 9. (2) A chief officer under Solomon, 1 Kgs. iv. 5. (3) Tenth king of Judah, commonly called Uzziah, 2 Kgs. xiv. 21 ; xv. 1–27 ; 1 Chr. iii. 12. (4) A son of Ethan, 1 Chr. ii. 8. (5) A son of Jehu, 1 Chr. ii. 38, 39. (6) A high priest under Abijah and Asa, 1 Chr. vi. 10. (7) A wrongly inserted name, 1 Chr. vi. 13. (8) An ancestor of Samuel, vi. 36. (9) A prophet in Asa's reign, 2 Chr. xv. 1. (10) Son of King Jehoshaphat, 2 Chr. xxi. 2. (11) Another son of Jehoshaphat, 2 Chr. xxi. 2. (12) For Ahaziah, 2 Chr. xxii. 6. (13) A captain of Judah, 2 Chr. xxiii. 1. (14) High priest in reign of Uzziah, 2 Chr. xxvi. 17–20. (15) A captain of Ephraim in reign of Ahaz, 2 Chr. xxviii. 12. (16) A Levite, 2 Chr. xxix. 12. (17) Another Levite, 2 Chr. xxix. 12. (18) High priest in time of Hezekiah, 2 Chr. xxxi. 10–13. (19) One who helped to rebuild the walls of Jerusalem, Neh. iii. 23, 24. (20) Leader of a returned family, Neh. vii. 7. (21) A Levite who helped Ezra, Neh. viii. 7. (22) A co-covenanter with Nehemiah, Neh. x. 2. (23) Jer. xliii. 2, for Jezaniah. (24) Hebrew name of Abed-nego, Dan. i. 6.

Ăz''ạ-rī'as. A frequent name in Esdras.

Ā'zaz (*strong*). A Reubenite, 1 Chr. v. 8.

Ăz''ạ-zī'ah (*whom God strengthens*). (1) A Levite musician, 1 Chr. xv. 21. (2) A chief of Ephraim, 1 Chr. xxvii. 20. (3) Custodian of tithes and offerings under Hezekiah, 2 Chr. xxxi. 13.

Ăz-băz'ạ-rĕth. Probably Esarhaddon, 1 Esdr. v. 69.

Ăz'bŭk (*devastation*). Father of Nehemiah, Neh. iii. 16.

Ȧ-zē'kah (*dug over*). A town of Judah, Josh. x. 10, 11.

Ā'zel (*noble*). A descendant of Saul, 1 Chr. viii. 37, 38 ; ix. 43, 44.

Ā′zem (*bone*) A city of Judah and Simeon, Josh. xv. 29; xix. 3. EZEM, elsewhere.

Ā-zē′tas. A returned Hebrew family, 1 Esdr. v. 15.

Ăz′gad (*strength of fortune*). (1) Head of a large returned family, Ez. ii. 12; viii. 12; Neh. vii. 17. (2) A co-covenanter with Nehemiah, Neh. x. 15.

Ā′zĭ-el (*whom God comforts*). A Levite, 1 Chr. xv. 20; Jaaziel in vs. 18.

Ā-zī′zȧ (*strong*). A returned captive, Ez. x. 27.

Ăz′ma-vĕth (*strong unto death*). (1) One of David's mighty men, 2 Sam. xxiii. 31; 1 Chr. xi. 33. (2) A descendant of Mephibosheth, 1 Chr. viii. 36; ix. 42. (3) A Benjamite, 1 Chr. xii. 3. (4) David's treasurer, 1 Chr. xxvii. 25. (5) A place in Benjamin, Ez. ii. 24; Neh. zii. 29. The Beth-azmaveth of Neh. vii. 28.

Ăz′mŏn (*strong*). A place in southern Palestine, Num. xxxiv. 4, 5; Josh. xv. 4.

Ăz′nŏth=tā′bôr (*summits of Tabor*). A boundary of Naphtali, Josh. xix. 34.

Ā′zôr (*helper*). One of Christ's ancestors, Matt. i. 13, 14.

Ā-zō′tus. Greek form of Ashdod in Acts viii. 40. [ASHDOD.]

Ăz′rĭ-el (*help of God*). (1) Head of Manassite family, 1 Chr. v. 24. (2) A Naphtalite, 1 Chr. xxvii. 19. (3) Father cf Seraiah, Jer. xxxvi. 26.

Ăz′rĭ-kam (*avenging help*). (1) A descendant of Zerubbabel, 1 Chr. iii. 23. (2) A descendant of Saul, 1 Chr. viii. 38; ix. 44. (3) A Levite, 1 Chr. ix. 14; Neh. xi. 15. (4) Prefect of King Ahaz's palace, 2 Chr. xxviii. 7.

Ā-zū′bah (*forsaken*). (1) Wife of Caleb, 1 Chr. ii. 18, 19. (2) Mother of Jehoshaphat, 1 Kgs. xxii. 42; 2 Chr. xx. 31.

Ā′zur (*helper*). (1) Father of the false prophet Hananiah, Jer. xxviii. 1. (2) Father of one of the princes against whom Ezekiel prophesied, Ezek. xi. 1.

Ăz′zah (*strong*). In Deut. ii. 23; 1 Kgs. iv. 24; Jer. xxv. 20, for GAZA.

Ăz′zan (*very strong*). A chief of Issachar, Num. xxxiv. 26.

Ăz'zur (*helper*). A co-covenanter with Nehemiah, Neh. x. 17. Azur, elsewhere.

B

Bā'al (*lord*). (1) Baal, Bel, or Belus, supreme male god of Phœnicians and Canaanites, worshipped with self-torture and human offerings, Jer. xix. 5. Even house-tops were temples, 2 Kgs. xxiii. 12, Jer. xxxii. 29. Hebrews infected with the worship, Num. xxii. 41; xxv. 3-18; Deut. iv. 16. Became the court religion, 1 Kgs. xvi. 31-33. xviii. 19-28; 2 Kgs. x. 22; xvii. 16. Bel in Isa. xlvi. 1. Baalim, plural form, in Judg. ii. 11; x. 10, and elsewhere. (2) A Reubenite, 1 Chr. v. 5. (3) Grandson of Saul, 1 Chr. viii. 30; ix. 36. (4) A town of Simeon; Bealoth and Baalath-beer, 1 Chr. iv. 33.

Bā'al-ah (*mistress*). (1) For Kirjath-jearim in Josh. xv. 9, 10; Baale, 2 Sam. vi. 2; Kirjath-baal, Josh. xv. 60; xviii. 14. (2) A town in south Judah, Josh. xv. 29. Balah in Josh. xix. 3; and Bilhah in 1 Chr. iv. 29.

Bā'al-ath (*mistress*). A town in Dan, Josh. xix. 44; 1 Kgs. ix. 18; 2 Chr. viii. 6.

Bā'al-ath=bē'ĕr (*lord of the well*). [BAAL.] (4) [BEALOTH.]

Bā'al=bē'rith (*Baal of the covenant*). Form of Baal worshipped by the Shechemites, Judg. viii. 33; ix. 4.

Bā'ă-lē of Jū'dah. Name for Kirjath-jearim. [BAALAH.]

Bā'al=gad (*troop of Baal*). Northern limit of Joshua's conquest, Josh. xi. 17; xii. 7; xiii. 5.

Bā'al=hā'mŏn (*lord of a multitude*). Solomon had a vineyard there, S. of Sol. viii. 11.

Bā'al=hā'nan (*lord of Hanan*). (1) A king of Edom, Gen. xxxvi. 38, 39; 1 Chr. i. 49, 50. (2) Superintendent of David's groves, 1 Chr. xxvii. 28.

Bā'al=hā'zôr (*village of Baal*). The shearing-place where Absalom killed Amnon, 2 Sam. xiii. 23.

Bā'al=hĕr'mŏn (*lord of Hermon*). A peak of Hermon, Judg. iii. 3; 1 Chr. v. 23.

Bā'al-ī (*my lord*). My idol! A repudiated word of endearment, Hos. ii. 16.

Bā′al-ĭm. [BAAL.]

Bā′a̱-lĭs (*son of exultation*). A king of the Ammonites, Jer. xl. 14.

Bā′al=mē′on (*lord of the house*). A Reubenite town, Num. xxxii. 38; 1 Chr. v. 8; Ezek. xxv. 9.

Bā′al=pē′or (*lord of the opening*). The form of Baal worship in Peor, Num. xxv. 3–5, 18. Israelites shared in it, Deut. iv. 3; Josh. xxii. 17; Ps. cvi. 28; Hos. ix. 10.

Bā′al=pĕr′a̱-zĭm (*lord of divisions*). Scene of David's victory over the Philistines, 2 Sam. v. 20; 1 Chr. xiv. 11. Mount Perazim in Isa. xxviii. 21.

Bā′al=shal′ī-shȧ. An unknown place, 2 Kgs. iv. 42.

Bā′al=tā′mär (*lord of palms*). A place in Benjamin, Judg. xx. 33.

Bā′al=zē′bŭb (*god of the fly*). The form of Baal worshipped at Ekron, 2 Kgs. i. 16.

Bā′al=zē′phon (*lord of the north*). A place on western coast of Red Sea near where the Israelites crossed, Ex. xiv. 2; Num. xxxiii. 7.

Bā′a̱-nȧ (*son of affliction*). (1) Son of Solomon's commissary in Jezreel, 1 Kgs. iv. 12. (2) Father of Zadok, Neh. iii. 4.

Bā′a̱-nah (*son of affliction*). (1) Co-murderer of Ish-bosheth, killed by David, 2 Sam. iv. 2–9. (2) Father of one of David's mighty men, 2 Sam. xxiii. 29; 1 Chr. xi. 30. (3) 1 Kgs. iv. 16; Baana in vs. 12. (4) One of the returned, Ez. ii. 2; Neh. vii. 7.

Bā′a̱-rȧh (*brutish*). Wife of Shaharaim, 1 Chr. viii. 8.

Bā′′a̱-sē′ĭah (*work of Jehovah*). A Levite, 1 Chr. vi. 40.

Bā′a̱-shȧ (*bravery*). Third king of Israel, 1 Kgs. xv. 27–34; xvi. Warred continually with King Asa, 1 Kgs. xv. 33, and ruled wickedly for 24 years, B. C. 953 to 931. Family cut off according to prophecy, 1 Kgs. xvi. 3–11.

Bā′bel (*confusion*). One of Nimrod's cities in the plain of Shinar, Gen. x. 10. [BABYLON.]

Bā′bel, Tower of. That brick structure, built in the plain of Shinar, and intended to prevent the very confusion and dispersion it brought about, Gen. xi. 4–9.

Băb′y̆-lon (*Greek form of Babel*). Capital city Babylonian empires. Situate on both sides of the Euphrates, 200 miles above its junction with the Tigris, Gen. x. 10; xi. 4–9; Jer. li. 58; Isa. xlv. 1–3. Once the capital of Assyria, 2 Chr. xxxiii. 11. Reached height of its splendor and strength under Nebuchadnezzar, Isa. xiii. 19; xiv. 4; xlvii. 5; Jer. li. 41. Chief home of the captive Jews. Captured by Cyrus the Persian, through his leader Darius, B. C. 539, as prophesied in Jer. li. 31, 39, and narrated in Dan. v. Its decay dates from that date. The Babylon of 1 Pet. v. 13 is conjectural. In Rev. xiv. 8; xvii. 18, Babylon types the power of Rome.

Băb′′y̆-lō′nĭ-anş. Inhabitants of Babylon, Ez. iv. 9.

Băb′′y̆-lō′nish Găr′mĕnt (*robe of Shinar*). A richly embroidered robe worn in Babylon and prized by other peoples, Josh. vii. 21.

Bā′cà (*weeping*). Perhaps a figurative " valley; " but if real, probably Gehenna, Ps. lxxxiv. 6.

Băc′chĭ-dēs. A noted Syrian general, 1 Macc. vii. 8.

Băc-chū′rus. One of the "holy singers," 1 Esdr. ix. 24.

Băc′chus. [DIONYSUS.]

Bă-çē′nor. A Jewish captain, 2 Macc. xii. 35.

Băch′rites. Becherites, Num. xxvi. 35.

Bădg′ers′ Skins (*striped skins*). The badger not found in Palestine. Seal, porpoise, or sheep skins may be meant, Ex. xxv. 5; xxxv. 7.

Băg (*swelling*). The bag of 2 Kgs. v. 23; xii. 10, was for holding money; that of Deut. xxv. 13–15 for carrying weights. Sack was the Hebrew grain-bag, Gen. xlii. 25. The shepherd's bag was for carrying feeble lambs, Zech. xi. 15–17. The bag of Judas was probably a small chest, John xii. 6; xiii. 29.

Bā-gō′as (*eunuch*). An attendant of Holofernes, Judith xii. 1–3.

Bă-hū′rim (*low grounds*). A village between the Jordan and Jerusalem, 2 Sam. iii. 16; xvi. 5; xvii. 18; 1 Kgs. ii. 8.

Bā′jith (*house*). Temple of the gods of Moab, Isa. xv. 2.

Băk-băk'kar (*pleasing*). A descendant of Asaph, 1 Chr. ix. 15.

Băk'bŭk (*bottle*). His children returned, Ez. ii. 51.

Băk''bŭk-ī'ah (*destruction by Jehovah*). A Levite porter, Neh. xi. 17 ; xii. 9, 25.

Bāke. Baking done at home and by the women, Lev. xxvi. 26 ; 1 Sam. viii. 13 ; 2 Sam. xiii. 8 ; Jer. vii. 18. Perhaps public bakeries in Hos. vii. 4–7.

Bā'laam (*glutton*). Son of Beor, or Bosor, Deut. xxiii. 4. A man of note and given to prophecy. Slain in battle by the Hebrews, Num. xxii.-xxiv., xxxi. ; Rev. ii. 14.

Bā'lăc, Rev. ii. 14. [BALAK.]

Băl'a-dăn. [MERODACH-BALADAN.]

Bā'lah, Josh. xix. 3. Short form of Baalah.

Bā'lăk (*destroyer*). The king of Moab who hired Balaam to curse Israel, Num. xxii.-xxiv. ; Josh. xxiv. 9 ; Judg. xi. 25. Balac in Rev. ii. 14.

Băl'ăn-çes (*two scales*). Were in general use among the ancients for weighing gold and silver, and in traffic, Lev. xix. 36 ; Mic. vi. 11 ; Hos. xii. 7.

Băld'ness (*ball-like*). Priests forbidden to make themselves bald, Lev. xxi. 5 ; Deut. xiv. 1 ; Ezek. xliv. 20. "Bald-head" a cry of contempt, 2 Kgs. ii. 23 ; as indicating leprosy, Lev. xiii. 40–43. Voluntary baldness a sign of misery, Isa. iii. 24 ; Ezek. vii. 18 ; or else the conclusion of the Nazarite vow, Num. vi. 9.

Bălm (*balsam*). The Balm of Gilead, or Mecca balsam, exudes an agreeable balsamic resin, highly prized in the East as an unguent and cosmetic, as the crushed leaves were for their odor, Gen. xxxvii. 25 ; xliii. 11 ; Jer. viii. 22 ; xlvi. 11 ; Ezek. xxvii. 17.

Băl-thā'sar, Bar. i. 11, 12. [BELSHAZZAR.]

Bā'mah (*high place*). Applied to places of idolatrous worship, Ezek. xx. 29.

Bā'mŏth, Num. xxi. 19. [BAMOTH-BAAL.]

Bā'mŏth=bā'al (*heights of Baal*). A sanctuary of Baal in Moab, Josh. xiii. 17. Bamoth in Num. xxi. 19.

Band. Tenth part of a Roman legion ; called also "cohort," Matt. xxvii. 27 ; Acts xxi. 31.

Bā'nī (*built*). (1) One of David's captains, 2 Sam. xxiii. 36. (2) A forefather of Ethan, 1 Chr. vi. 46.

(3) A Judahite, 1 Chr. ix. 4. (4) "Children of Bani" returned, Ez. ii. 10; x. 29–34; Neh. x. 14. (5) A son of Bani, Ez. x. 38. (6) Three others, Levites, Neh. iii. 17; viii. 7; xi. 22.

Băn'ner. [ENSIGN.]

Băn'quet (*sitting*). A favorite part of social enjoyment and religious festivity among Hebrews. The posture was usually sitting, Gen. xxi. 8; xl. 20. Morning banquets a mark of excess, Eccles. x. 16; Isa. v. 11. Banquet incidents were foods, wines, flowers, fine robes, music vocal and instrumental, dancing, jests, riddles and merriment, Prov. ix. 2; 2 Sam. xix. 35; Neh. viii. 10; Eccl. x. 19; Isa. v. 12; xxv. 6; Matt. xxii. 11; Luke xv. 25. [FEASTS.]

Băp'tism (*dipping, bathing*). The sacrament ordinance or rite commanded by Christ, Matt. xxviii. 19, in which water is used to initiate the recipient into the Christian Church. Christ did not baptize, John iv. 2. John's baptism with water, Christ's " with the Holy Ghost and with fire," Matt. iii. 1–12; Luke iii. 16. Jesus baptized by John, Matt. iii. 13–17. Outpouring of the Holy Spirit, Acts ii. John's baptized persons re-baptized, Acts xix. 1–6; xviii. 25, 26.

Bă-răb'bas (*son of Abba*). The prisoner at Jerusalem when Christ was condemned, Matt. xxvii. 16–28; Mark xv. 7; Luke xxiii. 18; John xviii. 40.

Băr'ă-chel (*blessed of God*). Father of Elihu, Job xxxii. 2–6.

Băr''a-chi'as, Matt. xxiii. 35. [ZECHARIAS.]

Bā'rak (*lightning*). A Hebrew chieftain, Judg. iv.

Băr-bā'rĭ-an (*bearded*). In N. T. sense one not a Greek, Acts xxviii. 2; Rom. i. 14; 1 Cor. xiv. 11.

Băr-hū'mīte, 2 Sam. xxiii. 31; of BAHURIM.

Bă-rī'ah (*fugitive*). Son of Shemaiah, 1 Chr. iii. 22.

Băr''=jē'şus (*son of Jesus*), Acts xiii. 6. [ELYMAS.]

Băr''=jō'nả (*son of Jonah*), Matt. xvi. 17. [PETER.]

Băr'kŏs (*painter*). "Children of Barkos" returned, Ez. ii. 53; Neh. vii. 55.

Băr'lěy. Much cultivated by the Hebrews, Ex. ix. 31; Lev. xxvii. 16; Deut. viii. 8; Ruth ii. 7. Used for bread chiefly among the poor, Judg. vii. 13; 2 Kgs. iv. 42; John vi. 9–13; and for fodder, 1 Kgs. iv. 28. Barley harvest preceded wheat harvest, Ruth i. 22; ii. 23; 2 Sam xxi. 9, 10

Bär′na̱-bǎs (*son of comfort*). Joseph or Joses, a convert of Cyprus, and companion of Paul, Acts iv. 36; ix. 27; xi. 25, 26; xv. 22–39.

Bä̱-rō′dis. Servant of Solomon, 1 Esdr. v. 34.

Bär′sa̱-bǎs. [JOSEPH, JUDAS.]

Bär′ta̱-cŭs. Soldier of Darius, 1 Esdr. iv. 29.

Bär-thŏl′ŏ-mew (*son of Tolmai*). One of the twelve apostles, Matt. x. 3; Mark iii. 18; Luke vi. 14; Acts i. 13; perhaps Nathanael in John i. 45.

Bär″ti̱-mæ′us (*son of Timæus*). A blind beggar of Jericho, Mark x. 46–52.

Bā′ru̱ch (*blessed*). (1) Jeremiah's friend, amanuensis and fellow prisoner, Jer. xxxvi. 4–32; xxxii. 12; xliii. 3–7. (2) Nehemiah's assistant, Neh. iii. 20. (3) A co-covenanter, Neh. x. 6. (4) A Judahite, Neh. xi. 5. (5) Eighth Apocryphal book.

Bär-zĭl′la̱-ī (*strong*). (1) A Gileadite, 2 Sam. xvii. 27; xix. 32–39. (2) Father-in-law of Michal, 2 Sam. xxi. 8. (3) Son-in-law of Barzillai, Ez. ii. 61; Neh. vii. 63.

Bǎs′cȧ-mȧ. A place in Gilead, 1 Macc. xiii. 23.

Bā′shăn (*thin soil*). A country east of Jordan between Gilead on the south and Hermon on the north, Deut. iii. 10–13; Josh. xii. 4, 5; xiii. 12–30. Conquered by the Israelites, Num. xxi. 33, and allotted to the half tribe of Manasseh, Josh. xiii. 29, 30

Bā′shăn=hā′voth=jā′ĭr (*Bashan of the villages of Jair*). Name given to Argob in Bashan, Deut. iii. 14. Havoth-Jair, Num. xxxii. 41.

Bǎsh′ĕ-mǎth (*pleasing*). Wife of Esau, Gen. xxvi. 34; xxxvi. 3, 4, 13. Mahalath, Gen. xxviii. 9.

Bā′sin. One of the smaller vessels of the tabernacle, for holding the blood of the sacrificial victims. A larger vessel in John xiii. 5.

Bǎs′ket. Mostly of wicker, and variously used for bread, Gen. xl. 16–19; Ex. xxix. 2, 3, 23; Lev. viii. 2; Matt. xiv. 20; xv. 37; first fruits, Deut. xxvi. 2–4; fruits, Jer. xxiv. 1, 2; bulky articles, 2 Kgs. x. 7; Ps. lxxxi. 6.

Băs'măth (*pleasing*). Daughter of Solomon, 1 Kgs. iv. 15.

Băs'tărd. Not applied to one born out of wedlock, but to issue within the prohibited degrees, Deut. xxiii. 2.

Băt. An unclean beast. Same as our bat, Lev. xi. 19; Deut. xiv. 18; Isa. ii. 20.

Băth. A Jewish liquid measure, varying from 4¾ to 6½ gallons.

Băth, Bā'thing. Part of the Jewish ritual of purification, Lev. xiv. 8; xv. 5, 16; xvii. 15; xxii. 6; Num. xix. 7; 2 Sam. xi. 2–4; 2 Kgs. v. 10. Customary after mourning, Ruth iii. 3; 2 Sam. xii. 20. Public bathing pools usually sheltered by porticos, 2 Kgs. xx. 20; Neh. iii. 15; Isa. xxii. 11; John v. 2; ix. 7.

Băth=răb'bim (*daughter of many*). A gate of ancient Heshbon, S. of Sol. vii. 4.

Băth'=shĕ-bā'' (*daughter of the oath*). Wife of David, and mother of Solomon, 2 Sam. xi; 1 Kgs. i. 15; ii. 13–22. Bathshua in 1 Chr. iii. 5.

Băth'=shụ-ā'' [BATHSHEBA.]

Băt'tĕr-ing=ram. A heavy beam of hard wood, with the end sometimes shaped like a ram, used for battering down the gates and walls of a city, Ezek. iv. 2; xxi. 22.

Băt'tle=axe. [ARMS.]

Băt'tle-ment. The barrier around the flat-roofed houses of the East, Deut. xxii. 8; Jer. v. 10.

Băv'ă-ī. A builder, Neh. iii. 18.

Bāy=tree, Ps. xxxvii. 35. The laurel, or sweet-bay (*Laurus nobilis*).

Băz'lith (*stripping*). His descendants returned, Neh. vii. 54; Ez. ii. 52.

Băz'lŭth. [BAZLITH.]

Bdĕl'li-um (*del'i-um*) (*a plant and its gum*). A fragrant gum resin. But in Gen. ii. 12 and Num. xi. 7, a precious stone.

Bea'con (*signal*). A lighted signal for warning, Isa. xxx. 17.

Bō''ạ-lī'ah (*Jehovah is Baal*). A friend of David, 1 Chr. xii. 5.

Bē'ă-lŏth (*mistresses*). A town of south Judah, Josh. xv. 24.

Bē′an. A Bedouin tribe, 1 Macc. v. 4.

Beans, Much cultivated in Palestine, as food for man and beast, 2 Sam. xvii. 28; Ezek. iv. 9.

Bear, Found in Syria and the mountains of Lebanon, 2 Sam. xvii. 8; 2 Kgs. ii. 24; Prov. xvii. 12.

Beard (*barbed*). Badge of manhood. Tearing, cutting, or neglecting, a sign of mourning, Ez. ix. 3, Isa. xv. 2; l. 6; Jer. xli. 5; xlviii. 37. To insult it a gross outrage, 2 Sam. x. 4. Taken hold of in salutation, 2 Sam. xx. 9. Removed in leprosy, Lev. xiv. 9.

Bĕb′ă-ī (*fatherly*). (1) Head of a returned family, Ez. ii. 11; Neh. vii. 16; x. 15. (2) Father of Zechariah, Ez. viii. 11.

Bē′chĕr (*first born*). (1) Second son of Benjamin, Gen. xlvi. 21; 1 Chr. vii. 6. (2) An Ephraimite, Num. xxvi. 35. Bered in 1 Chr. vii. 20.

Bē-chō′răth (*first fruits*). An ancestor of Saul, 1 Sam. ix. 1.

Bĕc′tĭ-leth. A plain, Judith ii. 21.

Bed. The Jewish bed consisted of a mattress and coverings, Gen. xlvii. 31; 1 Sam. xix. 13; Matt. ix. 6. Placed on the floor, or on a bench, 2 Kgs. i. 4; xx. 2; Ps. cxxxii. 3; Am. iii. 12; and later became ornamental and canopied, Am. vi. 4; Esth. i. 6. For bed-chamber furnishings *see* 2 Kgs. iv. 10.

Bē′dăd (*alone*). Father of Hadad, king of Edom, Gen. xxxvi. 35; 1 Chr. i. 46.

Bē′dăn (*according to judgment*). (1) A judge of Israel, 1 Sam. xii. 11. (2) A son of Gilead, 1 Chr. vii. 17.

Bĕ-dē′jah. A son of Bani, Ez. x. 35.

Bee. Honey bees and honey abounded in Palestine, Deut. i. 44; 1 Kgs. xiv. 3; Ps. lxxxi. 16; Isa. vii. 15, 18.

Bē′′ĕl-ī′a-dă (*Baal knows*). A son of David, 1 Chr. xiv. 7; Eliada in 2 Sam. v. 16 and 1 Chr. iii. 8.

Bē-ĕl=tĕth′mus. An officer of Artaxerxes, 1 Esdr. ii. 16.

Bĕ-ĕl′ze-bŭb, properly **Bĕ-ĕl′ze-bŭl** (*lord of the house*). N. T. form of Baalzebub, "lord of the fly." It personified Satan, and the general sovereignty of evil spirits, Matt. x. 25; xii. 24; Mark iii. 22; Luke xi. 15.

Bē′er (*a well*). (1) A halting place of the Israelites, Num. xxi. 16–18. (2) Place to which Jotham fled, Judg. ix. 21.

Bĕ-ē′rà (*a well*). Son of Zophar, 1 Chr. vii. 37.

Bĕ-ē′rah (*well*). A Reubenite, 1 Chr. v. 6.

Bĕ-er=ē′lim (*well of Elim*), Isa. xv. 8. [BEER.]

Bĕ-ē′rī (*my well*). (1) Father-in-law of Esau, Gen. xxvi. 34. (2) Father of Hosea, Hos. i. 1.

Bē′er=Lă-hāi′=roi (*well of the living*). Hagar's well, Gen. xvi. 6–14; xxiv. 62; xxv. 11.

Bĕ-ē′rŏth (*wells*). (1) A Hivite city, Josh. ix. 17. (2) A halting place of the Israelites, Deut. x. 6. Benejaakan in Num. xxxiii. 31.

Bē′er=shē′bà (*well of the oath*). An old place in southern Palestine; so named by Abraham, Gen. xxi. 31-33; or Isaac, Gen. xxvi. 32, 33.

Bĕ-ĕsh′=te̞-rah′′ (*house of Ashterah*). A city of Manasseh, Josh. xxi. 27.

Bee′tle (*biting animal*). A species of locust is evidently meant in Lev. xi. 21, 22.

Beeves. Same as cattle, when limited to the bovine species, Lev. xxii. 19.

Bĕg′gar (*asker*). Pauperism was discouraged, Lev. xix. 10; xxv. 5, 6; Deut. xxiv. 19. Poor invited to feasts, Deut. xiv. 29; xxvi. 12. Beggars abhorred, Ps. cix. 10. In N. T. times beggars had a fixed place to beg, Mark x. 46; Acts iii. 2; Luke xvi. 20.

Bĕ-hē′mŏth (*water-ox*). From the poet's description a hippopotamus is meant, Job xl. 15-24.

Bē′kah. A half shekel, valued at about thirty-three cents.

Bĕl. [BAAL.]

Bē′là (*destroying*). (1) A city of the plain; afterwards called Zoar, Gen. xiv. 2; xix. 22. (2) A king of Edom, Gen. xxxvi. 31-33; 1 Chr. i. 43. (3) Eldest son of Benjamin, Gen. xlvi. 21; and founder of the Belaites, Num. xxvi. 38; 1 Chr. vii. 6; viii. 1. (4) Son of Azaz, 1 Chr. v. 8.

Bē′lah. [BELA, 3.]

Bē′la̞-ītes, Num. xxvi. 38. [BELA, 3.]

Bē′lĭ-al (*lawlessness*). A vile, worthless person, reckless of God and man, Deut. xiii. 13; Judg. xix. 22; 1 Sam. ii. 12. Hence, Satan, 2 Cor. vi. 15.

Bĕl′lows (*bag, blow-skin*), though crude, did not differ in principle and use from ours, Jer. vi. 29.

Bĕlls (*bellowers*). Bells of gold were appended to priestly robes, Ex. xxviii. 33–35. Attached to anklets, Isa. iii. 16–18. Horses ornamented with bells, Zech. xiv. 20.

Bĕl-mā′im, Bĕl′men. A town of Samaria, Judith iv. 5.

Bĕl-shăz′zar (*prince of Bel*). Last king of Babylon ; ruling at time of the great feast and handwriting on the wall, B. C. 539, Dan. v.

Bĕl′′te̞=shăz′zar (*protected by Bel*). Name given to Daniel by Nebuchadnezzar, Dan. i. 7.

Bĕn (*son*). A Levite, and porter, appointed to carry the ark, 1 Chr. xv. 18.

Be̞-nā′i̞ah (*son of the Lord*). (1) Son of Jehoiada, 1 Chr. xxvii. 5 ; captain in David's bodyguard, 2 Sam. viii. 18 ; and commander-in-chief of Solomon's army, 1 Kgs. i. 36 ; ii. 34–46. (2) One of David's mighty men, 2 Sam. xxiii. 30 ; 1 Chr. xi. 31 ; and chief of eleventh monthly course, 1 Chr. xxvii. 14. (3) A priest and trumpeter, 1 Chr. xv. 18, 20 ; xvi. 5. (4) A priest, 1 Chr. xv. 24 ; xvi. 6. (5) A Levite, 2 Chr. xx. 14. (6) A Levite, 2 Chr. xxxi. 13. (7) Prince of a family of Simeon, 1 Chr. iv. 36. (8) Four of the returned, Ez. x. 25, 30, 35, 43. (9) Father of Pelatiah, Ezek. xi. 1, 13.

Bĕn′′=am′mī (*son of my people*). Grandson of Lot, and progenitor of the Ammonites, Gen. xix. 38.

Bĕn′e̞=bē′răk (*sons of lightning*). A city of Dan, Josh. xix. 45.

Bĕn′e̞=jā′a-kăn (*sons of Jaakan*). A desert tribe, Num. xxxiii. 31, 32. [BEEROTH.] Akan in Gen. xxxvi. 27.

Bĕn′e̞=kē′dem. "People of the East," Gen. xxix. 1 ; Judg. vi. 3, 33 ; vii. 12 ; viii. 10 ; Job i. 3.

Bĕn=hā′dăd (*son of Hadad*). (1) King of Syria, B. C. 950, called Benhadad I. Conqueror of northern Israel, 1 Kgs. xv. 18. (2) Benhadad II., son and successor of former, 1 Kgs. xx. 1. Defeated by Jehoram, 2 Kgs. vi. 8–33. Murdered by his servants, 2 Kgs. viii. 1–15 ; B. C. 890. (3) Benhadad III., son and successor of Hazael on Syrian throne, about B. C. 840. Defeated by King Joash, 2 Kgs. xiii. 3–24.

Bĕn=hā′il (*son of strength*). A prince in Judah, 2 Chr. xvii. 7.

Bĕn=hā′năn (*son of grace*). Son of Shimon, 1 Chr. iv. 20.

Bĕn′ĭ-nū (*our son*). A co-covenanter, Neh. x. 13.

Bĕn′ja-min (*son of the right hand*). (1) Youngest of Jacob's children. First named Benoni, afterwards Benjamin, Gen. xxxv. 16–18. Beloved by Jacob, Gen. xlii. ; visited Egypt, Gen. xliii. ; tribe distinguished as Jacob prophesied, Gen. xlix. 27 ; 1 Sam. xx. 20, 36 ; 2 Sam. ħ. 22 ; Judg. xx. 16 ; 1 Chr. viii. 40. Their allotment described in Josh. xviii. 11–28. Tribe awfully visited, Judg. xx., xxi. (2) Head of a Benjamite family, 1 Chr. vii. 10. (3) A returned captive, Ez. x. 32.

Bĕ′nō (*his son*). A Levite, 1 Chr. xxiv. 26, 27.

Bĕn=ō′nī (*son of my sorrow*), Gen. xxxv. 18. [BENJAMIN.]

Bĕn=zō′heth (*son of Zoheth*). A descendant of Judah, 1 Chr. iv. 20.

Bĕ′ŏn, Num. xxxii. 3. [BAAL-MEON.]

Bĕ′or (*burning*). (1) Father of Bela, an early king of Edom, Gen. xxxvi. 32. (2) Father of Balaam, Num. xxii. 5 ; xxiv. 3, 15 ; xxxi. 8 ; Deut. xxiii. 4 ; Josh. xiii. 22 ; xxiv. 9 ; Micah vi. 5. Bosor in N. T.

Bĕ′rå (*son of evil*). A king of Sodom, Gen. xiv. 2–22.

Bĕr′ă-chah (*blessing*). (1) A Benjamite, 1 Chr. xii. 3. (2) The valley in which Jehoshaphat celebrated his victory, 2 Chr. xx. 26.

Bĕr″a-chī′ah (*God has blessed*). Father of Asaph, 1 Chr. vi. 39.

Bĕr″a-ī′ah (*created by God*). A Benjamite, 1 Chr. viii. 21.

Bĕ-rē′å (*watered*). (1) A city of Macedonia, Acts xvii. 1–15. (2) A Syrian city, now Aleppo, 2 Macc. xiii. 4. (3) A place in Judea, 1 Macc. ix. 4.

Bĕr″e-chī′ah (*blessed of Jehovah*). (1) A descendant of David, 1 Chr. iii. 20. (2) A Levite, 1 Chr. ix. 16. (3) Father of Asaph, 1 Chr. xv. 17. (4) A door-keeper for the Ark, 1 Chr. xv. 23. (5) An Ephraimite, 2 Chr. xxviii. 12. (6) Father of a builder, Neh. iii. 4, 30 ; vi. 18. (7) Father of Zechariah, Zech. i. 1–7.

Bē'red (*hail*). (1) A place in south Palestine, Gen. xvi. 14. (2) An Ephraimite, 1 Chr. vii. 20.

Bĕr''ĕ-nī'çe. [BERNICE.]

Bē'rī (*well*). An Asherite, 1 Chr. vii. 36.

Bĕ̄-rī'ah (*evil*). (1) A descendant of Asher, Gen. xlvi. 17 ; Num. xxvi. 44, 45 ; 1 Chr. vii. 30, 31. (2) An Ephraimite, 1 Chr. vii. 23. (3) A chief of Benjamin, 1 Chr. viii. 13, 16. (4) A Levite, 1 Chr. xxiii. 10, 11.

Bĕ̄-rī'ītes, Num. xxvi. 44. Descendants of Beriah (1).

Bē'rītes. A people in north Palestine, 2 Sam. xx. 14.

Bē'rith (*covenant*), Judg. ix. 46. [BAAL-BERITH.]

Bĕr-nī'çe (*bringing victory*). Eldest daughter of Herod Agrippa, Acts xii. 1, and sister of the younger Agrippi, Acts xxv. 13–23 ; xxvi. 30.

Bĕ-rō'dăch=băl'a̱-dăn, 2 Kgs. xx. 12. [MERODACH-BALADAN.]

Bĕ-rō'thah (*of a well*). A boundary town of north Palestine, Ezek. xlvii. 16.

Bĕr'o̱-thāi (*my wells*). A city of north Palestine, 2 Sam. viii. 8.

Bē'rŏth-īte, 1 Chr. xi. 39, of Beeroth.

Bĕr'yl (*beril*) (*jewel*). The first stone in fourth row of a high priest's breastplate, Ex. xxviii. 20.

Bē'sāi (*sword*). His children returned, Ez. ii. 49 ; Neh. vii. 52.

Bĕs''ŏ-dē'i̱ah (*in the Lord's secret*). Father of an architect, Neh. iii. 6.

Bē'sŏm (*broom*). Twig broom ı̇or sweeping, Isa. xiv. 23.

Bē'sôr (*cool*). A brook in south Judah, 1 Sam. xxx. 9–21.

Bē'tah (*confidence*). A city of Zoba, 2 Sam. viii. 8. Tibhath in 1 Chr. xviii. 8.

Bĕt'a̱-nȧ. A place close to oak of Abraham, Judith i. 9.

Bē'ten (*raised*). Border city of Asher, Josh. xix. 25.

Bĕth (*house*). Used in combinations.

Beth''=ab'ȧ-rȧ (*house at the ford*). A place beyond, or at, Jordan where John baptized Christ, John i. 28.

Bĕth″=ā′năth (*house of reply*). City of Naphtali, Judg. i. 33.

Bĕth″=ā′nŏth (*house of reply*). A mountain town of Judah, Josh. xv. 59.

Bĕth′ă-ný (*house of affliction*). A village on the slope of Olivet close to Bethphage, Matt. xxi. 17; Mark xi. ; Luke xix. 29; John xi. 18. Now *Lazarieh.*

Bĕth″=ăr′ă-bah (*house of the desert*). A city of Judah and Benjamin, Josh. xv. 61; xviii. 22.

Bĕth″=ā′răm, properly BETHHARAN (*house of height*). A town of Gad, Josh. xiii. 27.

Bĕth″=är′bel (*house of ambush*). Scene of the massacre by Shalman, Hos x. 14.

Bĕth″=ā′ven (*house of idols*). A place in Benjamin, Josh. vii. 2; xviii. 12; 1 Sam. xiii. 5; xiv. 23. Stands for Bethel in Hos. iv. 15; v. 8; x. 5.

Bĕth″=ăz′ma-veth (*house of Azmaveth*). A town of Benjamin, Neh. vii. 28; Azmaveth and Bethsamos, elsewhere.

Bĕth″=bā′al=mē′on (*house of Baal-meon*). A place in Reuben, Josh. xiii. 17. Beon in Num. xxxii. 3; Baal-meon in xxxii. 38.

Bĕth″=bā′rah (*house of the ford*), Judg. vii. 24. [BETH-ABARA.]

Bĕth″=bā′sī. A town near Jericho, 1 Macc. ix. 62-64.

Bĕth″=bĭr′e̜-ī (*house of my creation*). A town in south Simeon, 1 Chr. iv. 31. Beth-lebaoth in Josh. xix. 6.

Bĕth′=căr (*house of the lamb*). A place where the Israelites' pursuit ended, 1 Sam. vii 11.

Bĕth″=dā′gon (*house of Dagon*). (1) Town in Judah, Josh. xv. 41. (2) Town in Asher, Josh. xix. 27.

Bĕth″=dĭb″la-thā′im (*house of dried figs*). A town of Moab, Jer. xlviii. 22. [ALMON-DIBLATHAIM.]

Bĕth′=el (*house of God*). (1) City of Palestine, 12 mls. N. of Jerusalem, Gen. xii. 8; xiii. 3, 4; scene of Jacob's vision, then called Luz, Gen. xxviii. 11-19; xxxi. 13; xxxv. 1-8; Judg. i. 23; residence of "sons of the prophets" and priests, 2 Kgs. ii. 2, 3; xvii. 27, 28. Now *Beitin.* (2) A town in south Judah, Josh. xii. 16; 1 Sam. xxx. 27; Chesil in Josh.

xv. 30; Bethul in **xix.** 4; and Bethuel in 1 Chr. iv. 30. (3) Mount Bethel, near Bethel, Josh. xvi. 1; 1 Sam. xiii. 2.

Bĕth″=ē′mĕk (*house of the valley*). A boundary of Asher, Josh. xix. 27.

Bē′thĕr. Figurative mountains, S. of Sol. ii. 17.

Bĕ̇-thĕṣ′dȧ (*house of mercy*). A pool near the sheep-gate, Jerusalem, John v. 2.

Bĕth″=ē′zĕl (*neighbor's house*). A place in Philistia, Mic. i. 11.

Bĕth″=gā′dĕr (*house of a wall*). A doubtful place or person, 1 Chr. ii. 51.

Bĕth″=gā′mŭl (*camel-house*). A town of Moab, Jer. xlviii. 23.

Bĕth″=gil′gal, Neh. xii. 29. [GILGAL.]

Bĕth″=hăc′çĕ-rĕm (*house of the vine*). A beacon station near Tekoa, Neh. iii. 14; Jer. vi. 1.

Bĕth″=hā′ran, Num. xxxii. 36. [BETH-ARAM.]

Bĕth″=hŏg′la, and **Hŏg′lah** (*partridge-house*). A place in boundary of Judah and Benjamin, Josh. xv. 6; xviii. 19-21.

Bĕth″=hō′rŏn (*cave-house*). A town of Benjamin, Josh. xvi. 3, 5; 1 Kgs. ix. 17; 1 Chr. vii. 24.

Bĕth″=jĕsh′ĭ-mŏth and **Jĕs′ĭ-mŏth** (*house of deserts*). A town of Moab, allotted to Reuben, Num. xxxiii. 49; Josh. xii. 3; xiii. 20.

Bĕth″=lĕb′ạ-ŏth (*house of lionesses*), Josh. xix. 6. [BETH-BIREI.]

Bĕth′=lĕ-hĕm, Beth′lĕ-hĕm (*house of bread*). (1) A town of Palestine, six miles S. of Jerusalem. First called Ephrath or Ephratah, Gen. xxxv. 16-19; xlviii. 7. Called Bethlehem-judah after the conquest, Judg. xvii. 7. Home of Ruth, Ruth i. 19. Birthplace of David, 1 Sam. xvii. 12. Here Christ was born, Matt. ii. 1, 2; Luke ii. 15-18. (2) A town in Zebulun, Josh. xix. 15.

Bĕth″=lō′mŏn, 1 Esdr. v. 17. [BETHLEHEM.]

Bĕth″mā′a-chah, 2 Sam. xx. 14, 15. Same as Abel, Abel-maim, and Abel-beth-maachah.

Bĕth″=mär′că-bŏth (*house of chariots*). A town of Simeon, Josh. xix. 5; 1 Chr. iv. 31. Madmannah in Josh. xv. 31.

Bĕth″=mē′on, Jer. xlviii. 23. Contraction of Beth-baal-meon.

Běth″=nĭm′rah (*house of leopards*). A fenced city of Gad, Num. xxxii. 36. Nimrah in vs. 3.

Běth″=pā′let (*house of expulsion*). A town in south Judah, Josh. xv. 27. Bethphelet in Neh. xi. 26.

Běth″=păz′zez (*house of dispersion*). A town of Issachar, Josh. xix. 21.

Běth=pē′or (*house of Peor*). A spot opposite Jericho, dedicated to Baal-peor, Deut. iii. 29; iv. 46; Josh. xiii. 20.

Běth′pha-ġē̇ (*house of figs*). A place on Olivet, close to Bethany, Matt. xxi. 1; Luke xix. 29; Mark xi. 1.

Běth″=phē′let, Neh. xi. 26. [BETH-PALET.]

Běth″=rā′pha (*house of health*). Son of Eshton, 1 Chr. iv. 12.

Běth″=rē′hŏb (*house of Rehob*). A province of Aram, or Syria, 2 Sam. x. 6. Rehob in vs. 8.

Běth-sā′ĭ-dȧ (*fishing-house*). A fishing-village on Sea of Galilee, and west of Jordan. Birthplace of Andrew, Peter and Philip, Matt. xi. 21; John i. 44; xii. 21. Bethsaida, where the five thousand were fed, Mark vi. 31–53; Luke ix. 10–17, appears to have been on eastward side of Jordan.

Běth″=sā′mos, 1 Esdr. v. 18. [BETH-AZMAVETH.]

Běth=shăn′, 1 Macc. v. 52. [BETH-SHEAN.]

Běth″=shē′ăn, **Běth′=săn**, **Běth′=shăn** (*house of rest*). A city of Manasseh, Josh. xvii. 11; Judg. i. 27; 1 Chr. vii. 29; Bethshan in 1 Sam. xxxi. 10–12. A commissary district of Solomon, 1 Kgs. iv. 12. Now Beisan.

Běth″=shē′mĕsh (*house of the sun*). (1) A Levitical town of N. Judah, Josh. xv. 10; xxi. 16. Now Ainshems. (2) A border city of Issachar, Josh. xix. 22. (3) A fenced city of Naphtali, Josh. xix. 38; Judg. i. 33. (4) Probably Heliopolis, Egypt, Jer. xliii. 13.

Běth″=shĭt′tah (*house of the acacia*). The place where Gideon's pursuit ended, Judg. vii. 22.

Běth″=sū′rȧ, 1 Macc. iv. 29. [BETH-ZUR.]

Běth″=tăp′pu-ah (*house of apples*). A town of Judah, near Hebron. Now Teffuh, Josh. xv. 53.

Běth-u′el (*filiation of God*). (1) Father of Laban and Rebekah, Gen. xxii. 22, 23; xxiv. 15, 24, 47; xxviii. 2–5. (2) [BETHUL.]

Bē′thŭl (*dweller in God*). A town of Simeon, Josh. xix. 4; Chesil in Josh. xv. 30; Bethuel in 1 Chr. iv. 30.

Bē-thu′lĭ-à. Scene of Judith's exploits, Judith iv. 6; vi. 11–14.

Bĕth′=zûr (*house of rock*). Now Beit Sûr, 4 mls. N. of Hebron, Josh. xv. 58; 2 Chr. xi. 7.

Bē-tō′lĭ-us, 1 Esdr. v. 21. [BETHEL.]

Bĕt′′ŏ-mĕs′them. A town near Esdraelon, Judith iv. 6.

Bĕt′ŏ-nim (*bellies*). A town of Gad, Josh. xiii. 26.

Bē-trōth′ (*in promise*). To pledge troth, *i. e.*, engage to marry. A betrothed woman was regarded as the lawful wife of her spouse, and he could not break off the match without a divorce, while she, if unfaithful, would be considered an adulteress.

Beū′lah (*married*). The land of Israel when the Jewish Church is again in its true relation to God, Isa. lxii. 4.

Bē′zāi (*conqueror*). His children returned, Ez. ii. 17; Neh. vii. 23.

Bē-zăl′ĕ-el (*in the shadow of God*). (1) A Tabernacle architect, Ex. xxxi. 1–6. (2) A returned Jew, Ez. x. 30.

Bē′zek (*lightning*). (1) A place in Judah, Judg. i. 1–5. (2) Where Saul numbered Israel, 1 Sam. xi. 8.

Bē′zer (*ore*). (1) A city of refuge east of Jordan, Deut. iv. 43; Josh. xx. 8. (2) An Asherite, 1 Chr. vii. 37.

Bē′zeth. Encampment of Bacchides, 1 Macc. vii. 19.

Bī′ble (*the book*). The term applied, not further back than the fifth century, to that collection of *biblia*, or holy books, which comprises the Old and New Testaments.

Bĭch′rī (*first-born*). A Benjamite, 2 Sam. xx. 1.

Bĭd′kär (*stabber*). One of Jehu's captains, 2 Kgs. ix. 25.

Bier (*that bears*). The frame on which a dead body was carried to the grave, Luke vii. 14; 2 Chr. xvi. 14.

Bĭg′thả, Bĭg′thăn, Bĭg′than-å (*gift of God*). A chamberlain of King Ahasuerus, Esth. i 10. Bigthan in ii. 21 ; Bigthana in vi. 2.

Bĭg′vạ-ī (*happy*). (1) His children returned, Ez. ii. 14 ; viii. 14 ; Neh. vii. 19. (2) A chief under Zerubbabel, Ezra ii. 2 ; Neh. vii. 7 ; x. 16.

Bĭl′dăd (*son of strife*). The Shuhite friend of Job ii. 11 ; viii., xviii., xxv.

Bĭl′ĕ-ăm (*foreigners*). A town of Manasseh, 1 Chr vi. 70.

Bĭl′gah (*first-born*). (1) Head of the fifteenth temple course, 1 Chr. xxiv. 14. (2) A returned priest, Neh. xii. 5, 18. Bilgai in x. 8.

Bĭl′gạ-ī, Neh. x. 8. [BILGAH.]

Bĭl′hah (*timid*). (1) Mother of Dan and Naphtali, Gen. xxix. 29 ; xxx. 3-8 ; xxxv. 25 ; xlvi. 25 ; 1 Chr. vii. 13. (2) A town of Simeon, 1 Chr. iv. 29.

Bĭl′hăn (*modest*). (1) A Horite chief, Gen. xxxvi. 27. (2) A Benjamite, 1 Chr. vii. 10.

Bĭl′shăn (*eloquent*). A returned captive, Ez. ii. 2 ; Neh. vii. 7.

Bĭm′hăl (*circumcised*). A son of Japhlet, 1 Chr. vii. 33.

Bĭn′ẹ-å (*fountain*). A descendant of Saul, 1 Chr. viii. 37.

Bĭn′nụ-ī (*building*). Name of five returned captives, Ez. viii. 33 ; x. 30, 38 ; Neh. vii. 15 ; x. 9.

Birds. Many birds of Palestine similar to our own. The "speckled bird" of Jer. xii. 9 means a vulture. Birds were snared, Ps. cxxiv. 7 ; Prov. vii. 23 ; Am. iii. 5. Used for curing leprosy, Lev. xiv. 2-7. List of birds not to be eaten, Lev. xi. 13-19 ; Deut. xiv. 11-19.

Bĭr′shả (*son of godliness*). A king of Gomorrah, Gen. xiv. 2.

Birth′days. Observed among ancients by feasts, Gen. xl. 20 ; Job i. 4 ; Hos. vii. 5 ; Matt. xiv. 6-10.

Birth′right. Among Jews the first-born son enjoyed the right of consecration, Ex. xxii. 29 ; great dignity, Gen. xlix. 3 ; a double portion of the paternal estate, Deut. xxi. 17 ; right to royal succession, 2 Chr. xxi. 3.

Bĭr′za-vĭth. An Asherite, 1 Chr. vii. 31.

Bĭsh′ŏp (*looking upon, or over*). Greek *episkopos*, overseer. An officer of the Apostolic church, identical with presbyter, or elder, Acts xx. 17, 18; 1 Tim. iii. 1-13; v. 17; Tit. i. 5-8; 1 Pet. v; 1 Thess. v. 12; James v. 14.

Bĭsh'ŏp-rĭc''. The jurisdiction and charge of a bishop, Acts i. 20; 1 Tim. iii. 1.

Bĭth'ĭ-ah (*daughter of the Lord*) Daughter of a Pharaoh, 1 Chr. iv. 18.

Bĭth'rŏn (*ravine*). A place east of Jordan, 2 Sam. ii. 29.

Bĭ-thўn'ĭ-à. A province of Asia Minor, bordering on the Euxine (Black) sea and west of Pontus, Acts xvi. 7; 1 Pet. i. 1. Capital, Nice or Nicæa.

Bĭt'ter Herbs. A part of the passover feast, Ex. xii. 8.

Bĭt'tern. A bird of the heron family, solitary in its habits, and noted for its melancholy night booming, Isa. xiv. 23; xxxiv. 11; Zeph. ii. 14.

Bĭz-jŏth'jah (*contempt*). A town of south Judah, Josh. xv. 28.

Bĭz'thà (*eunuch*). A eunuch, Esth. i. 10.

Blains (*boils*). The ulcerous inflammations which constituted the sixth Egyptian plague, Ex. ix. 9-11; Deut. xxviii. 27, 35.

Blăs'phē-mў (*injurious speaking*). Speaking evil of God, Lev. xxiv. 11; Ps. lxxiv. 18; Isa. lii. 5; Matt. xii. 32; Acts xviii. 6; Rom. ii. 24; Col. iii. 8. Royalty could be blasphemed, 1 Kgs. xxi. 10. Punished by stoning, Lev. xxiv. 11-14.

Blăs'tus (*that buds*). Chamberlain of Herod Agrippa, Acts xii. 20.

Blĕm'ish (*wound, stain*). For ceremonial blemishes *see* Lev. xxi. 18-20; xxii. 20-24.

Blind'ness. Blind treated with compassion, Lev. xix. 14; Deut xxvii. 18. A punishment, Judg. xvi. 21; 1 Sam. xi. 2; 2 Kgs. xxv. 7.

Blood. The vital fluid, Gen. ix. 4. Forbidden as food, Ex. xxix. 12; Lev. vii. 26; xvii. 11-13. For N. T. atoning blood *see* Heb. ix, x.; Acts xx. 28; Rom. v. 9; Eph. i. 7; Col. i. 14; Heb. vii. 27; 1 John i. 7.

Bō''ăn-êr'ges (*sons of thunder*). A name given by Christ to James and John, sons of Zebedee, Mark iii. 17.

Boar. Found wild in the thickets of Jordan and on the Lebanon ranges, Ps. lxxx. 13.

Bō'ăz (*lovely*). (1) The Bethlehemite who married Ruth. *See* Book of Ruth; Matt i. 5. (2) A brazen pillar in the porch of Solomon's temple, 1 Kgs. vii. 21; 2 Chr. iii. 17, Jer. lii. 21.

Bŏch'e-rụ (*young*). Son of Azel, 1 Chr. viii. 38.

Bō'chim (*weepers*). A place near Gilgal, Judg. ii. 1-5.

Booth (*hut*). Temporary structures, usually of boughs, Gen. xxxiii. 17; Lev. xxiii. 42.

Boot'y (*dealt out*). Spoils of war, regulated as in Num. xxxi. 26-47; 1 Sam. xxx. 24, 25.

Bō'oz, Matt. i. 5; Luke iii. 32. [BOAZ.]

Bŏs'căth, 2 Kgs. xxii. 1. [BOZKATH.]

Bos'om (*buz'um*). To lean on, implied great intimacy, John xiii. 23. Figuratively, Paradise, Luke xvi. 23; xxiii. 43.

Bō'sŏr. Greek form of Beor, 2 Pet. ii. 15.

Bŏs'ŏ-rȧ. Bozrah, 1 Macc. v. 26, 28.

Bŏs'ses (*humps*). Knobs on shields and bucklers, Job xv. 26.

Bŏtch. [BLAIN.]

Bŏt'tle (*little boot*). Primitive bottles, either of skin or earthenware, Gen. xxi. 14; Jer. xix. 1; Matt. ix. 17; of different sizes and shapes. Tear bottles used, Ps. lvi. 8.

Bō'han (*thumb*). A Reubenite, Josh. xv. 6; xviii. 17.

Boil. Burning inflammation, Lev. xiii. 23.

Bŏnd'age. [SLAVE.]

Bŏll'ed (*budded*). Podded, as flax, Ex. ix. 31.

Book (*beech*). Letters were at first engraved on stone, brick, or metal, Deut. xxvii. 2, 3, Job xix. 24; later, on papyrus, bark of trees, tablets of wax, cloth of linen or cotton, the latter in long rolls, or "scrolls," which were the books of the Hebrews.

Bōw. Besides the bow and arrow the bow-gun was used by the ancients as an offensive weapon, 1 Macc. vi. 20. [ARCHERY.] [ARMS.]

Bŏw. The Eastern mode of salutation by kneeling on one knee and bending the head forward, Gen. xxxvii. 10; 1 Kgs. i. 53; ii. 19.

Bŏw'els. Used figuratively for the emotions, Col. iii. 12; 1 John iii. 17.

Box=tree. The evergreen, whose wood is so prized by engravers, Isa. xli. 19; lx. 13.

Bō'zĕz (*height*). Sharp rocks mentioned in 1 Sam. xiv. 4, 5.

Bŏz'kăth (*craggy*). A lowland city of Judah, Josh. xv. 39; 2 Kgs. xxii. 1.

Bŏz'rah (*strong-hold*). (1) Ancient capital of Edom, Gen. xxxvi. 33; Isa. xxxiv. 6; lxiii. 1; Jer. xlix. 13, 22. (2) A city of Moab, Jer. xlviii. 24.

Brāce'let. A wrist and arm ornament worn by both sexes, Gen. xxiv. 30; Ezek. xvi. 11. A badge of royalty, and worn above elbow, 2 Sam. i. 10.

Brăm'ble (*blackberry*). [Thorns.]

Brass. An alloy of copper and zinc, not known to the Jews. The brass of Scripture was probably copper, or a copper alloy, Gen. iv. 22; Deut. viii. 9; Judg. xvi. 21; 2 Kgs. xxv 7; 1 Sam. xvii. 5; Job xxviii. 2; 1 Cor. xiii. 1.

Brā'zen Serpent. [Serpent.]

Breach'es (*broken*). Creeks, bays, and river-mouths; havens in case of storm, Judg. v. 17; Josh. xix. 29.

Bread (*brewed, baked*). Early used, Gen. xviii. 5, 6; Ex. xii. 34; Jer. vii. 18. Made of wheat, barley, rye, fitches, and spelt, in loaves or rolls, leavened or unleavened; the kneading being in troughs, bowls, or on flat plates, and the baking in portable ovens of earthenware, or upon heated stones, or on the coals.

Breast'plate. The breastplate of the high priest, Ex. xxviii. 15, was of embroidered stuff, some 10 inches square; its upper corners fastened with gold or lace to the ephod, its lower to the girdle, Ex. xxviii. 28. Adorned with 12 precious stones, Ex. xxviii. 12-29.

Breech'es (*broken, i. e. crotched*). Drawers or light trousers worn by priests, reaching from loins to thighs, Ex. xxviii. 42.

Brick (*fragment*). Bricks were made of clay, mixed with straw, usually larger than our bricks, and burned in a kiln or dried in the sun, Gen. xi. 3; Ex. i. 14; v. 7, 2 Sam. xii. 31; Jer. xliii. 9.

Bride, Bridegroom. [Marriage.]

Brĭg′an-dine (*brawl*), Jer. xlvi. 4; elsewhere as habergeon.

Brĭm′stone (*burn-stone*). Sulphur, Gen. xix. 24, of frequent figurative use, Job xviii. 15; Ps. xi. 6; Isa. xxxiv 9; Rev. xxi. 8.

Bŭck′ler (*cheek*). The small round shield used to catch blows. [ARMOR.]

Bŭk′kī (*void*). (1) A prince of Dan, Num. **xxxiv.** 22. (2) Fifth from Aaron in line of high priests, 1 Chr. vi. 5, 51.

Bŭk-kī′ah (*wasting*). A Temple musician, 1 Chr. xxv. 4, 13.

Bŭl (*rain*). Marchesvan or Bul, the second month of the Hebrew civil and eighth of the sacred year, corresponding to parts of October and November, 1 Kgs. vi. 38.

Bŭl′bŭl. The Persian nightingale, common in the Jordan valley; also the titmouse, in the Latin version.

Bull, Bullock (*bellow*). A term used generically for ox, cattle, etc., Ps. xxii. 12. Bullock in Isa. lxv. 25; cow in Ezek. iv. 15; oxen in Gen. xii. 16. The "wild bull" of Isa. li. 20, and the "wild ox" of Deut. xiv. 5, mean probably the oryx.

Bul′rush (*large rush*). The bulrush of Ex. ii. 3–5 is supposed to be the papyrus, from which paper was made, Job viii. 11.

Bū′nah (*discretion*). A descendant of Judah, 1 Chr. ii. 25.

Bŭn′nĭ (*built*). (1) A Levite, Neh. ix. 4. (2) A co-covenanter with Nehemiah, Neh. x. 15. (3) A Levite, Neh. xi. 15.

Bŭr′ĭ-al, Bŭr-y̆ (*mounding*). Place, a cave or hewn rock, Gen. xxiii. 4; xxv. 9; l. 5–13; Matt. xxvii. 60. Body washed, Acts ix. 37; swathed and spiced, Matt. xxvii. 59; Mark xv. 46; xvi. 1. Head covered separately, 2 Chr. xvi. 14; John xix. 40; pall-bearers and mourners, relatives and friends, 2 Sam. iii. 31; Luke vii. 12; sometimes hired mourners, Jer. ix. 17; Ezek. xxiv. 17; Matt. ix. 23.

Burnt offering. The offering which was wholly consumed by fire. For ceremonies *see* Lev. viii., ix., xiv., xxix.

Bush. Supposably the dwarf acacia, Ex. iii. 2–6.

In Deut. xxxiii. 16, Mark xii. 26, Luke xx. 37, the reference is to the locality.

Bush'el (*little box*). Hebrew *seah*, twenty pints.

Bŭt'ler (*bottler*). Officer of a royal household in charge of the wines and drinking vessels, Gen. xl. 1–13; xli. 9; "cup-bearer," Neh. i. 11; 1 Kgs. x. 5.

Bŭt'ter (*cow-cheese*). A curd, or curded milk, evidently meant, Gen. xviii. 8; Job xxix. 6; Judg. v. 25.

Bŭt'ter-fly. Nine Hebrew words confusedly translated locust and associated insects. Butterfly a natural incident to caterpillar life.

Bŭz (*despised*). (1) Progenitor of Elihu, Gen. xxii. 21. (2) A Gadite, 1 Chr. v. 14. (3) Land of Buz, Jer. xxv. 23.

Bŭz'ite. Elihu so called, Job xxxii. 2, 6. [ELI-HU, 1.]

Bū'zī (*despised*). Father of Ezekiel, Ezek. i. 3.

C

Căb. A Jewish dry measure, about a quart, 2 Kgs. vi. 25.

Căb'bon (*understanding*). A town in lowlands of Judah, Josh. xv. 40.

Căb'ins. Cells in a dungeon, Jer. xxxvii. 16.

Cā'bŭl (*displeasing*). (1) A boundary of Asher, Josh. xix. 27. (2) The district given to Hiram by Solomon, 1 Kgs. ix. 10-14.

Căd'dis. Joannan, 1 Macc. ii. 2.

Cā'des, 1 Macc. xi. 63. [KEDESH.]

Căd'mi-el, 1 Esdr. v. 26. [KADMIEL.]|

Çæ'şar (*hairy, or elephant*). With Julius Cæsar and Augustus Cæsar a surname, but with the latter it became official and remained so till the death of Nero. In Luke ii. 1, Augustus Cæsar is meant; in Luke iii. 1, Tiberius Cæsar; in Acts xi. 28, Claudius Cæsar; in Acts xxv. 8, Phil. iv. 22, Nero.

Çæs''ą-rē'å (*for Cæsar*). Political capital of Palestine, on Mediterranean, and official residence of Herodian kings and Roman procurators; home of Philip and Cornelius, Acts viii. 40; x., xi. 1-18.

Çæs''ą-rē'å Phĭ-lĭp'pī. A city of Galilee marking the northern limit of Christ's pilgrimage, and probable scene of the configuration, Matt. xvi. 13-20 xvii. 1-10; Mark viii. 27.

Cāge (*hollow*). Bird-trap in Jer. v. 27; prison in Rev. xviii. 2.

Cā'ĭa-phăs (*depression*). Appointed high priest by Valerius, and reappointed by Pontius Pilate; A. D. 27–36. Deposed by Vitellius, Matt. xxvi. 3–57; John xi. 49–51; xviii. 13–28; Acts iv. 6.

Cāin (*possession*). (1) Eldest son of Adam, Gen. iv. (2) A city in lowlands of Judah, Josh. xv. 57.

Că-ī'nan (*possessor*). (1) Son of Enos, Gen. v. 9; Luke iii. 36. Kenan in 1 Chr. i. 2. (2) Son of Arphaxad, Luke iii. 36.

Cāke. [BREAD.]

Cā'lah (*old age*). City of Assyria, Gen. x. 11.

Căl''ă-mŏl'ă-lus. A compound of Elam, Lod, and Hadidad, 1 Esdr. v. 22.

Căl'a-mus (*reed*). Ex. xxx. 23, S. of Sol. iv. 14, Ezek. xxvii. 19, identified with the lemon-grass, or sweet-flag. "Sweet cane" in Isa. xliii. 24, Jer. vi. 20.

Căl'cŏl (*nourishment*). A Judahite, 1 Chr. ii. 6.

Căl'drŏn (*hot*). A vessel for boiling meats, 1 Sam. ii. 14; 2 Chr. xxxv. 13; Job xli. 20; Micah iii. 3.

Cā'leb (*capable*). (1) Son of Hezron, 1 Chr. ii. 18, 19, 42, 50. Chelubai in ii. 9. (2) The spy of Judah, Num. xiii. 6; Josh. xiv., xv. ; 1 Sam. xxx. 14. (3) Son of Hur, 1 Chr. ii. 50. (4) Caleb's district, 1 Sam. xxx. 14.

Cālf. Fatted calf a luxury, Gen. xviii. 7; 1 Sam. xxviii. 24; Am. vi. 4; Luke xv. 23. Molten calf, Ex. xxxii. 4; 1 Kgs. xii. 28, gilded structures. Calf worship denounced, Hos. viii., x., xiii. 2. "Calves of our lips," Hos. xiv. 2, fruits of our lips.

Căl-lis'thĕ-nēs. Friend of Nicanor, 2 Macc. viii. 33.

Căl'neh, Căl'nō (*fortress*). A city of Nimrod, Gen. x. 10; Am. vi. 2; Isa. x. 9. Canneh in Ezek. xxvii. 23.

Căl'phī. A general, 1 Macc. xi. 70.

Căl'vă-rў (*skull*). Latin for Greek *Kranion*, "skull" (referring to shape), and Hebrew "Golgotha." Spot of crucifixion. Calvary, only in Luke xxiii. 33.

Căm'el (*carrier*). The Arabian, or one-humped camel, generally meant. Used for carriage, and source of wealth, Gen. xii. 16; Judg. vii. 12; 2 Chr. xiv. 15; Job i. 3; xlii. 12; Isa. xxx. 6. An unclean beast, Lev. xi. 4. Hair used for clothing, 2 Kgs. i. 8; Zech. xiii. 4; Matt. iii. 4. Figuratively for something beyond human power, Matt. xix. 24; xxiii. 24.

Cā'mŏn (*straw*). Burial place of Jair, Judg. x. 5.

Cămp. [ENCAMPMENT.]

Căm'phīre. The gum of the camphor-tree. But in S. of Sol. i. 14; iv. 13; the cyprus flower or henna.

Cā'nā (*reedy*). A town of Galilee, 7 mls. N. of Nazareth, John ii. 1-11; iv. 46; xxi. 2.

Cā'nāan (*low*). (1) Fourth son of Ham, Gen. x. 6-19; 1 Chr. i. 8-13. (2) The country between the Mediterranean and Jordan, given by God to the Israelites, Ex. vi. 4; Lev. xxv. 38. "Holy Land," after the captivity, Zech. ii. 13. Palestine, from Philistia.

Cā'nāan-īte. Dwellers in Canaan, and all tribes known to the Israelites at time of conquest, Gen. x. 18-20; xiii. 7; xiv. 7; xv. 20; Num. xiii. 29; Josh. xi. 3; xxiv. 11.

Căn'dā-çē (*queen of servants*). The Ethiopian queen whose servant was converted, Acts viii. 27.

Căn'dle-stĭck. The golden candlestick rather a lamp, Ex. xxv. 31-37; xxxvii. 17-24. Ten candelabra used instead, in Solomon's temple, 1 Kgs. vii. 49.

Cāne. [CALAMUS.]

Cănk'er-worm (*cancer-worm*). A variety of caterpillar. But in Joel i. 4; ii. 25; Nah. iii. 15, 16, probably an undeveloped locust.

Căn'neh. Ezek. xxvii. 23. [CALNEH.]

Căn'on (*cane, rule*). Word first applied to the Scriptures by Amphilochius about A. D. 380, Gal. vi. 16; Phil. iii. 16. O. T. canon fixed by the Jews, and accepted by Christ and his times. N. T. canon ratified by third council of Carthage, A. D. 397.

Căn'ō-pў (*bed with mosquito curtains*). Judith x. 21; xiii. 9; xvi. 19.

Căn'tĭ-cles (*song of songs*). The Latinized title of "The Song of Solomon."

Că-pĕr'nā-ŭm (*hamlet of Nahum*). A city on N. W. shore of Sea of Galilee. Chief residence of Christ and his apostles, Matt. iv. 12-16; viii. 5; ix. 1; xvii. 24; Mark ii. 1; Luke vii. 1-5; John vi. 17.

Căph'ar (*hamlet*). Common Hebrew prefix.

Căph''ăr-săl'ā-ma. A battlefield, 1 Macc. vii. 31.

Că-phĕn'ā-tha. A suburb of Jerusalem, 1 Macc. xii. 37.

Căph′tôr, Căph′tŏ-rĭm. Either Philistines or Copts of Egypt, Gen. x. 14; Deut. ii. 23; Jer. xlvii. 4; Am. ix. 7.

Căp′′pạ-dō′çĭ-à (*fine horses*). Largest Roman province in Asia Minor, with Cæsarea as metropolis, Acts ii. 9; 1 Pet. i. 1.

Căp′tain (*head*). Title for a leader of a band of ten, fifty, hundred or thousand, Deut. i. 15; Josh. x. 24; Judg. xi. 6, 11. Also a civic meaning, Isa. i. 10; iii. 3. "Captain of the Guard," Acts xxviii. 16, was commander of the Prætorian troop of Rome. "Captain of the Temple," Acts iv. 1, was chief of the Temple watchmen.

Căp′tĭve (*taken*). Captives in war treated with great cruelty in early times, Gen. xiv. 14; Judg. i. 7; 1 Sam. xi. 2; 2 Sam. viii. 2; 2 Kgs. xxv. 7. Later, treated as servants and slaves, 1 Kgs. xx. 31–34.

Căp-tĭv′ĭ-ty. Six partial captivities mentioned in Judges. Israel had several, 2 Kgs. xv. 29; 1 Chr. v. 26, the final one being that by Shalmaneser, B. C. 721, 2 Kgs. xvii. 6. Judah was captive to Assyria B. C. 713, and finally to Nebuchadnezzar B. C. 606–562. This captivity broken, Ez. i. 11. Last captivity was to Rome, A. D. 71.

Căr′bŭn-cle (*little coal*). A gem of deep red color, Isa. liv. 12. A stone in the high-priest's breastplate, Ex. xxviii. 17; xxxix. 10.

Căr′cas. A eunuch, Esth. i. 10.

Căr′chĕ-mĭsh (*fortress of Chemosh*). A city on the Euphrates, Isa. x. 5–9; 2 Chr. xxxv. 20–23; Jer. xlvi. 2.

Cȧ-rē′ah (*bald*). Father of Johannan, 2 Kgs. xxv. 23. Kareah, elsewhere.

Cā′rĭ-à. Southwest province of Asia Minor. Cnidus and Miletus were in it, Acts xx. 15; xxvii. 7.

Căr′mel (*fruitful*). (1) The promontory which forms the bay of Acre, 1 Kgs. xviii.; 2 Kgs. ii. 25; iv. 25; Isa. xxxiii. 9; xxxv. 2. (2) A city of Judah, 1 Sam. xv. 12; xxv. 2–44; 2 Chr. xxvi. 10.

Căr′mĭ (*vine dresser*). (1) Progenitor of the Carmites, Gen. xlvi. 9; Ex. vi. 14; Num. xxvi. 6; 1 Chr. v. 3. (2) Father of Achan, Josh. vii. 1, 18; 1 Chr. ii. 7.

Căr′nă-im. City in Manasseh, 1 Macc. v. 26–44.

Căr′pĕn-tĕr (*cart-wright*). Carpentry an early

art, Gen. vi. 14-16; Ex. xxv. 23; xxvii. 1-15. David and Solomon employed foreign wood-workers, 2 Sam. v. 11; 1 Kgs. v. 6. Joseph a carpenter, Matt. xiii. 55; and Christ, Mark vi. 3.

Căr'pus (*fruit*). Paul's friend, 2 Tim. iv. 13.

Căr'rĭage (*car*). Baggage, Judg. xviii. 21; Isa. x. 28; xlvi. 1; Acts xxi. 15.

Cär-shē'nà (*distinguished*). A Persian, Esth. i. 14.

Cärt (*carry*). A two-wheeled vehicle usually drawn by oxen, 1 Sam. vi. 7-15; Amos ii. 13.

Cär'vĭng (*cutting*). Carving and engraving in much request, Ex. xxxi. 5; xxxv. 33; 1 Kgs. vi. 18; 2 Chr. ii. 7-14; Ps. lxxiv. 6; Zech. iii. 9.

Cāse'ment (*house-frame*). The latticed opening of the Kiosk, or summer house, of the East, Prov. vii. 6; S. of Sol. ii. 9; Judg. v. 28.

Că-sĭph'ĭ-à (*white*). An unknown place, Ez. viii. 17.

Căs'leu, 1 Macc. i. 54. [CHISLEU.]

Căs-lu'hĭm (*fortified*). A Mizraite people, Gen. x. 14; 1 Chr. i. 12.

Căs'phor. City of Gilead, 1 Macc. v. 26.

Căs'pis, 2 Macc. xii. 13. [CASPHOR.]

Căs'sĭa (*that peels*) The cinnamon cassia in Ex. xxx. 24; Ezek. xxvii. 19. In Ps. xlv. 8, the shrub is unidentified.

Căs'tle (*fort*). The "Tower of Antonia," N. W. corner of the Temple at Jerusalem, Acts xxi. 34, 37; xxii. 24; xxiii. 10, 16, 32.

Căs'tŏr and **Pŏl'lux.** Two mythologic heroes; figurehead and name of Paul's ship, Acts xxviii. 11.

Căt'er-pĭl'lar (*hairy consumer*). The larva of the butterfly, 1 Kgs. viii. 37; 2 Chr. vi. 28; Ps. lxxviii. 46; Isa. xxxiii. 4; Joel i. 4.

Căts. Only in Baruch vi. 22.

Căt'tle (*capital*). Domestic bovine animals, as oxen, cows, bulls, and calves; also any live-stock, Gen. xiii. 2; Ex. xii. 29; xxxiv. 19; Num. xx. 19; xxxii. 16; Ps. l. 10; Job. i. 3. [BULL.]

Cạu'dà, Clauda in R. V.

Caul (*kŏl*) (*cap*). A net for a woman's hair, Isa. iii. 18. In Hos. xiii. 8, the membrane around the heart.

Cāve (*hollow*). Used for storage houses, dwellings, hiding and burial places, Gen. xix. 30; Josh. x. 16; Judg. vi. 2; 1 Sam. xiii. 6; xxii. 1; xxiv. 3; 2 Sam. xxiii. 13; 1 Kgs. xviii. 4; Heb. xi. 38.

Çĕ'dȧr (*resinous*). A cone-bearing tree whose reddish fragrant wood was much prized, 1 Kgs. vii. 2; Ps. xcii. 12; S. of Sol. v. 15; Isa. ii. 13; Ezek. xxxi. 6.

Çĕ'drŏn (*turbid*). (1) A brook, Kedron or Kidron, below the eastern wall of Jerusalem, John xviii. 1.

Çeī'lăn. His sons returned, 1 Esdr. v. 15.

Çĕil'ing (*heavens*). Hebrew temple ceilings were generally of cedar, richly carved, 1 Kgs. vi. 9–15; vii. 3; 2 Chr. iii. 5–9.

Çĕn'chrĕ-ȧ (*millet*). The eastern harbor of Corinth, Acts xviii. 18. Seat of a Christian church, Rom. xvi. 1.

Çĕn''dō-bē'us. A Syrian general, 1 Macc. xv. 38.

Çĕn'sẽr (*set on fire*). A small portable vessel of copper, Num. xvi. 39; Lev. xvi. 12, or gold, 1 Kgs. vii. 50; Heb. ix. 4, for carrying the coals on which incense was burned.

Çĕn'sus (*assess*). Twelve different censuses noted in the O. T., Ex. xxxviii. 26; Num. i. 2; xxvi.; 2 Sam. xxiv. 9; 2 Chr. ii. 17, 18; 1 Kgs. xii. 21; 2 Chr. xiii. 3; xiv. 8; xvii. 14; xxv. 5, 6; xxvi. 13; Ez. ii. 64; viii. 1–14. The census in Luke ii. 1–3, was for taxation.

Çĕn-tū'rĭ-ŏn (*hundred*). A Roman officer who had command of a hundred soldiers, Matt. viii. 5; Mark xv. 39; Luke vii. 1–10; Acts x. 1.

Çē'phas (*stone*). Name given to Peter, John i. 42.

Çē'ras, 1 Esdr. v. 29. [KEROS.]

Çē'tab. A doubtful name, 1 Esdr. v. 30.

Chā'bris. Ruler of Bethulia, Judith vi. 15.

Chā'dĭ-as. Her citizens returned, 1 Esdr. v. 20.

Chaff. Was separated from the grain by throwing all into the air from sheets, or forks, the wind carrying away the chaff, Ps. i. 4; Isa. xvii. 13; Hos. xiii. 3; Zeph. ii. 2.

Chains (*links*). Used for ornament on man and beast, and for fetters, Gen. xli. 42; Judg. viii. 21; xvi. 21; 2 Sam. iii. 34; 2 Kgs. xxv. 7; Isa. iii. 19; Acts xii. 6; xxi. 33; xxviii. 20.

Chăl''çē-dō'nў (*from Chalcedon*). A many-colored precious stone of the agate variety, Rev. xxi. 19.

Chăl'cŏl, 1 Kgs. iv. 31. [CALCOL.]

Chăl-dē'å, Chăl-dæ'å (*as demons*). The country lying along the Euphrates on both sides, and between it and the Tigris, for three or four hundred miles back from their mouths, Gen. x. 10; xi. 31; Job i. 17.

Chăl-dē'ăns, Chăl'deeş. The people of that country having Babylon for its capital, Dan. i. 4, v. 15; ix. 1.

Chälk=stōnes. Possibly burnt lime, Isa. xxvii. 9.

Chām'bĕr (*vault, arched*). Sleeping apartment, Gen. xliii. 30; 2 Sam. xviii. 33; Ps. xix. 5; Dan. vi. 10; Acts ix. 37. Dining room, Mark xiv. 14; Luke xxii. 12.

Chām'bĕr-ing. Amorous intrigue, Rom. xiii. 13.

Chām'bĕr-lain (*man of the chamber*). Officer in charge of the king's chamber, 2 Kgs. xxiii. 11; Esth. i. 10, 12, 15; Dan. i. 8-11. A more dignified office, in Acts xii. 20; Rom. xvi. 23.

Chȧ-mē'lē-ŏn (*ground lion*). A species of lizard, arboreal in habit. But the word thus translated implies a frog, Lev. xi. 30.

Chăm'ois (*sham-my*) (*buck*). The chamois not known in Palestine. A wild sheep, or goat, may be meant, Deut. xiv. 5.

Chā'năan. Greek spelling of Canaan, Acts vii. 11; xiii. 19; Judith v. 3.

Chăn'çĕl-lŏr (*usher of a law-court*). A keeper of the king's seal, Ez. iv. 8.

Chăp'ĭ-ter (*head*). The ornamental head of a pillar, Ex. xxxvi. 38; xxxviii. 17; 1 Kgs. vii. 31, 38.

Chăp'man (*cheap-man*). A trader, 1 Kgs. x. 15; 2 Chr. ix. 14.

Chär''a-ăth'ā-lar, 1 Esdr. v. 36. [CHERUB.]

Chär'a-cȧ. An obscure place, 2 Macc. xii. 17.

Chär'a-shĭm, Valley of (*ravine of craftsmen*). Where Joab's ancestors lived, 1 Chr. iv. 14.

Chär'chĕ-mĭsh, 2 Chr. xxxv. 20; **Chär'chă-mĭs,** 1 Esdr. i. 25. [CARCHEMISH.]

Chär'cus, 1 Esdr. v. 32. [BARKOS.]

Chär'ger (*car*). A dish for receiving water and blood, and for presenting offerings of flour and oil, Num. vii. 13, 79; later, a large service plate, Matt. xiv. 8.

Chär'ĭ-ot (*car*). A two-wheeled vehicle, used for travel and war, Gen. xli. 43; xlvi. 29; 1 Kgs. xviii. 44; 2 Kgs. v. 9. In use by enemies of Israel, Josh. xi. 4; Judg. iv. 3; 1 Sam. xiii. 5. Adopted for war by David and Solomon, 2 Sam. viii. 4; 1 Kgs. ix. 19; x. 26; xxii. 34; 2 Kgs. ix. 16; Isa. xxxi. 1.

Chär'mis. Ruler of Bethulia, Judith vi. 15.

Chär'ran, Acts vii. 2-4. [HARAN.]

Chăs'ĕ-ba, 1 Esdr. v. 31. [GAZERA.]

Chē'bär (*strength*). A river of Chaldea; seat of Ezekiel's visions, Ezek. i. 3; iii. 15, 23.

Chĕd''ŏr-lā'o-mēr (*handful of sheaves*). King of Elam, Gen. xiv. 1-24.

Cheese. The Hebrew words imply curds, or curdled milk, 1 Sam. xvii. 18; Job x. 10; 2 Sam. xvii. 29.

Chē'lăl (*perfect*). A returned captive, Ez. x. 30.

Chĕl'çi-as. Hilkiah, Bar. i. 7.

Chĕl'lụh (*perfection*). A returned captive, Ez. x. 35.

Chĕl'lus. A place west of Jordan, Judith i. 9.

Chē'lŭb (*basket*). (1) A Judahite, 1 Chr. iv. 11. (2) Father of one of David's overseers, 1 Chr. xxvii. 26.

Chĕ-lū'bāi (*capable*). Caleb, 1 Chr. ii. 9.

Chĕm'a-rims (*black ones*). Sun-worshippers, Zeph. i. 4.

Chē'mosh (*subduer*). National god of Moab, and Ammon, Num. xxi. 29; Judg. xi. 23, 24; 1 Kgs. xi. 7; 2 Kgs. xxiii. 13.

Chĕ-nā'ă-nah (*merchant*). (1) Father of Zedekiah, 1 Kgs. xxii. 11. (2) A Benjamite, 1 Chr. vii. 10.

Chĕn'a-nī (*contraction of Chenaniah*). A Levite, Neh. ix. 4.

Chĕn''a-nī'ah (*made by God*). A Levite, 1 Chr. xv. 22.

Chē'phär=hă-ăm'mo-nāi. "Hamlet of the Ammonites," in Benjamin, 2 Chr. xviii. 24.

Chĕ-phī'rah (*hamlet*). A Gibeonite city, Josh. ix. 17; Ez. ii. 25; Neh. vii. 29.

Chē'ran (*lyre*). A Horite, Gen. xxxvi. 26; 1 Chr. i. 41.

Chē'rĕ-as. A general, 2 Macc. x. 32–37.

Chĕr'ĕth-ĭms, Ezek. xxv. 16. [CHERETHITES.]

Chĕr'ĕth-ītes (*executioners*). A portion of David's body guard, 2 Sam. viii. 18; xv. 18; xx. 7, 23; 1 Kgs. i. 38, 44; 1 Chr. xviii. 17.

Chē'rĭth (*cutting*). The place where Elijah was fed by ravens, 1 Kgs. xvii. 3–5.

Chē'rub. A place in Babylonia, Ez. ii. 59; Neh. vii. 61.

Chĕr'ub, Chĕr'u-bĭm (*terrible*). Guards of Paradise, Gen. iii. 24; and the mercy seat, Ex. xxv. 18. Wrought in gold or wood, Ex. xxxvi. 35; xxxvii. 7–9. Of immense size in Solomon's Temple, 1 Kgs. vi. 27. Four-winged and four-faced, Ezek. i. 6; x. 14; Rev. iv. 8.

Chès'ă-lon (*hopes*). A landmark of Judah, Josh. xv. 10.

Chē'sed (*gain*). Fourth son of Nahor, Gen. xxii. 22.

Chē'sĭl (*fool*). A place in south Judah, Josh. xv. 30.

Chĕst (*box*). A coffin, Gen. l. 26. Treasure chest, 2 Kgs. xii. 9; 2 Chr. xxiv. 8–11. Trunk or packing-case, Ezek. xxvii. 24. In all other places, "Ark."

Chĕst'nut=tree, Gen. xxx. 37; Ezek. xxxi. 8; the plane-tree is meant.

Chē-sŭl'lŏth (*loins*). Town of Issachar, Josh. xix. 18.

Chĕt-tī'ĭm, 1 Macc. i. 1. [CHITTIM.]

Chē'zĭb (*lying*), Gen. xxxviii. 5. Probably Achzib.

Chī'don (*dart*). Spot where the accident befel the Ark, 1 Chr. xiii. 9–13. Nachon, 2 Sam. vi. 6.

Chief of Asia, Acts xix. 31. [ASIAARCH.]

Chief Priest. [HIGH PRIEST.]

Chĭl'dren. Children an honor, childlessness a misfortune, Gen. xvi. 2; Deut. vii. 14; 1 Sam. i. 6; 2 Sam. vi. 23; 2 Kgs. iv. 14; Ps. cxxvii. 3; Isa. xlvii. 9, Jer. xx. 15. Males circumcised on eighth day, Lev. xii. 3. Weaning an occasion of rejoicing, Gen. xxi. 8.

Chĭl'ẹ-ăb (*like the father*). Son of David, 2 Sam. iii. 3.

Chil'i-on (*sickly*). Husband of Orpah, Ruth 1:2-4.

Chĭl'măd (*closed*). A country on the Euphrates, Ezek. xxvii. 23.

Chĭm'ham (*longing*). A friend of David, 2 Sam. xix. 37, 38; Jer. xli. 17.

Chĭn'nẹ-rĕth, Chĭn'nẹ-rŏth. (1) A city on or near coast of Sea of Galilee, Josh. xi. 2. (2) Old name for the inland sea known as Lake Gennesareth, or Sea of Galilee, Num. xxxiv. 11; Deut. iii. 17; Josh. xiii. 27.

Chī'os (*open*). The island of Scio, Acts xx. 15.

Chĭs'lĕū. Ninth month of the Jewish sacred, and third of the civil, year, corresponding to parts of Nov. and Dec., Neh. i. 1.

Chĭs'lon (*hope*). A Benjamite, Num. xxxiv. 21.

Chĭs'lŏth=tā'bôr, Josh. xix. 12. [CHESULLOTH.]

Chĭt'tim, Kĭt'tim (*bruisers*). Descendants of Javan, and their country, supposably Cyprus, Gen. x. 4; Num. xxiv. 24; 1 Chr. i. 7; Isa. xxiii. 1–12.

Chī'ŭn. An Israelite idol, Am. v. 26. [REMPHAN.]

Chlō'ẹ (*green herb*). A Christian woman of Corinth, 1 Cor. i. 11.

Chō'bà, Chō'bāi. A place in Bethulia, Judith vi. 4; xv. 4.

Chŏr-ā'shan. A haunt of David, 1 Sam. xxx. 30.

Chŏ-rā'zin (*secret*). A city on the coast of the Sea of Galilee, Matt. xi. 21; Luke x. 13.

Chō'zẹ-bà. Descendants of Judah, 1 Chr. iv. 22.

Christ. The Anointed; the Messiah. A title of Jesus, the Saviour: at first with the article, "The Christ;" later, as part of a proper name, "Jesus Christ." [JESUS.]

Chris'tian. Follower of Christ. First so called at Antioch, Syria, A. D. 43, Acts xi. 26; xxvi. 28.

Chrŏn'i-cles ("*words of days*," *annals*). Thirteenth and fourteenth of O. T. Books. Originally one book called Paraleipomena, "things omitted." A supplement to Kings, compiled, no doubt, by Ezra. The history covers a period of 3500 years.

Chrȳs′ō-līte (*gold stone*). Evidently the yellow topaz, Rev. xxi. 20.

Chrȳs″ō-prā′sus (*golden leek*). An apple-green variety of chalcedony, Rev. xxi. 20.

Chŭb. Allies of Egypt, Ezek. xxx. 5.

Chŭn (*ready*). A city that supplied brass to Solomon, 2 Sam. viii. 8.

Chŭrch (*assembly*). A congregation of religious worshippers, Acts vii. 38; Matt. xvi. 18. Visible, Acts ii.; Col. i. 24. Invisible, Heb. xii. 23.

Chŭrn-ing, Prov. xxx. 33. The milk was enclosed in skin bags, which were shaken or trodden.

Chū′shan=rĭsh″a-thā′im (*great conqueror*). A king of Mesopotamia, Judg. iii. 8–10.

Chū′si. A place, Judith vii. 18.

Chū′zȧ (*seer*). Steward of Herod, Luke viii. 3; xxiv. 10.

Çĭ-lĭ′çĭa (*rolling*). A province of Asia Minor. Chief city, Tarsus, birthplace of Paul, Acts ix. 11, 30; xv. 41.

Çĭn′nȧ-mŏn (*dried*). Inner bark of the cinnamon-tree, Ex. xxx. 23; Rev. xviii. 13. A perfume, Prov. vii. 17.

Çĭn′ne̶-rŏth. A district of Naphtali, 1 Kgs. xv. 20. [CHINNERETH.]

Çĭr′a-mȧ. Returned Jews, 1 Esdr. v. 20.

Çĭr″cŭːn-çĭ′şion (*cutting around*). Cutting off the foreskin. A rite, performed on males on eighth day after birth, Gen. xvii.; Lev. xii. 3; Ex. xii. 44; John vii. 22. Antagonized by Christianity, Acts xv.; 1 Cor. vii. 18; Gal. v. 2.

Çĭs, Acts xiii. 21. [KISH.]

Çī′sai, Esther xi. 12. [KISH.]

Çĭs′tern (*chest*). Common and necessary in the East. Sometimes synonymous with "wells," Num. xxi. 22, and "pits," Gen. xxxvii. 22; 2 Sam. xvii. 18; Eccl. xii. 6; Jer. xxxviii. 6.

Çĭt′ĭms, 1 Macc. viii. 5. [CHITTIM.]

Çĭt′ĭ-zĕn-ship. Roman citizenship exempted from imprisonment or scourging without trial, and gave the right of appeal to the Emperor, Acts xvi. 37; xxii. 28, 29; xxv. 11.

Çĭt′ȳ (*place for citizens*). Cain and Nimrod city-builders, Gen. iv. 17 ; x. 9–11. "Fenced cities," fortified cities, 2 Kgs. x. 2 ; Isa. xxvi. 1. "City of David," Jerusalem, Bethlehem, 1 Chr. xi. 5 ; Luke ii. 11. "City of God," Jerusalem, Ps. xlvi. 4 ; Neh. xi. 1. "Cities of Refuge," six in number, Deut. xix. 7–9 ; Num. xxxv. 6–15.

Clau'då (*lamentable*). A small island near Crete, Acts xxvii. 16.

Clau'dĭ-å (*lame*). A female friend of Paul and Timothy, 2 Tim. iv. 21.

Clau'dĭ-us (*lame*). Claudius Cæsar. Fifth Roman Emperor. Reign, A. D. 41–54. Banished the Jews from Rome, Acts xviii. 2.

Clau'dĭ-us Lys'ĭ-as. [LYSIAS.]

Clāy. Used variously, Ps. xviii. 42 ; Isa. lvii. 20 ; Jer. xxxviii. 6 ; John ix. 6 ; for making pottery, Isa. xli. 25 ; for brick-making, 2 Sam. xii. 31 ; for sealing, Job xxxviii. 14 ; for writing tablets.

Clĕan and **Un'clean.** Words applied to personal and ceremonial conditions, and to edibility of animals. Gen. vii. 2 ; Lev. xi.–xv. ; Num. xix. ; Ex. xxii. 31 ; xxxiv. 15–26.

Clĕm'ent (*mild*). A co-worker with Paul, Phil. iv. 3.

Clē'o-pas (*renowned father*). One of the two disciples to whom Christ appeared, Luke xxiv. 18.

Clē'o-phas (*renowned*). Husband of Mary, John xix. 25. Called also Alphæus.

Clŏth. Skins first supplied the place of cloth. Art of weaving cloth early known, Ex. xxxv. 25. Judg. v. 30.

Clō'thing. [DRESS.]

Clôud (*round mass*). A prominent feature in Oriental imagery, Prov. xvi. 15 ; Isa. xxv. 5 ; Job xxx. 15. A token of Divine presence and protection, Ex. xvi. 10 ; Num. xii. 5.

Clôut'ed. Worn out and patched, Josh. ix. 5.

Cnī'dus (*ni'dus*) (*age*). The peninsula of Caria, and the city upon it, Acts xxvii. 7 ; 1 Macc. xv. 23.

Cōal (*glow*). The coal of scripture is charcoal, or embers, Prov. xxvi. 21 ; John xviii. 18 ; xxi. 9 ; heated stones, 1 Kgs. xix. 6 ; Isa. vi. 6 ; metaphorical, 2 Sam. xxii. 9–13 ; Ps. xviii. 8, 12, 13 ; Rom. xii. 20.

Coast (*rib*). Often used as border or boundary, Judg. xi. 20 ; 1 Sam. v. 6 ; Matt. viii. 34.

Coat (*coarse mantle*). [DRESS.]

Cock. The crowing of the cock in Matt. xxvi. 34 ; Mark xiv. 30 ; Luke xxii. 34, indicated the third watch of the night, from midnight to daylight.

Cock'a-trice (*crocodile like.*) The basilisk, Jer. viii. 17 ; Isa. xi. 8 ; xiv. 29 ; lix. 5 ; in all which some species of hissing, venomous serpent is meant.

Cock'le (*stinking*). A weed that grows among grain ; doubtless the tare, identified as darnel, Job xxxi. 40.

Cœl'e=Sўr'i-å and **Çĕl'o=Sўr'i-å** (*hollow Syria*). That part of Syria lying between the Libanus and Anti-Libanus ranges, 1 Macc. x. 69.

Cof'fer (*basket*). A movable box hanging from the side of a cart, 1 Sam. vi. 8, 11, 15.

Cof'fin (*basket*). [BURIAL.]

Co'hŏrt (*company*). [ARMY.]

Col-ho'zeh (*all-seeing*). A man of Judah, Neh. iii. 15 ; xi. 5.

Co'li-us, 1 Esdr. ix. 23. [KELAIAH.]

Col'lar. "Collars " in Judg. viii. 26, and " chains " in Isa. iii. 19, should be " ear-drops."

Col'lĕġe (*collected*). That part of Jerusalem north of the old city, 2 Kgs. xxii. 14.

Col'lops (*tender meat*). Slices of meat, Job xv. 27.

Col'o-ny (*cultivated*). Philippi, colonized by Rome, Acts xvi. 12.

Col'ors (*tints*). Royal colors, purple, Judg. viii. 26 ; Esth. viii. 15 ; Luke xvi. 19 ; Rev. xvii. 4 ; blue, Ex. xxv. 4 ; Esth. i. 6. Vermilion used for beams, walls and ceilings, Jer. xxii. 14 ; Ezek. xxiii. 14.

Co-lŏs'sĕ (*punishment*). A city of Phrygia. Paul wrote to the church there, Col. i. 2 ; iv. 13.

Co-lŏs'si-ans, Epistle to. Written by Paul from Rome, A. D. 61 or 62, and delivered by Tychicus, Acts xxviii. 16 ; Col. iv. 7, 8.

Colt (*young camel or ass*). The young of camels and asses, Gen. xxxii. 15 ; xlix. 11 ; Judg. x. 4 ; Job xi. 12 ; Matt. xxi. 2–7.

Com'fŏrt-er (*brave together*). Defender and

helper. Applied to the Holy Ghost, and Christ, John xiv. 16.

Cŏm'merce (*buying together.*) Limited among Hebrews, Gen. xiii. 2; xxiv. 22, 53. Outside enterprises a failure, 1 Kgs. xxii. 48–9. Used some foreign articles, Ez. iii. 7; Neh. xiii. 16; supplied some, 1 Kgs. v. 11; Acts xii. 20. Temple commerce led to Christ's rebuke, Matt. xxi. 12; John ii. 14.

Cŏm-mū'nion (*bound together*). Mutual love, confidence and fellowship, 1 Cor. x. 16; 2 Cor. xiii. 14; 1 John i. 3. The Lord's supper called the "holy communion."

Cŏm'pass (*encircle*). To make a circuit, 2 Sam. v. 23; Acts xxviii. 13.

Cŏn-a-nī'ah (*made by Jehovah*). A Levite, 2 Chr. xxxv. 9.

Cŏn-çī'şion (*cutting off*). A sarcastic use by Paul of the word circumcision, Phil. iii. 2.

Cŏn'cū-bine (*lying with*). In the Jewish economy, a secondary wife, betrothed according to custom, Gen. xxi. 14; xxv. 6; Ex. xxi. 7; Deut. xxi. 10–14. Concubinage repudiated in N. T., Matt. xix. 4–9; 1 Cor. vii. 2–4.

Cŏn'duit (*wit*) (*conductor*). A water pipe or aqueduct, 2 Kgs. xviii. 17; xx. 20; Isa. vii. 3; xxxvi. 2; ditch, Job xxxviii. 25.

Cō'nĕy, Cō'nў (*rabbit*). The small rabbit-like animal known as the *Hyrax Syriacus*, Lev. xi. 5; Deut. xiv. 7; Prov. xxx. 26.

Cŏn''grē-gā'tion (*collected together*). Biblically, the Hebrew nationality, Num. xv. 15. Generally, collected Jewry, Ex. xii. 19. A popular assembly, Acts xix. 32, 39, 41. A religious assembly, or church, Acts vii. 38.

Cō-nī'ah. [JECONIAH.]

Cŏn''ŏ-nī'ah (*the Lord's appointed*). Treasurer of tithes, 2 Chr. xxxi. 12, 13.

Cŏn'sĕ-crāte (*together sacred*). The tribe of Levi consecrated to the priesthood, Ex. xxxii. 28, 29; Lev. vii. 37. Consecrate vessels, Josh. vi. 19; profits, Mic. iv. 13; fields, Lev. xxvii. 28; cattle, 2 Chr. xxix. 33; persons, Num. vi. 9–13; nations, Ex. xix. 6.

Cŏn''vō-cā'tion (*called together*). The "congregation," when called in a purely religious capacity, Ex. xii. 16; Lev. xxiii. 2; Num. xxviii. 18.

Cook'ing. Done by both sexes, Gen. xviii. 6–8; later by servantage, 1 Sam. viii. 13. Kids, lambs and calves furnished meat for guests, Gen. xviii. 7; Luke xv. 23.

Cō'ŏs (*summit*), Acts xxi. 1. [Cos.]

Cō'ping. The top and projecting layer of a wall, 1 Kgs. vii. 9.

Cŏp'per (*from Cyprus*). The "brass" of the Bible. Known to antediluvians, Gen. iv. 22. Used largely in the temple, 1 Chr. xxii. 3–14; and for vessels, ornaments and mirrors, Ex. xxxviii. 8; helmets and spears, 1 Sam. xvii. 5, 6; 2 Sam. xxi. 16.

Cŏr. [HOMER.]

Cŏr'al. Used by Hebrews for beads and ornaments. Ranked among precious stones, Job xxviii. 18; Ezek. xxvii. 16.

Cŏr'ban (*offering*). The offering in fulfilment of a vow, Lev. xxvii.; Num. xxx. The plea of corban reprehended by Christ, Matt. xv. 3–9.

Cŏr'be, 1 Esdr. v. 22. [ZACCAI.]

Cŏrd (*string*). Variously made and used, Isa. xix. 9; scourge, John ii. 15; ship-ropes, Acts xxvii. 32.

Cō'rĕ, Ecclus. xlv. 18; Jude 11. [KORAH.]

Cō''rĭ-ăn'der (*smelling like a bed-bug*). A plant of the parsley family producing aromatic seeds. Ex. xvi. 31; Num. xi. 7.

Cŏr'inth (*ornament*). Anciently Ephyra; capital of Achaia. Destroyed by Rome, B. C. 146. Rebuilt by Julius Cæsar, B. C. 46, as a Roman colony. Paul founded a church there, Acts xviii. 1; xx. 2, 3.

Cŏr-ĭn'thĭ-ans, Epistles to. I. written by Paul at Ephesus, 1 Cor. xvi. 8; treats of church organization, social practices, holy observances, and doctrinal affairs. II. written a few months afterwards, at suggestion of Titus; largely refers to Paul's right to preach and teach, 2 Cor. vii. 5; ix. 2.

Cŏr'mō-rant (*sea raven*). A large, greedy waterbird, pronounced "unclean." Lev. xi. 17; Deut. xiv. 17. Doubtless "pelican" in Isa. xxxiv. 11; Zeph ii. 14.

Cŏrn (*kernel*). In a Bible sense, grain of all kinds

except our maize, or Indian corn. Used largely in figurative speech, Gen. xli. 22; Ex. ix. 32; Deut. xi. 14; xviii. 4; xxviii. 51; 2 Chr. ii. 15; Isa. xxviii. 25; Ezek. xxvii. 17; Matt. xii. 1.

Côr-nē′lĭus (*of a horn*). A Roman centurion and first Gentile convert, Acts x. 1–33.

Côr′ner (*horned*). Grain-field corners not allowed to be wholly reaped, Lev. xix. 9; xxiii. 22. "Legal corner," one sixtieth of the field. "Length and breadth" of a country, Num. xxiv. 17; Jer. xlviii. 45. "Cornerstone," chief stone in a foundation, Job xxxviii. 6. Figuratively in Isa. xxviii. 16; Matt. xxi. 42.

Côr′net (*horn*). The curved signal horn of the Jews, usually made of the horn of a ram, ox, chamois, or wild goat, Lev. xxv. 9; Ezek. xxxiii. 4, 5; 1 Chr. xv. 28.

Cŏs, Cō′ŏs (*summit*). A small island of the Grecian archipelago, Acts xxi. 1.

Cō′sam (*diviner*). One of Christ's ancestors, Luke iii. 28.

Cōte (*cot, den*). A sheepfold, 2 Chr. xxxii. 28.

Cŏt′tage (*cot*). A rustic tent or shelter, Isa. xxiv. 20.

Cŏt′ton (*wool-plant*). Not known to Hebrews. Cotton garments mentioned on the Rosetta stone.

Cŏuch (*placed*). [BED.]

Cŏun′çĭl (*called together*). In N. T., (1) The Sanhedrim, Matt. xxvi. 49. (2) Lesser courts, Matt. x. 17; Mark xiii. 9. (3) A jury of councillors, Acts xxv. 12. [SANHEDRIM.]

Cōur′ses (*running*). Priests divided into twenty-four classes, courses, or orders, 1 Chr. xxiv. [ABIA.]

Cōurt (*enclosure*). The enclosed space within the limits of Oriental houses. The outer area of the tabernacle and temple, Ex. xxvii. 9; Lev. vi. 16; 2 Sam. xvii. 18; 1 Kgs. vi. 36; 2 Kgs. xxiii. 12; 2 Chr. xxxiii. 5.

Cou′tha. One of the returned, 1 Esdr. v. 32.

Cŏv′ē-nant (*coming together*). Ratified by eating together, oaths, witnesses, gifts, pillars, Gen. ix. 15; xxi. 30, 31; xxxi. 50–52. Covenant of the law through Moses, Ex. xx. 24; of the gospel through Christ, Gal. iii.; Heb. viii.

Côv′et (*desire*). Rightful desire, 1 Cor. xii. 31, good. Wrongful desire, sinful, Ex. xx. 17; xviii. 21; Prov. xxviii. 16; Luke xii. 15–34; 1 Tim. vi. 9, 10.

Cow. Cow and calf not to be killed on same day, Lev. xxii. 28. Symbol of plenty, Isa. vii. 21.

Côz (*thorn*). A Judahite, 1 Chr. iv. 8.

Côz′bī (*liar*). Daughter of Zur, Num. xxv. 15–18.

Crăck′nels (*that cracks*). Hard brittle cakes, 1 Kgs. xiv. 3.

Crāne. A large, long-necked, heron-like bird, of gray plumage, noisy on the wing, Isa. xxxviii. 14; Jer. viii. 7.

Crā′tes. Governor of Cyprus, 2 Macc. iv. 29.

Crē-āte′, Crē-ā′tion (*make, made*). To produce out of nothing by Almighty fiat, Gen. i. ii. The universe.

Crĕs′çenṣ (*increasing*). Assistant of Paul, 2 Tim. iv. 10.

Crēte (*carnal*). Now Candia. One of the largest islands in the Grecian archipelago. Paul founded a church there in charge of Titus, Acts ii. 11; xxvii. 1–12; Tit. i. 5–13.

Crētes. Inhabitants of Crete, Acts ii. 11.

Crĭb. A stall for cattle, and the manger or rack for hay or straw, Job xxxix. 9; Prov. xiv. 4; Isa. i. 3.

Crĭm′son (*carmine*). A deep-red color; or a red tinged with blue, Jer. iv. 30.

Crĭsp′ing=pins (*curling pins*). Crimping pins, Isa. iii. 22.

Crĭs′pus (*curled*). Chief ruler of the synagogue at Corinth, Acts xviii. 8. Baptized by Paul, 1 Cor. i. 14.

Crŏss (*across*). A gibbet of wood of various forms, Deut. xxi. 23; John xix. 17; Gal. iii. 13. Now a sacred emblem.

Crown (*curved*). A head-dress, Ezek. xvi. 12· Head-dress of priests, kings, and queens, Ex. xxviii. 36–38; 2 Chr. xxiii. 11; Esth. ii. 17. Symbol of power, honor, and eternal life, Prov. xii. 4; Lam. v. 16; 1 Pet. v. 4.

Crū″cĭ-fix′ĭon (*fixing to the cross*). A method of death punishment by fixing to a cross, Gen. xl. 19; Esth. vii. 10. Limbs sometimes broken to hasten death, John xix. 31. Sepulture denied, Deut. xxi. 22, 23, but an exception allowed in Christ's case, Matt. xxvii. 58.

Crū′cĭ-fy. [CRUCIFIXION.]

Crūse (*pot*). A bottle, flask, or jug for holding liquids, 1 Sam. xxvi. 11; 1 Kgs. xvii. 12; xix. 6.

Crȳs′tal (*frost*). A disputed original, variously translated crystal, Job xxviii. 17; frost, Gen. xxxi. 40; ice, Job xxxviii. 29.

Cū′bit (*elbow*). Distance from the elbow to end of the middle finger, or about 21.8 inches, Gen. vi. 15; 1 Sam. xvii. 4.

Cuck′oo (*crower*). A mistranslation; and perhaps the storm-petrel is meant, Lev. xi. 16; Deut. xiv. 15.

Cū′cŭm-ber (*cumberer*). Much used for food in the East, Num. xi. 5; Isa. i. 8.

Cŭm′min. An annual of the parsley family, producing aromatic seeds, Isa. xxviii. 25; Matt. xxiii. 23.

Cŭn′ning (*test*). Skilful, Gen. xxv. 27; 1 Sam. xvi. 16.

Cŭp (*coop*, *tub*). A drinking vessel of various designs, made of horn, clay, or metal, Gen. xliv. 2; 1 Sam. xvi. 13; 1 Kgs. vii. 26. Used figuratively in Ps. xxiii. 5; Isa. li. 17; Rev. xiv. 10; Matt. xx. 22; xxvi. 39.

Cŭp′beär″er. [BUTLER.]

Cŭsh (*black*). (1) Oldest son of Ham, Gen. x. 6, 8; 1 Chr. i. 8–10. (2) That indefinite country translated Ethiopia in Gen. ii. 13. (3) The country settled by Ham's descendants, Gen. x. 6–8; Isa. xviii. 1; Jer. xiii. 23; Dan. xi. 43. (4) A Benjamite, Ps. vii. title.

Cu′shan (*blackness*), Hab. iii. 7. Some refer it to Cush.

Cu′shī (*Ethiopian*). (1) A foreigner in David's army, 2 Sam. xviii. 21–32. (2) An ancestor of Jehudi, Jer. xxxvi. 14. (3) Father of Zephaniah, Zeph. i. 1.

Cŭth (*burning*). The land in Persia whence colonists came into Samaria, 2 Kgs. xvii. 30. **Cuthah in vs. 24.**

Cū'thah, Cŭth-ītes, 2 Kgs. xvii. 24. [CUTH.]

Cŭt'tings, Of the flesh, forbidden by Levitical law, Lev. xix. 28; xxi. 5; Deut. xiv. 1.

Çȳ'ă-mon. A place near Carmel, Judith vii. 3.

Çȳm'bal (*hollow of a vessel*). Metallic plates, slightly concave, used as musical instruments, by striking them together, 1 Chr. xiii. 8; xvi. 5; Ps. cl. 5; 1 Cor. xiii. 1.

Çȳ'press (*from Cyprus*). Not indigenous to Palestine. Juniper may be meant, Isa. xliv. 14.

Çȳp'rĭ-an. Dweller in Cyprus, 2 Macc. iv. 29.

Çȳ'prus (*fairness*). A large island in N. E. angle of the Mediterranean. Christianity introduced quite early, Acts xi. 19. Birthplace of Barnabas, Acts iv. 36. Paul visited it, Acts xiii. 4-13.

Çȳ-rē'nĕ (*wall*). Capital of Cyrenaica. in northern Africa, and corresponding to Tripoli. Simon was of Cyrene, Matt. xxvii. 32; Mark xv. 21. Cyreneans present at Pentecost, Acts ii. 10; vi. 9.

Çȳ-rē'nĭ-us (*of Cyrene*). Roman governor of Syria, B. C. 4-1, and A. D. 6-11; Luke ii. 2; Acts v. 37.

Çȳ'rus (*sun*). Founder of the Persian empire, Dan. vi. 28; xi. 13; 2 Chr. xxxvi. 22. United Media to Persia. Conquered Babylon, B. C. 538, and reigned over the consolidated empire till B. C. 529. A guardian and liberator of captive Jews, Isa. xliv. 28; xlv. 1-7. Daniel was his favorite minister. *See* Dan., also Ez. i. 1-4; iii. 7; iv. 3; v. 13-17; vi. 3.

D

Dăb'a-reh, Josh. xxi. 28. [DABERATH.]

Dăb'ba-shĕth (*hump*). A boundary of Zebulun, Josh. xix. 11.

Dăb'e-răth (*pasture*). A Levitical city, Josh. xix. 12.

Dăb'rĭ-á. A swift scribe, 2 Esdr. xiv. 24.

Dȧ-cō'bī, 1 Esdr. v. 28. [AKKUB.]

Dăd-dē'us, or **Săd-dē'us,** 1 Esdr. viii. 45, 46. [IDDO.]

Dā'gŏn (*fish*). National male idol of the Philistines, 1 Chr. x. 10. Noted temples at Ashdod, 1 Sam. v. 1-7; Gaza, Judg. xvi. 23; Beth-dagon, Josh. xv. 41; and in Asher, Josh. xix. 27. Represented with human hands and face and a fish's body.

Dai'san, 1 Esdr. v. 31. [REZIN.]

Dăl''a-ī'ah (*freed by God*). A Judahite, 1 Chr. iii. 24.

Dāle, the **King's**. A valley near Jerusalem, Gen. xiv. 17; 2 Sam. xviii. 18.

Dăl''ma-nū'thă. A town on Sea of Galilee, Mark viii. 10.

Dăl-mā'tĭ-à (*-she-a*) (*deceitful*). A province of Illyricum, 2 Tim. iv. 10; Rom. xv. 19.

Dăl'phon (*swift*). Son of Haman, Esth. ix. 7.

Dăm'a-rĭs (*heifer*). An Athenian woman converted by Paul, Acts xvii. 34.

Dă-măs'cus. A city of Asia, 133 miles N. E. of Jerusalem, Gen. xiv. 15; xv. 2. Adjacent region called "Syria of Damascus," 2 Sam. viii. 5. Taken by David, 2 Sam. viii. 6; and by Jeroboam, 2 Kgs. xiv. 28. Scene of Paul's conversion, Acts ix. 1-27; xxii. 1-16.

Dăm-nā'tion (*condemnation*). Consignment to everlasting perdition, Matt. xxiii. 33; Mark iii. 29; John v. 29; 2 Pet. ii. 3.

Dăn (*judge*). (1) Fifth son of Jacob, Gen. xxx. 6; xlix. 16. Allotment, Josh. xix. 40-46. Portion of the tribe moved north, Josh. xix. 47, 48; Judg. xviii. (2) Changed name of Laish, or Leshem, Josh. xix. 47; Judg. xviii. 29. (3) A place in Arabia, Ezek. xxvii. 19.

Dăn'ītes. Members of the tribe of Dan, Judg. xiii. 2; 1 Chr. xii. 35.

Dăn=jā'an (*Danite*). Probably the northern Danites, 2 Sam. xxiv. 6.

Dănce (*drag along*). (1) In Hebrew, "leaping for joy." Not a measured step, Ps. xxx. 11. Common on festal occasions, Ex. xv. 20, 21; Judg. xi. 34; 1 Sam. xviii. 6, 7; 2 Sam. vi. 14; Jer. xxxi. 4; Luke vi. 23; xv. 25; Acts iii. 8. (2) A musical instrument, Ps. cl. 3-5. "Pipe," in margin.

Dăn'iel (*judgment of God*). (1) Fourth of the

greater prophets. Carried captive to Babylon, B. C. 604; and named Belteshazzar, Dan. i., ii. Made a governor under Darius, Dan. vi. 2. Last vision on the Tigris in third year of Cyrus, B. C. 534, x. 1-4. (2) Second son of David, 1 Chr. iii. 1. (3) Son of Ithamar, Ez. viii. 2. (4) A co-covenanter, Neh. x. 6.

Dăn'ịel, Book of. First six chapters historic. Chapters vii.-xii. contain the earliest model of apocalyptic literature. Largely acknowledged in N. T., Matt. xxiv. 15; Luke i. 19, 26; Heb. xi. 33, 34. "The Song of the Three Holy Children," "History of Susanna," and "History of Bel and the Dragon," are apocryphal additions to Daniel's writings.

Dăn'nah (*judging*). A city of Judah, Josh. xv. 49.

Dăph'ne (*bay-tree*). Sanctuary of Apollo, near Antioch, 2 Macc. iv. 33.

Dā'rȧ, 1 Chr. ii. 6. [DARDA.]

Dăr'dȧ (*pearl of wisdom*). One of four famed for wisdom, 1 Kgs. iv. 31.

Dăr'ic (*kingly*). A Persian coin of gold and silver; former worth about five dollars; latter fifty cents. "Dram," in 1 Chr. xxix. 7; Ez. ii. 69; Neh. vii. 70-72.

Dȧ-rī'us (*Persian* "*dara,*" *king*). (1) Darius the Mede, Dan. v. 31; vi.; ix. 1; xi. 1. Captured Babylon from Belshazzar, B. C. 538. (2) Darius Hystaspes, King of Persia, B. C. 521-486. He restored the captive Jews, Ez. iv. 5, 24; vi. 14, 15; Hag. i. 1, 15; Zech. i. 1, 7; vii. 1. (3) Darius the Persian, Neh. xii. 22. Darius Codomanus, B. C. 336-330, last king of Persia.

Dărk'ness (*blackness*). Absence of light, Gen. i. 2; 9th plague, Ex. x. 20-23; State of misery, Job xviii. 6; God's dwelling, Ex. xx. 21; 1 Kgs. viii. 12; typical of national convulsion, Acts ii. 19, 20; state of the fallen, Matt. viii. 12; ignorance, John i. 5; sympathetic, Luke xxiii. 44.

Dăr'kon (*scatterer*). His children returned, Ez. ii. 56; Neh. vii. 58.

Dāte (*like a finger*). Fruit of the date-palm, 2 Chr. xxxi. 5, marg. [PALM.]

Dā'than (*of a spring*). A Reubenite chief and conspirator, Num. xvi.; xxvi. 9; Deut. xi. 6.

Dăth′ĕ-ma. Ramoth-gilead, 1 Macc. v. 9.

Daugh′ter (*milk*). Daughter or any female descendant, Gen. xxiv. 48; female inhabitant, Gen. vi. 2; Isa. x. 32; xxiii. 12; Luke xxiii. 28; singing birds, Eccl. xii. 4.

Dā′vid (*well-beloved*). Youngest son of Jesse, 1 Sam. xvi. 8–12, born at Bethlehem. Anointed king by Samuel, 1 Sam. xvi. 13. Re-anointed at Hebron, 2 Sam. ii. 4. United his kingdom and raised it to great strength and splendor. Died at the age of 70, B. C. 1015, after a reign of seven and a half years over Judah and thirty-three years over the entire kingdom of Israel. History told in 1 Sam. xvi. to 1 Kgs. ii.

Dā′vid, City of. [JERUSALEM.]

Dāy (*shining*). Natural Hebrew day from sunset to sunset, Gen. i. 5; Ex. xii. 18. Sabbath the only day named; others numbered, Lev. xxiii. 32. Morning, noon, and evening divisions, Ps. lv. 17. Hours introduced, Dan. iii. 6; John xi. 9. Indefinite time, Gen. ii. 4; of birth, Job iii. 1; of ruin, Hos. i. 11; of judgment, Joel i. 15; of Christ's kingdom, John viii. 56.

Dāys′man. Umpire or moderator, Job ix. 33.

Dāy′spring. Dawn, Job xxxviii. 12; Luke i. 78.

Dāy′star. Morning star, 2 Pet. i. 19.

Dēa′con (*servant*). A subordinate minister or officer in early Christian Church, Acts vi. 1–6. Qualifications in 1 Tim. iii. 8–12.

Dēa′cŏn-ess. A female officer in early Church, Rom. xvi. 1; 1 Tim. v. 10.

Dĕad Sea. Not so called until the second century. In O. T. "Salt Sea" and "Sea of the Plain." [SALT SEA.]

Dĕarth. [FAMINE.]

Dē′bĭr (*oracle*). (1) A Levitical city of Judah, Josh. xxi. 15; Kirjath-sepher, Josh. xv. 15; Kirjath-sannah, xv. 49. (2) A northern boundary of Judah, Josh. xv. 7. (3) A boundary of Gad, Josh. xiii. 26. (4) A king of Eglon, Josh. x. 3–26.

Dĕb′o-rah (*bee*). (1) ·Nurse of Rebekah, Gen. xxxv. 8; xxiv. 59. (2) Prophetess and Judge, Judg. iv. 5–14; v. (3) Grandmother of Tobit, Tob. i. 8.

Dĕbt'ŏr (*ower*). Lands or the person might be taken for debt, and held till the year of jubilee, Ex. xxi. 2; Lev. xxv. 29-34; 2 Kgs. iv. 1; Neh. v. 3-5.

Dĕ-căp'ŏ-lis (*ten cities*). A Roman province embracing parts of Syria and Palestine, Matt. iv. 25; Mark v. 20; vii. 31.

De-çi'şion, Valley of. Joel iii. 14. "Valley of Jehoshaphat," "or judgment," as in verses 2 and 12.

Dē'dan (*low*). (1) Grandson of Cush, Gen. x. 7. (2) Son of Jokshan, Gen. xxv. 3. Both founders of Arabian or Idumean tribes, Isa. xxi. 13; Ezek. xxxviii. 13.

Ded'a-nĭm. Descendants of Dedan, Isa. xxi. 13.

Dĕd''ĭ-cā'tion (*declaration*). Devoting person, place or thing to holy use, Ex. xl.; Num. vii.; 2 Sam. viii. 11; 1 Kgs. viii.; Ez. vi.; Neh. xii. 27; "Feast of Dedication" commemorated the purging of the temple, John x. 22; 1 Macc. iv. 52-59.

Dēep. Abyss, or abode, of lost spirits, Luke viii. 31; Rom. x. 7. "Bottomless pit," Rev. ix. 1, 2, 11; xi. 7.

Dēer (*wild*), Deut. xiv. 5; 1 Kgs. iv. 23. [FAL-LOW-DEER.]

Dĕ-grēe' (*step or grade down*). Rank or station, Ps. lxii. 9; 1 Tim. iii. 13. "Song of Degrees," title to Pss. cxx.–cxxxiv.

Dĕ-hā'vītes. Colonists planted in Samaria, Ez. iv. 9.

Dē'kär (*lancer*). Father of one of Solomon's commissaries, 1 Kgs. iv. 9.

Del''a-ī'ah (*freed by God*). (1) Leader of the 23d priestly course, 1 Chr. xxiv. 18. (2) Returned Jews, Ez. ii. 60; Neh. vii. 62. (3) Father of Shemaiah, Neh. vi. 10. (4) A courtier, Jer. xxxvi. 12.

Dĕ-lī'lah (*longing*). A woman of Sorek, employed to discover the secret of Samson's strength, Judg. xvi. 4-20.

Dĕl'ūge (*washing away*). The usual modern word for Noah's flood, Gen. vi.–viii.

Dē'lus (*suddenly visible*). Smallest of the Cyclades islands, 1 Macc. xv. 23.

Dē'mas (*popular*). A friend of Paul at Rome, Col. iv. 14; 2 Tim. iv. 10.

Dĕ-mē'trĭ-us (*belonging to Ceres*). (1) A silver-smith at Ephesus, Acts xix. 24–30. (2) A disciple, 3 John, 12. (3) Demetrius (I.) Soter, of Syria, 1 Macc. x. 48-50. (4) Demetrius (II.) Nicator, 1 Macc. x.

Dĕ-nā'rĭ-us (*ten asses*). A Roman silver coin worth about 15 cents. The "penny" of N. T., Matt. xx. 2.

Dĕp'ū-tў (*selected*). In N. T., a proconsul, or governor, Acts xiii. 7, 8, 12.

Dĕr'bĕ (*sting*). A city of Lycaonia in Asia Minor, Acts xiv. 20 ; xx. 4.

Dĕs'ert (*deserted*). An arid sandy plain, or wild mountainous waste, Ex. xxiii. 31 ; Deut. xi. 24 ; Ps. lxv. 12.

Dĕs'să-ū. A village, 2 Macc. xiv. 16.

Deū'el (*knowledge of God*). Father of Eliasaph, Num. i. 14. Reuel in ii. 14.

Deū''te-rŏn'o-mў. So called because it "repeats the law." Fifth book of O. T. and last of the Pentateuch. Authorship ascribed to Moses, except last chapter. Chapters i.-iv. 40, rehearse the wanderings ; v.-xxvi. recapitulate the law ; the others deliver the law into keeping of the Levites, and describe the death of Moses.

Dĕv'il (*slanderer*). The Hebrew Satan, "adversary," Matt. xvi. 23 ; Mark viii. 33 ; Luke xxii. 3 ; Rev. xx. 2. The devil of bodily possession was rather the polluting power of disease — dumbness, Matt. ix. 32 ; blindness, xii. 22 ; epilepsy, Mark ix. 17-27 ; insanity, Matt. viii. 28 ; murderous antipathy, John vii. 20.

Dĕw. Source of fertility, Gen. xxvii. 28 ; Judg. vi 37-40 ; object of rich imagery, Deut. xxxii. 2 ; Job xxix. 19 ; Ps. cxxxiii. 3.

Dī'al (*daily*). An instrument for telling the time of day, 2 Kgs. xx. 11 ; Isa. xxxviii. 8.

Dī'a-mônd (*adamant*). Pure crystallized carbon. Third stone in second row of high-priest's breastplate, Ex. xxviii. 18 ; Ezek. xxviii. 13.

Di-ăn'à (*safety*). A Roman goddess. Artemis of the Greeks. Her temple at Ephesus regarded as one of the seven wonders of the world, Acts xix. 24-28.

Dĭb'la-ĭm (*two cakes*). Mother-in-law of Hosea, Hos. i. 3.

Dĭb′lăth. Unidentified place, Ezek. vi. 14.

Dī′bŏn (*wasting*). (1) A town of Gad, Num. xxxii. 3, 34. Dibon-gad, Num. xxxiii. 45, 46. Accounted to Reuben, Josh. xiii. 9, 17. Now Dhiban, within the gateway of which the famous Moabite stone was found in 1868. (2) A town in south Judah, Neh. xi. 25.

Dī′bon=găd. [DIBON, 1.]

Dĭb′rī (*orator*). A Danite, Lev. xxiv. 11.

Dĭd′y̆-mus (*twin*). Surname of Thomas, John xi. 16; xx. 24; xxi. 2.

Dĭk′lah (*palm*). A son of Joktan, Gen. x. 27; 1 Chr. i. 21.

Dĭl′ĕ-an (*cucumber*). A lowland city of Judah, Josh. xv. 38.

Dĭm′nah (*dung*). A Levitical city, Josh. xxi. 35.

Dī′mon (*reddish*). A stream of Moab, Isa. xv. 9.

Dĭ-mō′nah (*dunghill*) A city in south Judah, Josh. xv. 22.

Dī′nah (*judged*). First daughter of Jacob and Leah, Gen. xxx. 21; xxxiv.

Dī′na̤-ītes. Cuthean colonists in Samaria, Ez. iv. 9.

Dĭn′hă-bah. A capital of Edom, Gen. xxxvi. 32; 1 Chr. i. 43.

Dī′′ŏ-nȳs′ĭus (*devotee of Dionysos, or Bacchus*). A member of the court of Areopagus at Athens, Acts xvii. 34.

Dī′′ŏ-nȳs′us (*Bacchus*). Bacchus, 2 Macc. xiv. 33.

Dī′os=cŏr-ĭn′thĭ-us (*Corinthian Jove*). A month in the Cretan calendar, 2 Macc. xi. 21.

Dĭ-ot′rĕ-phēs (*nourished by Jupiter*). A Christian, 3 John 9.

Dĭs-çī′ple (*learner*). Follower of Christ, Matt. x. 24; of John, Matt. ix. 14. Applied specially to the twelve, Matt. x. 1; xi. 1; xx. 17.

Dĭṣ′cus (*round plate*). The quoit, 2 Macc. iv. 14.

Dĭs-cov′er (*uncover*). Uncovering, making bare, Ps. xxix. 9; Isa. xxii. 8; Mic. i. 6.

Dĭs-ēaṣ′eṣ (*uneasy*). Visitations of plagues and pestilences frequent in Bible lands, Gen. vii. viii.; Ex. xii. 21–29; 2 Kgs. xix. 35; 1 Chr. xxi. 12; Acts

xii. 23. Principal bodily diseases were, ophthalmia, leprosy, brain and malarial fevers, lung disorders.

Dī'shan (*antelope*). Youngest son of Seir, Gen. xxxvi. 21.

Dī'shon (*antelope*). Sons of Seir, Gen. xxxvi. 21–30.

Dĭs''pĕn-sā'tion (*weighing out*), 1 Cor. ix. 17 ; Eph. i. 10; iii. 2; Col. i. 25. In these instances, authority to preach and teach.

Dĭs-pĕr'sion (*scattering*). The breaking up of the Jewish kingdoms and scattering of the tribes by conquest, James i. 1 ; 1 Pet. i. 1.

Dĭs'taff (*flax-staff*). The staff around which flax was wound for spinning, Prov. xxxi. 19.

Dī'vēs (*rich*). A popular name for the rich man in Luke xvi. 19–31.

Dĭv''ĭ-nā'tion (*belonging to a god*). In Scripture, the false use of means to discover the divine will; by rods, Hos. iv. 12 ; arrows, Ezek. xxi. 21 ; cups, Gen. xliv. 5 ; the liver, Ezek. xxi. 21 ; dreams, Deut. xiii. 3 ; Zech. x. 2 ; consulting oracles, Isa. xli. 21–24 ; xliv. 7. Faith in divination forbidden, Lev. xix. 26.

Dĭ-vôrçe' (*turning asunder*). Allowed by Mosaic law, Deut. xxiv. 1–4, yet forbidden in certain cases, xxii. 19, 29. Christ regarded adultery as an only cause for divorce, Matt. v. 31, 32 ; xix. 9 ; Mark x. 11; Luke xvi. 18.

Dĭz'a-hăb (*gold region*). Scene of one of Moses' addresses, Deut. i. 1.

Dŏc'tor (*teacher*). A teacher of the Law of Moses, Luke ii. 46 ; v. 17. Teacher of the Christian faith, 1 Cor. xii. 28.

Dō'cus. Springs near Jericho, 1 Macc. xvi. 15.

Dŏd'a-ī (*loving*). Leader of David's second military course, 1 Chr. xxvii. 4.

Dŏd'a-nĭm (*leaders*). Descendants of Javan, Gen. x. 4 ; 1 Chr. i. 7.

Dŏd'a-vah. Father of Eliezer, 2 Chr. xx. 37.

Dō'dō (*loving*). (1) Father of one of David's captains, 2 Sam. xxiii. 24. (2) Father of Eleazar, 2 Sam. xxiii. 9 ; 1 Chr. xi. 12. (3) Grandfather of Tola, Judg. x. 1.

Dō'eg (*fearful*). An overseer of Saul's herds, 1 Sam. xxi. 7; xxii. 9–22.

Dŏg. An unclean animal, Ex. xi. 7; xxii. 31; Deut. xxiii. 18; regarded with contempt, 1 Sam. xvii. 43; xxiv. 14; 2 Sam. ix. 8; 2 Kgs. viii. 13; Matt. vii. 6; Rev. xxii. 15; guards, Isa. lvi. 10; Job xxx. 1; scavengers, 1 Kgs. xiv. 11; xxi. 19–23; xxii. 38; enemies, Ps. xxii. 16–20.

Dōor (*through*). [GATE.]

Dŏph'kah (*drover*). A desert station of the Israelites, Num. xxxiii. 12.

Dôr (*dwelling*). A city on the coast north of Cæsarea, Josh. xi. 2; xii. 23; xvii. 11; Judg. i. 27; 1 Kgs. iv. 11.

Dō'rȧ, 1 Macc. xv. 11. [DOR.]

Dŏr'cas (*gazelle*). The woman of Joppa whom Peter raised from the dead, Acts ix. 36–42. [TABITHA.]

Dō-rȳm'ē-nēs. Father of Ptolemy Macron, 1 Macc. iii. 38.

Dō-sĭth'ē-us. (1) A Jewish captain, 2 Macc. xii. 19–35. (2) A priest, Esth. xi. 1, 2.

Dō'tha-ĭm, Judith iv. 6. [DOTHAN.]

Dō'than (*two wells*). The place where Joseph was sold, Gen. xxxvii. 17; 2 Kgs. vi. 13.

Do You To Wit. To make known, 2 Cor. viii. 1.

Dove (*diver*). Clean by the law and offered as a sacrifice by the poor, Gen. xv. 9; Lev. v. 7; xii. 6–8; Luke ii. 24; symbol of innocence, Matt. x. 16; harbinger of God, Gen. viii.; emblem of Holy Spirit, Matt. iii. 16.

Dove's Dŭng. Eaten as a last resort, in time of famine, 2 Kgs. vi. 25.

Dow'rȳ (*gift*). The consideration paid the father of the bride by the bridegroom, Gen. xxix. 18; xxxiv. 12; 1 Sam. xviii. 25; Hos. iii. 2.

Drăch'mȧ, Drăchm (*handful*). A silver coin of Greece, corresponding to the Roman denarius, and worth about fifteen and a half cents. A piece of silver, Luke xv. 8, 9.

Drăg'on (*serpent*). An animal of the lizard species. Evidently a wild beast, as a jackal, in Job xxx. 29; Isa. xxxiv. 13; Ps. xliv. 19; Jer. ix. 11;

Mic. i. 8; sea-serpent, Gen. i. 21; land-serpent, Ex. vii. 9–12; Deut. xxxii. 33; devil, Rev. xii. 3–17.

Dråg′on Well. Possibly Gihon, Neh. ii. 13.

Dråm (*handful*), 1 Chr. xxix. 7; Ez. ii. 69; Neh. vii. 70–72. [DARIC.]

Dråught House. Cesspool, 2 Kgs. x. 27; Matt. xv. 17.

Drēam (*phantom*). Seriously regarded by ancients, Gen. xl. Divine method of approach, Gen. xx. 3–7; 1 Sam. xxviii. 6; Acts xxvii. 22–25. Interpretation of an exceptional gift, Gen. xl. 5–23; xli. 14–45; Dan. iv. 19–27.

Drĕss (*keeping straight*). Of leaves, Gen. iii. 7; skins, iii. 21; woolens, xxxviii. 12; Ex. xxv. 4; Lev. xiii. 47; linen, 1 Chr. iv. 21; silk, Rev. xviii. 12; mixed materials forbidden, Lev. xix. 19; colors rich, Ex. xxxv. 25; Luke xvi. 19; no sexual interchanges, Deut. xxii. 5; common inner dresses, armless shirt, second tunic, linen wrapper, Mark xiv. 51; outer, for men, woolen wrap, 2 Sam. xv. 30; Esth. vi. 12; for women, a long shawl, Ruth iii. 15; Isa. iii. 22–24; Jer. xiii. 22; girdled, Matt. xxiv. 18; Acts xii. 8; 1 Kgs. xviii. 46; poor man's bedclothes, Ex. xxii. 26, 27.

Drĭnk offering. The pouring of a small quantity of wine on the daily morning and evening sacrificial lamb, Ex. xxix. 40; Lev. xxiii. 18.

Drĭnk, Strong. Use of, not uncommon among Hebrews, Gen. ix. 21; xix. 34, 35; Ps. cvii. 27; Isa. xxiv. 20; xlix. 26; li. 17–22; John ii. 1–11; but under prohibitions, Prov. xx. 1; Isa. v. 11.

Drŏm′e̥-dā-ry (*running*). Post camel of the East, usually the one-humped species, as distinguished from the two-humped, or Bactrian, camel, 1 Kgs. iv. 28; Isa. lx. 6; Jer. ii. 23; Mic. i. 13.

Dru̥-sĭl′lå (*watered by dew*). Daughter of Herod Agrippa I., Acts xii. 1–4, 20–23; xxiv. 24.

Du̥ke (*leader*). Hereditary chief or sheikh of Edom, Gen. xxxvi. 15–43.

Dŭl′çi-mer (*sweet song*). The bagpipe and not the stringed dulcimer is meant, Dan. iii. 5–15.

Du̥′mah (*silence*). (1) A son of Ishmael, Gen. xxv. 14; 1 Chr. i. 30. (2) A town in Judah, Josh. xv. 52. (3) A region, Isa. xxi. 11.

Dŭng (*excrement*). Dung of cattle used for fuel, Ezek. iv. 12. Manure made from straw, Isa. xxv. 10. A fertilizer, Luke xiii. 8.

Dŭn′geon (*tower, keep*). [PRISON.]

Dụ′rå (*circle*). A plain of Babylon, Dan. iii. 1.

Dŭst (*storm breath*). Symbol of mourning, Josh. vii. 6; Isa. xlvii. 1; feebleness, Gen. xviii. 27; Job xxx. 19; countless numbers, Gen. xiii. 16; low condition, 1 Sam. ii. 8; rage, 2 Sam. xvi. 13; Acts xxii. 23; renunciation, Matt. x. 14; Mark vi. 11; Acts xiii. 51. A sand storm, Deut. xxviii. 24.

Dwĕll′ings. [HOUSES.]

E

Ēa′gle *dark-colored*). The eagle of Scripture is probably the griffon vulture, Mic. i. 16; Matt. xxiv. 28; Luke xvii. 37; unclean, Lev. xi. 13; Deut. xiv. 12; noted for height and rapidity of flight, Prov. xxiii. 5; 2 Sam. i. 23; Job ix. 26; Deut. xxviii. 49; Jer. iv. 13; great age, Ps. ciii. 5; care of young, Ex. xix. 4; Deut. xxxii. 11, 12; Isa. xl. 31.

Ē′ạ-nēs. A returned captive, 1 Esdr. ix. 21.

Ēar′ing (*plowing*). Earing time was plowing time, Gen. xlv. 6; Ex. xxxiv. 21; Deut. xxi. 4; 1 Sam. viii. 12.

Ĕarn′est (*pledge*). Pledge, Gen. xxxviii. 17; surety, Prov. xvii. 18; hostage, 2 Kgs. xiv. 14; deposit or advance, 2 Cor. i. 22; Eph. i. 14.

Ĕar′rings. Included "nose-rings;" worn by both sexes; Gen. xxxv. 4; Ex. xxxii. 2; Judg. viii. 24; Job xlii. 11; offerings, Num. xxxi. 50.

Ĕarth (*producer*). The world, Gen. i. 1; dry land, i. 10; the soil, ii. 7.

Ĕarth′en-wåre. [POTTERY.]

Ĕarth′quāke (*earth-shaking*). A natural and historic phenomenon, in Am. i. 1; Zech. xiv. 5; 1 Kgs. xix. 11, 12; Matt. xxvii. 51. Token of God's wrath, Judg. v. 4; 2 Sam. xxii. 8; Ps. lxxvii. 18; xcvii. 4; civ. 32; Am. viii. 8; Hab. iii. 10.

Ēast (*dawn*). The Hebrew idea was "before" "in front of," "to the East," Gen. xxix. 1; Num. xxiii. 7; Job i. 3; Ezek. xlvii. 8; Matt. ii. 1.

Ĕast'er (*Eastre, Saxon goddess*). The day commemorative of Christ's resurrection. Wrongly associated with the Saxon Eastre festival, and the Jewish Passover feast, but corrected in R. V., Acts xii. 4.

Ĕast Sea. Ezek. xlvii. 18; Joel ii. 20. The Dead Sea.

Ĕat. Offensive to eat or drink outside of certain limits, Gen. xliii. 32; Matt. ix. 11; John iv. 9.

Ē'bal (*stone*). (1) Son of Shobal, Gen. xxxvi. 23. (2) Son of Joktan, 1 Chr. i. 22. Obal, Gen. x. 28.

Ē'bal, Mount. The mount of curses in Samaria, Deut. xi. 29; Josh. viii. 30–35.

Ē'bed (*servant*). (1) Father of Gaal, Judg. ix. 26–35. (2) One of the returned, Ez. viii. 6.

Ē'bĕd=mē'lĕch (*king's servant*). An Ethiopian, Jer. xxxviii. 12; xxxix. 15–18.

Ĕb''en=ē'zẽr (*stone of help*). A memorial stone, 1 Sam. iv. 1–5; vii. 12.

Ē'bẽr (*beyond*) (1) Great-grandson of Shem, Gen. x. 24; 1 Chr. i. 19. (2) A Benjamite, 1 Chr. viii. 12. (3) A priest, Neh. xii. 20.

Ē-bī'ạ-săph (*father that adds*). A Levite, 1 Chr. vi. 23, 37.

Ĕb'ŏ-nў (*stone-like*). A hard, heavy, dark wood, used for ornamental work and musical instruments, Ezek. xxvii. 15.

Ē-brō'nah (*gateway*). A desert encampment, Num. xxxiii. 34.

Ē-cā'nus. A swift scribe, 2 Esdr. xiv. 24.

Ĕc-băt'ạ-nả (*egress*). Greek for Achmetha, Ez. vi. 2, marg.

Ĕc-clē''sị-ăs'tēs (*preacher*). Twenty-first book of O. T. Authorship ascribed to Solomon. An old man's confession of the vanities of life.

Ĕc-clē''sị-ăs'tị-cus (*of the assembly*). The Latin name of the "Wisdom of Jesus, Son of Sirach," seventh of the Apocryphal books.

Ĕd (*witness*). A word, Josh. xxii. 34.

Ē'där (*flock*). A tower, Gen. xxxv. 21.

Ĕd-dī'as, 1 Esdr. ix. 26. [JEZIAH.]

Ē'dĕn (*pleasure*). (1) First residence of man, Gen. ii. 15. Paradise. Site not fixed. (2) A mart of Mesopotamia, 2 Kgs. xix. 12; Isa. xxxvii. 12. (3)

Beth-eden, Am. i. 5.   (4) A Levite, 2 Chr. xxix. 12.
(5) Another Levite, 2 Chr. xxxi. 15.

Ē′dĕr (*flock*). (1) A town of Judah, Josh. xv. 21.
(2) A Levite, 1 Chr. xxiii. 23 ; xxiv. 30.

Ē′dēṣ, 1 Esdr. ix. 35. [JADDUA.]

Ĕd′nȧ. Wife of Raguel, Tob. vii. 2-16.

Ē′dom (*red*). Called also Idumea and Mount Seir.
Name given to Esau, his country and people, Gen.
xxxii. 3-19 ; xxxiii. 1-16. It lay to the south of Palestine and Moab.

Ĕd′rĕ-ī (*fortress*). (1) A capital of Bashan, Num.
xxi. 33 ; Deut. iii. 10 ; Josh. xii. 4. (2) Town of northern Palestine, Josh. xix. 37.

Ĕg′lah (*heifer*). A wife of David, 2 Sam. iii. 5 ;
1 Chr. iii. 3.

Ĕg′lȧ-ĭm (*ponds*). A place in Moab, Isa. xv. 8.

Ĕg′lŏn (*calf-like*). (1) A King of Moab, Judg. iii.
12-23.   (2) A lowland town of Judah, Josh. x. 3-5 ;
xv. 39.

Ē′gȳpt (*Coptic land*). Northeastern country of
Africa ; the Hebrew "Mizraim," Gen. x. 6, and
"Land of Ham," Ps. cv. 23, 27. Bondage place of
Israelites, Ex. i.-xiv. Noted for Nile river, rich soil
and gigantic ruins. Ancient religion monotheistic,
with sun as central object ; and attributes of nature
in form of trinities. Vast temples and numerous
priests. Kings called Pharaohs, who perpetuated
their reigns in obelisks, temples, sculptures, sphinxes,
pyramids, etc. In intimate commerce with Hebrews,
1 Kgs. iii. 1. Conquered Judea, 1 Kgs. xiv. 25, 26.
Frequently mentioned in Scripture.

Ē′hī, Gen. xlvi. 21. [AHIRAM.]

Ē′hŭd (*united*). (1) Son of Bilhan, 1 Chr. vii. 10.
(2) A judge of Israel, Judg. iii. 15-21.

Ē′kĕr (*tearing up*). A Judahite, 1 Chr. ii. 27.

Ĕk′rĕ-bel. A place in Esdraelon, Judith vii. 18.

Ĕk′rŏn (*migration*). One of the five Philistine
cities, Josh. xiii. 3 ; xv. 45 ; xix. 43 ; 1 Sam. v. 10.

Ĕk′rŏn-ītes. Inhabitants of Ekron, Josh. xiii. 3.

Ē′lȧ, 1 Esdr. ix. 27. [ELAM.]

Ĕl′ȧ-dah (*eternity of God*). An Ephraimite, 1
Chr. vii. 20.

Ē′lah (*oak*). (1) Son and successor of Baasha on

the throne of Israel, B. C. 928-27, 1 Kgs. xvi. 8-10. (2) Father of Hosea, 2 Kgs. xv. 30; xvii. 1. (3) A duke of Edom, Gen. xxxvi. 41. (4) Father of Solomon's commissary, 1 Kgs. iv. 18. (5) Son of Caleb, 1 Chr. iv. 15. (6) A chief of Benjamin, 1 Chr. ix. 8. (7) The valley in which David slew Goliath, 1 Sam. xvii. 2-19.

Ē'lăm (age). (1) Son of Shem, Gen. x. 22, and his country, xiv. 1-9; Dan. viii. 2, in Mesopotamia. (2) A chief of Benjamin, 1 Chr. viii. 24. (3) A Korhite Levite, 1 Chr. xxvi. 3. (4) Persons whose children returned, Ez. ii. 7, 31; Neh. vii. 12, 34. (5) A priest, Neh. x. 14.

Ē'lăm-ītes. Inhabitants of Elam, Ez. iv. 9.

Ĕl'a-sah (whom God made). (1) A priest, Ez. x. 22. (2) Son of Shaphan, Jer. xxix. 3.

Ē'lăth, E'lŏth (oaks). A city of Edom, Deut. ii. 8; Seat of Solomon's navy, 1 Kgs. ix. 26; 2 Chr. viii. 17.

Ĕl=bĕth'=el (God of Bethel). Place where God appeared to Jacob, Gen. xxxv. 7.

Ĕl'çĭ-à. Progenitor of Judith, Judith viii. 1.

Ĕl'da-ah (called of God). Last son of Midian, Gen. xxv. 4; 1 Chr. i. 33.

Ĕl'dăd (loved of God). One of the seventy assistants of Moses, Num. xi. 16, 26-29.

Ĕl'dĕr (old man). Highest in tribal authority, Gen. xxiv. 2; l. 7; Ex. iii. 16; iv. 29; Num. xxii. 7. One of the 70 justiciars, Num. xi. 25, or Sanhedrim, Judg. ii. 7; 2 Sam. xvii. 4; Jer. xxix. 1. An official in early Christian church, like presbyter or bishop, Acts xx. 17, 28.

Ē'le-ăd (praised of God). An Ephraimite, 1 Chr. vii. 21.

Ē''le-ā'leh (ascent of God). A Moabite town, assigned to Reuben, Num. xxxii. 3, 37; Isa. xv. 4; Jer. xlviii. 34.

Ē-lē'a-sà. A place near Ashdod, 1 Macc. ix. 5-18.

Ē-lē'a-sah (made by God). (1) A Judahite, 1 Chr. ii. 39. (2) A descendant of Saul, 1 Chr. viii. 37; ix. 43.

Ē''le-ā'zar (help of God). (1) Third son of Aaron, Ex. vi. 23. Chief of the Levites, Num. iii. 32; and high priest, Num. xx. 28. (2) Son of Abinadab, 1 Sam. vii. 1. (3) One of David's mighty men, 2 Sam. xxiii. 9; 1 Chr. xi. 12. (4) A Levite, 1 Chr. xxiii. 21. (5) A priest, Neh. xii. 42. (6) Son of Phinehas, Ez. viii. 33. (7) Son of Parosh, Ez. x. 25. (8) Surnamed Avaran, 1 Macc. vi. 43. (9) A scribe, 2 Macc. vi. 18. (10) Father of Jason, 1 Macc. viii. 17. (11) Son of Eliud, Matt. i. 15.

Ē″le-a-zū′rus, 1 Esdr. ix. 24. [ELIASHIB.]

Ē-lĕct′ (*chosen out*). One called to everlasting life; the saved collectively, Matt. xxiv. 22; Mark xiii. 27; Luke xviii. 7; Rom. viii. 33; Tit. i. 1. The "elect lady," 2 John i. 1, probably refers to the Christian church.

Ēl=e-lō′hĕ=Ĭs′ra-el (*strength of the God of Israel*). Name of Jacob's altar, Gen. xxxiii. 19, 20.

Ē′leph (*ox*). A town of Benjamin, Josh. xviii. 28.

Ĕl′e-phănt (*ox*). The Hebrew *eleph* means an ox, 1 Kgs. x. 22; 2 Chr. ix. 21; Job xl. 15, margins.

Ē-leu′thĕ-rus. A Syrian river, 1 Macc. xi. 7.

Ĕl-hā′nan (*grace of God*). (1) A noted Hebrew warrior, 2 Sam. xxi. 19; 1 Chr. xx. 5. (2) One of David's body-guard, 2 Sam. xxiii. 24.

Ē′lī (*going up*). A descendant of Aaron, Lev. x. 12. First of a line of high priests, 1 Sam. i. 9–17; ii. 22–36; iii. 1–14; and Judge of Israel for 40 years, iv. 14–18. Line extinguished, 1 Kgs. ii. 26, 27.

Ē′lī, Ē′lī, lā′mä sā-băch-thā′nī. The Lord's cry upon the cross, Matt. xxvii. 46; Mark xv. 34, "My God, my God, why hast thou forsaken me?" Ps. xxii. 1.

Ē-lī′ab (*God is father*). (1) A Chief of Zebulun, Num. i. 9. (2) A Reubenite, Num. xxvi. 8, 9. (3) A Levite musician, 1 Chr. xv. 18–20. (4) Eldest brother of David, 1 Chr. ii. 13. (5) A Gadite leader, 1 Chr. xii. 9. (6) An ancestor of Samuel, 1 Chr. vi. 27. (7) Son of Nathaniel, Judith viii. 1.

Ē-lī′a-dȧ (*known of God*). (1) A younger son of David, 2 Sam. v. 16; 1 Chr. iii. 8. (2) A Benjamite general, 2 Chr. xvii. 17.

Ē-lī′a-dah. Father of Rezon, 1 Kgs. xi. 23–25.

Ē-lī′ah (*God the Lord*). (1) A Benjamite chief, 1 Chr. viii. 27. (2) One of the returned, Ez. x. 26.

Ē-lī′ah-bȧ (*hidden by God*). One of David's guard, 2 Sam. xxiii. 32; 1 Chr. xi. 33.

Ė-lī'a-kĭm (*raised of God*). (1) Master of Hezekiah's household, 2 Kgs. xviii. 18–37; Isa. xxxvi. 3. (2) Original name of King Jehoiakim, 2 Kgs. xxiii. 34; 2 Chr. xxxvi. 4. (3) A priest, Neh. xii. 41. (4) Forefather of Joseph, Matt. i. 13. (5) Father of Jonan, Luke iii. 30, 31.

Ė-lī'a̱-lī, 1 Esdr. ix. 34. [BINNUI.]

Ė-lī'ăm (*God's people*). (1) Father of Bathsheba, 2 Sam. xi. 3. (2) One of David's warriors, 2 Sam. xxiii. 34.

Ė-lī'as. N. T. form of Elijah. [ELIJAH.]

Ė-lī'a-săph (*God increaseth*). (1) Chief of Dan, Num. i. 14; ii. 14; vii. 42; x. 20. (2) A Levite chief, Num. iii. 24.

Ė-lī'a-shĭb (*restored of God*). (1) Eleventh priest of "order of governors," 1 Chr. xxiv. 12. (2) A Judahite, 1 Chr. iii. 24. (3) High priest, Neh. iii. 1–21. (4) Three of the returned, Ez. x. 24, 27, 36.

Ė-lī'a-thah (*to whom God comes*). Leader of the twentieth temple course, 1 Chr. xxv. 4, 27.

Ė-lī'dad (*beloved of God*). A Benjamite, Num. xxxiv. 21.

Ė-lī'el (*God, my God*). (1) A chief of Manasseh, 1 Chr. v. 24. (2) A forefather of Samuel, 1 Chr. vi. 34. (3, 4) Two chiefs of Benjamin, 1 Chr. viii. 20, 22. (5, 6) Two heroes of David's guard, 1 Chr. xi. 46, 47. (7) A Gadite, 1 Chr. xii. 11. (8) A Levite, 1 Chr. xv. 9–11. (9) Overseer of Temple offerings, 2 Chr. xxxi. 13.

Ė'lĭ-ē'na-ī (*eyes toward God*). A chief of Benjamin, 1 Chr. viii. 20.

Ė'lĭ-ē'zĕr (*help of God*). Servant of Abraham, Gen. xv. 2, 3. (2) Second son of Moses, Ex. xviii. 4; 1 Chr. xxiii. 15–17; xxvi. 25. (3) A chief of Benjamin, 1 Chr. vii. 8. (4) A priest, 1 Chr. xv. 24. (5) A Reubenite chief, 1 Chr. xxvii. 16. (6) A prophet, 2 Chr. xx. 37. (7) Messenger of Ezra, Ez. viii. 16. (8, 9, 10) Returned Jews, Ez. x. 18, 23, 31. (11) Ancestor of Christ, Luke iii. 29.

Ėl'ĭ-hō-ē'nă-ī (*eyes toward God*). A returned leader, Ez. viii. 4.

Ėl'ĭ-hō'reph (*God his reward*). A scribe, 1 Kgs. iv. 3.

Ė-lī'hū (*God is his*). (1) A forefather of Samuel,

1 Sam. i. 1. (2) Eldest brother of David, 1 Chr. xxvii. 18. (3) A captain of Manasseh, 1 Chr. xii. 20. (4) A Levite door-keeper, 1 Chr. xxvi. 7. (5) One of Job's friends, Job xxxii. 2.

Ĕ-lī'jah (*God is God*). (1) The prophet; Elias in N. T., Matt. xvii. 3. A Tishbite of Gilead; appears suddenly; is fed by ravens; restores the widow's son, 1 Kgs. xvii. 1–24; invokes fire on the prophets of Baal, xviii. 17–40; anoints Hazael, Jehu, and Elisha, xix.; denounces Ahab and Jezebel, xxi. 17–24; is translated in a chariot of fire, 2 Kgs. ii.; reappears on the mount of Transfiguration, Luke ix. 28–35. (2) A son of Harim, Ez. x. 21.

Ĕl'i-kā (*rejected of God*). One of David's guard, 2 Sam. xxiii. 25.

Ē'lĭm (*oaks*). Second encampment of the Israelites after crossing the Red Sea, Ex. xv. 27; Num. xxxiii. 9.

Ĕ-lĭm'ĕ-lech (*my God is king*). Husband of Naomi, Ruth i. 1–3.

Ĕl''i-ō-ē'nă-ī (*eyes toward God*). (1) A descendant of David, 1 Chr. iii. 23, 24. (2) A Simeonite, 1 Chr. iv. 36. (3) A Levite doorkeeper, 1 Chr. xxvi. 3. (4) A Benjamite, 1 Chr. vii. 8. (5) Two priests, Ez. x. 22, 27.

Ĕl-i-ō'nas, 1 Esdr. ix. 22–32. [Elioenai.]

Ĕl'ĭ-phal (*judged of God*). Son of Ur, 1 Chr. xi. 35. Eliphelet, 2 Sam. xxiii. 34.

Ĕ-lĭph'a-lĕt (*God of deliverance*). A son of David, 2 Sam. v. 16; 1 Chr. xiv. 7.

Ĕl'ĭ-phăz (*God his strength*). (1) A son of Esau, Gen. xxxvi. 4; 1 Chr. i. 35, 36. (2) One of Job's friends, Job iv., v., xv., xxii.

Ĕ'lĭph'e-leh (*who exalts God*). A harper, 1 Chr. xv. 18–21.

Ĕ-lĭph'e-lĕt (*God of deliverance*). (1) One of David's warriors, 2 Sam. xxiii. 34. (2) Name of two sons of David, 1 Chr. iii. 6, 8. (3) A descendant of Saul, 1 Chr. viii. 39. (4) Two of the returned, Ez. viii. 13; x. 33.

Ĕ-lĭṣ'a-bĕth (*oath of God*). Wife of Zecharias, Luke i. 36–80.

Ĕl''ĭ-sē'us. Greek form of Elisha, Luke iv. 27.

Ė-lī'shả (*God his salvation*). Anointed prophet by Elijah, 1 Kgs. xix. 16-21. Prophesied in reigns of Jehoram, Jehu, Jehoahaz and Joash, a period of sixty years. Life and works in 2 Kgs. ii.-ix.; xiii. 14-21.

Ė-lī'shah (*God saves*). Eldest son of Javan, Gen. x. 4; Ezek. xxvii. 7.

Ė-lĭsh'ạ-mả (*whom God hears*). (1) Grandfather of Joshua, Num. i. 10. (2) Two sons of David, 2 Sam. v. 16; 1 Chr. iii. 6, 8. (3) A priest. 2 Chr. xvii. 8. (4) A Judahite, 1 Chr. ii. 41. (5) Grandfather of Ishmael, 2 Kgs. xxv. 25. (6) A scribe, Jer. xxxvi. 12, 20-21. (7) A priest, 2 Chr. xvii. 8.

Ė-lĭsh'ạ-phăt (*whom God judges*). Captain of a hundred, 2 Chr. xxiii. 1.

Ė-lish'ẹ-bả (*God her oath*). Wife of Aaron, Ex. vi. 23.

Ėl''ĭ-shụ'ả. A son of David, 2 Sam. v. 15; 1 Chr. xiv. 5. Elishama, 1 Chr. iii. 6-8.

Ė-lĭs'ĭ-mus, 1 Esdr. ix. 28. [ELIASHIB.]

Ė-lī'ū. A forefather of Judith, Judith viii. 1.

Ė-lī'ŭd (*God my praise*). Ancestor of Joseph, Matt. i. 15.

Ė-lĭz'ạ-phan (*protected of God*). (1) A Levite chief, Num. iii. 30; 1 Chr. xv. 8. Elzaphan, Ex. vi. 22; Lev. x. 4. (2) A chief of Zebulun, Num. xxxiv. 25.

Ė-lī'zŭr (*God his rock*). A prince of Reuben, Num. i. 5; ii. 10.

Ėl'kă-nah, Ėl'kŏ-nah (*provided of God*). (1) Grandson of Korah, Ex. vi. 24; 1 Chr. vi. 23. (2) Another descendant of Korah, 1 Chr. vi. 26, 35. (3) Another Levite, 1 Chr. vi. 27, 34; 1 Sam. i. 1-23; ii. 11, 20. (4) A Levite, 1 Chr. ix. 16. (5) A Korhite, 1 Chr. xii. 6. (6) An officer under Ahaz, 2 Chr. xxviii. 7.

Ėl'kosh (*my bow is of God*). Modern Alkush on the Tigris, Nahum i. 1.

Ėl'lạ-sär (*oak*). City of King Arioch, Gen. xiv. 1-9.

Ėlm, Hosea iv. 13; elsewhere translated "oak."

Ėl-mō'dăm (*measure*). Son of Er. Elmadam in R. V., Luke iii. 28.

Ėl'na-am (*God his delight*). Father of two of David's guard, 1 Chr. xi. 46.

Ėl'nạ-than (*gift of God*). (1) Grandfather of

Jehoiachin, 2 Kgs. xxiv. 8; Jer. xxvi. 22. (2) Names of three Levites, Ez. viii. 16.

Ė-lō′ī, Ė-lō′hī, Ĕl′ō-him. God. Eloi is also Aramaic form of Elias, or Elijah, Mark xv. 34.

Ē′lon (*oak*). (1) A Hittite, Gen. xxvi. 34; xxxvi. 2. (2) A son of Zebulun, Gen. xlvi. 14; Num. xxvi. 26. (3) A Zebulunite, Judg. xii. 11, 12. (4) A town of Dan, Josh. xix. 43.

Ē′lon=bĕth=hā′′năn (*oak of house of grace*). Part of one of Solomon's commissary districts, 1 Kgs. iv. 9.

Ē′lŏn-ītes, Num. xxvi. 26. [ELON, 2.]

Ė′lŏth, 1 Kgs. ix. 26; 2 Chr. viii. 17; xxvi. 2. [ELATH.]

Ĕl′pă-al (*wages of God*). A Benjamite, 1 Chr. viii. 11, 12.

Ĕl′pa-let, 1 Chr. xiv. 5. [ELIPHELET, 2.]

Ĕl-pā′ran. Oak of Paran, Gen. xiv. 6. [PARAN.]

Ĕl′tĕ-keh (*fear of God*). A city of Dan, Josh. xix. 44; xxi. 23.

Ĕl′tĕ-kon (*founded by God*). A town in Judah, Josh. xv. 59.

Ĕl′to-lăd (*kindred of God*). A city of Judah, and Simeon, Josh. xv. 30; xix. 4; Tolad, 1 Chr. iv. 29.

Ē′lŭl (*vine*). Twelfth month of Hebrew civil, and sixth of sacred, year, corresponding to parts of September and October, Neh. vi. 15.

Ė-lū′za-ī (*God my praise*). A Benjamite warrior, 1 Chr. xii. 5.

Ĕl′′ȳ-mæ′ans, Judith i. 6. [ELAMITES.]

Ĕl′ȳ-măs (*wise*). Arabic name of Bar-jesus, Acts xiii. 6-12.

Ĕl′za-băd (*gift of God*). (1) A Gadite, 1 Chr. xii. 12. (2) A Korhite Levite, 1 Chr. xxvi. 7.

Ĕl′za-phăn (*protected by God*). Second son of Uzziel, Ex. vi. 22; Lev. x. 4; 2 Chr. xxix. 13. Elizaphan in Num. iii. 30; 1 Chr. xv. 8.

Ĕm-bälm′ (*to put in balsam*). Embalming carried to great perfection by the Egyptians, whom the Jews feebly imitated, Gen. l. 2-26.

Ĕm-brôi′der (*to work a border*). Ex. xxviii. 39; xxxv. 35; xxxviii. 23. Possibly nothing beyond the common weaver's art is meant. "Cunning work," Ex. xxvi. 1, implies embroidery.

Ĕm'ĕr-ăld. A bright green variety of beryl. The emerald of Ex. xxviii. 18 ; xxxix. 11 ; Ezek. xxvii. 16 ; xxviii. 13 ; Rev. iv. 3 ; xxi. 19, is supposably the carbuncle, a fiery garnet.

Ĕm'ė-rŏds (*flowing with blood*). Hemorrhoids or piles, Deut. xxviii. 27 ; 1 Sam. v. 6–12 ; vi. 4–11.

Ē'mĭms (*terrors*). A race of Anakim east of Dead Sea, Gen. xiv. 5 ; Deut. ii. 10, 11.

Ĕm-măn'ū-el, Matt. i. 23. [IMMANUEL.]

Ĕm'ma-us (*warm springs*). A village of Palestine, 7½ mls. from Jerusalem, Luke xxiv. 13–33.

Ĕm'mer, 1 Esdr. ix. 21. [IMMER.]

Ĕm'môr (*ass*), Acts vii. 16. [HAMOR.]

Ĕn. A fountain. Used in compounds.

Ĕn-ā'bled. Qualified, 1 Tim. i. 12.

Ē'nam (*two fountains*). A city of Judah, Josh. xv. 34.

Ē'nan (*eyes*). A prince of Naphtali, Num. i. 15 ; ii. 29 ; vii. 78, 83 ; x. 27.

Ē-năs'ĭ-bus, 1 Esdr. ix. 34. [ELIASHIB.]

Ĕn-cămp'ment (*field*). Halting place of army or caravan, Ex. xiv. 19 ; xvi. 13 ; Num. ii., iii. ; Josh. x. 5.

Ĕn-chănt'ment (*song-spell*). Enchantments unlawful, Lev. xix. 26 ; Deut. xviii. 10–12 ; as Egyptian trickery, Ex. vii. 11–22 ; viii. 7 ; Balaam's omens, Num. xxiv. 1 ; muttered spells, 2 Kgs. ix. 22 ; Mic. v. 12 ; Nah. iii. 4 ; serpent charming, Eccl. x. 11 ; magical spells, Isa. xlvii. 9–12 ; auguries, Jer. xxvii. 9. [DIVINATION.]

Ĕn'=dôr (*fountain of Dor*). A village of Manasseh, Josh. xvii. 11 ; Ps. lxxxiii. 9, 10 ; 1 Sam. xxviii.

Ĕn=eg'la-ĭm (*fountain of two calves*). An unknown place, Ezek. xlvii. 10.

Ĕn''ė-mĕs'sär. Shalmaneser, Tob. i. 2, 15.

Ē-nē'nĭ-us. A returned leader, 1 Esdr. v. 8.

Ĕn-găd'dī, Ecclus. xxiv. 14. [ENGEDI.]

Ĕn=găn'nĭm (*fount of the garden*). (1) A city of Judah, Josh. xv. 34. (2) A Levitical city, Josh. xix. 21 ; xxi. 29.

Ēn=gē′dī (*fount of the kid*). A town on west shore of Dead Sea, Josh. xv. 62; Ezek. xlvii. 10; 1 Sam. xxiv. 1–7; S. of Sol. i. 14. Hazezon-tamar, Gen. xiv. 7; 2 Chr. xx. 2.

Ēn′gīne (*skilled product*). The ballista for throwing spears, arrows, stones, 2 Chr. xxvi. 15; the catapult, Ezek. xxvi. 9; battering ram, Ezek. iv. 2; xxi. 22.

Ēn-grā′vĕr (*digger in*). The commandments were engraved, Ex. xxxii. 16; also stones and signets, Ex. xxviii. 11, 21, 36; Job xix. 24; Acts xvii. 29. Graven images were objects of idolatry, Ex. xx. 4; xxxii. 4.

Ēn=hăd′dah (*fountain*). A city of Issachar, Josh. xix. 21.

Ēn=hak′kŏ-rē (*fount of the caller*). Samson's fountain, Judg. xv. 19.

Ēn=hā′zôr (*fount of Hazor*). A fenced city in Naphtali, Josh. xix. 37.

Ēn=mish′pat (*fount of judgment*). Gen. xiv. 7. [KADESH.]

Ē′nŏch (*dedicated*). (1) A son of Cain, Gen. iv. 17. (2) Father of Methuselah, Gen. v. 18–24; Heb. xi. 5–13; Jude 14. (3) "Behemoth," 2 Esdr. vi. 49–51.

Ē′non (*springs*). John i. 28; iii. 23. [ÆNON.]

Ē′nos (*mortal*). Son of Seth, Gen. iv. 26; v. 6–11; Luke iii. 38. Enosh, 1 Chr. i. 1.

Ē′nosh, 1 Chr. i. 1. [ENOS.]

Ēn=rĭm′mon (*fount of the pomegranate*). A settlement of returned Jews, Neh. xi. 29.

Ēn=rō′gel (*fuller's fount*). A celebrated spring, Josh. xv. 7; xviii. 16; 2 Sam. xvii. 17; 1 Kgs. i. 9.

Ēn=shē′mesh (*fount of the sun*). A spring, Josh. xv. 7; xviii. 17.

Ēn′sīgn (*mark upon*). A simple device, elevated on a pole, bearing some emblem to distinguish the tribes and army divisions, Num. i. 52; S. of Sol. ii. 4; Isa. xiii. 2; xviii. 3.

Ēn=sūe′. Pursue, 1 Pet. iii. 11.

Ēn=tăp′pu-ah (*fount of the apple*). Tappuah in Manasseh, Josh. xvii. 7.

Ĕp′a-phrăs (*lovely*). A Roman friend of Paul, Col. i. 7; iv. 12.

Ē-pæn'ĕ-tus (*praised*). A Christian at Rome, Rom. xvi. 5.

Ē-păph''ro-dī'tus (*lovely*). Probably Epaphras. Phil. ii. 25; iv. 18

Ē'phah (*gloomy*). (1) First son of Midian, Gen. xxv. 4; 1 Chr. i. 33; Isa. lx. 6. (2) Caleb's concubine, 1 Chr. ii. 46. (3) A Judahite, 1 Chr. ii. 47. (4) A Hebrew dry measure, estimated at 2⅓ to 3¼ pecks, Ruth ii. 17; Num. v. ¹5. (5) A Hebrew liquid measure equal to 7½ gallons.

Ē'phāi (*gloomy*). His sons were captains left behind in Judah, Jer. xl. 8.

Ē'pher (*calf*). (1) A son of Midian, Gen. xxv. 4; 1 Kgs. iv. 10. (2) A son of Ezra, 1 Chr. iv. 17. A chief of Manasseh, 1 Chr. v. 24.

Ē'phes=dam'mim (*border of blood*). A Philistine encampment, 1 Sam. xvii. 1. Pasdammim, 1 Chr. xi. 13. [ELAH.]

Ē-phē'sĭaņs. (1) Inhabitants of Ephesus, Acts xix. 28. (2) Epistle to, written by Paul to the Christians at Ephesus, about A. D 61 or 62, and while he was a prisoner at Rome. Forwarded by Tychicus, Eph. vi. 21. Of general import.

Ĕph'ĕ-sŭs (*desirable*). Capital of Ionia, on the Ægean Sea. Noted for its commerce, learning, and architecture. Paul visited it, Acts xviii. 1–20, and founded a church there, to which he addressed one of his best epistles, Acts xix. 1–10; xx. 17–38.

Ĕph'lăl (*judgment*). A Judahite, 1 Chr. ii. 37.

Ĕph'ŏd (*clothe*). (1) A sleeveless linen garment for priests, covering breast and back, Ex. xxviii. 4–35; 1 Sam. xxii. 18, with onyx clasp at shoulder, and breastplate at breast, crossing. Worn later by other than priests, 1 Chr. xv. 27. [BREASTPLATE.] (2) A Manassite, Num. xxxiv. 23.

Ĕph'phă-thă (*be opened*). Christ's utterance in Mark vii. 34.

Ē'phrȧ-ĭm (*doubly fruitful*). (1) Second son of Joseph, Gen. xli. 52. Obtained Jacob's blessing, Gen. xlviii. 8–20. Tribe numerous, Num. i. 33; xxvi. 37. Allotment as in Josh. xvi. 1–10. (2) Site of Absalom's sheep-farm, 2 Sam. xiii. 23. (3) Place to which Christ retired, John xi. 54. (4) A gate of Jerusalem, 2 Kgs. xiv. 13; 2 Chr. xxv. 23; Neh. viii.

16; xii. 39. (5) "Mount of," in Ephraim, 1 Sam. i. 1. (6) "The wood of," east of Jordan, 2 Sam. xviii. 6.

Ē'phrā-ĭm-ītes''. Members of the tribe of Ephraim, Judg. xii. 5. Sometimes Ephrathites.

Ē'phră-ĭn (*doubly fruitful*). A city of Israel, 2 Chr. xiii. 19.

Ĕph'ra-tah, Ĕph'rath (*fruitful*). (1) Second wife of Caleb, 1 Chr. ii. 19, 50. (2) Ancient name of Bethlehem-judah, Gen. xxxv. 16, 19; xlviii. 7.

Ĕph'rath-ītes. (1) Inhabitants of Bethlehem, or Ephrath, Ruth i. 2. (2) Ephraimites, Judg. xii. 5; 1 Sam. i. 1; 1 Kgs. xi. 26.

Ĕph'ron (*fawn-like*). (1) A Hittite who sold Machpelah to Abraham, Gen. xxiii. 8–20; xlix. 29; l. 13. (2) Landmarks of Judah, Josh. xv. 9. (3) A city east of Jordan, 1 Macc. v. 46–52.

Ĕp''ĭ-cū-rē'anş (*followers of Epicurus*). A sect of pleasure-loving philosophers at Athens, Acts xvii. 18.

Ē-pĭph'a-nēş, 1 Macc. i. 10. [ANTIOCHUS, 4.]

Ē-pĭs'tle (*sending to*). In O. T. a letter, 2 Sam. xi. 14; 2 Kgs. v. 5, 6; 2 Chr. xxi. 12; Ez. iv. 6–11. In N. T., a formal tract containing Christian doctrine and salutary advice.

Ĕr (*watchman*). (1) First-born of Judah, Gen. xxxviii. 3–7; Num. xxvi. 19. (2) A descendant of Shelah, 1 Chr. iv. 21. (3) Son of Jose, Luke iii. 28.

Ē'răn (*watchful*). Founder of the Eranites, Num. xxvi. 36.

Ē-răs'tŭs (*beloved*). (1) A friend of Paul at Ephesus, Acts xix. 22; 2 Tim. iv. 20. (2) A Corinthian convert, Rom. xvi. 23.

Ē'rĕch (*healthy*). A city of Shinar, Gen. x. 10.

Ē'rī (*watching*). A son of Gad, Gen. xlvi. 16, and founder of the Erites, Num. xxvi. 16.

Ē-şā'ĭas. N. T. name of Isaiah, Matt. iii. 3.

Ē''sar-hăd'don (*conqueror*). A king of Assyria, 2 Kgs. xix. 37; 2 Chr. xxxiii. 11. He united Babylon to Assyria and reigned over both B. C. 680–667.

Ē'şau (*hairy*). Eldest son of Isaac and twin brother of Jacob, Gen. xxv. 25. Called also Edom. Sold his birthright to Jacob, Gen. xxv. 26–34; xxxvi. 1–10. Gave his name, Edom, to a country and to his descendants, Gen. xxvi., xxxvi. [EDOM.]

Ē′say, Ecclus. xlviii. 20–22. [ISAIAH.]

Eṣ″dra-ē′lon. Greek for Jezreel, Judith iii. 9; iv. 6.

Ĕṣ′dras. (1) A scribe in 1 and 2 Esdras. (2) First and second books of the Apocrypha. First a supplement to Ezra; second a series of visions.

Ē′sĕk (*strife*). A well in Gerar, Gen. xxvi. 20.

Ĕsh=bā′al (*Baal's man*). Ishbosheth, Saul's fourth son, 1 Chr. viii. 33; ix. 39.

Ĕsh′băn (*wise man*). Son of Dishon, Gen. xxxvi. 26; 1 Chr. i. 41.

Ĕsh′cŏl (*bunch of grapes*). (1) Brother of Mamre, Gen. xiv. 13–24. (2) A valley or brook near Hebron, Num. xiii. 22–27; xxxii. 9; Deut. i. 24.

Ē′shĕ-an (*slope*). A city of Judah, Josh. xv. 52.

Ē′shĕk (*oppression*). A descendant of Saul, 1 Chr. viii. 39.

Ĕsh′ka-lŏn-ītes″, Josh. xiii. 3. [ASHKELON.]

Ĕsh′tă-ŏl (*a way*). Town in Judah and Dan, Josh. xv. 33; xix. 41; burial place of Samson, Judg. xiii. 25; xvi. 31; xviii. 2–11.

Ĕsh′tă-ul-ītes″. Families of Kirjath-jearim, 1 Chr. ii. 53.

Ĕsh″te-mō′å, Ĕsh′te-mōh (*bosom of a woman*). A Levitical town of Judah, Josh. xv. 50; xxi. 14; 1 Sam. xxx. 28.

Ĕsh′ton (*weak*). A Judahite, 1 Chr. iv. 11, 12.

Ĕs′lī (*reserved*). Ancestor of Joseph, Luke iii. 25.

Ē-sō′rå. Hazor or Zorah, Judith iv. 4.

Ĕs-pouṣe′ (*promise*). [BETROTH.]

Ĕs′rom, Matt. i. 3; Luke iii. 33. [HEZRON.]

Ĕs-sēne′ (*priest*). Member of a Jewish ascetic sect, the Essenes.

Ĕs-tāte′ (*standing*). In Mark vi. 21, a class or order representing the government. The "estate of the elders," Acts xxii. 5, was a body of advisers co-operating with the Sanhedrim.

Ĕs′thĕr (*star*). Persian name of Hadassah, Mordecai's cousin, who married King Ahasuerus, and saved the lives of her countrymen. Her book, seventeenth of O. T., tells her story.

Ē'tam (*lair*). (1) A village in Simeon, 1 Chr. iv. 32. (2) Favorite resort of Solomon, 2 Chr. xi. 6; Judg. xv. 8–19. (3) A doubtful name, 1 Chr. iv. 3.

Ē'tham (*sea bound*). An Israèlite encampment, Ex. xiii. 20; Num. xxxiii. 6-8.

Ē'than (*strong*). (1) One noted for wisdom, 1 Kgs. iv. 31; 1 Chr. ii. 6; title to Ps. lxxxix. (2) A Levite singer, 1 Chr. vi. 44; xv. 17–19. (3) An ancestor of Asaph, 1 Chr. vi. 42.

Ĕth'a̤-nĭm (*flowing*). Seventh month (Tisri) of Jewish sacred, and first of civil, year; corresponding to parts of Sept. and Oct., 1 Kgs. viii. 2.

Ĕth'bā-al (*favored of Baal*). King of Sidon, 1 Kgs. xvi. 31.

Ē'thĕr (*plenty*). Town in Judah and Simeon, Josh. xv. 42; xix. 7.

Ē″thĭ-ō'pĭ-a̤ (*burnt faces*). Greek and Roman for Hebrew "Cush." The unbounded country south of Egypt, Ezek. xxix. 10; settled by Hamites, Gen. x. 6; merchants, Isa. xlv. 14; Jer. xiii. 23; Job xxviii. 19; wealthy, Acts viii. 27-37; strongly military, 2 Chr. xii. 3; xiv. 9–12; 2 Kgs. xvii. 4.

Ē″thĭ-ō'pĭ-an̯s. Dwellers in Ethiopia; Cushites, Num. xii. 1; 2 Chr. xiv. 9; Jer. xxxviii. 7; xxxix. 16; Acts viii. 27-37.

Ĕth'nan (*hire*). A Judahite, 1 Chr. iv. 5-7.

Ĕth'nī (*liberal*). A Levite, 1 Chr. vi. 41.

Eū-bū'lus (*prudent*). A Roman Christian, 2 Tim. iv. 21.

Eū-ĕr'gĕ-tē̯s (*benefactor*). A common Grecian surname, and title of honor; applied especially to the Ptolemies.

Eū'nă-tan, 1 Esdr. viii. 44. [ELNATHAN.]

Eū'nĭçe (*good victory*). Mother of Timothy, Acts xvi. 1; 2 Tim. i. 5.

Eū'nŭch (*couch guardian*). A castrated male. Eunuchs became court officials, 2 Kgs. ix. 32; Esth. ii. 3; Acts viii. 27; could not enter the congregation, Deut. xxiii. 1. A celibate, Matt. xix. 12.

Eū-ō'dĭ-as (*fragrant*). Euodia in R. V.; a Christian woman of Philippi, Phil. iv. 2.

Eū-phrā'tēs (*fructifying*). A great river of western Asia, rising in Armenia and emptying into the Persian Gulf. Boundary of Eden, Gen. ii. 14; "great river," Gen. xv. 18; Deut. i. 7; eastern boundary of the promised land, Deut. xi. 24; Josh. i. 4; 1 Chr. v. 9; and of David's conquests, 2 Sam. viii. 3; 1 Chr. xviii. 3. *See* also, Jer. xiii. 4-7; xlvi. 2-10; li. 63; Ps. cxxxvii. 1; Rev. ix. 14; xvi. 12.

Eū-pŏl'e-mus. An envoy, 1 Macc. viii. 17.

Eū-rŏc'lȳ-don. A stormy northeast wind of the Levant, Acts xxvii. 14.

Eū'tȳ-chus (*fortunate*). A sleepy youth of Troas, Acts xx. 6-12.

Ė-vặn'ġĕl-ĭst (*publisher of glad tidings*). One of the four writers of the gospels Matthew, Mark, Luke and John. A preacher of the gospel inferior in authority to the Apostles, Acts viii. 14-19, and apparently to the prophets, Eph. iv. 11, yet superior to the pastor and teacher, Acts xxi. 8; Eph. iv. 11; 2 Tim. iv. 5. A travelling and corresponding missionary, Acts xx. 4, 5.

Ēve (*life*). The first woman; made *of* man and *for* him, Gen. ii. 18-25; iii.-iv.

Ēve'nĭng (*decline of day*). Two evenings recognized, one before, the other after, sunset, Gen. xxiv. 63; Ex. xii. 6; Num. ix. 3; xxviii. 4.

Ē'vī (*desire*). A King of Midian, Num. xxxi. 8; Josh. xiii. 21.

Ē'vĭl=mė-rō'dach (*fool of Merodach*). King of Babylon, B. C. 561-559, 2 Kgs. xxv. 27; Jer. lii. 31-34.

Ĕx″cŏm-mū″nĭ-cā'tion (*putting out of the community*). Threefold in Jewry. (1) Temporary suspension. (2) Further temporary suspension. (3) Final cutting off. Now rests on Matt. xvi. 19; xviii. 17; 1 Cor. v. 11; 2 Cor. ii. 5-11; 1 Cor. i. 20; Tit. iii. 10.

Ĕx″ē-cū'tion-ẽr (*a follower out*). In O. T. a position of dignity, Gen. xxxvii. 36, marg.; 1 Kgs. ii. 25, 34. Even in Mark vi. 27, the executioner belonged to the king's body-guard.

Ĕx'ȯ-dus (*going out*). Second Book of the Bible and Pentateuch. Written by Moses. Historic from i to xviii. 27 ; legislative from xix. to end. Its history covers the period (about 142 years) of Jewish preparation to leave Egypt, the departure, the desert wanderings and the arrival at Sinai. Its legislation comprises the giving of the law at Sinai, directions for the priesthood, the establishment of the tabernacle and its service.

Ĕx′ŏr-çĭsts (*swearers out*). Those who pretended to drive out evil spirits by prayers and conjurations, Matt. xii. 27 ; Mark ix. 38 ; Acts xix. 13.

Ĕx″pĭ-ā′tion, Feast of. [ATONEMENT.]

Eye. Putting out the eye a warfare custom, especially with dangerous prisoners. Judg. xvi. 21 ; 1 Sam. xi. 2 ; 2 Kgs. xxv. 7. Painting the eyelids a fashion, 2 Kgs. ix. 30 ; Jer. iv. 30 ; Ezek. xxiii. 40. "Eyeservice," reluctant service, Col. iii. 22 ; Eph. vi. 6.

Ē′zär, 1 Chr. i. 38. [EZER, 1.]

Ĕz′bă-ī (*shining*). Father of one of David's mighty men, 1 Chr. xi. 37.

Ĕz′bŏn (*bright*). (1) A son of Gad, Gen. xlvi. 16 ; Ozni in Num. xxvi. 16. (2) A Benjamite, 1 Chr. vii. 7.

Ĕz-ē-chī′as, 2 Esdr. vii. 40. [HEZEKIAH.]

Ĕz-ē-çī′as, 1 Esdr. ix. 43. [HILKIAH.]

Ĕz-ē-kī′as, 2 Macc. xv. 22 ; Matt. i. 9, 10. [HEZEKIAH.]

Ė-zē′kĭ-ĕl (*strength of God*). One of the four greater prophets ; carried captive to Babylon B. C. 598 ; entered the prophetic calling in fifth year of his captivity, Ezek. i. 1–3. Chapters i.–xxiv. of his book contain predictions before the fall of Jerusalem, and xxv.–xlviii. predictions after that event. The visions of the Temple, xl.–xlviii., are a unique feature of the book.

Ē′zĕl (*going away*). Scene of the parting of David and Jonathan, 1 Sam. xx. 19.

Ē′zĕm (*bone*). A town of Simeon, 1 Chr. iv. 29 ; Azem in Josh. xix. 3.

Ē′zĕr (*help*). (1) A Horite duke, Gen. xxxvi. 21, 27, 30 ; 1 Chr. iv. 4. (2) An Ephraimite, 1 Chr. vii. 21. (3) A Gadite, 1 Chr. xii. 9. (4) A Levite, Neh. iii. 19. (5) A priest, Neh. xii. 42.

Ĕz″ĕ-rī′as, Ė-zī′as, 1 Esdr. viii 1, 2. [AZARIAH.]

Ē'zĭ-on=gā'bĕr, or **gė'bĕr** (*backbone of a giant*). An Israelite encampment, Num. xxxiii. 35, 36; Deut. ii. 8. Compare 1 Kgs. ix. 26; 2 Chr. viii. 17; 1 Kgs. xxii. 48.

Ĕz'nīte, 2 Sam. xxiii. 8, for Tachmonite in same verse and Hachmonite in 1 Chr. xi. 11.

Ĕz'rȧ (*help*). The famous scribe and priest, resident at Babylon, who returned to Jerusalem with his countrymen, B. C. 458, where he began instant reforms. He collected and revised the previous O. T. writings and largely settled the O. T. canon. His book, 15th of O. T., tells the story of the return and the establishment of a new order of things at Jerusalem and in Judea.

Ĕz'ra-hite''. A title applied to Ethan and Heman, 1 Kgs. iv. 31; Ps. lxxxviii. title; lxxxix. title.

Ĕz'rī (*my help*). A superintendent of David's farm laborers, 1 Chr. xxvii. 26.

F

Fā'ble (*spoken*). A narrative in which inanimate things are personalized, Judg. ix. 8-15; 2 Kgs. xiv. 9.

Fair Hā'vens. A harbor of Crete, Acts xxvii. 8-13.

Fairs (*holidays*). Wares, Ezek. xxvii. 12-33.

Făl'low=deer (*yellowish brown*). The bubalis or African deer, Deut. xiv. 5; 1 Kgs. iv. 23. Some say the Arabian wild ox.

Făl'low (*yellow*). Plowed land left to mellow. Tillage, Prov. xiii. 23. Figurative, Jer. iv. 3; Hos. x. 12. The Sabbatical, or fallow year; year of land-rest, Lev. xxv. 1-7; Deut. xxxi. 9-14.

Făm'ĭne (*hunger*). Generally foretold and regarded as a judgment, Gen. xii. 10; xxvi. 1; xli. 54-56; 2 Kgs. vii.

Făn (*winnower*). Winnowing shovel or fork used to throw chaff up into the wind, to separate it from the kernels, Isa. xxx. 24; Matt. iii. 12.

Fȧr'thǐng. Two Roman bronze coins. One, Matt. v. 26; Mark xii. 42, worth ¼ of a cent; the other, Matt. x. 29; Luke xii. 6, worth 1½ cents.

Fȧsts (*keep*). One legal fast, the Atonement, kept by Jews, Lev. xvi. 29-34; Deut. ix. 9; Jonah iii. 5; Zech. vii. 1-7. Special fasts observed, 1 Sam. vii. 6; Jer. xxxvi. 6-10; Esth. iv. 16; Matt. ix. 14; Mark ii. 18; Luke v. 33; Acts x. 30; xiii. 3.

Făt (*fed*). Forbidden food, as belonging to God, Lev. iii. 3-17; vii. 3, 23; Neh. viii. 10; yet fatted cattle enjoyed, 1 Kgs. iv. 23; Luke xv. 23. Vat is meant in Joel ii. 24; iii. 13; Hag. ii. 16.

Fȧ'ther (*sire*). Source of authority, Gen. iii. 16; 1 Cor. xi. 3. Disrespect of, condemned, Ex. xxi. 15-17; xxii. 17; Lev. xx. 9; 1 Tim. i. 9. Parental obedience bears a promise, Ex. xx. 12. Father also a priest, Gen. viii. 20. Any ancestor, Deut. i. 11; Matt. xxiii. 30. A title, Judg. xvii. 10; 1 Sam. x. 12; Acts vii. 2. Protector, Ps. lxviii. 5. Author and founder, Gen. iv. 21; Rom. iv. 12. Divine appellation, Deut. xxxii. 6; Matt. vi. 4; Rom. i. 7.

Făth'om (*embrace*). Space to which a man can extend his arms; about 6 feet, Acts xxvii. 28.

Fēasts (*joyful*). Observed for joyous events, Gen. xxi. 8; xxix. 22; xl. 20; Mark vi. 21, 22. Numerous religious feasts, Ex. xii. 16; Lev. xxiii. 21-24; Jude 12.

Fēet. To wash, a sign of hospitality, Gen. xviii. 4; 1 Sam. xxv. 41; John xiii. 5, 6. To remove shoes, a reverence, Ex. iii. 5; sign of mourning, Ezek. xxiv. 17.

Fē'lix (*happy*). A procurator of Judea, Acts xxiii. 26.

Fĕnced Cities (*defenced*). Walled or palisaded cities. [CITY.]

Fĕr'ret (*thief*). A domesticated animal of the weasel family used for catching rats, Lev. xi 30.

Fĕs'tŭs. Procurator, Acts xxiv. 27.

Fĕt'ters (*shackles*). Instruments of brass or iron for fastening feet of prisoners, Ps. cv. 18; cxlix. 8.

Fiēld. Open area beyond the enclosed gardens or vineyards, Gen. iv. 8; xxiv. 63; Deut. xxii. 25. Landmarks, sacred, Deut. xix. 14; Job xxiv. 2; Prov. xxii. 28.

Fĭg, Fĭg=tree. Common in Palestine, Deut. viii. 8; Isa. xxxiv. 4; 1 Kgs. iv. 25. Pressed figs, 1 Sam. xxv. 18. Fruit appears before leaves, Matt. xxi. 19.

Fĭr. A tree of the pine family, 2 Sam. vi. 5; 1 Kgs. v. 8; S. of Sol. i. 17.

Fīre. Symbol of God's presence, Gen. iv. 4, 5; xv. 17; Ex. iii. 2; Judg. xiii. 19, 20. Worshipped, 2 Kgs. xvii. 17; punishment, Lev. xx. 14; xxi. 9. Christ comes in, 2 Thess. i. 8. World destroyed by, 2 Pet. iii. 7.

Fīre=pan. The censer and snuff-dish of the temple, Ex. xxv. 38; xxvii. 3; xxxvii. 23; xxxviii. 3; 2 Kgs. xxv. 15.

Fĭr'kin (*fourth*). A Greek measure equal to Hebrew bath, 4 to 6 gals., John ii. 6.

Firm'a-ment (*made firm*). Overhead expanse, Gen. i. 17; solid, Ex. xxiv. 10; with windows and doors, Gen. vii. 11; Isa. xxiv. 18; Ps. lxxviii. 23.

First=born. Consecrated to God, Ex. xiii. 2; received a double portion, Deut. xxi. 17. Paid redemption money after the priesthood started, Num. iii. 12, 13; xviii. 15, 16.

First=fruits were offerings and priest's perquisites, Ex. xxii. 29; xxiii. 19; xxxiv. 26; Lev. ii. 12; xxiii. 10-12; Num. xviii. 12; Deut. xviii. 3, 4.

Fĭsh, Fĭsh-ing. Grand division of animal kingdom, Gen. i. 21, 22. Without scales, unclean, Lev. xi. 9–12. Plenty in waters of Palestine, Luke v. 5. Worship of, prohibited, Deut. iv. 18. Caught with nets, hooks, and spears, Hab. i. 15; Luke v. 5-7; Job xli. 7.

Fĭsh=gate. A Jerusalem gate, 2 Chr. xxxiii. 14.

Fĭsh=hooks. [FISH.]

Fĭsh=pools. Should read "pools," S. of Sol. vii. 4.

Fĭtch'es (*vetches*). "Spelt," Ezek. iv. 9. "Fennel," or black cummin, Isa. xxviii. 25-27.

Flăg (*fluttering*). Embraces many water plants, Ex. ii. 3-5; Isa. xix. 6.

Flăg'on (*flask*). Small vessel for liquids, Isa. xxii. 24; 2 Sam. vi. 19; 1 Chr. xvi. 3; S. of Sol. ii. 5.

Flăx (*flexible*). Grown and used largely in East, Ex. ix. 31; Josh. ii. 6; Isa. xix. 9. For lamp wicks, Isa. xlii. 3; Matt. xii. 20. Spinning honorable, Prov. xxxi. 13, 19, 24.

Flēa. Pests throughout the East, 1 Sam. xxiv. 14; xxvi. 20.

Flĕsh. Everything living, Gen. vi. 13–19 ; mankind, vi. 12 ; the body, Col. ii. 5 ; 1 Pet. iv. 6 ; seat of appetites, Rom. viii. 1, 5, 9 ; Gal. v. 17–19 ; Eph. ii. 3. Used much figuratively.

Flĕsh=hooks. Three-tined hooks for taking meat from a boiling vessel, Ex. xxxviii. 3 ; 1 Sam. ii. 13, 14.

Flĭnt. Quartz ; abounds in Palestine, Ps. cxiv. 8. Types abundance, Deut. xxxii. 13 ; firmness, Isa. l. 7 ; Ezek. iii. 9.

Flōats. Rafts for floating timber, 1 Kgs. v. 9 ; 2 Chr. ii. 16.

Flŏck. [SHEEP.]

Flood (*flow*). The Noachian deluge ; "the flood," Gen. vi.–viii ; Matt. xxiv. 37 ; 2 Pet. ii. 5 ; iii. 6. [NOAH.]

Flōor. [AGRICULTURE.]

Flŏur. [BREAD.]

Flūte (*blow, flow*). Flute or " pipe," made of reeds or copper, and similar to those of to-day, Dan. iii. 5–15 ; 1 Kgs. i. 40.

Flŭx (*flow*). Violent dysentery, Acts xxviii. 8.

Fly. Of many varieties in East, and very noisome, Ex. viii. 21–31 ; Ps. lxxviii. 45 ; Eccl. x. 1 ; Isa. vii. 18.

Food (*feed*). Vegetable foods, soups, eggs, curds, honey, bread, etc., preferred by Hebrews to animal food, Lev. xxvi. 26 ; Ps. cv. 16 ; Ezek. iv. 16. Animal food a feature of entertainments, Gen. xviii. 7 ; 1 Sam. xvi. 20 ; Luke xv. 23. Fish used, Num. xi. 5 ; Matt. xiii. 47, 48 ; xv. 34.

Foot. Used in pumping water from Nile, Deut. xi. 10.

Foot'men. Swift runners, couriers, 1 Sam. xxii. 17 ; 1 Kgs. xiv. 28 ; 2 Kgs. xi. 4.

Foot'stool. Kings used them, 2 Chr. ix. 18. God's footstool, 1 Chr. xxviii. 2 ; Ps. xcix. 5.

Fŏre'hĕad. Unveiled women " hard of forehead," Gen. xxiv. 65 ; Ezek. iii. 7–9 ; Jer. iii. 3. Mark of beast on forehead, Rev. xiii. 16 ; God's name there, Rev. xxii. 4.

Fŏr'eĭgn-er (*out of doors*). One not of Hebrew stock, Ex. xii. 45; Eph. ii. 12.

Fōre=knowl'edge. God's knowledge of the future, Acts ii. 23; xv. 18; 1 Pet. i. 2.

Fōre=rŭn'ner. Preparer of the way "within the veil," Heb. vi. 19, 20.

Fŏr'est. Woodland and waste land, 1 Sam. xxii. 5. "House of the Forest" was built of cedars thereof, 1 Kgs. vii. 2.

Fŏrks, 1 Sam. xiii. 21. [FLESH-HOOKS.]

Fŏr''nĭ-cā'tion (*crime under the arch*). Crime of impurity between unmarried persons. Figuratively, infidelity to God, Ezek. xvi. 2; Jer. ii. 20; Matt. v. 32.

Fŏr''tū''nā'tus (*fortunate*). A Corinthian friend of Paul, 1 Cor. xvi. 17, and postscript.

Fŏun'tain (*font*). Springs of Palestine many but uncertain, Deut. viii. 7. They furnish many figures of speech, Ps. xxxvi. 8, 9; Isa. xlix. 10; Jer. ii. 13; John iv. 10; Rev. vii. 17.

Fowl (*flying*). The Hebrew original embraces birds in general, Gen. i. 20; 1 Kgs. iv. 23. The Greek provides the domestic limitation, Luke xii. 24.

Fŏx (*hairy*). The jackal meant, as it is gregarious and feeds on carcasses, Judg. xv. 4; Ps. lxiii. 10; S. of Sol. ii. 15; Ezek. xiii. 4; Luke ix. 58.

Frănk'ĭn-çense (*free burning*). The yellowish gum used in sacrificial fumigation, Ex. xxx. 7-9; Lev. xvi. 12, 13; Rev. viii. 3. A mixture of gums and spices in Ex. xxx. 34-38.

Frĭn'ǧeş (*fibres*). The ornamental hem of the outer garment. Wearing enjoined, Num. xv. 37-40; Deut. xxii. 12; Matt. ix. 20; xiv. 36.

Frŏg. The Egyptian species akin to our own. Source of one of the plagues, Ex. viii. 2-14. Elsewhere only in Ps. lxxviii. 45; cv. 30; Rev. xvi. 13.

Frŏnt'lets (*little foreheads*). Phylacteries in Greek. Parchment strips inscribed with texts, Ex. xiii. 2-17; Deut. vi. 4-22; enclosed in calf-skin case, worn at prayers on forehead or left arm, Matt. xxiii. 5; Mark vii. 3, 4; Luke v. 33.

Fụl'ler (*tramper on*). Fuller's art used for cleaning clothes. They were placed in vessels of water impregnated with natron or soap and trodden with the feet, Prov. xxv. 20; Jer. ii. 22; Mal. iii. 2. Chalk and fuller's earth used for bleaching, 2 Kgs. xviii. 17; Isa. vii. 3; xxxvi. 2.

Fŭ'nĕr-al. [BURIAL.]

Fŭr'long (*furrow long*). In N. T. for Greek stadium, 600 feet long, Luke xxiv. 13.

Fŭr'nace (*oven*). Oven in Gen. xv. 17; Neh. iii. 11. Smelting furnace or lime-kiln in Gen. xix. 28; Ex. ix. 8; Isa. xxxiii. 12. Refining furnace in Prov. xvii. 3. Furnace like a brick-kiln in Dan. iii. 15-27.

Fŭr'nĭ-tṳre (*provided*). Oriental furniture scanty, 2 Kgs. iv. 10-13. Camel's trappings in Gen. xxxi. 34. [BED.]

Fŭr'row (*ridge*). Usual meaning, except in Hos. x. 10, where it means transgressions.

G

Gā'al (*contempt*). Son of Ebed, Judg. ix. 26-41.

Gā'ăsh (*earthquake*). The hill on which Joshua was buried, Josh. xxiv. 30; 2 Sam. xxiii. 30.

Gā'bà, Josh. xviii. 24; Ez. ii. 26. [GEBA.]

Găb'ā-el. Ancestor of Tobit, Tob. i. 1, 14.

Găb'ba̱-ī (*gatherer*). A Benjamite family, Neh. xi. 8.

Găb'ba̱-thà (*elevated*). The pavement on which Christ was sentenced, John xix. 13.

Găb'dēs, 1 Esdr. v. 20. [GEBA.]

Gā'brĭ-as. Brother of Tobit, Tob. i. 14; iv. 20.

Gā'brĭ-el (*man of God*). The announcing angel, Luke i. 11, 19, 26, 38; Dan. viii. 16; ix. 21.

Găd (*troop*). (1) Jacob's seventh son, Gen. xxx. 11-13; xlix. 19; Num. i. 24, 25. Tribe settled east of Jordan, and became a fierce, warlike people. Carried captive by Tiglath-pileser, 1 Chr. v. 26. (2) A prophet and David's seer, 1 Sam. xxii. 5; 1 Chr. xxi. 9-19; xxix. 29; 2 Chr. xxix. 25.

Găd'a-rà (*walled*). A city six miles S. E. of Sea of Galilee. Now Um-keis.

Găd'a-rēnes, Gĕr'gĕ-sēnes, Gĕr'a-sēnes. A people east of the Sea of Galilee, Matt. viii. 28 - 34: Mark v. 1-20; Luke viii. 26-40.

Găd'dī (*fortunate*). One of the spies, Num. xiii. 11.

Găd'dĭel (*fortune of God*). Another of the spies, Num. xiii. 10.

Gā'dī (*of Gad*). Father of King Menahem, 2 Kgs. xv. 15, 17.

Gā'hăm (*browned*). Son of Nahor, Gen. xxii. 24.

Gā'här (*hiding place*). His sons returned, Ez. ii. 47.

Gā'ius, Cā'ius (*lord*). (1) Of Macedonia, a friend of Paul, Acts xix. 29. (2) Of Derbe, co-worker with Paul, Acts xx. 4. (3) Of Corinth, baptized by Paul, Rom. xvi. 23; 1 Cor. i. 14. (4) John's third epistle addressed to Gaius.

Găl'a-ad. Greek form of Gilead.

Gā'lăl (*prominence*). Three Levites, 1 Chr. ix. 15, 16; Neh. xi. 17.

Gă-lā'tĭà (*land of the Galli, Gauls*). A central province of Asia Minor, and part of Paul's missionary field, Acts xvi. 6; xviii. 23; 2 Tim. iv. 10.

Gă-lā'tĭans, Epistle to. Written by Paul to people of Galatia, A. D. 56 or 57, to strengthen their faith in the divinity of his mission, unfold his doctrine of justification by faith, and urge persistency in Christian work.

Găl-bā'num (*fat*). A gum-resin of yellowish color, and pungent, disagreeable odor when burning, Ex. xxx. 34.

Găl'ë-ed (*heap of witness*). Memorial heap of Jacob, Gen. xxxi. 47, 48.

Găl'gă-là, 1 Macc. ix. 1. [GILGAL.]

Găl'ĭ-lee (*circle*). Originally the circuit containing the 20 towns given by Solomon to Hiram, Josh. xx. 7; 1 Kgs. ix. 11; 2 Kgs. xv. 29. In time of Christ, one of the largest provinces of Palestine, in which he spent the greater part of his life and ministry. Luke xiii. 1; xxiii. 6; John i. 43–47; Acts i. 11.

Găl'ĭ-lee, Sea of. [GENNESARET.]

Gall (*yellow, bitter*). The fluid secreted by the liver. Bitter, Job xvi. 13; poison, xx. 14, 25; Deut. xxxii. 33; "hemlock" in Hos. x. 4; probably myrrh, in Matt. xxvii. 34; as in Mark xv. 23; great troubles, Jer. viii. 14; Acts viii. 23.

Găl'lĕr-ўฺ (*show*). An eastern veranda or portico; but panel work in S. of Sol. i. 17; or pillared walk, Ezek. xli. 15.

Găl'ley, Isa. xxxiii. 21. [SHIP.]

Găl'lĭm (*heaps*). A village of Benjamin, 1 Sam. xxv. 44; Isa. x. 30.

Găl'lĭ-ō (*who lives on milk*). Roman proconsul of Achaia, A. D. 53, Acts xviii. 12–17.

Găl'lōws. [PUNISHMENT]

Găm'ặ-el, 1 Esdr. viii. 29. [DANIEL.]

Gȧ-mā'lĭ-el (*recompense of God*). (1) A prince of Manasseh, Num. i. 10; ii. 20; vii. 54; x. 23. (2) A learned president of the Sanhedrim, and Paul's legal preceptor, Acts v. 34; xxii. 3.

Gāmes (*sports*). Simple among Hebrews. Falconry, Job xli. 5; foot-racing, Ps. xix. 5; Eccl. ix. 11; bow and sling contests, 1 Sam. xx. 20; Judg. xx. 16; 1 Chr. xii. 2; dancing, Matt. xi. 16, 17; joking, Prov. xxvi. 19; Jer. xv. 17.

Găm'ma-dĭms (*dwarfs*). Perhaps watchmen, Ezek. xxvii. 11.

Gā'mŭl (*weaned*). Leader of the 22d priestly course, 1 Chr. xxiv. 17.

Gär. Sons of, in 1 Esdr. v. 34.

Gär'den (*yard*). In Hebrew sense, enclosures for fruits, etc., well watered, Gen. ii. 10; xiii. 10; xxi. 33; Num. xxiv. 6; Job viii. 16; hedged, Isa. v. 5; walled, Prov. xxiv. 31; protected, Isa. i. 8; Job xxvii. 18; Mark xii. i.

Gā'rĕb (*scab*). (1) One of David's warriors, 2 Sam. xxiii. 38; 1 Chr. xi. 40. (2) A hill near Jerusalem, Jer. xxxi. 39.

Gär'ĭ-zĭm, 2 Macc. v. 23. [GERIZIM.]

Gär'lic (*spear leek*). A bulbous plant similar to an onion and leek, Num. xi. 5.

Gär'ment. [DRESS.]

Gär'mīte. A Judahite, 1 Chr. iv. 19.

Gär'rĭ-sŏn (*warning*). In Hebrew sense, a place manned, provisioned, and fortified, 1 Sam. xiii. 23; 2 Sam. xxiii. 14; 1 Chr. xi. 16; guards in 2 Chr. xvii. 2; 1 Chr. xviii. 13.

Găsh'mŭ, Neh. vi. 6. [GESHEM]

Gā'tam (*burnt valley*). A duke of Edom, Gen. xxxvi. 11, 16.

Gāte (*opening*). Those of walled cities made of wood, iron, or brass, Judg. xvi. 3; Deut. iii. 5; Ps. cvii. 16; Acts xii. 10; flanked by towers, 2 Sam. xviii. 24, 33; market and judgment places near, 2 Sam. xv. 2; 2 Kgs. vii. 1; Job xxix. 7; Deut. xvii. 5; xxv. 7; Am. v. 10; Ruth iv. 1–12; symbol of power, Gen. xxii. 17; Isa. xxiv. 12; Matt. xvi. 18; the city itself, Deut. xii. 12.

Găth (*wine press*). A city of Philistia, Josh. xiii. 3; 1 Sam. vi. 17; home of Goliath, 1 Sam. xvii. 4; refuge of David, 1 Sam. xxi. 10.

Găth=hē'phĕr, Gĭt'tah=hē'phĕr (*wine press of Hepher*). A town in Zebulun, now el Meshed, Josh. xix. 13; 2 Kgs. xiv. 25.

Găth=rĭm'mon (*high wine press*). (1) A Levitical city of Dan, Josh. xxi. 24; 1 Chr. vi. 69. (2) A Levite town of Manasseh, Josh. xxi. 25. Bileam, 1 Chr. vi. 70.

Gā'zȧ (*strong*). Hebrew Azzah, now Ghuzzeh. A city of Philistia, Gen. x. 19; assigned to Judah, Josh. x. 41; xv. 47; Judg. i. 18; scene of Samson's exploits, Judg. xvi.; 1 Kgs. iv. 24; Acts viii. 26.

Găz'ȧ-rȧ, 1 Macc. ix. 52. [GEZER.]

Gā'zăth-ītes. Inhabitants of Gaza, Josh. xiii. 3.

Gā'zĕr, 2 Sam. v. 25; 1 Chr. xiv. 16. [GEZER.]

Găz'ė-rȧ. (1) 1 Macc. iv. 15. [GEZER.] (2) His sons returned, 1 Esdr. v. 31.

Gā'zĕz (*shearer*). Son of Caleb, 1 Chr. ii. 46.

Gā'zītes. Inhabitants of Gaza, Judg. xvi. 2.

Găz'zam (*consuming*). His descendants returned, Ez. ii. 48; Neh. vii. 51.

Gē'bȧ (*hill*). Gaba in Josh. xviii. 24; now Jeba, 6 miles N. of Jerusalem. A Levitical city of Benjamin, Josh. xxi. 17; 1 Chr. vi. 60; 1 Sam. xiii. 3; 1 Kgs. xv. 22; 2 Kgs. xxiii. 8; Isa. x. 29.

Gē'bal (*mountain*). A maritime town of Phœnicia, near Tyre, Ezek. xxvii. 9. Inhabitants called Giblites, Josh. xiii. 5.

Gē'bĕr (*man*). Two of Solomon's commissaries, 1 Kgs. iv. 13, 19.

Gē'bim (*ditches*). A place near Jerusalem, Isa. x. 31.

Gĕc'ko. The fan-footed lizard of Palestine. "Ferret," in A. V., Lev. xi. 30; "Gecko" in R. V.

Gĕd''a-lī'ah (*God my greatness*). (1) A governor of Judea, 2 Kgs. xxv. 22; and friend c. Jeremiah, Jer. xl. 5, 6; xli. 2. (2) A Levite harpist, 1 Chr. xxv. 3. (3) A priest, Ez. x. 18. (4) A persecutor of Jeremiah, Jer. xxxviii. 1. (5) Grandfather of Zephaniah, Zeph. i. 1.

Gĕd'dur, 1 Esdr. v. 30. [Gahar.]

Gĕd'e-on. Greek form of Gideon, Heb. xi. 32.

Gē'dêr (*wall*). Its king was conquered by Joshua, Josh. xii. 13.

Gē-dē'rah (*sheepfold*). A town in lowlands of Judah, Josh. xv. 36.

Gĕd'ĕ-răth-īte''. Inhabitant of Gederah, 1 Chr. xii. 4.

Gĕd'ĕ-rīte. Inhabitant of Geder, 1 Chr. xxvii. 28.

Gĕ-dē'rŏth (*sheepfolds*). A city in lowlands of Judah, Josh. xv. 41; 2 Chr. xxviii. 18.

Gĕd''ĕ-rŏth-ā'im (*two sheepfolds*). A town in lowlands of Judah, Josh. xv. 36.

Gē'dôr (*wall*). (1) A hill town of Judah, Josh. xv. 58. (2) A town of Benjamin, 1 Chr. xii. 7. (3) 1 Chr. iv. 39, probably Gerar. (4) An ancestor of Saul, 1 Chr. viii. 31.

Gē-hā'zī (*valley of vision*). Messenger of Elisha, 2 Kgs. iv. 12-37; v. 20-27; viii. 4.

Gē-hĕn'nå. [Hinnom.]

Gĕl'ī-lŏth (*circuit*). A landmark of Benjamin, Josh. xviii. 17.

Gĕ-măl'lī (*camel driver*). Father of Ammiel, Num. xiii. 12.

Gĕm''a-rī'ah (*perfected by God*). (1) Son of Shaphan, Jer. xxxvi. 10-27. (2) Messenger of King Hezekiah, Jer. xxix. 3, 4.

Gĕms. [Stones, Precious.]

Gĕn''ĕ-ăl'ŏ-gy (*birth record*). In Hebrew, "book of generations," Gen. v.; x.; 1 Chr. i.-viii.; ix. 1; Matt. i. 1-17; Luke iii. 23-38.

Gĕn''ĕr-ā'tion (*begotten*). In plural, the genealogical register, Gen. ii. 4; v. 1; Matt. i. 1; family history, Gen. vi. 9; xxv. 12; men of the existing age, Lev. iii. 17; Isa. liii. 8; Matt. xxiv. 34; Acts ii. 40.

Găn'ĕ-sĭs (*beginning*). First book of the Bible and Pentateuch. Chapters i.-xi. give history of Creation, Adam, Deluge, Noah, first inhabitants, Babel. Balance devoted to history of the patriarchs Abraham, Isaac, Jacob and Joseph. Covers a period of nearly 2500 years. Authorship attributed to Moses.

Găn-nĕs'ạ-rĕt (*garden of the prince*). (1) Land of, the small crescent country N. W. of Sea of Galilee, Matt. xiv. 34; Mark vi. 53. (2) Lake of, "Sea of Chinnereth," in O. T., Num. xxxiv. 11; Josh. xii. 3; and "Sea of Galilee," in N. T.; enlargement of Jordan river; 13 miles long, 6 wide, 700 below bed of ocean. "Lake of Gennesaret," Luke v. 1; "Sea of Tiberias," John vi. 1; "the sea," Matt. iv. 15.

Găn-nĕs'ạ-rĕth. [GENNESARET.]

Găn-nē'ŭs. Father of Apollonius, 2 Macc. xii. 2.

Găn'tīleṣ (*nations*). In O. T. sense, all peoples not Jewish, Gen. x. 5; xiv. 1; Neh. v. 8. In N. T., Greeks and Romans seem to type Gentiles, Luke ii. 32; Acts xxvi. 17–20; Rom. i. 14–16; ix. 24. "Isles of the Gentiles," Gen. x. 5, supposed to embrace Asia Minor and Europe.

Gẹ̆-nū'băth (*theft*). An Edomite, 1 Kgs. xi. 20.

Gē'on, Ecclus. xxiv. 27. [GIHON.]

Gē'rȧ (*grain*). (1) A Benjamite, Gen. xlvi. 21; 1 Chr. viii. 3–7. (2) Father of Ehud, Judg. iii. 15. (3) Father of Shimei, 2 Sam. xvi. 5; xix. 16; 1 Kgs. ii. 8.

Gē'rah. One twentieth of a shekel; about 3 cents, Ex. xxx. 13.

Gē'rär (*halting place*). A town of Philistia, Gen. x. 19; xx. 1; xxvi. 26; 2 Chr. xiv. 13, 14.

Gĕr''ȧ-sēneṣ'. For Gadarenes in Luke viii. 26, R. V.

Gĕr'gĕ-sēneṣ, Matt. viii. 28. [GADARENES, GERASENES.]

Gĕr'ĭ-zĭm (*cutters*). The mountain of blessings in Ephraim, Deut. xi. 29; xxvii. 12–26; xxviii.

Gĕr-rhē'nĭ-anṣ. Of Gerar, 2 Macc. xiii. 24.

Gĕr'shŏm (*exile*). (1) Son of Moses, Ex. ii. 22; xviii. 3. (2) A priest, Ez. viii. 2.

Gĕr'shŏn (*exile*). Eldest son of Levi, Gen. xlvi. 11; Ex. vi. 16: 1 Chr. vi. 1. Founder of the Gershonites. Given thirteen cities in Canaan, Josh. xxi. 6. Gershom in 1 Chr. vi. 62–71.

Gĕr′zītes. Dwellers south of Palestine, 1 Sam. xxvii. 8 marg.

Gē′sem, Judith i. 9. [Goshen.]

Gē′shăm (*filthy*). A descendant of Caleb, 1 Chr. ii. 47.

Gē′shem, Găsh′mū (*rain*). A scoffing Arabian, Neh. ii. 19; vi. 1, 2.

Gē′shŭr (*bridge*). A province of Syria peopled by Geshuri or Geshurites, Deut. iii. 14; Josh. xiii. 11; 2 Sam. iii. 3; xv. 8; 1 Chr. ii. 23.

Gĕsh′u-rī, Deut. iii. 14; Josh. xiii. 2. [Geshur.]

Gĕsh′u-rītes. Besides above, a people of Arabia and Philistia, Josh. xiii. 11; 1 Sam. xxvii. 8.

Gē′thĕr (*fear*). Son of Aram, Gen. x. 23; 1 Chr. i. 17.

Gĕth-sĕm′a-nē (*oil press*). Scene of Christ's agony and betrayal, at the foot of Olivet, near Jerusalem, Matt. xxvi. 36–56; Mark xiv. 26–52; Luke xxii. 39–49; John xviii. 1–13.

Gē-ū′el (*majesty of God*). The Gadite spy, Num. xiii. 15.

Gē′zĕr (*steep*). Gazer, Gazara, Gazera, and Gad. A Levitical city, Josh. x. 33; xii. 12; xvi. 3; xxi. 21; whose native people remained, Judg. i. 29.

Gĕz′rītes. [Gerzites.]

Ghōst (*that terrifies*). The spirit, Matt. xxvii. 50.

Gī′ah (*waterfall*). A hill near Ammah, 2 Sam. ii. 24.

Gī′ants (*sons of Gaea*). Huge men — Nephilim, Gibborim, Gen. vi. 4; Rephaim, xiv. 5; Emim, Anakim, Zuzim, etc., Num. xiii. 28–33; Deut. iii. 11; 1 Sam. xvii. 4.

Gĭb′bar (*huge*). His children returned, Ez. ii. 20.

Gĭb′be-thon (*high*). A Levitical town of Dan, Josh. xix. 44; xxi. 23; 1 Kgs. xv. 27; xvi. 17.

Gĭb′e-à (*hill*). A Judahite, 1 Chr. ii. 49.

Gĭb′e-ah (*hill*). (1) A town of Judah, Josh. xv. 57. (2) Place where the ark was left, 2 Sam. vi. 3, 4. (3) A place in Benjamin, Judg. xix. 12–15; xx. 19–25; 1 Sam. xiii. 2. (4) Saul's birthplace, 1 Sam. x. 26; xi.

4; xv. 34; xxii. 6; xxiii. 19; Isa. x. 29. (5) Probably Geba, Judg. xx. 31.

Gĭb′e-ath, Josh. xviii. 28. [GIBEAH, 3.]

Gĭb′e-on (*lofty hill*). A Hivite city of Canaan, given to Levites, Josh. ix. 3-15; x. 12, 13; xxi. 17; 2 Sam. ii. 12-24; xx. 8-10. Tabernacle set up there, 1 Chr. xvi. 39; 1 Kgs. iii. 4, 5; ix. 2; 2 Chr. i. 3, 13; Jer. xli. 12-16.

Gĭb′e-on-ītes″. Inhabitants of Gibeon, 2 Sam. xxi. 1-9.

Gĭb′lītes, Josh. xiii. 5. [GEBAL.]

Gĭd-dăl′tī (*trained up*). Son of Heman, and leader of 22d musical course, 1 Chr. xxv. 4.

Gĭd′del (*great*). His children returned, Ez. ii. 47, 56.

Gĭd′e-on (*destroyer*). The powerful warrior of Manasseh, and judge of Israel for 40 years, Judges vi.-viii.

Gĭd″e-ō′nī (*destroyer*). A Benjamite, Num. i. 11.

Gī′dom (*desolation*). A place near Rimmon, Judg. xx. 45.

Gier (*jer*) **Eagle** (*sacred eagle*). An unclean bird of prey; probably the Egyptian vulture, Lev. xi. 18: Deut. xiv. 17.

Gĭft (*given*). A common way of showing esteem and confidence and securing favors, Gen. xxxii. 13-15; xlv. 22, 23. Kings were donees, 1 Kgs. iv. 21; 2 Chr. xvii. 5. Not to give, a mark of contempt, 1 Sam. x. 27. Cattle given, Gen. xxxii. 13; garments, 2 Kgs. v. 23; money, 2 Sam. xviii. 11; perfumes, Matt. ii. 11.

Gī′hon (*stream*). (1) Second river of Paradise, Gen. ii. 13. (2) A spot, or pool, near Jerusalem, 1 Kgs. i. 33-38; 2 Chr. xxxii. 30; xxxiii. 14.

Gĭl′a-lāī (*weighty*). A musician, Neh. xii. 36.

Gĭl-bō′à (*fountain*). The mountain range east of Esdraelon and overlooking Jezreel, 1 Sam. xxviii. 4; xxxi. 1; 2 Sam. i. 6.

Gĭl′e-ăd (*rocky*). (1) Mount and Land of Gilead, east of Jordan, Gen. xxxi. 21-25; Num. xxxii. 1; Josh. xvii. 6. (2) A mountain near Jezreel, Judg. vii. 3. (3) Grandson of Manasseh, Num. xxvi. 29, 30. (4) Father of Jephthah, Judg. xi. 1, 2.

Gĭl'e-ăd-ītes⁄⁄. Manassites of Gilead, Num. xxvi. 29.

Gĭl'găl (*rolling*). (1) First encampment of Israelites west of Jordan, Josh. iv. 19, 20; v. 9, 10. Became a city and headquarters, Josh. ix. 6; xv. 7. Saul crowned there, 1 Sam. vii. 16; x. 8; xi. 14, 15. (2) Another Gilgal in Sharon plain, Josh. xii. 23. (3) Another near Bethel, 2 Kgs. iv. 38.

Gī'loh (*exile*). A town of Judah, Josh. xv. 51; 2 Sam. xv. 12.

Gī'lo-nīte. Inhabitant of Giloh, 2 Sam. xv. 12; xxiii. 34.

Gĭm'zō (*producing sycamores*). Now Jimzu, a village 2½ miles from Lydda, 2 Chr. xxviii. 18.

Gĭn (*engine*). A bird-trap, Isa. viii. 14; Am. iii. 5.

Gī'nath (*protection*). Father of Tibni, 1 Kgs. xvi. 21, 22.

Gĭn'nĕ-thō (*gardener*). A priest, Neh. xii. 4.

Gĭn'nĕ-thon (*gardener*). A priest, Neh. x. 6; xii. 16.

Gîr'dle (*gird*). Worn by men and women to hold the looser garments. Made of leather, 2 Kgs. i. 8; Matt. iii. 4; of linen, Jer. xiii. 1; Ezek. xvi. 10; embroidered, Dan. x. 5; Rev. i. 13; used for carrying swords and daggers, Judg. iii. 16; 2 Sam. xx. 8.

Gîr'ga-sīte, Gîr'ga-shītes. An original tribe of Canaan, Gen. x. 16; xv. 21; Deut. vii. 1.

Gĭs'på (*fondle*). An overseer, Neh. xi. 21.

Gĭt'tah=hē'phĕr, Josh. xix. 13. [GATH-HEPHER.]

Gĭt'ta-ĭm (*two wine presses*). An unknown place, 2 Sam. iv. 3.

Gĭt'tītes. Gathite followers of David, 2 Sam. xv. 18, 19. [GATH.]

Gĭt'tith. A musical instrument or melody, Ps. viii., lxxxi., lxxxiv., titles.

Gī'zō-nīte. Hashem, 1 Chr. xi. 34.

Glăss. Only once in O. T. as "crystal," Job xxviii. 17; N. T. "glass" mirrors were metal, 1 Cor. xiii. 12; 2 Cor. iii. 18; James i. 23; Rev. iv. 6.

Glēan'ing (*handful*). Field-gleanings were reserved for the poor, Lev. xix. 9, 10; Ruth ii. 2. [CORNER.]

Glēde (*glide*). An unclean bird of prey, Deut.

xiv. 13. The European kite ; but vulture in Lev. **xi.** 14.

Gnăt. A small insect ; figuratively mentioned in Matt. xxiii. 24.

Gōad (*gad, strike*). A rod spiked at the end for driving oxen, Judg. iii. 31 ; and iron-shod at the other end for cleaning plows, or even for plowing, 1 Sam. xiii. 21.

Gōat. Several varieties in Palestine, both wild and tame. An important source of food, clothing, and wealth, Gen. xxvii. 9 ; 1 Sam. xxiv. 2 ; xxv. 2 ; Job xxxix. 1. "Scape-goat," one of the two offered on Day of Atonement, over which the priest confessed the sins of Israel, and then let it escape to the wilderness, Lev. xvi. 7–26.

Gō'ath (*lowing*). An unknown place, Jer. xxxi. 39.

Gŏb (*cistern*). A battlefield, 2 Sam. xxi. 18, 19. Gezer in 1 Chr. xx. 4.

Gŏb'let (*little cask*). A wine cup.

God (*good*). In Hebrew, Jehovah, "the self-existent and eternal," and especially the covenant God. Generally rendered Lord. The ineffable name, not pronounced by the Jews, who substituted for it Adonai, "my Lord ; " or Elohim — God, the creator and moral governor — when Adonai was written with Jehovah.

God'head. The Supreme Being in all his nature and attributes, Acts xvii. 29 ; Rom. i. 20 ; Col. ii. 9.

Gŏg (*roof*). (1) A Reubenite, 1 Chr. v. 4. (2) [MAGOG.]

Gō'lan (*circuit*). A refuge city in Bashan, Deut. iv. 43 ; Josh. xx. 8 ; xxi. 27.

Gōld (*yellow*). Known early to Hebrews, Gen. ii. 11 ; used for ornaments, Gen. xxiv. 22 ; money, temple furniture and utensils, Ex. xxxvi. 34-38 ; 1 Kgs. vii. 48-50 ; emblem of purity and nobility, Job xxiii. 10 ; Lam. iv. 1. Obtained chiefly from Ophir, Job xxviii. 16 ; Parvaim, 2 Chr. iii. 6 ; Sheba and Raamah, Ezek. xxvii. 22.

Gŏl'gō-thȧ (*skull*). Hebrew name of the spot where Christ was crucified, Matt. xxvii. 33 ; Mark xv. 22 ; John xix. 17. [CALVARY.]

Gō-lī'ath (*splendor*). The Philistine giant who

defied the army of Israel, 1 Sam. xvii. 4–54. Another Goliath in 2 Sam. xxi. 19–22.

Gō′mer (*complete*). (1) Eldest son of Japheth, Gen. x. 2, 3; 1 Chr. i. 5, 6. (2) Wife of Hosea, Hos. i. 3.

Gŏ-mŏr′rah (*submersion*). Gomorrha in N. T. A city of the plain destroyed by fire, Gen. xiv. 1–11; xviii. 20; xix. 24–28; Deut. xxix. 23; xxxii. 32; Matt. x. 15; Mark vi. 11.

Gō′pher. The unknown wood of Noah's ark, Gen. vi. 14.

Gŏr′gĭ-as (*frightful*). A Syrian general, 1 Macc. iii. 38.

Gŏr-tȳ′na. Capital of Crete, 1 Macc. xv. 23.

Gō′shen (*drawing near*). (1) The extreme province of Egypt, northward toward Palestine; assigned to the Jews, Gen. xlv. 5–10; xlvi. 28–34; xlvii. 1–6; l. 8. (2) An undefined part of southern Palestine, Josh. x. 41; xi. 16. (3) A city of Judah, Josh. xv. 51.

Gŏs′pels (*good tidings*). The four initial books of N. T., containing the biographies of Christ.

Gŏth′′ō-lī′as. One who returned, 1 Esdr. viii. 33.

Gō-thŏn′ĭ-el. Father of Chabris, Judith vi. 15.

Gōurd (*encumberer*). A large plant family, covering the melon, pumpkin, squash, calabash, etc., Jonah iv. 6–10. A poisonous apple or cucumber, 2 Kgs. iv. 39–41.

Gŏv′ẽr-nôr (*director*). Often captain, chief, or civic official; but generally the political officer in charge of a province, Gen. xlii. 6; 1 Kgs. x. 15; Ez. viii. 36; Neh. ii. 9; Matt. xxvii. 2.

Gō′zan. Place or river in Mesopotamia, 2 Kgs. xvii. 6; xviii. 11; 1 Chr. v. 26.

Grā′bā, 1 Esdr. v. 29. [HAGABA.]

Grāpe (*hook, grab*). Grapes of Palestine noted for size and flavor, Gen. xlix. 11; Num. xiii. 24. Used for wine and food, 1 Sam. xxv. 18; xxx. 12; 2 Sam. xvi. 1; 1 Chr. xii. 40.

Grȧss (*for gnawing*). Large figurative use, Ps. xc. 5, 6; Isa. xl. 6, 8; James i. 10, 11; 1 Pet. i. 24; sometimes herbage in general, Isa. xv. 6; a fuel, Matt. vi. 30; Luke xii. 28.

Grȧss′hop-per. An insect of the locust species,

often translated locust, 2 Chr. vii. 13. A clean animal, Lev. xi. 22; timid, Job xxxix. 20; gregarious and destructive, Judg. vi. 5; vii. 12; Eccl. xii. 5; Jer. xlvi. 23; type of insignificance, Num. xiii. 33; Isa. xl. 22.

Grāve. [BURIAL.] [ENGRAVER.]

Grēaves (*shins*). Armor, metallic or leathern, to protect the shins from foot to knee, 1 Sam. xvii. 6.

Grēēçe, Grēēks, Grē′çians. The well known country in S. E. of Europe, called also Hellas. Javan in O. T., Gen. x. 2-5; Isa. lxvi. 19; Ezek. xxvii. 13, 19; but direct in Dan. viii. 21; x. 20; xi. 2; Joel iii. 6; Acts xx. 2. Greek the original N. T. language.

Grey′hound, Prov. xxx. 31. The original implies a "wrestler," not a quadruped.

Grīnd′ing. [MILL.]

Grōve. Except in Gen. xxi. 33, the Hebrew original means an idol; primitively set up and worshipped in groves, 1 Kgs. xviii. 19; 2 Kgs. xiii. 6.

Gŭd′go-dah, Deut. x. 7. [HOR-HAGIDGAD.]

Guĕst. [HOSPITALITY.]

Gū′nī (*painted*). (1) Son of Naphtali and founder of the Gunites, Gen. xlvi. 24; Num. xxvi. 48; 1 Chr. vii. 13. (2) A son of Gad, 1 Chr. v. 15.

Gûr (*whelp*). Spot where King Ahaziah was slain, 2 Kgs. ix. 27.

Gûr=bā′al (*abode of Baal*). A district south of Palestine, 2 Chr. xxvi. 7.

H

Hā″a-hăsh′ta-rī (*runner*). Son of Ashur, 1 Chr. iv. 6.

Hă-bā′ļah (*God hides*). His children returned, Ez. ii. 61.

Hă-băk′kŭk (*embrace*). A minor prophet during reigns of Jehoiakim and Josiah. His book, thirteenth of the prophetic, denounces Chaldea, and concludes with a striking poem and prayer.

Hăb″a-zī-nī′ah (*God's light*). A Rechabite, Jer. xxxv. 3.

Hăb′ba-cuc, B. and D. 33-39. [HABAKKUK.]

Hăb'ĕr-ġeon (*neck protector*). Coat of mail for neck and breast, Ex. xxviii. 32.

Hā'bôr (*fertile*). A tributary of the Euphrates, 2 Kgs. xvii. 6 ; 1 Chr. v. 26.

Hăch''a-lī'ah (*who waits*). Father of Nehemiah, Neh. i. 1.

Hăch'ĭ-lah (*dark hill*). A hill in Ziph, 1 Sam. xxiii. 19.

Hăch'mŏ-nī (*wise*). A Hachmonite, 1 Chr. xi. 11 ; xxvii. 32.

Hā'dăd (*brave*). (1) An Ishmaelite, 1 Chr. i. 30 ; Hadar, Gen. xxv. 15. (2) A king of Edom, Gen. xxxvi. 35 ; 1 Chr. i. 46. (3) Another king of Edom, 1 Chr. i. 50 ; Hadar, Gen. xxxvi. 39. (4) An Edomite, 1 Kgs. xi. 14–25.

Hăd''ăd-ē'zĕr, 2 Sam. viii. 3–12. [HADAREZER.]

Hā'dăd=rĭm'mon. From two Syrian idols. Spot of mourning for Josiah, Zech. xii. 11.

Hā'dar, Gen. xxv. 15 ; xxxvi. 39. [HADAD.]

Hăd''är-ē'zĕr (*Hadad's help*). A king of Zoba, 2 Sam. viii. 3 ; x. 16 ; 1 Chr. xviii. 7 ; xix. 16–19.

Hăd'a-shah (*new*). Town of Judah, Josh. xv. 37.

Hă-dăs'sah (*myrtle*). Hebrew name of Esther, Esth. ii. 7.

Hă-dăt'tah (*new*). Town of Judah, Josh. xv. 25.

Hā'des. Place of departed spirits. Greek equivalent of Hebrew " sheol," unseen world. Hell in A. V. ; Hades in R. V., Matt. xi. 23 ; xvi. 18 ; Acts ii. 31 ; Rev. i. 18.

Hā'dĭd (*sharp*). Place named in Ez. ii. 33 ; Neh. vii. 37.

Hăd'la-ī (*restful*). An Ephraimite, 2 Chr. xxviii. 12.

Hă-dō'ram (*power*). (1) Son of Joktan, Gen. x. 27. (2) An ambassador to David, 1 Chr. xviii. 10. (3) 2 Chr. x. 18. [ADONIRAM.]

Hā'drăch (*dwelling*). A Syrian country, Zech. ix. 1.

Hā'găb (*locust*). His sons returned, Ez. ii. 46.

Hăg'a-bă, Neh. vii. 48. Hagabah, Ez. ii. 45. [HAGAB.]

Hā'gar (*flight*). Abraham's concubine, Gen. xvi.

3; mother of Ishmael, xxi. 9–21. Type of law and bondage, Gal. iv. 24, 25.

Hā'gar-ītes, Hā'gar-ēnes. Ishmaelites, 1 Chr. v. 10–20; xxvii. 31; Ps. lxxxiii. 6.

Hăg'ḡa-ī (*festive*). A minor prophet. His book, fifteenth of the prophetic, exhorts the Jews to crown the work of Zerubbabel.

Hăg-ḡē'rī (*wanderer*), 1 Chr. xi. 38. [BANI.]

Hăg'ḡī (*festive*). Son of Gad, Gen. xlvi. 16.

Hăg-ḡī'ah (*Lord's feast*). A Levite, 1 Chr. vi. 30.

Hăg'ḡites. Of Haggi, Num. xxvi. 15.

Hăg'ḡīth (*dancer*). A wife of David, 2 Sam. iii. 4; 1 Kgs. i. 5.

Hā'ḡi-à, 1 Esdr. v. 34. [HATTIL.]

Hā'ī. Ancient form of Ai, Gen. xii. 8; xiii. 3.

Hāil. The seventh plague, Ex. ix. 18–29. God's weapon, Josh. x. 11; Rev. xvi. 21.

Hâir. Worn short with elderly men, long with young men, vowed men and women, Num. vi. 5–9; 2 Sam. xiv. 26; Luke vii. 38. Lepers shorn, Lev. xiv. 8, 9.

Hăk'ka-tăn (*little*). Father of Johanan, Ez. viii. 12.

Hăk'kŏz (*thorn*). Priest of 7th course, 1 Chr. xxiv. 10.

Hȧ-kū'phȧ (*bent*). His children returned, Ez. ii. 51.

Hā'lah. Probably Habor, 2 Kgs. xvii. 6.

Hā'lăk (*smooth*). An unlocated mountain, Josh. xi. 17; xii. 7.

Hūle. Haul, Luke xii. 58; Acts viii. 3.

Hăl'hŭl (*trembling*). Town of Judah, Josh. xv. 58.

Hā'lī (*necklace*). Border of Asher, Josh. xix. 25.

Hăl''i-căr-năs'sus. City of Caria, 1 Macc. xv. 23.

Hăll. Court of a high priest's house, Luke xxii. 55; Matt. xxvii. 27.

Hăl''le-lū'jȧh (*ya*). [ALLELUIA.]

Hăl-lō'hesh (*enchanter*). Co-covenanter with Nehemiah, Neh. x. 24.

Hȧ-lō'hesh (*enchanter*). A builder of the wall, Neh. iii. 12.

Hăm (*hot*). Third son of Noah, Gen. v. 32; ix. 22. Father of the Hamitic races, x. 6, etc.

Hā′man (*famed*). Prime minister of Ahasuerus, Esth.

Hā′math (*fortress*). Chief city of upper Syria, Gen. x. 18; Num. xxxiv. 8. Became part of Solomon's kingdom, 1 Kgs. viii. 65; 2 Chr. viii. 3, 4. Now Hamah.

Hăm′măth (*hot springs*). A town near Tiberias, Josh. xix. 35. Hammoth-Dor, Josh. xxi. 32. Hammon, 1 Chr. vi. 76.

Hăm-mĕd′a-thà (*double*). Father of Haman, Esth. iii. 1.

Hăm′me-lĕch (*king*). Hardly a proper name, Jer. xxxvi. 26; xxxviii. 6.

Hăm′mĕr. Same as now, Judg. iv. 21; Isa. xliv. 12. Mighty force, Jer. xxiii. 29; l. 23.

Hăm-mŏl′e-kĕth (*queen*). Sister of Gilead, 1 Chr. vii. 17, 18.

Hăm′mŏn (*warm springs*). (1) City in Asher, Josh. xix. 28. (2) Levitical city in Naphtali, 1 Chr. vi. 76.

Hăm′moth=dôr, Josh. xxi. 32. [HAMMATH].

Hà-mō′nah (*multitude*). Unknown city, Ezek. xxxix. 16.

Hā′mon=gŏg (*multitude of Gog*). Unlocated valley, Ezek. xxxix. 11–15.

Hā′mor (*ass*). Father of Shechem, Gen. xxxiii. 19; xxxiv. 26. Emmor, Acts vii. 16.

Hà-mū′el (*wrath*). A Simeonite, 1 Chr. iv. 26.

Hā′mŭl (*pity*). Son of Pharez, and founder of Hamulites, Gen. xlvi. 12.

Hā′mŭl-ītes, Num. xxvi. 21. [HAMUL.]

Hà-mū′tal (*like dew*). A wife of Josiah, 2 Kgs. xxiii. 31; Jer. lii. 1.

Hà-năm′e-el (*given of God*). Jeremiah's cousin, Jer. xxxii. 6–12.

Hā′nan (*merciful*). (1) A Benjamite, 1 Chr. viii. 23. (2) Descendant of Saul, 1 Chr. viii. 38. (3) One of David's guard, 1 Chr. xi. 43. (4) His sons returned, Ez. ii. 46. (5, 6, 7) Co-covenanters with Nehemiah, Neh. x. 10, 22, 26. (8) A tithe-keeper,

Neh. xiii. 13. (9) One who had temple rooms, **Jer.** xxxv. 4.

Hă-năn′e-el (*given of God*). A tower on wall of Jerusalem, Neh. iii. 1; xii. 39; Jer. xxxi. 38.

Hă-nā′nī (*gracious*). (1) Head of the 18th temple course, 1 Chr. xxv. 4, 25. (2) A seer, 2 Chr. xvi. 7–10. (3) A priest, Ez. x. 20. (4) Brother of Nehemiah, Neh. i. 2; vii. 2.

Hăn″ạ-nī′ah (*given of God*). (1) Leader of 16th temple course, 1 Chr. xxv. 4, 5, 23. (2) A general, 2 Chr. xxvi. 11. (3) Father of Zedekiah, Jer. xxxvi. 12. (4) A false prophet, Jer. xxviii. (5) Grandfather of Irijah, Jer. xxxvii. 13. (6) Hebrew name of Shadrach, Dan. i. 3–19. (7) Son of Zerubbabel, 1 Chr. iii. 19. Joanna in Luke. (8) A Benjamite, 1 Chr. viii. 24. (9) One of the returned, Ez. x. 28. (10) Others, Neh. iii. 8; vii. 2, 3; x. 23; xii. 12.

Hănd. Conspicuous in Hebrew ceremonial and other customs, Gen. xiv. 22; Deut. xxi. 6, 7; Matt. xxvii. 24; Job xxxi. 27; Isa. lxv. 2.

Hănd′breadth. Palm width; about four inches, Ex. xxv. 25.

Hănd′ī-craft. Though not noted for artisanship, Hebrew boys were taught trades, and reference is made to smiths, Gen. iv. 22; carpenters, Isa. xliv. 14; Matt. xiii. 55; masons, 1 Kgs. v. 18; ship-building, 1 Kgs. ix. 26; apothecaries, Ex. xxx. 25, 35; weavers, Ex. xxxv. 25, 26; dyers, Josh. ii. 18; barbers, Num. vi. 5–19; tent-makers, Acts xviii. 3; potters, Jer. xviii. 2–6; bakers, xxxvii. 21; engravers, Ex. xxviii. 9–11; tanners, Acts ix. 43.

Hănd′kĕr-chiefs. These, and napkins and aprons, signify about same as to-day, Luke xix. 20; John xi. 44; Acts xix. 12.

Hănd′stāves. Javelins, Ezek. xxxix. 9.

Hā′nēs. A city in Egypt, Isa. xxx. iv.

Hăng′ing, Hăng′ings. In strict law, culprits were strangled first, then hung, Num. xxv. 4; Deut. xxi. 22, 23. Hangings for doors and tabernacle use, quite the same as modern tapestries, Ex. xxvi. 9, 36; Num. iii. 26.

Hăn′ī-el (*grace of God*). An Asherite, 1 Chr. vii. 39.

Hăn'nah (*grace*). Mother of Samuel, 1 Sam. i., ii.

Hăn'na-thon (*gracious*). A city of Zebulun, Josh. xix. 14.

Hăn'nĭ-el (*grace of God*). A prince of Manasseh, Num. xxxiv. 23.

Hā'noch (*dedicated*). (1) Son of Midian, Gen. xxv. 4; Henoch, 1 Chr. i. 33. (2) A son of Reuben, and founder of Hanochites, Gen. xlvi. 9; Num. xxvi. 5.

Hā'nŭn (*gracious*). (1) A king of Ammon, 2 Sam. x. 1–6. (2) Two architects, Neh. iii. 13, 30.

Hăph-rā'im (*pits*). A city of Issachar, Josh. xix. 19.

Hā'rȧ (*hill*). No doubt Haran, 1 Chr. v. 26.

Hăr'ȧ-dah (*fear*). An Israelite encampment, Num. xxxiii. 24, 25.

Hā'ran (*mountainous*). (1) Brother of Abraham, Gen. xi. 26–31. (2) A Levite, 1 Chr. xxiii. 9. (3) Son of Caleb, 1 Chr. ii. 46. (4) The spot in Mesopotamia where Abraham located after leaving Ur, Gen. xi. 31, 32; xxiv. 10; xxvii. 43. Charran, Acts vii. 2–4.

Hā'ra-rīte. Three of David's guard so called, 2 Sam. xxiii. 11, 33.

Hăr-bō'nȧ (*ass driver*). A chamberlain, Esth. i. 10. Harbonah in vii. 9.

Hâre (*leaper*). A species of rabbit, wrongly thought to chew the cud, Lev. xi. 6; Deut. xiv. 7.

Hā'reph (*plucking*). Son of Caleb, 1 Chr. ii. 51.

Hā'reth (*thicket*). A forest of Judah, 1 Sam. xxii. 5.

Hăr''hȧ-ī'ah (*God's anger*). Father of Uzziel, Neh. iii. 8.

Hăr'has (*poor*). Ancestor of Shallum, 2 Kgs. xxii. 14.

Hăr'hŭr (*inflamed*). His children returned, Neh. vii. 53.

Hā'rim (*flat-nosed*). (1) Priestly head of third course, 1 Chr. xxiv. 8. (2) Name of several who returned, Ez. ii. 32, 39; x. 21; Neh. iii. 11; vii. 35, 42; x. 27; xii. 15.

Hā′riph (*plucking*). His children returned, Neh. vii. 24; x. 19.

Här′lot (*vagabond*). An abandoned woman, Gen. xxxviii. 15. Harlotry forbidden, Lev. xix. 29. Type of idolatry, Isa. i. 21; Ezek. xvi. Classed with publicans, Matt. xxi. 32.

Här″ma-gēd′don. R. V. for Armageddon.

Här′nĕ-phẽr (*panting*). An Asherite, 1 Chr. vii. 36.

Hā′rod (*fear*). A spring near Jezreel, Judg. vii. 1.

Hā′rod-īte. Two of David's guard, so called, 2 Sam. xxiii. 25.

Här′ŏ-eh (*seer*). Son of Shobal, 1 Chr. ii. 52.

Hȧ-rō′sheth (*handicraft*). A city of Naphtali, Judg. iv. 2–16.

Härp (*sickle shaped*). Prominent Jewish musical instrument, invented by Jubal, Gen. iv. 21; of various shapes and sizes; different number of strings; played with fingers or plectrum (quill).

Här′row (*rake*). "Threshing-machine," 2 Sam. xii. 31; 1 Chr. xx. 3. Pulverizer of ground, Isa. xxviii. 24; Job xxxix. 10, and elsewhere.

Här′shȧ (*deaf*). His children returned, Ez. ii. 52; Neh. vii. 54.

Härt. Male of the red deer, Deut. xii. 15; xiv. 5; 1 Kgs. iv. 23; S. of Sol. ii. 9.

Hā′rum (*high*). A Judahite, 1 Chr. iv. 8.

Hȧ-ru′maph (*slit-nosed*). Father of Jedaiah, Neh. iii. 10.

Här′ṳ-phīte, The. A friend of David, 1 Chr. xii. 5.

Hā′ruz (*careful*). Amon's grandfather Kgs. xxi. 19.

Här′vest. [AGRICULTURE.]

Hăs″a-dī′ah (*loved of God*). One of David's line, 1 Chr. iii. 20.

Hăs″e-nū′ah (*hated*). A Benjamite, 1 Chr. ix. 7.

Hăsh″a-bī′ah (*regarded*). (1) Two Levites, 1 Chr. vi. 45; ix. 14. (2) Leader of twelfth course, 1 Chr. xxv. 3, 19. (3) A Hebronite, 1 Chr. xxvi. 30. (4) Other Levites, 1 Chr. xxvii. 17; 2 Chr. xxxv. 9; Ez. viii. 19, 24; Neh. iii. 17; x. 11; xi. 15, 22; xii. 24.

Hă-shăb'nah (*regarded*). A co-covenanter with Nehemiah, Neh. x. 25.

Hăsh''ăb-nī'ah (*regarded*). (1) His son repaired the wall, Neh. iii. 10. (2) A Levite, Neh. ix. 5.

Hăsh-băd'a̤-nȧ (*judge*). Assistant to Ezra, Neh. viii. 4.

Hā'shem (*fat*). His sons were of David's guard, 1 Chr. xi. 34.

Hăsh-mō'nah (*fatness*). A desert station, Num. xxxiii. 29.

Hā'shub (*informed*). (1) Hasshub, a Levite, 1 Chr. ix. 14. (2) Other Levites and builders, Neh. iii. 11, 23; x. 23.

Hă-shṳ'bah (*informed*). One of David's line, 1 Chr. iii. 20.

Hā'shum (*rich*). (1) His children returned, Ez. ii. 19. (2) Assistant to Ezra, Neh. viii. 4.

Hă-shū'phȧ (*stripped*). His children returned, Ez. ii. 43; Neh. vii. 46.

Hăs'rah, 2 Chr. xxxiv. 22. [HARHAS.]

Hăs''sĕ-nā'ah (*thorny*). His sons built the fish-gate, Neh. iii. 3.

Hăs'shub. [HASHUB.]

Hă-sū'phȧ. [HASHUPHA.]

Hā'tăch. Chamberlain of Ahasuerus, Esth. iv. 5–10.

Hā'thăth (*fear*). Son of Othniel, 1 Chr. iv. 13.

Hăt'ĭ-phȧ (*captive*). His sons returned, Ez. ii. 54.

Hăt'ĭ-tȧ (*searching*). Returned porters, Ez. ii. 42.

Hăt'til (*doubtful*). His sons returned, Ez. ii. 57.

Hăt'tŭsh (*gathered*). (1) A Judahite, 1 Chr. iii. 22; Ez. viii. 2. (2) Others of the returned, Neh. iii. 10; x. 4; xii. 2.

Hau'ran (*caves*). Present Hauran, S. of Syria in Bashan, Ezek. xlvii. 16–18.

Hăv'ĭ-lah (*circle*). (1) Son of Cush, Gen. x. 7. (2) Son of Joktan, x. 29. (3) An unlocated region, Gen. ii. 11; xxv. 18; 1 Sam. xv. 7.

Hā'voth=jā'ir (*villages of Jair*). Villages in Gilead or Bashan, Num. xxxii. 41; Deut. iii. 14.

Hãwk (*havoc*). An unclean bird; species of falcon, Lev. xi. 16; Deut. xiv. 15; Job xxxix. 26.

Hãy (*cut*). Grass; but hardly cut and dried grass, Prov. xxvii. 25; Ps. lxxii. 6; Isa. xv. 6.

Hăz'a-el (*God sees*). A Syrian king, 1 Kgs. xix. 15; 2 Kgs. viii. 7–16; x. 32; xiii. 24.

Hă-zā'ĭah (*whom God sees*). A Judahite, Neh. xi. 5.

Hā'zar. [HAZER.]

Hā'zar=ăd'dar. [HAZER.]

Hā'zar=mā'veth. Son of Joktan, Gen. x. 26.

Hā'zel. The almond doubtless meant, Gen. xxx. 37.

Hăz''e-lĕl-pō'nī (*coming shadows*). Sister of Judahites, 1 Chr. iv. 3.

Hā'zer (*village*). In composition. (1) Hazar-addar, a landmark of Israel, Num. xxxiv. 4; Adar, Josh. xv. 3. (2) Hazar-enan, a boundary of Israel, Num. xxxiv. 9, 10. (3) Hazar-gaddah, a town of Judah, Josh. xv. 27. (4) Hazar-shual, in southern Judah, Josh. xv. 28. (5) Hazar-susah, in Judah, Josh. xix. 5; Hazar-susim, 1 Chr. iv. 31. (6) Hazar-hatticon, Ezek. xlvii. 16.

Hă-zē'rĭm, Deut. ii. 23. Villagers. [HAZER.]

Hă-zē'roth (*villages*). An Israelite encampment, Num. xi. 35; Deut. i. 1.

Hăz'e-zon=tā'mar (*felling of palms*). Old name of Engedi, Gen. xiv. 7. Hazazon-tamar, 2 Chr. xx. 2.

Hā'zĭ-el (*vision*). A Levite, 1 Chr. xxiii. 9.

Hā'zō (*vision*). Son of Nahor, Gen. xxii. 22.

Hā'zôr (*court*). (1) City of Naphtali, Josh. xi. 10; 1 Kgs. ix. 15; 2 Kgs. xv. 29. (2) Town of Judah, Josh. xv. 23–25. (3) Place in Benjamin, Neh. xi. 33.

Hĕad'dress. Sacerdotal and ornamental, Ex. xxviii. 40. Mantle or veil the usual head-dress.

Heãrth (*ground*). Hot stones, Gen. xviii. 6. Pan or brazier, Jer. xxxvi. 23.

Hēath (*country*). No heath in Palestine. Evidently a desert scrub, Jer. xvii. 6; xlviii. 6.

Hēa'then (*dwellers on the heath*). All except Jews, Ps. ii. 1. Non-believer, Matt. xviii. 17.

Hĕav'en (*heaved*). Firmament, Gen. i. 1; Matt.

v. 18.   Abode of God, 1 Kgs. viii. 30; Dan. ii. 28;
Matt. v. 45.   Paradise, Luke xxiii. 43.

Hē′bēr (*alliance*).   Eber, Luke iii. 35.   Others
in Gen. xlvi. 17; Num. xxvi. 45; Judg. iv. 17; 1
Chr. iv. 18; v. 13; vii. 31; viii. 17, 22.

Hē′brews.   "Abram the Hebrew," Gen. xiv.
13, that is, *eber*, the one who had "passed over" the
Euphrates, westward.   Hence, "seed" or descend-
ants of Abraham.   Among themselves, preferably,
Israelites, from Gen. xxxii. 28.   Jews, *i. e.* Judahites,
Judeans, after the captivity.

He′brews, Epistle to.   Written probably by
Paul, from Rome, A. D. 62 or 63, to overcome Hebrew
favoritism for the old law.

Hē′bron (*friendship*).   (1) Son of Kohath, Ex.
vi. 18; Num. iii. 19, 27.   (2) Person or place, 1 Chr.
ii. 42.   (3) Ancient city of Judah, 20 mls. S. of Jerusalem, Gen. xiii. 18; Num. xiii. 22; Arba in Josh.
xxi. 11; Judg. i. 10.

Hē′bron-ītes.   Kohathite Levites, Num. iii. 27;
xxvi. 58.

Hĕdge (*haw*).   In Hebrew sense, anything that
encloses — wall, fence, or thorn bushes, Num. xxii.
24; Prov. xxiv. 31; Hos. ii. 6.

Hĕg′a-ī, Hē′gē.   Chamberlain of Ahasuerus,
Esth. ii. 3, 8, 15.

Hĕif′ēr (*high-bullock*).   Red heifers sacrificial,
Num. xix. 10.   Frequent source of metaphor, Judg.
xiv. 18; Isa. xv. 5; Jer. xlvi. 20; Hos. iv. 16.

Heir (*inheritor*).   Eldest son became head of
tribe or family with largest share of paternal estate; sons of concubines given presents; daughters,
a marriage portion, Gen. xxi. 10, 14; xxiv. 36; xxv.
6; xxxi. 14; Judg. xi. 2, etc.   Real estate apportioned as in Deut. xxi. 17; Num. xxvii. 4–11.

Hē′lah (*rust*).   Wife of Ashur, 1 Chr. iv. 5.

Hē′lam (*fort*).   A battlefield, 2 Sam. x. 16, 17.

Hĕl′bah (*fertile*).   Town of Asher, Judg. i. 31.

Hĕl′bon (*fertile*).   A Syrian city, Ezek. xxvii. 18.

Hĕl-chī′ah, 1 Esdr. viii. 1.   [HILKIAH.]

Hĕl′da-ī (*worldly*).   (1) Captain of 12th course,
1 Chr. xxvii. 15.   (2) One who returned, Zech. vi.
10.   Helem in vs. 14.

Hē′lĕb, Hē′lĕd (*passing*). One of David's guard, 2 Sam. xxiii. 29 ; 1 Chr. xi. 30.

Hē′lek (*portion*). Founder of Helekites, Num. xxvi. 30.

Hē′lem (*strength*). (1) An Asherite, 1 Chr. vii. 35. (2) Probably Heldai, Zech. vi. 14.

Hē′leph (*exchange*). Starting point of Naphtali's boundary, Josh. xix. 33.

Hē′lez (*strong*). (1) Captain of 7th course and one of David's guard, 2 Sam. xxiii. 26 ; 1 Chr. xi. 27. (2) A Judahite, 1 Chr. ii. 39.

Hē′lī (*climbing*). Eli, father of Joseph, Luke iii. 23.

Hē′′lĭ-ō-dō′rus. A Syrian treasurer, 2 Macc. iii.

Hĕl′ka̤-ī (*portion*). A priest, Neh. xii. 15.

Hĕl′kăth (*part*). (1) Starting point of Asher's boundary, Josh. xix. 25. (2) Hĕl′kăth-hăz′zu-rĭm, a battlefield ; 2 Sam. ii. 16.

Hĕl-kī′as, 1 Esdr. i. 8. [HILKIAH.]

Hĕll (*conceal*). Hebrew "sheol ;" translated "grave," 1 Sam. ii. 6 ; "pit," Num. xvi. 30 ; "hell," Job xi. 8, in O. T. In N. T., Hades and Gehenna are translated hell, Acts ii. 27 ; Matt. v. 29. Gehenna, or Valley of Hinnom, alone implies a place of burning or torture.

Hĕl′lĕn-ist. A Grecian ; but limited to Greek-speaking Jews in Acts vi. 1 ; ix. 29 ; xi. 20.

Hĕl′met (*hide*). Armor, generally metal, for head, 1 Sam. xvii. 5 ; 2 Chr. xxvi. 14. [ARMOR.]

He′lon (*strong*). Father of Eliab, Num. i. 9 ; ii. 7.

Hĕm (*field*). Edge, or fringe, of a garment, Num. xv. 38, 39 ; Matt. xxiii. 5.

Hē′mam (*driving out*). Grandson of Seir, Gen. xxxvi. 22.

Hē′man (*trusty*). (1) Son of Zerah, 1 Chr. ii. 6. (2) Grandson of Samuel, 1 Chr. vi. 33 ; xv. 16–22 ; xxv. 5.

Hē′măth (*heat*). Person or place, 1 Chr. ii. 55. Hamath, 1 Chr. xiii. 5 ; Am. vi. 14.

Hĕm′dan (*pleasant*). Son of Dishon, Gen. xxxvi. 26. Amram, 1 Chr. i. 41.

Hĕm'lock. Not the bitter, poisonous hemlock as in Hos. x. 4; Am. vi. 12, but "gall," as elsewhere.

Hĕn (*rest*). (1) Son of Zephaniah, Zech. vi. 14. (2) The domestic fowl, common in Palestine, but mentioned only in Matt. xxiii. 37; Luke xiii. 34.

Hē'nȧ (*troubling*). A city of Mesopotamia, 2 Kgs. xviii. 34; xix. 13; Isa. xxxvii. 13.

Hĕn'ȧ-dăd (*favor of Hadad*). His sons returned, Ez. iii. 9; Neh. x. 9.

Hē'noch. (1) 1 Chr. i. 3. [ENOCH, 6.] (2) 1 Chr. i. 33. [HANOCH, 1.]

Hē'phĕr (*pit*). (1) Founder of Hepherites, Num. xxvi. 32; Josh. xii. 17. (2) Son of Ashur, 1 Chr. iv. 6. (3) One of David's guard, 1 Chr. xi. 36. (4) A place W. of Jordan, Josh. xii. 17.

Hĕph'zĭ-bah (*my delight in her*). (1) Name of restored Jerusalem, Isa. lxii. 4. (2) Wife of Hezekiah, 2 Kgs. xxi. 1.

Hĕr'ăld (*army ruler*). Crier, Dan. iii. 4; preacher, as in 1 Tim. ii. 7; 2 Pet. ii. 5.

Hĕr'cū-leş. The god "Melkart," 2 Macc. iv. 19.

Hĕrd. A collection of cattle. Herdsmen despised by Egyptians, Gen. xlvi. 34, but honored by Hebrews, 1 Sam. xi. 5; xxi. 7.

Hē'rēş (*sun*). A place in Dan, Judg. i. 35.

Hē'resh (*carpenter*). A Levite, 1 Chr. ix. 15.

Hĕr'mas, Hĕr'mēş (*Mercury*). Two friends of Paul, Rom. xvi. 14.

Hĕr-mŏg'e-nēş (*born of Mercury*). One who deserted Paul, 2 Tim. i. 15.

Hĕr'mŏn (*lofty*). Highest peak of Anti-Libanus range and northern landmark of Palestine, 10,000 ft. high, Deut. iii. 8; Josh. xi. 17.

Hĕr'mon-ītes. The three peaks of Hermon, Ps. xlii. 6.

Hĕr'od (*heroic*). (1) Herod the Great, tetrarch of Judea, B. C. 41; King of Judea, B. C. 41–4; liberal, yet tyrannical and cruel. Issued murderous edict against children of Bethlehem, Matt. ii. 16. (2) Herod Antipas, son of former; tetrarch of Galilee and Perea, B. C. 4–A. D. 39; murderer of John the Baptist, Matt. xiv. 1; Luke iii. 19; xxiii. 7–15; Acts xiii. 1. (3) Herod Philip, son of Herod the Great. Married Herodias, Matt. xiv. 3; Mark vi. 17; Luke

iii. 19. Lived and died in private life. (4) Herod Philip II., son of Herod the Great, and tetrarch of Batanea, Ituræa, etc., B. C. 4-A. D. 34, Luke iii. 1. (5) Herod Agrippa I., grandson of Herod the Great; tetrarch of Galilee; king of his grandfather's realm, A. D., 37-44, Acts xii. 1-19. (6) Herod Agrippa II., son of former, and king of consolidated tetrarchies, A. D. 50-100, Acts xxv. 13-27; xxvi. 1-28.

Hĕ-rō'dĭ-ans. A Jewish political party who favored the Herods and Roman dependence, Matt. xxii. 16; Mark iii. 6; viii. 15.

Hĕ-rō'dĭ-as. Granddaughter of Herod the Great. Wife of her uncle Herod Philip and her step-uncle. She requested the head of John the Baptist, Matt. xiv. 3-6; Mark vi. 17; Luke iii. 19.

Hĕ-rō'dĭ-on. Kinsman of Paul, Rom. xvi. 11.

Hĕr'on. A large aquatic bird, pronounced unclean, Lev. xi. 19; Deut. xiv. 18.

Hē'sed (*kindness*). Father of one of Solomon's commissaries, 1 Kgs. iv. 10.

Hĕsh'bŏn (*device*). An Amorite capital, N. E. of Dead Sea, Num. xxi. 26; Josh. xiii. 17; Isa. xv. 4.

Hĕsh'mŏn (*fertile*). Place in south Judah, Josh. xv. 27.

Hĕs'rŏn. [HEZRON.]

Hĕth (*fear*). Progenitor of the Hittites, Gen. x. 15; xxiii. 3-20; xxv. 10; xxvii. 46.

Hĕth'lŏn (*hiding place*). A mountain pass, probably Hamath, Ezek. xlvii. 15; xlviii. 1.

Hĕz'e-kī (*strong*). A Benjamite, 1 Chr. viii. 17.

Hĕz-e-kī'ah (*strength of God*). (1) Twelfth king of Judah, B. C. 726-698. Noted for abolition of idolatry and powerful resistance to neighboring nations, 2 Kgs. xviii.-xx.; 2 Chr. xxix.-xxxii. (2) Son of Neariah, 1 Chr. iii. 23. (3) [ATER.]

Hē'zĭ-on (*sight*). A king of Syria; probably Rezon, 1 Kgs. xv. 18; xi. 23.

Hē'zīr (*swine*). (1) Leader of 17th course, 1 Chr. xxiv. 15. (2) A co-covenanter, Neh. x. 20.

Hĕz'ra-ī (*enclosure*). One of David's guard, 2 Sam. xxiii. 35. Hezro, 1 Chr. xi. 37.

Hĕz'ron (*surrounded*). (1) A Reubenite, Gen. xlvi. 9. (2) Son of Pharez, Gen. xlvi. 12; Ruth iv. 18.

Hĕz′ron-ites. Reubenite and Judahite families, Num. xxvi. 6, 21.

Hĭd′da̤-ī (*joyful*). One of David's guard, 2 Sam. xxiii. 30.

Hĭd′dę-kel (*rapid*). Third river of Eden, no doubt Tigris, Gen. ii. 14; Dan. x. 4.

Hī′el (*God lives*). A Bethelite who rebuilt Jericho, 1 Kgs. xvi. 34.

Hī″ę-răp′o-lĭs (*holy city*). City of Phrygia, on the Meander near Colossæ, Col. iv. 13.

Hī-er′ę-el, 1 Esdr. ix. 21. [JEHIEL.]

Hī-er′ę-moth. Jeremoth, Ramoth, in Esdr.

Hī″ę-rŏn′ў̆-mus (*sacred name*). A Syrian general, 2 Macc. xii. 2.

Hĭg-gā′ion (*meditation*). Musical pause for meditation, Ps. ix. 16; xix. 14, xcii. 3, marg.

Hīgh Plā′ces. Altars, temples, and dedicated places originally on high ground, Gen. xii. 8; Judg. vi. 25; Isa. lxv. 7; Jer. iii. 6. When the groves and mounts of idolatry overshadowed true worship, "high places" became a reproach.

Hīgh Priēst. Chief priest, Aaron being the first. Originally a life office, limited to a line or family, Ex. xxviii. 1; Lev. xxi. 10; Num. iii. 32; xx. 8; Deut. x. 6.

Hī′len (*caves*). A Levitical city in Judah, 1 Chr. vi. 58.

Hĭl-kī′ah (*God my portion*). (1) Father of Eliakim, 2 Kgs. xviii. 37. (2) A high priest, 2 Kgs. xxii. 8. (3) Four Levites, 1 Chr. vi. 45; xxvi. 11; Neh. viii. 4; xii. 7, 21. (4) Father of Jeremiah, Jer. i. 1. (5) Father of an ambassador, Jer. xxix. 3.

Hĭl′lel (*praise*). Father of Abdon, Judg. xii. 13, 15.

Hĭn. A Hebrew liquid measure, about 1¼ gallons, Ex. xxx. 24.

Hīnd. Female of the red deer, Gen. xlix. 21; Ps. xxix. 9; Prov. v. 19.

Hĭnge (*hanged*). A pivot and socket for swinging doors, 1 Kgs. vii. 50; Prov. xxvi. 14.

Hĭn′nom (*wailing*). A narrow valley south and west of Jerusalem, Josh. xv. 8; xviii. 16, where Molech was worshipped, 1 Kgs. xi. 7; 2 Kgs. xvi. 3;

hence called Tophet, "drum," noise, Isa. xxx. 33; defiled, 2 Kgs. xxiii. 10, and called ge-Hinnom, gehenna, "place of Hinnom," to type a place of eternal torment. "Hell" in N. T., Matt. v. 22, 29; x. 28; xxiii. 15; Mark ix. 43; Luke xii. 5.

Hī'rah (*noble*). An Adullamite, Gen. xxxviii. 1, 12, 20.

Hī'ram, Hū'ram (*noble*). (1) King of Tyre who furnished men and material to David and Solomon, 2 Sam. v. 11; 1 Kgs. v.; 1 Chr. xiv. 1 (2) Hiram's chief architect, 1 Kgs. vii. 13, 40.

Hĭr-cā'nus. Son of Tobias, 2 Macc. iii. 11.

Hĭt'tītes. Descendants of Heth, Gen. x. 15; xxv. 9; Josh. iii. 10; 2 Sam. xi. 3.

Hī'vītes (*villagers*). Descendants of Canaan, Gen. x. 17; located at Shechem, xxxiv. 2; noted for craft, Josh. ix.

Hĭz-kī'ah (*strength*). Ancestor of Zephaniah, Zeph. i. 1.

Hĭz-kī'jah (*strength*). A co-covenanter, Neh. x. 17.

Hō'băb (*live*). Brother-in-law of Moses, Num. x. 29–32.

Hō'bah (*hiding*). A place beyond Damascus, Gen. xiv. 15.

Hŏd (*splendor*). Son of Zophah, 1 Chr. vii. 37

Hŏd-a̤-ī'ah (*praise ye*). A Judahite, 1 Chr. iii. 24.

Hŏd-a̤-vī'ah (*praise ye*). (1) A Manassite, 1 Chr v. 24. (2) A Benjamite, 1 Chr. ix. 7 (3) A Levite, Ez. ii. 40.

Hō'desh (*new moon*). A Benjamite woman, 1 Chr. viii. 9.

Hŏ-dē'vah, Neh. vii. 43. [HODAVIAH, 3.]

Hŏ-dī'ah (*splendor*). Wife of Ezra, 1 Chr. iv. 19. Jehudijah in vs. 18.

Hō'dī-jah (*splendor*). Three Levites, Neh. viii. 7; x. 13, 18.

Hŏg'lah (*quail*). Daughter of Zelophehad, Num. xxvi. 33.

Hō'ham (*driven*). A king of Hebron, Josh. x. 3.

Hōlm=tree. Holm-oak, Sus. 58.

Hŏl-ō-fĕr′nĕṣ. The general slain by Judith, Judith ii. 4, etc.

Hō′lŏn (*sandy*). (1) A town of Judah, Josh. xv. 51. (2) A city of Moab, Jer. xlviii. 21.

Hō′mam, 1 Chr. i. 39. [HEMAM.]

Hō′mĕr. A Hebrew liquid and dry measure, from 47 to 64 gals., according to time, and 6 to 8 bush., Ezek. xlv. 14.

Hon′ey. Bees numerous and honey plentiful in Palestine. Much used, Lev. xx. 24 ; Deut. xxxii. 13 ; Matt. iii. 4.

Hooks. Various kinds. Fishing, Job xli. 2 ; leading, 2 Kgs. xix. 28 ; pruning, Isa. ii. 4 ; hanging meats, Ezek. xl. 43 ; curtains, Ex. xxvi. 32–37 ; lifting boiled food, 1 Sam. ii. 13.

Hŏph′nī (*fighter*). Impious son of Eli, 1 Sam. i. 3 ; ii. 12–17 ; iii. 11–14 ; iv. 11.

Hôr (*hill*). (1) Mount in Edom on which Aaron died, Num. xx. 22–29 ; xxxiii. 37. (2) A peak of Lebanon range, Num. xxxiv. 7, 8.

Hō′ram (*hill*). King of Gezer, Josh. x. 33.

Hō′reb (*desert*). [SINAI.]

Hō′rem (*offered*). A place in Naphtali, Josh. xix. 38.

Hôr=hȧ-ḡĭd′gad (*cleft mountain*). A desert station of the Israelites, Num. xxxiii. 32.

Hō′rī (*cave-dweller*). (1) Grandson of Seir, Gen. xxxvi. 22. (2) A Simeonite, Num. xiii. 5.

Hō′rītes, Hōrims. Original people of Mt. Seir, Gen. xiv. 6.

Hôr′mah (*laid waste*). A Canaanite town in southern Judah, Josh. xv. 30 ; 1 Sam. xxx. 30.

Hôrn. Made of horn or metal, and of various shapes, sizes, and uses. Used much figuratively, Deut. xxxiii. 17 ; 1 Sam. xvi. 1 ; Job xvi. 15 ; Jer. xlviii. 25.

Hôr′net (*horner*). Plenty in Palestine, Ex. xxiii. 28 ; Deut. vii. 20 ; Josh. xxiv. 12.

Hŏr′′o-nā′im (*two caves*). City of Moab, Isa. xv. 5 ; Jer. xlviii. 3.

Hŏrse (*neigher*). Used chiefly for war, Ex. xiv. 9–23 ; 2 Chr. i. 14–17 ; ix. 25 ; Esth. vi. 8 ; for threshing, Isa. xxviii. 28.

Hŏrse′lēech (*adherer*). Found in stagnant waters of East, and fastens to nostrils of animals when drinking, Prov. xxx. 15.

Hō′sah (*refuge*). (1) City of Asher, Josh. xix. 29. (2) A Levite, 1 Chr. xxvi. 10.

Hŏ-săn′nȧ. "Save, we pray," Ps. cxviii. 25, 26. The cry when Christ entered Jerusalem, Matt. xxi. 9-15; Mark xi. 9, 10.

Hŏ-ṣē′ȧ (*help*). First of minor prophets. Prophetic career, B. c. 784–725, in Israel. Denounces the idolatries of Israel and Samaria. Style obscure.

Hŏsh″a-ī′ah (*helped by God*). (1) Nehemiah's assistant, Neh. xii. 32. (2) Jezaniah's father, Jer. xlii. 1.

Hŏsh-a′mȧ (*whom God hears*). Son of Jeconiah, 1 Chr. iii. 18.

Hŏ-shē′ȧ (*salvation*). (1) Nineteenth and last king of Israel, B. c. 730–721. Conquered and imprisoned by Shalmaneser, 2 Kgs. xv. 30; xvii. 1-6; Hos. xiii. 16. (2) Son of Nun, Deut. xxxii. 44. (3) An Ephraimite, 1 Chr. xxvii. 20. (4) A co-covenanter, Neh. x. 23.

Hŏs″pĭ-tăl′ĭ-ty (*guest treatment*). Regulated in Lev. xix. 33, 34; xxv. 14–17; Deut. xv. 7-11.

Hō′tham (*seal*). An Asherite, 1 Chr. vii. 32.

Hō′than (*seal*). Father of Shama, 1 Chr. xi. 44.

Hō′thir (*fulness*). Son of Heman, 1 Chr. xxv. 4, 28, and leader of 21st course

Hough (*hok*) (*hock*). Cutting the sinews of the hind. leg, hamstringing, Josh. xi. 6, 9; 2 Sam. viii. 4.

Hour (*time*). First division of Jewish day, morning, noon, evening, Ps. lv. 17. Night had three watches, Ex. xiv. 24; Judg. vii. 19; Lam. ii. 19. Later, day was, morning, heat, midday, evening. Hours introduced from Babylon, after captivity, Matt. xx. 1-10. An indefinite time, Dan. iii. 6; Matt. ix. 22.

House (*cover*). Prevailing Oriental style, low, flat roofed, with court in centre. A tent, palace, citadel, tomb, family, Gen. xii. 17; property, 1 Kgs. xiii. 8; lineage, Luke ii. 4; place of worship, Judg. xx. 18.

Hŭk′kŏk (*cut*). A border of Naphtali, Josh. xiv 34.

Hū′kŏk, 1 Chr. vi. 75. [HELKATH.]

Hŭl (*circle*). Grandson of Shem, Gen. x. 23.

Hŭl'dah (*weasel*). A prophetess, 2 Kgs. xxii. 14-20; 2 Chr. xxxiv. 22.

Hŭm'tah (*place of lizards*). A city of Judah, Josh. xv. 54.

Hŭnt'ing. Hebrews not a hunting people, yet various devices mentioned for capturing wild animals, 2 Sam. xxiii. 20; Job xviii. 9, 10; Prov. xxii. 5; Isa. li. 20; Am. iii. 5.

Hū'pham (*coast-man*). Founder of Huphamites, Num. xxvi. 39.

Hŭp'pah (*covered*). Leader of 13th priestly course, 1 Chr. xxiv. 13.

Hŭp'pim (*covered*). A Benjamite, 1 Chr. vii. 12.

Hûr (*hole*). (1) The man who helped stay the hands of Moses, Ex. xvii. 10; xxiv. 14. (2) A Judahite, Ex. xxxi. 2. (3) A king of Midian, Num. xxxi. 8. (4) Father of one of Solomon's commissaries, 1 Kgs. iv. 8. (5) Father of a wall-builder, Neh. iii. 9.

Hū'rāi (*weaver*). One of David's guard, 1 Chr. xi. 32.

Hū'ram (*noble*). (1) A Benjamite, 1 Chr. viii. 5. (2) Hiram, 2 Chr. ii. 3-13; iv. 11-16.

Hū'rī (*weaver*). A Gadite, 1 Chr. v. 14.

Hū'shah (*haste*). A Judahite, 1 Chr. iv. 4.

Hū'shāi (*haste*). A friend of David, 2 Sam. xv. 32; 1 Kgs. iv. 16.

Hū'sham (*haste*). A king of Edom, Gen. xxxvi. 34, 35.

Hū'shath-īte. Two of David's guard so called, 2 Sam. xxi. 18; xxiii. 27.

Hū'shim (*haste*). (1) Son of Dan, Gen. xlvi. 23. Shuham, Num. xxvi. 42. (2) A Benjamite, 1 Chr. vii. 12. (3) Wife of Shaharaim, 1 Chr. viii. 8, 11.

Hŭsks (*hulls*). The original means the carob, or locust bean, Luke xv. 16.

Hŭz (*strong*). Son of Nahor, Gen. xxii. 21.

Hŭz'zăb (*fixed*). A possible queen of Nineveh, Nah. ii. 7.

Hȳ-ē'na (*hog*). A bristled, fierce, carnivorous animal. "Zeboim," in 1 Sam. xiii. 18; Neh. xi. 34, means hyenas. So, it is thought, the original of " speckled bird," Jer. xii. 9, should be rendered.

Hȳ-dȧs′pēs (*watery*). A river in India, Judith i. 6.

Hȳ′′mĕ-næ′us (*hymeneal*). A convert and pervert, 1 Tim. i. 20 ; 2 Tim. ii. 17.

Hȳmn (*praise-song*). Spiritual song, Matt. xxvi. 30 ; Acts xvi. 25 ; Eph. v. 19 ; Col. iii. 16.

Hȳs′sop (*aromatic plant*). A bushy herb, of the mint family, Ex. xii. 22 ; Lev. xiv. 4, 6, 51 ; 1 Kgs. iv. 33 ; John xix. 29.

Hȳp′ŏ-crĭte (*stage-player*). Who feigns what he is not, Job viii. 13 ; Luke xii. 1.

I

Ĭb′här (*God's choice*). Son of David, 2 Sam. v. 15.

Ĭb′le-ăm (*destroying*). City of Manasseh, Josh. xvii. 11 ; Judg. i. 27.

Ĭb-nē′ĭah (*God builds*). A Benjamite, 1 Chr. ix. 8.

Ĭb-nī′jah (*God builds*). A Benjamite, 1 Chr. ix. 8.

Ĭb′rī (*Hebrew*). A Levite, 1 Chr. xxiv. 27.

Ĭb′zăn (*famous*). A judge of Israel, Judg. xii. 8–10.

Ĭ′=chạ-bŏd (*inglorious*). Son of Phinehas, 1 Sam. iv. 19–22 ; xiv. 3.

Ĭ-cō′nĭ-um (*image*). City of Lycaonia, visited twice by Paul, Acts xiii. 51 ; xiv. 1–22 ; xvi. 2 ; 2 Tim. iii. 11.

Ĭ-dā′lah (*memorial*). City of Zebulun, Josh. xix. 15.

Ĭd′băsh (*stout*). A Judahite, 1 Chr. iv. 3.

Ĭd′dō (*timely*). (1) Father of Ahinadab, 1 Kgs. iv. 14. (2) A Levite, 1 Chr. vi. 21. (3) A Manassite chief, 1 Chr. xxvii. 21. (4) A seer and chronicler, 2 Chr. ix. 29 ; xiii. 22. (5) Grandfather of Zechariah, Zech. i. 1, 7. (6) One of the returned, Ez. viii. 17.

Ĭ′dol, Ĭ-dŏl′ạ-try (*apparent*). An object of worship, other than God, Gen. xxxi. 19 ; idolatry forbidden, Ex. xx. 3, 4 ; xxxiv. 13 ; Deut. iv. 16–19 ; vii. 25, 26 ; yet existed largely, especially under the judges and later kings, Ex. xxxii. ; Judg. ii. 10–23 ; 1 Kgs. xi. 33 ; xii. 27–33 ; xiv. 22–24 ; Isa. lvii. 5–8.

Ĭ″dṳ-mē′á (*red*), Isa. xxxiv. 5. Idumæa, Mark iii. 8. Greek name of Edom.

Ĭ′găl (*redeemed*). (1) The spy of Issachar, Num. xiii. 7. (2) One of David's guard, 2 Sam. xxiii. 36.

Ĭg″da-lī′ah (*great*). "A man of God," Jer. xxxv. 4.

Ĭg′e-ăl (*redeemed*). A Judahite, 1 Chr. iii. 22.

Ĭ′ĭm (*heaps*). (1) Num. xxxiii. 45, Ije-abarim. (2) Town of southern Judah, Josh. xv. 29.

Ĭj″e=ăb′a-rĭm (*ruins of Abarim*). An Israelite encampment near Moab, Num. xxi. 11.

Ĭ′jon (*ruin*). Town of Naphtali, 1 Kgs. xv. 20; 2 Kgs. xv. 29.

Ĭk′kĕsh (*wicked*). Father of Ira, 2 Sam. xxiii. 26; 1 Chr. xi. 28; xxvii. 9.

Ĭ′lāi (*exalted*). One of David's guard, 1 Chr. xi. 29.

Ĭl-lȳr′ĭ-cŭm (*joy*). A country on E. shore of Adriatic, N. of Macedonia. Reached by Paul, Rom. xv. 19.

Ĭm′aġe (*likeness*). As in Gen. i. 26, 27; Col. i. 15. Also Idol.

Ĭm′lá (*full*). Father of Micaiah, 2 Chr. xviii. 7, 8. Imlah, 1 Kgs. xxii. 8, 9.

Ĭm-măn′ū-el (*God with us*). Name of the prophetic child, Isa. vii. 14. The Messiah, Matt. i. 23.

Ĭm′mĕr (*loquacious*). (1) A priestly family in charge of 16th course, 1 Chr. ix. 12; xxiv. 14. (2) Place in Babylonia, Ez. ii. 59; Neh. vii. 61.

Ĭm′ná (*lagging*). An Asherite, 1 Chr. vii. 35.

Ĭm′nah (*lagging*). (1) An Asherite, 1 Chr. vii. 30. (2) A Levite, 2 Chr. xxxi. 14.

Ĭm′rah (*stubborn*). An Asherite, 1 Chr. vii. 36.

Ĭm′rī (*talkative*). (1) A Judahite, 1 Chr. ix. 4. (2) Father of Zaccur, Neh. iii. 2.

Ĭn′çense (*set on fire*). A mixture of gums, spices, etc., Ex. xxx. 34–38, constituted the official incense. Burned morning and evening on the altar of incense, xxx. 1–10. Used also in idolatrous worship, 2 Chr. xxxiv. 25; Jer. xi. 12–17, and by angels, Rev. viii. 3.

Ĭnd′ia (*Indus*). The indefinite country which bounded the Persian empire on the east, Esth. i. 1; viii. 9.

In-hĕr′ĭ-tance (*heirship*). [HEIR.]

Ink, Ink′hôrn (*burnt in*). Ancient ink heavy and thick and carried in an ink-horn, Jer. xxxvi. 18; Ezek. ix. 2.

Inn (*in*). In O. T. a halting place for caravans, Gen. xlii. 27; Ex. iv. 24. In N. T. a caravansary afforded food and shelter for man and beast, Luke x. 34, 35.

In′stant (*stand in*). Urgent, Luke vii. 4; xxiii. 23; fervent, Acts xxvi. 7; Rom. xii. 12.

I-ō′nĭa. India in 1 Macc. viii. 8.

Iph″e-dē′jah (*free*). A Benjamite, 1 Chr. viii. 25.

Ir (*city*). A Benjamite, 1 Chr. vii. 12. Iri, vs. 7.

I′ra (*watchful*). (1) "Chief ruler about David," 2 Sam. xx. 26. (2) Two of David's warriors, 2 Sam. xxiii. 38; 1 Chr. xi. 28.

I′răd (*fleet*). Son of Enoch, Gen. iv. 18.

I′ram (*citizen*). A duke of Edom, Gen. xxxvi. 43: 1 Chr. i. 54.

I′rī (*watchful*). A Benjamite, 1 Chr. vii. 7.

I-rī′jah (*seen of God*). A ward-keeper, Jer. xxxvii. 13, 14.

Ir-nā′hăsh (*serpent city*). Unknown person or place, 1 Chr. iv. 12.

I′ron (*pious*). (1) City of Naphtali, Josh. xix. 38. (2) Iron, the metal, and copper early known, Gen. iv. 22. Prepared in furnaces, 1 Kgs. viii. 51; used for tools, Deut. xxvii. 5; weapons, 1 Sam. xvii. 7; implements, 2 Sam. xii. 31; war-chariots, Josh. xvii. 16, etc.

Ir′pĕ-el (*healed*). City of Benjamin, Josh. xviii. 27.

Ir-shē′mĕsh (*sun city*). A Danite city, Josh. xix. 41.

I′ru (*watch*). Son of Caleb, 1 Chr. iv. 15.

I′saac (*laughter*). Son of Abraham, Gen. xvii. 17–22. Second of the patriarchs, and father of Jacob and Esau, Gen. xxi.–xxxv.

I-ṣā′iah (*salvation of Jehovah*). Son of Amoz, Isa. i. 1, and first of greater prophets. His book, 23d of O. T., covers sixty years of prophecy, Isa. i. 1, at Jerusalem. It reproves the sins of the Jews and

other nations, and foreshadows the coming of Christ.
Called "prince of prophets." Poetically for Israel,
Am. vii. 9, 16.

Ĭs'cah (*who looks*). Sister of Lot, Gen. xi. 29.

Ĭs-căr'ĭ-ot. [JUDAS ISCARIOT.]

Ĭs'dă-el, 1 Esdr. v. 33. [GIDDEL.]

Ĭsh'bah (*praising*). A Judahite, 1 Chr. iv. 17.

Ĭsh'băk (*leaving*). Son of Abraham, and father
of northern Arabians, Gen. xxv. 2 ; 1 Chr. i. 32.

Ĭsh-bī=bē'nŏb (*dweller at Nob*). A Philistine
giant, 2 Sam. xxi. 16, 17.

Ĭsh=bō'sheth (*man of shame*). Son and successor of Saul. Original name, Esh-baal. Reigned two
years, then defeated by David, and assassinated, 2
Sam. ii. 8–11 ; iii. ; iv. 5–12.

Ĭsh'ī (*saving*). (1) Two Judahites, 1 Chr. ii. 31 ;
iv. 20. (2) A Simeonite, iv. 42. (3) A Manassite,
v. 24.

Ĭsh-ī'ah (*loaned*). Chief of Issachar, 1 Chr. vii. 3.

Ĭsh-ī'jah (*loaned*). A lay Israelite, Ez. x. 31.

Ĭsh'mă (*ruin*). A Judahite, 1 Chr. iv. 3.

Ĭsh'ma-el (*whom God hears*). (1) Son of Abraham and Hagar, Gen. xvi. 15, 16. Banished to wilderness ; became progenitor of Arabian tribes, Gen.
xxi. ; xxv. 9 ; xxxvii. 25–28. (2) Descendant of Saul,
1 Chr. viii. 38. (3) A Judahite, 2 Chr. xix. 11. (4)
A Judahite captain, 2 Chr. xxiii. 1. (5) A priest,
Ez. x. 22. (6) Crafty son of Nethaniah, 2 Kgs. xxv.
23–25 ; Jer. xli.

Ĭsh'ma-el-ītes''. Descendants of Ishmael, Judg.
viii. 24. Ishmeelites, Gen. xxxvii. 25 ; 1 Chr. ii. 17.

Ĭsh''ma-ī'ah (*God hears*). Ruler of Zebulun, 1
Chr. xxvii. 19.

Ĭsh'mĕ-rāi (*God keeps*). A Benjamite, 1 Chr.
viii. 18.

Ī'shod (*famed*). A Manassite, 1 Chr. vii. 18.

Ĭsh'păn (*bald*). A Benjamite, 1 Chr. viii. 22.

Ĭsh'=tŏb (*men of Tob*). Part of Aram, 2 Sam. x.
6–8. [TOB.]

Ĭsh'u-ah (*quiet*). An Asherite, Gen. xlvi. 17 ;
1 Chr. vii. 30.

Ĭsh'u-āi (*quiet*). Son of Asher, 1 Chr. vii. 30.

Ĭsh'u-ī (*quiet*). Son of Saul, 1 Sam. xiv. 49.

Īsle (*island*). Habitable place, Isa. xlii. 15; island, Gen. x. 5; Isa. xi. 11; coast lands, Isa. xx. 6; xxiii. 2, 6; Ezek. xxvii. 7.

Ĭs''ma-chī'ah (*supported*). Overseer of offerings, 2 Chr. xxxi. 13.

Ĭs'mă-el, 1 Esdr. ix. 22. [ISHMAEL.]

Ĭs''ma-ī'ah (*God hears*). A chief of Gibeon, 1 Chr. xii. 4.

Ĭs'pah (*bald*). A Benjamite, 1 Chr. viii. 16.

Ĭṣ'ra-el (*who prevails with God*). Name given to Jacob, Gen. xxxii. 28; xxxv. 10; became national, Ex. iii. 16; narrowed to northern kingdom after the revolt of the ten tribes from Judah, 1 Sam. xi. 8; 2 Sam. xx. 1; 1 Kgs. xii. 16, with Shechem as capital, 1 Kgs. xii. 25, and Tirzah as royal residence, xiv. 17; afterwards, capital at Samaria, xvi. 24. Kingdom lasted 254 years, with 19 kings, B. C. 975-721, when it fell a prey to the Assyrians. The returned of Israel blended with those of Judah.

Ĭṣ'ra-ĕl-ītes''. "Children of Israel." [ISRAEL.]

Ĭs'sa-char (*rewarded*). (1) Fifth son of Jacob by Leah, Gen. xxx. 17, 18. Tribe characteristics foretold, Gen. xlix. 14, 15. Place during march at east of Tabernacle, Num. ii. 5. Allotment N. of Manasseh, from Carmel to Jordan, Josh. xix. 17-23. (2) A temple porter, 1 Chr. xxvi. 5.

Ĭs'shĭ-ah (*loaned*). Descendant of Levi, 1 Chr. xxiv. 21. (2) A Levite, 1 Chr. xxiv. 25.

Ĭs''tăl-cū'rus, 1 Esdr. viii. 40. [ZABBUD.]

Ĭs'u-ah, 1 Chr. vii. 30. [JESUI.]

Ĭs'ui, Gen. xlvi. 17. [JESUI.]

Ĭt'a-lў (*kingdom of Italus*). In N. T. the whole of Italy between the Alps and sea, Acts xviii. 2; xxvii. 1; Heb. xiii. 24.

Ĭth'a-ī (*with God*). A Benjamite, 1 Chr. xi. 31.

Ĭth'a-mär (*land of palms*). Son of Aaron, Ex. vi. 23; xxviii. 1-43; Num. iii. 2-4. Eli was high priest of his line, 1 Chr. xxiv. 6.

Ĭth'ĭ-el (*God with me*). (1) Friend of Agur, Prov. xxx. 1. (2) A Benjamite, Neh. xi. 7.

Ĭth'mah (*orphan*). One of David's guard, 1 Chr. xi. 46.

Ĭth′nan (*given*). Town in south Judah, Josh. xv. 23.

Ĭth′rȧ (*plenty*). David's brother-in-law, 2 Sam. xvii. 25.

Ĭth′ran (*plenty*). (1) A Horite, Gen. xxxvi. 26. (2) An Asherite, 1 Chr. vii. 37.

Ĭth′rẹ-ăm (*populous*). Son of David, 2 Sam. iii. 5.

Ĭth′rīte. Two of David's warriors so called, 2 Sam. xxiii. 38 ; 1 Chr. xi. 40.

Ĭt′tah=kā′zin (*hour of a prince*). A landmark of Zebulun, Josh. xix. 13.

Ĭt′tạ-ī (*timely*). (1) One of David's generals, 2 Sam. xv. 19 ; xviii. 2–12. (2) One of David's guard, 2 Sam. xxiii. 29.

Ĭ″tu-ræ′ȧ. From Jetur, Gen. xxv. 15 ; 1 Chr. i. 31. A small province N. W. of Palestine, now Jedur, Luke iii. 1.

Ī′vah, Ā′va. An Assyrian city, possibly Hit, 2 Kgs. xviii. 34 ; xix. 13.

Ī′vŏ-rў (*elephant tooth*), Much used by Hebrews, 1 Kgs. x. 22 ; 2 Chr. ix. 17–21 ; Ezek. xxvii. 15.

Ĭz′ẹ-här, Num. iii. 19. [IZHAR.]

Ĭz′här (*oil*). Uncle of Moses, Ex. vi. 18–21 ; Num. iii. 19. Founder of Izharites, 1 Chr. xxiv. 22.

Ĭz″ra-hī′ah (*sparkling*). Descendant of Issachar, 1 Chr. vii. 3.

Ĭz′ra-hīte. A captain of David, so called, 1 Chr. xxvii. 8.

Ĭz′rī (*created*). Leader of the 4th musical course 1 Chr. xxv. 11.

J

Jā′a-kăn, Deut. x. 6. [JAKAN.]

Jȧ-ăk′ŏ-bah (*supplanter*). Prince of Simeon, 1 Chr. iv. 36.

Jȧ-ā′lah (*wild goat*). His children returned, Ez. ii. 56. Jaala, Neh. vii. 58.

Jȧ-ā′lam (*hidden*). Duke of Edom, Gen. xxxvi. 5, 18.

Jȧ-ā′nāi (*answered*). A Gadite, 1 Chr. v. 12.

Jă-är′ĕ=ŏr′e-gĭm (*weaver's forests*). Father of Elhanan, slayer of Goliath's brother, 2 Sam. xxi. 19.

Jā′a-sạu (*created*). Son of Bani, Ez. x. 37.

Jă-ā′sĭ-el (*created*). Son of Abner, 1 Chr. xxvii. 21.

Jă-ăz′′a-nī′ah (*heard of God*). (1) A Hebrew captain, 2 Kgs. xxv. 23. (2) A denounced prince, Ezek. xi. 1. (3) Son of Jeremiah, Jer. xxxv. 3. (4) Son of Shaphan, Ezek. viii. 11.

Jă-ā′zĕr, Jā′zĕr (*helped*). City and province of Gilead, Num. xxi. 32; xxxii. 1; Josh. xxi. 39; 1 Chr. xxvi. 31.

Jă′′a-zī′ah (*comforted*). A Levite, 1 Chr. xxiv. 26, 27.

Jă-ā′zĭ-el (*comforted*). A temple musician, 1 Chr. xv. 18.

Jā′băl (*stream*). Son of Lamech, Gen. iv. 20.

Jăb′bok (*flowing*). A tributary of Jordan, on east side; and northern boundary of Ammon, Gen. xxxii. 22; Num. xxi. 24; Deut. ii. 37.

Jā′besh (*dry*). (1) King Shallum's father, 2 Kgs. xv. 10, 13. (2) Jabesh-gilead, a city of Gilead, Judg. xxi. 8–14; 1 Sam. xi. 1–11; xxxi. 11–13.

Jā′bĕz (*sorrow*). Persons or places, 1 Chr. ii. 55; iv. 9, 10.

Jā′bin (*observed*). (1) King of Hazor, Josh. xi. 1–14. (2) Another king of Hazor, defeated by Barak, Judg. iv. 2–24.

Jăb′ne-el (*building of God*). (1) Stronghold in Judah, Josh. xv. 11; Jabneh, 2 Chr. xxvi. 6. (2) Place in Naphtali, Josh. xix. 33.

Jăb′neh. [JABNEEL.]

Jā′chan (*affliction*). A Gadite, 1 Chr. v. 13.

Jā′chin (*established*). (1) A temple pillar, 1 Kgs. vii. 21; 2 Chr. iii. 17. (2) Fourth son of Simeon, Gen. xlvi. 10. (3) Head of 21st priestly course, 1 Chr. ix. 10; xxiv. 17.

Jā′chin-ītes. Descendants of Jachin, Num. xxvi. 12.

Jā′cinth (*hyacinth*). Zircon, a vari-colored gem, Rev. ix. 17; xxi. 20.

Jā′cob (*supplanter*). Son of Isaac and second born twin with Esau, Gen. xxv. 24–34. Bought

Esau's birthright, fled to Padan-aram, married Rachel and Leah, wandered to Hebron, name changed
to Israel, drifted to Egypt, where he died, aged 147
years, Gen. xxv.-l.

Jȧ-cū′bus, 1 Esdr. ix. 48. [AKKUB, 4.]

Jā′dȧ (*knowing*). A Judahite, 1 Chr. ii. 28, 32.

Jȧ-dā′u̞ (*loving*). Son of Nebo, Ez. x. 43.

Jad-dū′ȧ (*known*). (1) A co-covenanter, Neh.
x. 21. (2) High priest, and last mentioned in O. T.,
Neh. xii. 11, 22.

Jā′don (*judge*). Assistant wall builder, Neh.
iii. 7.

Jā′el (*goat*). Heber's wife; murderess of Sisera,
Judg. iv. 17-23; v.

Jā′gŭr (*lodging*). Southern town of Judah,
Josh. xv. 21.

Jäh. Jehovah, in poetry, Ps. lxviii. 4.

Jā′hăth (*united*). (1) A Judahite, 1 Chr. iv. 2.
(2) Four Levites, 1 Chr. vi. 20; xxiii. 10, 11; xxiv.
22; 2 Chr. xxxiv. 12.

Jā′hăz (*trodden*). Place in Moab where Moses
conquered the Ammonites, Num. xxi. 23, 24; Deut.
ii. 32.

Jȧ-hā′zȧ, Josh. xiii. 18. [JAHAZ.]

Jȧ-hā′zah, Josh. xxi. 36. [JAHAZ.]

Jȧ″hȧ-zī′ah (*seen of God*). A priest, Ez. x. 15.

Jȧ-hā′zĭ-el (*seen of God*). (1) A Benjamite, 1
Chr. xii. 4. (2) A trumpeter, 1 Chr. xvi. 6. (3) A
Levite, 1 Chr. xxiii. 19; xxiv. 23. (4) A Levite, 2
Chr. xx. 14. (5) His sons returned, Ez. viii. 5.

Jäh′da-ī (*directed*). A Judahite, 1 Chr. ii. 47.

Jäh′dĭ-el (*joyful*). A Manassite, 1 Chr. v. 24.

Jäh′dō (*united*). A Gadite, 1 Chr. v. 14.

Jäh′lĕ-el (*hoping*). Founder of Jahleelites, Gen.
xlvi. 14; Num. xxvi. 26.

Jäh′ma-ī (*guarded*). Son of Tola, 1 Chr. vii. 2.

Jäh′zah, 1 Chr. vi. 78. [JAHAZ.]

Jäh′zĕ-el (*allotted*). Founder of the Jahzeelites,
Gen. xlvi. 24; Num. xxvi. 48.

Jäh′zĕ-rah (*led back*). A priest, 1 Chr. ix. 12.

Jäh′zĭ-el, 1 Chr. vii. 13. [JAHZEEL.]

Jā′ir (*enlightened*). (1) Conqueror of Argob and

part of Gilead, Num. xxxii. 41 ; Deut. iii. 14. (2) A judge of Israel, Judg. x. 3-5. (3) A Benjamite, Esth. ii. 5. (4) Father of Elhanan, 1 Chr. xx. 5.

Ja̍'ir-ite. Ira so called, 2 Sam. xx. 26.

Ja̤-i̍'rus (*enlightened*). Ruler of a synagogue, Luke viii. 41.

Ja̍'kan (*thoughtful*). A Horite, 1 Chr. i. 42. [JAAKAN, AKAN.]

Ja̍'keh (*pious*). Father of Agur, Prov. xxx. 1.

Ja̍'kim (*confirmed*). (1) Head of 12th course, 1 Chr. xxiv. 12. (2) A Benjamite, 1 Chr. viii. 19.

Ja̍'lon (*tarrying*). A Judahite, 1 Chr. iv. 17.

Jăm'brĕs. An Egyptian magician, Ex. vii. 9-13, 2 Tim. iii. 8, 9.

Jăm'brī. Supposably Ammonites, 1 Macc. ix. 36-41.

James (*Jacob*). (1) " The Greater " or " Elder," son of Zebedee and brother of John, Matt. iv. 21, 22. A fisherman of Galilee, called to the Apostolate about A. D. 28, and styled Boanerges, Matt. x. 2, 3 ; Mark iii. 14-18 ; Luke vi. 12-16 ; Acts i. 13. Labored at Jerusalem. Beheaded by Herod, A. D. 44. (2) " The Less," another Apostle, son of Alphæus, Matt. x. 3 ; Mark iii. 18 ; Luke vi. 15. (3) Christ's brother, or more likely cousin, and identical with James the Less, Gal. i. 19. Compare Matt. xiii. 55 ; Mark vi. 3; Acts xii. 17. Resident at Jerusalem and author of The Epistle of James, written before A. D. 62 to the scattered Jews, urging good works as the ground-work and evidence of faith.

Ja̍'min (*right hand*). (1) Founder of Jaminites, Gen. xlvi. 10 ; Ex. vi. 15 ; Num. xxvi. 12. A Judahite, 1 Chr. ii. 27. (3) Ezra's assistant, Neh. viii. 7.

Jăm'lech (*reigning*). A Simeonite chief, 1 Chr. iv. 34.

Jăm'nĭ-à, 1 Macc. iv. 15. [JABNEEL.]

Jăn'nà (*God-given*). Ancestor of Christ, Luke iii. 24.

Jăn'nĕs. An Egyptian magician, 2 Tim. iii. 8, 9; Ex. vii. 9-13.

Ja̤-nō̍'ah (*rest*). Town of Naphtali, 2 Kgs. xv. 29.

Ja̤-nō̍'hah (*rest*). Border town of Ephraim, Josh. xvi. 6, 7.

Jā'num (*sleeping*). Town of Judah, Josh. xv. 53.

Jā'pheth (*enlarged*). Son of Noah, Gen. v. 32; vi. 10; ix. 27; x. 21. His generations peopled the "isles of the Gentiles," and type the Indo-European and Caucasian races, Gen. x. 1–5.

Jǎ-phī'à (*splendor*). (1) A border of Zebulun, Josh. xix. 12. (2) King of Lachish, Josh. x. 3. (3) A son of David, 2 Sam. v. 15; 1 Chr. iii. 7.

Jǎph'let (*delivered*). An Asherite, 1 Chr. vii. 32, 33.

Jǎph-lē'tī. Landmark of Ephraim, Josh. xvi. 3.

Jā'phō, Josh. xix. 46. [JOPPA.]

Jā'rah (*honey*). Son of Micah, 1 Chr. ix. 42.

Jā'reb (*enemy*). Unknown person or place, Hos. v. 13; x. 6.

Jā'red (*descent*). Father of Enoch, Gen. v. 15–20; Luke iii. 37.

Jǎr-ĕ-sī'ah (*nourished*). A Benjamite, 1 Chr. viii. 27.

Jǎr'hà. An Egyptian servant, 1 Chr. ii. 34, 35.

Jā'rib (*enemy*). (1) A Simeonite, 1 Chr. iv. 24. (2) One who returned, Ez. viii. 16. (3) A priest, Ez. x. 18.

Jǎr'ĭ-moth, 1 Esdr. ix. 28. [JEREMOTH.]

Jǎr'mŭth (*high*). (1) Town of lower Judah, Josh. x. 3; xv. 35. (2) A Levitical city of Issachar, Josh. xxi. 29.

Jǎ-rō'ah (*moon*). A Gadite, 1 Chr. v. 14.

Jā'shen (*sleeping*). His sons were in David's guard, 2 Sam. xxiii. 32.

Jā'shěr (*upright*). Book of, wholly lost, Josh. x. 13; 2 Sam. i. 18.

Jǎ-shō'bẹ-ǎm (*turned to*). A chief of David's captains, 1 Chr. xi. 11; xii. 6; xxvii. 2. Adino, 2 Sam. xxiii. 8.

Jǎsh'ŭb (*he turns*). (1) Founder of Jashubites, Num. xxvi. 24; 1 Chr. vii. 1; Job, Gen. xlvi. 13. (2) Son of Bani, Ez. x. 29.

Jǎsh'u-bī=lē'hĕm (*turning back for food*). Person or place of Judah, 1 Chr. iv. 22.

Jā'sĭ-el (*created*). One of David's heroes, 1 Chr. xi. 47.

Jā'sọn (*healer*). (1) Son of Eleazar, 1 Macc.

viii. 17. (2) Father of Antipater, xii. 16. (3) **An** historian, 2 Macc. ii. 23. (4) High priest, 2 Macc. iv. 7–26. (5) A friend of Paul, Acts xvii. 5–9.

Jăs'pĕr. A colored quartz. Last stone in high priest's breastplate, and first in New Jerusalem foundation, Ex. xxviii. 20 ; Rev. xxi. 19.

Jăth'nĭ-el (*God-given*). A Levite, 1 Chr. xxvi. 2.

Jăt'tĭr (*prominent*). Town of south Judah, Josh. xv. 48 ; xxi. 14 ; 1 Sam. xxx. 27.

Jā'văn (*clay*). (1) Fourth son of Japheth, and type of Ionians and Grecians, Gen. x. 2–5 ; 1 Chr. i. 5–7. (2) An Arabian trading post, Ezek. xxvii. 13, 19.

Jăve'lĭn. A short, light spear. [ARMS.]

Jā'zär, 1 Macc. v. 8. [JAAZER.]

Jā'zĕr, Num. xxxii. 1–3 ; Josh. xxi. 39. [JAAZER.]

Jā'zĭz (*moved*). Herdsman of David, 1 Chr. xxvii. 31.

Jĕ'a-rĭm (*woods*). Border mountain of Judah, Josh. xv. 10.

Jĕ-ăt'e-rāi (*led*). A Levite, 1 Chr. vi. 21.

Jĕ''bĕr-e-chī'ah (*blessed*). Father of Zechariah, Isa. viii. 2.

Jē'bus (*threshing floor*). Original name of Jerusalem ; the "threshing floor" of the Jebushi or Jebusites, Josh. xv. 8 ; xviii. 16, 28 ; Judg. xix. 10, 11 ; 1 Chr. xi. 4, 5.

Jĕb'u-sīte, Jĕ-bū'sī. Original people of Jebus, Deut. vii. 1 ; Josh. xi. 3 ; 2 Sam. v. 6–10 ; xxiv, 16–25.

Jĕc''a-mī'ah (*gathered*). One of David's line, 1 Chr. iii. 18.

Jĕch''o-lī'ah (*enabled*). Mother of King Azariah, 2 Kgs. xv. 2. Jecoliah, 2 Chr. xxvi. 3.

Jĕch''o-nī'as, Matt. i. 11, 12 ; Esth. xi. 4. Greek form of Jeconiah and Jehoiachin.

Jĕc''o-lī'ah, 2 Chr. xxvi. 3. [JECHOLIAH.]

Jĕc''o-nī'ah, 1 Chr. iii. 16 ; Jer. xxiv. 1. [JEHOI-ACHIN.]

Jĕ-dā'ĭah (*praise God*). (1) Head of 2d temple course, 1 Chr. xxiv. 7. (2) A priest, Zech. vi. 10–14. (3) A Simeonite, 1 Chr. iv. 37. (4) A wall-repairer, Neh. iii. 10.

Jĕ-dĭ'a-el (*known of God*). (1) A Benjamite, 1 Chr. vii. 6–11. (2) One of David's guard, 1 Chr. xi. 45. (3) A Manassite chief, 1 Chr. xii. 20. (4) A Levite, 1 Chr. xxvi. 1, 2.

Jĕ-dĭ'dah (*beloved*). Mother of King Josiah, 2 Kgs. xxii. 1.

Jĕd″ĭ-dĭ'ah (*beloved of God*). Name given to Solomon by Nathan, 2 Sam. xii. 25.

Jĕd'u-thŭn (*praising*). A leader of the temple choir, 1 Chr. xxv. 6 ; Ps. xxxix., lxii., lxxvii., title.

Jĕ-ē'zẽr (*father of help*). A Manassite, Num. xxvi. 30. Abiezer, elsewhere.

Jĕ-ē'zẽr-ītes. Descendants of above.

Jē'gar=sā-hȧ-dū'thȧ (*testimonial heap*). Heap of compact between Jacob and Laban, Gen. xxxi. 47.

Jĕ″hȧ-lē'lĕ-el (*who praises*). A Judahite, 1 Chr. iv. 16.

Jĕ-hăl'ĕ-lĕl (*who praises*). A Levite, 2 Chr. xxix. 12.

Jĕh-dē'ĭah (*made joyful*). (1) A Levite, 1 Chr. xxiv. 20. (2) David's herdsman, 1 Chr. xxvii. 30.

Jĕ-hĕz'ĕ-kĕl (*made strong*). Head of the 20th priestly course, 1 Chr. xxiv. 16.

Jĕ-hī'ah (*God lives*). A doorkeeper of the ark, 1 Chr. xv. 24.

Jĕ-hī'el (*God lives*). (1) A Levite, 1 Chr. xv. 18, 20. (2) A treasurer, 1 Chr. xxiii. 8. (3) Son of Jehoshaphat, 2 Chr. xxi. 2. (4) An officer of David, 1 Chr. xxvii. 32. (5) A Levite, 2 Chr. xxix. 14. (6) Ruler of God's house, 2 Chr. xxxv. 8. (7) An overseer, 2 Chr. xxxi. 13. (8) Returned captives, Ez. viii. 9 ; x. 2, 21, 26.

Jĕ-hī'el (*treasured*). (1) Father of Gibeon, 1 Chr. ix. 35. (2) One of David's guard, 1 Chr. xi. 44.

Jĕ-hī'e-lī. A Levite family, 1 Chr. xxvi. 21, 22.

Jĕ″hĭz-kī'ah (*strengthened*). An Ephraimite, 2 Chr. xxviii. 12.

Jĕ-hō'a-dah (*adorned*). A descendant of Saul, 1 Chr. viii. 36.

Jĕ″hŏ-ăd'dan (*adorned*). Mother of King Amaziah, 2 Kgs. xiv. 2 ; 2 Chr. xxv. 1

Jĕ-hō'a-hăz (*possession*). (1) Son and successor of Jehu on throne of Israel, B. C. 856–840, 2 Kgs. xiii.

1–9. Reign disastrous. (2) Son and successor of Josiah on throne of Judah. Reigned 3 months, B. C. 610. Called Shallum. Deposed and died in Egypt, Jer. xxii. 11, 12. (3) Ahaziah, Azariah, 2 Chr. xxi. 17 ; xxii. 1, 6.

Jĕ-hō'ash. [JOASH.]

Jĕ''hŏ-hā'nan (*God-given*). (1) A temple porter, 1 Chr. xxvi. 3. (2) A general of Judah, 2 Chr. xvii. 15 ; xxiii. 1. (3) Returned Levites, Ez. x. 28 ; Neh. xii. 13, 42.

Jĕ-hoi'a-chin (*God-appointed*). Jeconiah, 1 Chr. iii. 17 ; Coniah, Jer. xxii. 24 ; Jechonias, Matt. i. 12. Son and successor of Jehoiakim on throne of Judah. Reigned 100 days, B. C. 597 ; carried prisoner to Babylon ; released after 36 years' captivity, 2 Kgs. xxiv. 6–16 ; Jer. xxix. 2 ; Ezek. xvii. 12.

Jĕ-hoi'a-dȧ (*known of God*). (1) Father of Benaiah, 2 Sam. viii. 18 ; 1 Kgs. i., ii. (2) An Aaronite leader, 1 Chr. xii. 27. (3) No doubt same as (1), 1 Chr. xxvii. 34. (4) High priest and religious reformer under Athaliah and Joash, 2 Kgs. xi. 4–21; xii. 1–16. (5) Second priest, or sagan, Jer. xxix. 25–29. (6) A wall-repairer, Neh. iii. 6.

Jĕ-hoi'a-kĭm (*God-established*). Eliakim, son of Josiah ; name changed to Jehoiakim ; successor to Jehoahaz, and 19th king of Judah, B. C. 609–598. Nearly entire reign one of vassalage to Egypt or Babylon, 2 Kgs. xxiii. 34–37 ; xxiv. 1–6 ; Jer. xxii. 18, 19 ; xxxvi. 30–32.

Jĕ-hoi'a-rĭb (*God-defended*). Head of 1st temple course, 1 Chr. xxiv. 7.

Jĕ-hŏn'a-dȧb, Jŏn'a-dȧb (*God-impelled*). Son of Rechab, and adherent of Jehu, 2 Kgs. x. 15–23 ; Jer. xxxv. 6.

Jĕ-hŏn'a-than (*God-given*). (1) David's storehouse keeper, 1 Chr. xxvii. 25. (2) A Levite teacher, 2 Chr. xvii. 8. (3) A priest, Neh. xii. 18.

Jĕ-hō'ram, Jō'ram (*God-exalted*). (1) Son of Ahab and successor to Ahaziah on throne of Israel, B. C. 896–884. Victoriously allied with Judah, but defeated and slain in Jehu's revolt. Last of Ahab's line, 1 Kgs. xxi. 21–29 ; xxii. 50 ; 2 Kgs. i. 17, 18 ; ii.-ix. (2) Son and successor of Jehoshaphat on throne of Judah, B. C. 893–885. Murderer and Baal worshipper. Reign calamitous. Died a terrible death, 2 Chr. xxi.

Jĕ″hŏ-shăb′e-ăth, 2 Chr. xxii. 11. [JEHOSH-EBA.]

Jĕ-hŏsh′a-phăt (*judged of God*). (1) Recorder under David and Solomon, 2 Sam. viii. 16; 1 Kgs. iv. 3. (2) A trumpeter, 1 Chr. xv. 24. (3) Solomon's purveyor, 1 Kgs. iv. 17. (4) Father of Jehu, 2 Kgs. ix. 2-14. (5) Valley of Cedron, or else a visionary spot, Joel iii. 2-12. (6) Son and successor of Asa on throne of Judah, B. C. 914-890. A God-fearing king, in close alliance with Israel, 1 Kgs. xv. 24; 2 Kgs. viii. 16; 2 Chr. xvii.-xxi.

Jĕ-hŏsh′e-bȧ (*oath of God*). Daughter of king Joram and wife of Jehoiada, the high priest, 2 Kgs. xi. 2; 2 Chr. xxii. 11.

Jĕ-hŏsh′u-ȧ. Full form of Joshua, Num. xiii. 16; Jehoshuah, 1 Chr. vii. 27.

Jĕ-hō′vah. "He that is." "I am," Ex. iii. 14. The self-existent and eternal one. Hebrew word for God, generally rendered "Lord." Not pronounced; but Adonai, "Lord," or Elohim, "God," substituted, Ex. vi. 3. [GOD.]

Jĕ-hō′vah=jī′reh (*God will provide*). Abraham's name for spot where Isaac was offered, Gen. xxii. 14.

Jĕ-hō′vah=nĭs′sī (*God my banner*). The altar built in honor of Joshua's victory, Ex. xvii. 15.

Jĕ-hō′vah=shā′lom (*God is peace*). Gideon's altar in Ophrah, Judg. vi. 24.

Jĕ-hŏz′a-băd (*God-given*). (1) A storekeeper and porter, 1 Chr. xxvi. 4. (2) Co-murderer of King Joash, 2 Kgs. xii. 21. (3) A Benjamite captain, 2 Chr. xvii. 18.

Jĕ-hŏz′a-dăk (*God justifies*). Captive father of Jeshua, the high priest, 1 Chr. vi. 14, 15; Ez. iii. 2.

Jē′hū (*who exists*). (1) Prophet of Judah, 1 Kgs. xvi. 1-7. (2) Tenth king of Israel, B. C. 884-856. He extirpated Ahab's line according to the prophecies, 1 Kgs. xix. 16, 17; 2 Kgs. ix., x. (3) A Judahite, 1 Chr. ii. 38. (4) A Simeonite, 1 Chr. iv. 35. (5) A Benjamite, 1 Chr. xii. 3.

Jĕ-hŭb′bah (*hidden*). An Asherite, 1 Chr. vii. 34.

Jē′hū-cal (*mighty*). Messenger to Jeremiah, Jer. xxxvii. 3.

Jē'hŭd (*famed*). Town of Dan, Josh. xix. 45.

Jĕ-hū'dī (*Jew*). A messenger, Jer. xxxvi. 14-23.

Jē''hū-dī'jah (*Jewess*). Mother of Jered, 1 Chr. iv. 18.

Jē'hŭsh (*collector*). Son of Eshek, 1 Chr. viii. 39.

Jĕ-ī'el (*God's treasure*). (1) Reubenite chief, 1 Chr. v. 7. (2) Levites, 1 Chr. xv. 18; 2 Chr. xx. 14; xxvi. 11; xxix. 13; xxxv. 9; Ez. viii. 13; x. 43.

Jĕ-kăb'zĕ-el (*gathered*). Kabzeel, in south Judah, Neh. xi. 25; Josh. xv. 21; 2 Sam. xxiii. 20.

Jĕk''a-mē'am (*who gathers*). A Levite, 1 Chr. xxiii. 19; xxiv. 23.

Jĕk''a-mī'ah (*gathered*). A Judahite, 1 Chr. ii. 41.

Jĕ-kū'thĭ-el (*piety*). A Judahite, 1 Chr. iv. 18.

Jĕ-mī'ma (*dove*). Job's daughter, Job xlii. 14.

Jĕm'nă-an, Judith ii. 28. [JABNEEL.]

Jĕ-mū'el (*God's day*). A Simeonite, Gen. xlvi. 10; Ex. vi. 15.

Jĕph'thă-ĕ, Heb. xi. 32. Greek form of Jephthah.

Jĕph'thah (*set free*). A judge of Israel, B. C. 1143-1137, Judg. xi., xii.

Jĕ-phŭn'neh (*favorably regarded*). (1) Father of Caleb the spy, Num. xiii. 6. (2) An Asherite, 1 Chr. vii. 38.

Jē'räh (*moon*). Son of Joktan, Gen. x. 26; 1 Chr. i. 20.

Jĕ-räh'me-el (*God's mercy*). (1) Son of Hezron, 1 Chr. ii. 9, 42. (2) A Levite, 1 Chr. xxiv. 29. (3) An official of Jehoiakim, Jer. xxxvi. 26.

Jĕ-räh'me-el-ītes''. Descendants of above (1), 1 Sam. xxvii. 10.

Jĕr'ĕ-cus, 1 Esdr. v. 22. [JERICHO.]

Jē'rĕd (*descent*). (1) Father of Enoch, 1 Chr. i. 2. (2) A Judahite, 1 Chr. iv. 18.

Jĕr'e-mäi (*mountaineer*). A layman, Ez. x. 33.

Jĕr''e-mī'ah (*exalted*). (1) Second of greater prophets. His prophecies cover reigns of Josiah, Jehoiakim, and Zedekiah, B. C. 628-586, and constitute the 24th O. T. book. Life one of vicissitude. Prophecies noted for boldness and beauty, and chiefly denunciative of Judah and her policy. Withdrew to

Egypt, where he probably died.   (2) Seven others in O. T., 2 Kgs. xxiii. 31; 1 Chr. xii. 4–13; v. 24; Neh. x. 2; xii. 1, 12, 34; Jer. xxxv. 3.

Jĕr″e-mī′as, Jĕr′e-my̆. Greek form of Jeremiah, Matt. ii. 17; xvi. 14; xxvii. 9.

Jĕr′e-mŏth (*heights*). Persons in 1 Chr. viii. 14; xxiii. 23; xxv. 22; Ez. x. 26, 27.

Jĕ-rī′ah (*founded*). A chief of the house of Hebron, 1 Chr. xxiii. 19; xxiv. 23.

Jĕr′ĭ-bāi (*defended*). One of David's guard, 1 Chr. xi. 46.

Jĕr′ĭ-chō (*fragrance*). Ancient city of Canaan, 5 miles W. of Jordan and 18 from Jerusalem. Strongly fortified, and conquered by Joshua. Fell to Benjamin, Deut. xxxiv. 3; Num. xxii. 1; Josh. vi.; xvi. 7; xviii. 21; 1 Kgs. xvi. 34; Matt. xx. 29; Mark x. 46.

Jĕ′rĭ-el (*founded*). An Issacharite, 1 Chr. vii. 2.

Jĕ-rī′jah, 1 Chr. xxvi. 31.   [JERIAH.]

Jĕr′ĭ-mŏth (*heights*). Persons in 1 Chr. vii. 8; xii. 5; xxiv. 30; xxv. 4, 22; xxvii. 19; 2 Chr. xi. 18; xxxi. 13.

Jĕ′rĭ-ŏth (*curtains*). Caleb's wife, 1 Chr. ii. 18.

Jĕr″o-bō′am (*many-peopled*). (1) First king of Israel after the division, B. C. 975–954. Plotter for Solomon's throne, 1 Kgs. xi. 26–40; fled to Egypt; returned on death of Solomon; set up kingdom of ten tribes; established idolatry; warred with Judah; defeated by Abijah; soon after died, 1 Kgs. xii.–xiv.; 2 Chr. x.–xiii.   (2) Jeroboam II., 13th king of Israel. Successor to Joash. Reigned B. C. 825–784. Idolatrous, but mighty and illustrious. Raised Israel to greatest splendor, 2 Kgs. xiv. 23–29; xv. 8, 9; Am. i.; ii. 6–16.

Jĕr′o-hăm (*cherished*). (1) Father of Elkanah, 1 Sam. i. 1; 1 Chr. vi. 27. (2) A Benjamite, 1 Chr. viii. 27; ix. 8. (3) Father of Adaiah, 1 Chr. ix. 12. (4) Others in 1 Chr. xii. 7; xxvii. 22; 2 Chr. xxiii. 1.

Jĕ-rŭb′ba-ăl (*contender with Baal*). Surname of Gideon, Judg. vi. 32.

Jĕ-rŭb′be-shĕth (*strife with the idol*). Another surname of Gideon, 2 Sam. xi. 21.

Jĕr′u-el (*founded*). Unknown battlefield, 2 Chr xx. 16.

Jĕ-ru̇'să-lĕm (*place of peace*). Capital of Hebrew monarchy and of kingdom of Judah, 24 miles west of Jordan and 37 east of the Mediterranean. "Salem," Ps. lxxvi. 2, and perhaps, Gen. xiv. 18. "Jebus," Judg. xix. 10, 11. "Jebus-salem," Jerusalem, Josh. x. 1. "City of David," Zion, 1 Kgs. viii. 1; 2 Kgs. xiv. 20. "City of Judah," 2 Chr. xxv. 28. "City of God," Ps. xlvi. 4. "City of the great King," Ps. xlviii. 2. "The holy city," Neh. xi. 1. Captured and rebuilt by David, and made his capital, 2 Sam. v. 6–13; 1 Chr. xi. 4–9. Destroyed by Nebuchadnezzar, B. C. 588. Rebuilt by returned captives. Captured by Alexander the Great, B. C. 332; by Antiochus, B. C. 203; by Rome, B. C. 63.

Jĕ-ru̇'să-lĕm, New. Metaphorically, the spiritual church, Rev. iii. 12; xxi.; compare Gal. iv. 26; Heb. xii. 22.

Jĕ-ru̇'shȧ (*possessed*). Daughter of Zadok, 2 Kgs. xv. 33. Jerushah, 2 Chr. xxvii. 1.

Jĕ-sā'iah (*saved*). (1) Grandson of Zerubbabel, 1 Chr. iii. 21. (2) A Benjamite, Neh. xi. 7.

Jĕ-shā'iah (*God's help*). (1) Head of 8th singing course, 1 Chr. xxv. 3, 15. (2) A Levite, 1 Chr. xxvi. 25. Isshiah, xxiv. 21. (3) Two who returned, Ez. viii. 7, 19.

Jĕsh'a̱-nah (*old*). Unidentified town, 2 Chr. xiii. 19.

Jĕ-shăr'e-lah (*right*). Head of 7th singing course, 1 Chr. xxv. 14. Asarelah, vs. 2.

Jĕ-shĕb'e-ăb (*father's seat*). Head of 14th priestly course, 1 Chr. xxiv. 13.

Jĕ'shĕr (*right*). Son of Caleb, 1 Chr. ii. 18.

Jĕsh'ĭ-mŏn (*waste*). Perhaps desert or plain, Num. xxi. 20; xxiii. 28.

Jĕ-shĭsh'a-ī (*ancient*). A Gadite, 1 Chr. v. 14.

Jĕsh''ŏ-ha-ī'ah (*bowed*). A Simeonite, 1 Chr. iv. 36.

Jĕsh'u-ȧ (*saviour*). (1) Joshua, Neh. viii. 17. (2) Priest of 9th course, Ez. ii. 36; Neh. vii. 39. Jeshuah, 1 Chr. xxiv. 11. (3) A Levite, 2 Chr. xxxi. 15. (4) High priest and returned captive, called also Joshua and Jesus, Zech. iii.; vi. 9–15. (5) Other Levites and returned captives, Ez. ii. 6, 40; viii. 33;

Neh. iii. 19; viii. 7. (6) A town peopled by returned captives, Neh. xi. 26.

Jĕsh'u-rŭn (*blessed*). Symbolically, Israel, Deut. xxxii. 15; xᵊxiii. 5, 26. Jesurun, Isa. xliv. 2.

Jĕ-sī'ah (*loaned*). (1) One of David's warriors, 1 Chr. xii. 6. (2) Jeshaiah, 1 Chr. xxiii. 20.

Jē-sĭm'i-el (*set up*). A Simeonite, 1 Chr. iv. 36.

Jĕs'sẹ (*strong*). Father of David, 1 Sam. xvi. 1–18.

Jĕs'su-ē, 1 Esdr. v. 26. [JESHUA.] Jesu, viii. 63.

Jes'u-ī (*level*). Founder of Jesuites, Num. xxvi. 44. Isui, Gen. xlvi. 17. Ishuai, 1 Chr. vii. 30.

Jē'ṣus (*saviour*). (1) Greek form of Joshua, Jeshua, contraction of Jehoshua, Num. xiii. 16; Acts vii. 45. (2) Compiler of the Apocryphal book. Ecclesiasticus. (3) Justus, Paul's friend, Col. iv. 11,

Jē'ṣŭs Chrīst. Jesus the Saviour; Christ, or Messiah, the anointed. Jesus the Christ. Name given to the long promised prophet and king, Matt. xi. 3; Acts xix. 4. Only begotten of God. Born of Mary at Bethlehem, B. C. 5; reared at Nazareth, baptized at age of 30, Luke iii. 23. Ministerial career, extending over Galilee, Judea, and Perea, began A. D. 27 and ended with the crucifixion, April 7, A. D. 30. Matthew, Mark, and Luke record his Galilean ministry; John his Judean ministry. The four gospels embrace Christ's biography.

Jē'thĕr (*who excels*). (1) Son of Gideon, Judg. viii. 20. (2) Father of Amasa, 1 Chr. ii. 17. (3) Others in 1 Chr. ii. 32; iv. 17; vii. 38.

Jē'thĕth (*nail*). A duke of Edom, Gen. xxxvi. 40.

Jĕth'lah (*high*). City of Dan, Josh. xix. 42.

Je'thrŏ (*his excellence*). Honorary title, Ex. iii. 1, of Reuel, Ex. ii. 18, or Raguel, Num. x. 29, the father-in-law of Moses, Ex. xviii.

Jē'tŭr, Gen. xxv. 15; 1 Chr. i. 31. [ITURÆA.]

Jĕ-ū'el (*treasured*). A Judahite, 1 Chr. ix. 6.

Jē'ŭsh (*assembler*). (1) Son of Esau, Gen. xxxvi. 5, 14, 18. (2) A Benjamite, 1 Chr. vii. 10. (3) A Levite, 1 Chr. xxiii. 10, 11. (4) Son of Rehoboam, 2 Chr. xi. 18, 19.

Jē'ŭz (*assembler*). A Benjamite, 1 Chr. viii. 10.

Jew. Contraction of Judah. Man of Judea, 2 Kgs. xvi. 6; xxv. 25. After captivity, Hebrews in general, Ez. iv. 12; Dan. iii. 8-12. Antithesis of Christian in N. T., John; Rom. i. 16.

Jew'el (*joy*). Ornament, Gen. xxiv. 22; Num. xxxi. 50.

Jew'ess. Hebrew woman, Acts xvi. 1.

Jew'ry. Judah, Judea, Jewish dynasty, Dan. v. 13.

Jĕz''a-nī'ah (*heard*). A Jewish captive, Jer. xl. 7-12. Jaazaniah, 2 Kgs. xxv. 23.

Jĕz'e-bĕl (*chaste*). Idolatrous wife of Ahab, 1 Kgs. xvi. 29-33; xvii.-xxi.; 2 Kgs. ix. 30-37.

Jĕ-zē'lus, 1 Esdr. viii. 32-35. [JAHAZIEL.]

Jē'zer (*help*). A Naphtalite, Gen. xlvi. 24; founder of Jezerites, Num. xxvi. 49.

Jĕ-zī'ah (*sprinkled*). One with a foreign wife, Ez. x. 25.

Jē'zi-el (*sprinkled*). A Benjamite, 1 Chr. xii. 3.

Jĕz-lī'ah (*preserved*). A Benjamite, 1 Chr. viii. 18.

Jĕz'o-ar (*white*). A Judahite, 1 Chr. iv. 7.

Jĕz''ra-hī'ah (*brought forth*). A Levite singer, Neh. xii. 42.

Jĕz're-el (*seed of God*). (1) A Judahite, 1 Chr. iv. 3. (2) A city in plain of Jezreel. Ahab's royal residence, Josh. xix. 18; 1 Kgs. xxi. 1; 2 Kgs. ix. 30. (3) Valley of, stretches from Jezreel to Jordan. Greek form, Esdraelon. (4) Town of Judah, Josh. xv. 56; 1 Sam. xxvii. 3. (5) Son of Hosea, Hos. i. 4.

Jĭb'sam (*pleasant*). An Issacharite, 1 Chr. vii. 2.

Jĭd'laph (*weeping*). Son of Nahor, Gen. xxii. 22.

Jĭm'nà (*prosperity*). Son of Asher and founder of Jimnites, Num. xxvi. 44. Jimnah, Gen. xlvi. 17. Imnah, 1 Chr. vii. 30.

Jĭph'tah. Lowland city of Judah, Josh. xv. 43.

Jĭph'thah=el (*God opens*). Valley between Zebulun and Asher, Josh. xix. 14, 27.

Jō'ăb (*God his father*). (1) General-in-chief of David's army, 2 Sam. ii. 18-32; iii., xviii., xx., xxiv.; 1 Kgs. ii. (2) Son of Seraiah, 1 Chr. iv. 14. (3) One who returned, Ez. ii. 6.

Jō'a-chaz, 1 Esdr. i. 34. [JEHOAHAZ.]

Jō'a-chĭm, Bar. i. 3. [JEHOIAKIM.]

Jō″a-dā′nus. Son of Jeshua, 1 Esdr. ix. 19.

Jō′ah (*God's brother*). (1) Hezekiah's recorder, 2 Kgs. xviii. 18. (2) Josiah's recorder, 2 Chr. xxxiv. 8. (3) Levites, 1 Chr. vi. 21; xxvi. 4; 2 Chr. xxix. 12.

Jō′a-hăz (*held of God*). Father of Joah, 2 Chr. xxxiv. 8.

Jŏ-ăn′nà (*God-given*). (1) An ancestor of Christ, Luke iii. 27. (2) Wife of Chusa, Luke viii. 3; xxiv. 10.

Jō′ash (*God-given*), 2 Kgs. xiii. 1. Jehoash, 2 Kgs. xii. 1. (1) Son of Ahaziah and his successor on throne of Judah, B. c. 878–839. Cruel and idolatrous. Murdered by his servants, 2 Kgs. xi., xii.; 2 Chr. xxiv. (2) Son and successor of Jehoahaz on throne of Israel, B. c. 840–825. Successful warrior, 2 Kgs. xiii. 9–25; xiv. 1–16; 2 Chr. xxv. 17–25. (3) Father of Gideon, Judg. vi. 11–31. (4) Son of Ahab, 2 Chr. xviii. 25. (5) A Judahite, 1 Chr. iv. 22. (6) One of David's heroes, 1 Chr. xii. 3. (7) Son of Becher, 1 Chr. vii. 8. (8) Officer of David, 1 Chr. xxvii. 28.

Jō′a-thăm, Matt. i. 9. [JOTHAM.]

Jŏb (*persecuted*). (1) The pious and wealthy patriarch of Uz, whose poem constitutes the 18th O. T. book, and first of the poetical. It is a dramatic narrative of his life of vicissitude, the gist being, whether goodness can exist irrespective of reward. Poetry noted for its sublimity, pathos, and beauty. Authorship disputed. Oldest of sacred writings. (2) Son of Issachar, Gen. xlvi. 13. Jashub, 1 Chr. vii. 1.

Jō′băb (*desert*). (1) Son of Joktan, Gen. x. 29. (2) King of Edom, Gen. xxxvi. 33. (3) King of Madon, Josh. xi. 1. (4) Two Benjamites, 1 Chr. viii. 9, 18.

Jŏch′e-bed (*glorified*). Mother of Moses, Ex. vi. 20; Num. xxvi. 59.

Jō′dà, 1 Esdr. v. 58. [JUDAH.]

Jō′ed (*witnessed*). A Benjamite, Neh. xi. 7.

Jō′el (*Jehovah his God*). (1) Son of Pethuel and second of minor prophets. Probably of Judah and contemporary with Uzziah, B. c. 810–758. His book, 29th of O. T., depicts calamities, rises into exhortation, and foreshadows the Messiah. (2) Son of Samuel, 1 Sam. viii. 2. (3) Others in 1 Chr. iv. 35; **v.**

4, 8, 12; vi. 36; vii. 3; xi. 38; xv. 7; xxiii. 8; xxvii. 20; 2 Chr. xxix. 12; Ez. x. 43; Neh. xi. 9.

Jŏ-ē'lah (*helped*). A Benjamite chief, 1 Chr. xii. 7.

Jŏ-ē'zĕr (*aided*). A Benjamite, 1 Chr. xii. 6.

Jŏg'be-hah (*high*). City of Gad, E. of Jordan, Num. xxxii. 35.

Jŏg'lī (*exiled*). A prince of Dan, Num. xxxiv. 22.

Jō'hå (*given life*). (1) A Benjamite, 1 Chr. viii. 16. (2) One of David's guard, 1 Chr. xi. 45.

Jŏ-hā'nan (*God's mercy*). (1) A Judahite captain who escaped captivity, 2 Kgs. xxv. 23, and carried Jeremiah and other Jews into Egypt, Jer. xl.–xliii. (2) Others in 1 Chr. iii. 15, 24; vi. 9, 10; xii. 4, 12; 2 Chr. xxviii. 12; Ez. viii. 12; x. 6; Neh. vi. 18.

Jŏhn (*God's gift*). Johanan, contraction of Jehohanan. (1) Kinsman of the high priest, Acts iv. 6. (2) Hebrew name of Mark, Acts xii. 25; xiii. 5; xv. 37. (3) John the Baptist, son of Zacharias. Birth foretold, Luke i. Born about six months before Christ. Retired to wilderness. Emerged to preach and baptize. Baptized Jesus, Matt. iii. Imprisoned by Herod, Luke iii. 1–22. Beheaded, Matt. xiv. 1–12. (4) John, Apostle and Evangelist; son of Zebedee, Matt. iv. 21; a fisherman of Galilee, Luke v. 1–10; a favorite apostle, noted for zeal and firmness, John xiii. 23; xix. 26; xx. 2; xxi. 7. He remained at Jerusalem till about A. D. 65, when he went to Ephesus. Banished to Patmos, and released A. D. 96. His writings, doubtless done at Ephesus, are the fourth Gospel, giving Christ's ministry in Judea; his three epistles, and Revelation. (5) A frequent name among the Maccabees, 1 Macc.

Joi'a-då (*favored*). A high priest, Neh. xii. 10, 11, 22; xiii. 28.

Joi'a-kĭm (*exalted*). A high priest, Neh. xii. 10.

Joi'a-rĭb (*defended*). Two who returned, Ez. viii. 16; Neh. xii. 6, 19.

Jŏk'de-ăm (*peopled*). City of Judah, Josh. xv. 56.

Jō'kĭm (*exalted*) A Judahite, 1 Chr. iv 22.

Jŏk'me-ăm (*gathered*). Levitical city in Ephraim, 1 Chr. vi. 68.

Jŏk′ne̯-ăm (*gathered*). Levitical city in Zebulun, Josh. xxi. 34.

Jŏk′shan (*fowler*). Son of Abraham, Gen. xxv. 2, 3; 1 Chr. i. 32.

Jŏk′tan (*small*). Son of Eber and progenitor of Joktanite Arabs, Gen. x. 25; 1 Chr. i. 19.

Jŏk′the̯-el (*subdued*). (1) City in Judah, Josh. xv. 38. (2) An Edomite stronghold, 2 Kgs. xiv. 7.

Jō′nȧ (*dove*). Father of Apostle Peter, Matt. xvi. 17; John i. 42.

Jŏn′a̯-dăb (*God-impelled*). (1) David's subtle nephew, 2 Sam. xiii. 3, 32–35. (2) Jer. xxxv. 6–19, Jehonadab.

Jō′nah (*dove*). Son of Amittai. Commissioned to denounce Nineveh. His book, 32d of O. T. and 5th of minor prophets, narrates his refusal, escape from drowning, final acceptance and successful ministry. Its lesson is God's providence over all nations.

Jō′nan (*grace*). Ancestor of Christ, Luke iii. 30.

Jō′nas. Greek form of Jonah, Matt. xii. 39–41; Luke xi. 30–32.

Jŏn′a̯-than (*God-given*). (1) A Levite, Judg. xvii. 7–13; xviii. (2) Eldest son of Saul, and friend of David, 1 Sam. xiii. 2, 3; xviii. 1-4; xix. 1-7; xx. Fell in battle of Gilboa. David's lament, 2 Sam. i. 17-27. (3) Others in 2 Sam. xv. 27, 36; xxi. 20, 21; xxiii. 32; 1 Chr. ii. 32, 33; xxvii. 32; Ez. viii. 6; x. 15; Neh. xii. 11, 14, 35; Jer. xxxvii. 15, 20; xl. 8.

Jŏn′a̯-thas, Tob. v. 13. [JONATHAN.]

Jō′nath=ē″lem=re̯-chō′kim (*a dumb dove of distant places*). Title to, and probably melody of, Ps. lvi.

Jŏp′pȧ (*beauty*). Mediterranean seaport of Jerusalem; now Jaffa, 1 Kgs. v. 9; 2 Chr. ii. 16; Ez. iii. 7.

Jŏp′pē. For Joppa in Apoc.

Jō′rah (*rain*). His family returned, Ez. ii. 18.

Jō′ra̯-ī (*taught of God*). A Gadite chief, 1 Chr. v. 13.

Jō′ram (*exalted*). (1) Short form of Jehoram, king of Israel, 2 Kgs. viii. 16, etc.; and of Jehoram, king of Judah, 2 Kgs. viii. 21, etc.; Matt. i. 8. (2) Son of Toi, 2 Sam. viii. 10. (3) A Levite, 1 Chr. xxvi. 25.

Jôr'dan (*descender*). Chief river of Palestine, rising in the Anti-Libanus range, flowing southward, enlarging into Sea of Galilee, emptying into Dead Sea. A swift, narrow, yet fordable stream, with an entire course of about 200 miles, Gen. xiii. 10; Josh. ii. 7; Judg. iii. 28; 2 Sam. x. 17; Matt. iii. 13.

Jō'rim (*exalted*). An ancestor of Christ, Luke iii. 29.

Jŏr'ko-ăm. A person or place, 1 Chr. ii. 44.

Jŏs'a-băd (*dowered*). (1) One of David's warriors, 1 Chr. xii. 4. (2) Persons in 1 Esdr.

Jŏs'a-phăt, Matt. i. 8. [JEHOSHAPHAT.]

Jō'se. An ancestor of Christ, Luke iii. 29.

Jŏs'e-děch, Hag. i. 1. [JEHOZADAK.]

Jō'ṣeph (*increase*). (1) Son of Jacob and Rachel, Gen. xxxvii. 3; sold into Egypt; promoted to high office by the Pharoah; rescued his family from famine; settled them in Goshen; died at advanced age; bones carried back to Shechem, Gen. xxxvii.–l. (2) An Issacharite, Num. xiii. 7. (3) Two who returned, Ez. x. 42; Neh. xii. 14. (4) Three of Christ's ancestors, Luke iii. 24, 26, 30. (5) Husband of Mary, and a carpenter at Nazareth, Matt. i. 19; xiii. 55; Luke iii. 23; John i. 45. (6) Of Arimathea, a member of the Sanhedrim, who acknowledged Christ, Matt. xxvii. 57–59; Mark xv. 43; Luke xxiii. 51. (7) The apostle Barsabas, substituted for Judas, Acts i. 23. (8) Frequent name in Apoc.

Jō'ṣeṣ (*helped*). (1) One of Christ's brethren, Matt. xiii. 55; xxvii. 56; Mark vi. 3; xv. 40, 47. (2) Barnabas, Acts iv. 36.

Jō'shah (*dwelling*). A Simeonite chief, 1 Chr. iv. 34.

Jŏsh'a-phăt (*judged*). One of David's guard, 1 Chr. xi. 43.

Jŏsh''a-vī'ah (*dwelling*). One of David's guard, 1 Chr. xi. 46.

Jŏsh-běk'a-shah (*hard seat*). Head of 17th musical course, 1 Chr. xxv. 4, 24.

Jŏsh'u-à (*saviour*). (1) Jehoshuah, 1 Chr. vii. 27. Oshea, Num. xiii. 8. Jesus, Acts vii. 45; Heb. iv. 8. Son of Nun, of tribe of Ephraim. The great warrior of the Israelites during the desert wanderings and conquest and apportionment of Canaan, Ex. xvii. 9–14;

1 Chr. vii. 27; Num. xiii. 8, 16; xxvii. 18–23. His book, 6th of O. T., contains the history of his conquests and governorship, B. C. 1451–1426. (2) A Bethshemite, 1 Sam. vi. 14. (3) A governor of Jerusalem, 2 Kgs. xxiii. 8. (4) A high priest, Hag. i. 1, 14.

Jŏ-sī′ah (*God-healed*). (1) Son and successor of Amon on throne of Judah, B. C. 641–610. He abolished idolatry, propagated the newly discovered law, aided Assyria against Egypt, and fell in the celebrated battle of Esdraelon, 2 Kgs. xxii.–xxiii. 1–30; 2 Chr. xxxiv.–xxxv. (2) Son of Zephaniah, Zech. vi. 10.

Jŏ-sī′as. (1) Greek form of Josiah, 1 Esdr. i. 1; Matt. i. 10, 11. (2) 1 Esdr. viii. 33. [JESHAIAH.]

Jŏs′′ĭ-bī′ah (*dwelling*). A chief of Simeon, 1 Chr. iv. 35.

Jŏs′′ĭ-phī′ah (*increase*). His family returned, Ez. viii. 10.

Jŏt. The Greek i, iota. A little thing, Matt. v. 18.

Jŏt′bah (*goodness*). Residence of Haruz, 2 Kgs. xxi. 19.

Jŏt′băth (*goodness*). Jotbathah, Num. xxxiii. 33. An Israelite encampment, Deut. x. 7.

Jō′tham (*God is upright*). (1) Youngest son of Gideon and author of the bramble fable, Judg. ix. 5–21. (2) Son and successor of Uzziah, or Azariah, on throne of Judah, B. C. 758–741. Reign prosperous, 2 Kgs. xv. 5, 6, 32–36; 2 Chr. xxvii. (3) A Judahite, 1 Chr. ii. 47.

Joûr′ney (*daily*). A day's journey, indefinite. Sabbath day's journey, 2000 paces, or ¾ of a mile from the walls of a city, Deut. i. 2; Acts i. 12.

Jŏz′a-băd (*God-given*). (1) Two Manassite chiefs, 1 Chr. xii. 20. (2) Five Levites, 2 Chr. xxxi. 13; xxxv. 9; Ez. viii. 33; x. 22; Neh. viii. 7; xi. 16.

Jŏz′a-chär (*remembered*). Zabad, 2 Chr. xxiv. 26. One of Joash's murderers, 2 Kgs. xii. 21.

Jŏz′a-dăk, Ez. iii. 2, 8, etc.; Neh. xii. 26. [JEHOZADAK.]

Jū′băl (*music*). Son of Lamech, and inventor of harp and organ, Gen. iv. 19–21.

Jū′bĭ-lēe (*blast of trumpets*). Year of, celebrated every fiftieth year; ushered in by blowing of trumpets; land rested; alienated lands reverted; slaves freed; outer circle of seventh or sabbatical system, year, month, and day, Lev. xxv. 8–55.

Jū′cal, Jer. xxxviii. 1. [JEHUCAL.]

Jū′dä (*praised*). (1) Ancestors of Christ, Luke iii. 26, 30. (2) One of Christ's brethren, Mark vi. 3. (3) The patriarch Judah, Luke iii. 33. (4) The tribe of Judah, Heb. vii. 14; Rev. v. 5.

Jū-dæ′à, Jū-dē′à (*from Judah*). Vaguely, Joshua's conquest, Matt. xix. 1; Mark x. 1, or Canaanite land. Limitedly, the part occupied by returned captives; the "Jewry" of Dan. v. 13; the "province" of Ez. v. 8; Neh. xi. 3. "Land of Judea" in Apoc. A Roman province jointly with Syria, with a procurator, after A. D. 6.

Jū′dah (*praise*). (1) Fourth son of Jacob, Gen. xxix. 35; xxxvii. 26–28; xliii. 3–10; xliv. 14–34. His tribe the largest, Num. i. 26, 27. Allotted the southern section of Canaan, Josh. xv. 1–63. (2) Kingdom of, formed on disruption of Solomon's empire, out of Judah, Benjamin, Simeon, and part of Dan, with Jerusalem as capital, B. C. 975. Had 19 kings, and lasted for 389 years, till reduced by Nebuchadnezzar, B. C. 586. Outlived its rival, Israel, some 135 years. (3) City of Jerusalem, 2 Chr. xxv. 28. (4) A town in Naphtali, Josh. xix. 34. (5) Persons in Ez. iii. 9; x. 23; Neh. xi. 9.

Jū′das. Greek form of Judah. (1) Judah, Matt. i. 2, 3. (2) Iscariot, or of Kerioth. Betrayer of Christ, Matt. x. 4; Mark iii. 19; Luke vi. 16; John vi. 71; xii. 6; xiii. 29. (3) Man of Damascus, Acts ix. 11. (4) Barsabas, chief among the brethren, and prophet, Acts xv. 22, 32. (5) A Galilean apostate, Acts v. 37. (6) Frequent name in Apoc.

Jūde, Jude i. 1. Judas, brother of James the Less, Luke vi. 16; John xiv. 22; Acts i. 13; Matt. xiii. 55. Thaddæus, Lebbæus, Matt. x. 3; Mark iii. 18. An Apostle and author of the epistle which bears his name, 26th N. T. book. Written about A. D. 65. Place not known.

Jŭdg′es. Governors of Israel between Joshua and the kings. They were called of God, elective or usurpative. Qualification, martial or moral prowess. Rule arbitrary. Fifteen are recorded. Period, B. C. 1400 – 1091, about 310 years. Book of Judges, 7th of O. T., probably compiled by Samuel. Its history is that of a tumultuous period, completing Joshua's conquests and leading to legitimate kingly rule.

Jŭdg′mĕnt Hạll. Pilate's residence in Jerusalem, John xviii. 28, 33 ; xix. 9. Prætorium or court, Acts xxiii. 35.

Jū′dith (*praised, Jewess*). (1) Wife of Esau, Gen. xxvi. 34. (2) Heroine of the 4th Apocryphal book.

Jū′el, Apoc. [JOEL.]

Jū′lĭà (*feminine of Julius*). A Christian woman at Rome, Rom. xvi. 15.

Jū′lĭus (*soft-haired*). A Roman centurion, Acts xxvii. 1–3, 43.

Jū′nĭà (*youth*). Roman friend of Paul, Rom. xvi. 7.

Jū′nĭ-pĕr (*young producer*). Not the evergreen, but the desert broom-shrub, 1 Kgs. xix. 4, 5 ; Job xxx. 4 ; Ps. cxx. 4.

Jū′pĭ-tẽr (*father Jove*). Supreme god of Greeks and Romans, Acts xiv. 12 ; xix. 35.

Jū′shăb=hē′sĕd (*requited love*). Son of Zerubbabel, 1 Chr. iii. 20.

Jŭs″tĭ-fĭ-cā′tion. Pardon and acceptance of the just through faith, Rom. iii. 20–31 ; iv. 25.

Jŭs′tus (*just*). (1) Surname of Joseph, or Barsabas, Acts i. 23. (2) A Corinthian convert, Acts xviii. 7. (3) Surname of Jesus, a friend of Paul, Col. iv. 11.

Jŭt′tah (*extended*). A Levitical city in mountains of Judah ; now Yutta, Josh. xv. 55 ; xxi. 16.

K

Kăb′ze-el (*gathered*). A city of Judah, Josh. xv. 21. Jekabzeel, Neh. xi. 25.

Kā′desh (*holy*). Halting place of Israelites near borders of Canaan, and scene of Miriam's death, Num. xiii. 26 ; xx. 1. Kadesh-barnea, Deut. ii. 14 ; Josh. xv. 3. Enmishpat, Gen. xiv. 7.

Kăd′mĭ-el (*before God*). One who returned, Ez. iii. 9 ; Neh. ix. 4.

Kăd′mŏn-ītes (*eastern*). Ancient Canaanites, Gen. xv. 19.

Kăl′la-ī (*runner*). A priest, Neh. xii. 20.

Kā′nah (*reedy*). (1) A boundary of Asher, Josh. xix. 28. (2) Boundary stream between Ephraim and Manasseh, Josh. xvi. 8; xvii. 9.

Kå-rē′ah (*bald*). Father of Johanan, Jer. xl. 8–16.

Kär′ka-å (*floor*). A southern boundary of Judah, Josh. xv. 3.

Kär′kôr (*foundation*). Scene of Gideon's victory, Judg. viii. 10.

Kär′tah (*city*). Levitical city in Zebulun, Josh. xxi. 34.

Kär′tan, Josh. xxi. 32. [KIRJATHAIM.]

Kăt′tath (*small*). Town of Zebulun, Josh. xix. 15.

Kē′där (*dark*). Son of Ishmael and founder of Arabic tribe, Gen. xxv. 13; Isa. xxi. 13–17; Ezek. xxvii. 21.

Ked′e-mah (*eastward*). Son of Ishmael, Gen. xxv. 15; 1 Chr. i. 31.

Kĕd′e-mŏth (*eastern*). Levitical town of Reuben, Josh. xiii. 18; xxi. 37; 1 Chr. vi. 79.

Kē′desh (*sacred*). (1) Josh. xv. 23. [KADESH.] (2) Levitical city in Issachar, Josh. xii. 22; 1 Chr. vi. 72. (3) City of refuge in Naphtali, Josh. xix. 37; Judg. iv. 6; 2 Kgs. xv. 29. Now Kades.

Kē′dron. [KIDRON.]

Kĕ-hĕl′a-thah (*assembly*). A desert encampment, Num. xxxiii. 22, 23.

Kēi′lah (*fortress*). (1) Lowland town of Judah, Josh. xv. 44; 1 Sam. xxiii. 1–13; Neh. iii. 17, 18. (2) Person or place, 1 Chr. iv. 19.

Kĕ-lā′jah, Ez. x. 23. [KELITA.]

Kĕl′ī-tå (*dwarf*). Assistant of Ezra, Neh. viii. 7.

Kĕ-mū′el (*helper*). (1) Son of Nahor, Gen. xxii. 21. (2) A prince of Ephraim, Num. xxxiv. 24. (3) A Levite, 1 Chr. xxvii. 17.

Kē′nan, 1 Chr. i. 2. [CAINAN.]

Kē′nath (*possession*). A city or section of Gilead, Num. xxxii. 42.

Kē′năz (*hunting*). (1) A duke of Edom, Gen. xxxvi. 15, and founder of Kenezites, Josh. xiv. 14.

(2) Father of Othniel, Josh. xv. 17. (3) Grandson of Caleb, 1 Chr. iv. 15.

Kĕn'ez-īte (*hunter*). Kenizzite, Gen. xv. 19. An ancient Edomite tribe, Num. xxxii. 12; Josh. xiv. 6, 14.

Kĕn'ītes (*smiths*). A Midianite tribe allied to Israelites, Gen. xv. 19; Num. xxiv. 21, 22; Judg. iv. 11.

Kĕr'ĕn=hăp'puch (*horn of beauty*). Third daughter of Job, Job xlii. 14.

Kē'rī-ŏth (*cities*). (1) A town of Judah, Josh. xv. 25. (2) A city of Moab, Jer. xlviii. 24.

Kē'ros (*crooked*). His children returned, Ez. ii. 44.

Kĕt'tle (*deep vessel*). Used for cooking and sacrifices, 1 Sam. ii. 14. Basket, Jer. xxiv. 2; caldron, 2 Chr. xxxv. 13; pot, Job xli. 20.

Kē̆-tū'rah (*incense*). A wife of Abraham, Gen. xxv. 1; 1 Chr. i. 32.

Kē̆-zī'à (*cassia*). Job's second daughter, Job xlii. 14.

Kē'ziz (*end*). A town of Benjamin, Josh. xviii. 21.

Kĭb'roth=hăt-tā'a̱-vah (*graves of lust*). A desert encampment of the Israelites, Num. xi. 31–35.

Kĭb'za̱-im (*heaps*). Levitical city in Ephraim, Josh. xxi. 22. Jokmeam, 1 Chr. vi 68.

Kĭd. Young goat. An offering, Num. vii. 12–82. A favorite meat, Gen. xxxviii. 17; 1 Sam. xvi. 20.

Kĭd'ron (*turbid*). The brook or ravine between Jerusalem and Olivet, 2 Sam. xv. 23; 2 Kgs. xxiii. 6. Cedron, John xviii. 1.

Kī'nah (*dirge*). City of south Judah, Josh. xv. 22.

Kīne. Plural of cow, Gen. xli. 17–21.

King (*tribe*). Title of Hebrew rulers from Saul to Zedekiah, B. C. 1095–588. Other rulers, Gen. xxxvi. 31; Ex. iii. 19; Num. xxxi. 8. Supreme ruler, 1 Tim. i. 17; vi. 15.

Kings. Eleventh and twelfth O. T. books. Originally one. Compilation credited to Ezra or Jeremiah. 1 Kings gives history of Hebrew kingdoms from Solomon, B. C. 1015, to Jehoshaphat, B. C. 890. 2 Kings completes the history, B. C. 890–588.

Kĭr (*fortress*). An unlocated eastern country, 2 Kgs. xvi. 9; Am. ix. 7.

Kĭr=hăr′a-sĕth (*brick fortress*). A stronghold of Moab, 2 Kgs. iii. 25. Kirhareseth, Isa. xvi. 7. Kirharesh, Isa. xvi. 11. Kirheres, Jer. xlviii. 31, 36. Kir of Moab, Isa. xv. 1.

Kĭr″ĭ-a-thā′ĭm, Jer. xlviii. 1, 23; Ezek. xxv. 9. [KIRJATHAIM.]

Kĭr″ĭ-ạth-ĭ-ā′rĭ-us, 1 Esdr. v. 19. [KIRJATH-JEARIM.]

Kĭr′ĭ-ŏth, Am. ii. 2. [KERIOTH.]

Kĭr′jath (*city*). City in Benjamin, Josh. xviii. 28.

Kĭr″jath-ā′im (*double city*). (1) A Moabite town, Num. xxxii. 37. (2) Levitical town in Naphtali, Josh. xiii. 19; 1 Chr. vi. 76.

Kĭr′jath=ăr′bà (*city of Arba*). Old name of Hebron, Gen. xxiii. 2; Josh. xiv. 15.

Kĭr′jath=ā′rim, Ez. ii. 25. [KIRJATH-JEARIM.]

Kĭr′jath=bā′al, Josh. xv. 60; xviii. 14. [KIRJATH-JEARIM.]

Kĭr′jath=hū′zoth (*city of streets*). City in Moab, Num. xxii. 39.

Kĭr′jath=jē′a-rĭm (*city of woods*). A Gibeonite city which fell to Judah, Josh. ix. 17; Judg. xviii. 12. Baalah, Josh. xv. 9. Kirjath-baal, xviii. 14.

Kĭr′jath=san′nah (*palm city*). [DEBIR.]

Kĭr′jath=sē′phĕr (*city of books*). [DEBIR.]

Kir of Mō′ab. [KIR-HARASETH.]

Kĭsh (*bow*). (1) Father of Saul, 1 Sam. x. 21. (2) A Benjamite, 1 Chr. viii. 30. (3) A Levite, 1 Chr. xxiii. 21. (4) A Levite, 2 Chr. xxix. 12. (5) Ancestor of Mordecai, Esth. ii. 5.

Kĭsh′ī (*bow*). A Levite, 1 Chr. vi. 44.

Kĭsh′ĭ-ŏn (*hardness*). Levitical city in Issachar, Josh. xix. 20.

Kī′shŏn (*crooked*). (1) Josh. xxi. 28. [KISHION.] (2) The brook or wady which drains the valley of Esdraelon, Judg. iv. 7–13; v. 21; 1 Kgs. xviii. 40. Kison, Ps. lxxxiii. 9.

Kī′son, Ps. lxxxiii. 9. [KISHON.]

Kĭss. Form of salutation, Gen. xxix. 13; token of allegiance, 1 Sam. x. 1; pledge of Christian brotherhood, Rom. xvi. 16; 1 Pet. v. 14.

Kīte (*quick of wing*). An unclean bird of the hawk species, Lev. xi. 14; Deut. xiv. 13. Vulture, Job xxviii. 7.

Kĭth'lish (*wall*). Lowland town in Judah, Josh. xv. 40.

Kĭt'rŏn (*knotty*). Town in Zebulun, Judg. i. 30.

Kĭt'tim, Gen. x. 4; 1 Chr. i. 7. [CHITTIM.]

Knĕad'ing=troughs. Were bowls, or leather surfaces, Gen. xviii. 6; Ex. xii. 34.

Knīfe (*waster*). Primitively of stone or bone; later of metal. Little used at meals. For killing and cutting, Lev. viii. 20; sharpening pens, Jer. xxxvi. 23; pruning, Isa. xviii. 5; lancing, 1 Kgs. xviii. 28.

Knŏp (*knob*). Ornamental knobs, or reliefs, Ex. xxv. 31–36; 1 Kgs. vi. 18.

Kō'à (*male camel*). An eastern prince, Ezek. xxiii. 23.

Kō'hath (*assembly*). Second son of Levi, and head of the house of Kohathite Levites, Gen. xlvi. 11; Ex. vi. 16, 18; Num. iii. 27; xxvi. 57; Josh. xxi. 4–42.

Kŏl''a-ī'ah (*God's voice*). (1) A Benjamite, Neh. xi. 7. (2) Father of the false prophet Ahab, Jer. xxix. 21.

Kō'rah (*baldness*). (1) Dukes of Edom, Gen. xxxvi. 5–18. (2) Son of Hebron, 1 Chr. ii. 43. (3) Leader of the rebellion against Moses, Num. xvi.; xxvi. 9–11.

Kō'rah-ītes. Descendants of Korah, 1 Chr. ix. 19. Korhites, 2 Chr. xx. 19. Korathites, Num. xxvi. 58.

Kō'rḛ (*quail*). (1) A Korahite, 1 Chr. ix. 19. (2) Korhites, 1 Chr. xxvi. 1–19. (3) A Levite, 2 Chr. xxxi. 14.

Kŏz (*thorn*). (1) A Judahite, 1 Chr. iv. 8. [COZ.] (2) A priest, 1 Chr. xxiv. 10. [HAKKOZ.] (3) Returned captives, Ez. ii. 61; Neh. iii. 4, 21.

Kŭsh-ā'jah, 1 Chr. xv. 17. [KISHI.]

L

Lā′a-dah (*order*). A Judahite, 1 Chr. iv. 21.

Lā′a-dăn (*ordered*). (1) An Ephraimite, 1 Chr. vii. 26. (2) Son of Gershon, 1 Chr. xxiii. 7–9; xxvi. 21. Libni, elsewhere.

Lā′ban (*white*). (1) Father-in-law of Jacob, Gen. xxiv.-xxx. (2) A landmark, Deut. i. 1.

Lăb′a-nà, 1 Esdr. v. 29. [LEBANA.]

Lăç″e-dē-mō′nĭ-anṣ. Inhabitants of Lacedemon. Spartans, 1 Macc. xii. 2–21.

Lā′chish (*impregnable*). An Amorite city in southern Judah, Josh. x.; 2 Kgs. xviii. 17; xix. 8; 2 Chr. xi. 9; Neh. xi. 30.

Lā̊-cū′nus. A returned captive, 1 Esdr. ix. 31.

Lā′dan, 1 Esdr. v. 37. [DELAIAH.]

Lā′el (*of God*). A Gershonite, Num. iii. 24.

Lā′hăd (*oppression*). A Judahite, 1 Chr. iv. 2.

Lā̊-hāi′=roi (*well of the living God*). Well of Hagar's relief, Gen. xxiv. 62; xxv. 11.

Lăh′mam (*bread*). Lowland town of Judah, Josh. xv. 40.

Lăh′mī (*warrior*). Brother of Goliath, 1 Chr. xx. 5.

Lā′ish (*lion*). (1) A northern Danite city, Judg. xviii. 7–29; Isa. x. 30. (2) Father of Phaltiel, 1 Sam. xxv. 44; 2 Sam. iii. 15. Leshem, Josh. xix. 47.

Lā′kŭm (*fortress*). A border of Naphtali, Josh. xix. 33.

Lămb. Young of sheep or goat. Favorite sacrifices, Ex. xxix. 38–41; Num. xxviii. 9–29.

Lā′mech (*strong*). (1) Father of Noah, Gen. v. 28–32. (2) Father of Jubal, inventor of the harp and organ, Gen. iv. 18–26.

Lăm″ĕn-tā′tionṣ (*weepings*). Twenty-fifth O. T. book. An elegiac poem by Jeremiah, on the destruction of Jerusalem.

Lămp (*shine*). The temple candlestick, Ex. xxv. 31–40; 1 Kgs. vii. 49. Torches, Judg. vii. 16. Oriental lamps of many shapes and ornamental. Fed with oil, tallow, wax, etc., Matt. xxv. 1.

Lăn'çet (*little lance*). Light spear, 1 Kgs. xviii. 28.

Lănd'märks, Were trees, stones, towns, mountains, streams, etc. Removal forbidden, Deut. xix. 14; Prov. xxii. 28.

Lăn'guāge (*tongue*). Originally one, Gen. xi. 1. Diversified at Babel, Gen. xi. 7-9.

Lăn'tĕrn (*shining*). Covered candle or lamp, John xviii. 3.

Lă-ŏd''ĭ-çē'ȧ (*just people*). Ancient Diospolis; modern Eski-hissar. A city of Phrygia, and seat of an early Christian church, Col. ii. 1; iv. 15; Rev. i. 11; iii. 14-22.

Lăp'ĭ-dŏth (*lamps*). Husband of Deborah, Judg. iv. 4.

Lăp'wĭng. An unclean bird, thought to be the beautiful migratory hoopoe, Lev. xi. 19.

Lȧ-sē'ȧ. City in Crete, Acts xxvii. 8.

Lā'shȧ (*cleft*). A Canaanite border, Gen. x. 19.

Lȧ-shâr'on (*plain*). A Canaanite town, Josh. xii. 18.

Lăs'thĕ-nē̦s. A Cretan, 1 Macc. xi. 31.

Lătch'et (*lace*). Sandal lacings, or fastenings, Gen. xiv. 23; Mark i. 7.

Lăt'in. Language of Latium, *i. e.* the Romans, Luke xxiii. 38; John xix. 20.

Lăt'tiçe (*lath*). Open work of wood or metal; also window, blind, or screen, Judg. v. 28; 2 Kgs. i. 2; Prov. vii. 6.

Lā'ver (*wash*). Brazen vessel holding water for priestly washings—hands, feet, and the sacrifices, Ex. xxx. 18-21; xxxviii. 8; 1 Kgs. vii. 38-40; 2 Chr. iv. 6.

Lȧw (*rule*). In Scripture, reference is nearly always to the Hebrew civil, moral, and ceremonial law, Matt. v. 17; John i. 17; Acts xxv. 8.

Lȧw'yĕr. Scribe or divine who expounded the Mosaic law in school or synagogue, Matt. xxii. 35; Luke x. 25.

Lăz'ȧ-rus (*whom God helps*). Abbreviation of Eleazar. (1) Brother of Mary and Martha, John xi. 1; xii. 1-11. (2) Type of poverty and distress in the parable, Luke xvi. 19-31.

Lĕad. Early known, imported and used by

Hebrews, Ex. xv. 10; Num. xxxi. 22; Job xix. 24; Ezek. xxvii. 12.

Lēaf. Of trees, Gen. viii. 11; Matt. xxi. 19; double doors, 1 Kgs. vi. 34; of books, Jer. xxxvi. 23; prosperity, Jer. xvii. 8; decay, Job xiii. 25.

Lē′ah (*weary*). Jacob's wife through deceit of her father, Laban, Gen. xxix., xxx., xlix. 31.

Lēas′ing (*lying*). Falsehood, Ps. iv. 2; v. 6.

Lĕath′er. Used by Hebrews, 2 Kgs. i. 8; Matt. iii. 4.

Lĕav′en (*raise*). Old fermented dough used to lighten new dough, Matt. xiii. 33. Passover bread unleavened, Ex. xii. 15-17. Corrupt doctrines, Matt. xvi. 6; evil passions, 1 Cor. v. 7, 8.

Lĕb′a-nä (*white*). His children returned, Neh. vii. 48. Lebanah, Ez. ii. 45.

Lĕb′a-non (*white*). Two mountain ranges running N. E., between which was Cœlo-Syria. The western is Libanus, or Lebanon proper. The eastern is Anti-Libanus, and skirted Palestine on the north, Deut. i. 7; Josh. i. 4. Many scripture allusions, Isa. x. 34; Jer. xxii. 23.

Lĕb′a-ŏth (*lionesses*). Boundary town of southern Judah, Josh. xv. 32.

Lĕb-bæ′us (*brave*). Thaddæus, the apostle Jude, Matt. x. 3, Mark iii. 18.

Lĕ-bō′nah (*incense*). Place north of Bethel, Judg. xxi. 19.

Lē′cah (*walking*). Person or place, 1 Chr. iv. 21.

Lēech. [HORSE-LEECH.]

Lēek. Closely allied to the onion, Num. xi. 5.

Lēes (*dregs*). Sediment of liquor. Settled, pure wine, Isa. xxv. 6; sloth, Jer. xlviii. 11; extreme suffering, Ps. lxxv. 8.

Lē′gį͏on (*gathered*). Division of Roman army; when full, 6200 men and 730 horse. N. T. use indefinite, Matt. xxvi. 53; Mark v. 9.

Lē′hă-bĭm (*flame*). A Mizraite tribe; Libyans, Gen. x. 13. Lubim, 2 Chr. xii. 3.

Lē′hī (*jawbone*). Where Samson slew the Philistines, Judg. xv. 9, 19.

Lĕm′u-el (*dedicated*). The unknown king in Prov. xxxi. 1-9.

Lĕn′tĭl (*little lens*). A podded food plant, like the pea or bean, Gen. xxv. 34; 2 Sam. xvii. 28.

Lĕop'ard (*lion-panther*). This fierce, spotted beast of the cat species once found in Jordan jungles, Jer. xiii. 23; Dan. vii. 6; S. of Sol. iv. 8.

Lĕp'ẽr (*peeled*). Who has leprosy; a loathsome, incurable skin disease, common in East, Ex. iv. 6; treatment of, Lev. xiv. 3–32; Luke xvii. 12–19.

Lē'shem, Josh. xix. 47. [LAISH.]

Lĕt'tus, 1 Esdr. viii. 29. [HATTUSH.]

Lĕ-tū'shim (*hammered*). Son of Dedan, and his Arabian tribe, Gen. xxv. 3.

Lĕ-ŭm'mim (*nations*). Son of Dedan, and his Arabian tribe, Gen. xxv. 3.

Lē'vī (*joined*). (1) Third son of Jacob, Gen. xxix. 34; avenged Dinah's wrong, xxxiv. 25–31; cursed, xlix. 5–7; went to Egypt, Ex. vi. 16; blessed, Ex. xxxii. 25–28. (2) Two of Christ's ancestors, Luke iii. 24, 29. (3) Original name of Matthew, Mark ii. 14; Luke v. 27, 29; compare Matt. ix. 9.

Lĕ-vī'a-than (*aquatic monster*). The crocodile is described in Job xli.; and probably meant in Ps. lxxiv. 14; civ. 26.

Lē'vītes. Descendants of Levi, Ex. vi. 16–25; Lev. xxv. 32, etc.; Num. xxxv. 2–8; Josh. xxi. 3. In above, the tribe is meant. But Levites came to mean the priestly branch, *i. e.*, descendants of Aaron, Josh. iii. 3; 1 Kgs. viii. 4; Ez. ii. 70; John i. 19. Three Levitical lines, Kohathite, Gershonite, Merarite, Num. iii. 17. Assigned 48 cities among the other tribes, Num. xxxv.

Lĕ-vĭt'i-cus (*for Levites*). Third book of Bible and Pentateuch, containing the ceremonial law for guidance of Levites. Authorship ascribed to Moses and Aaron.

Lĭb'ā-nus. Greek form of Lebanon, 1 Esdr. iv. 48.

Lĭb'ẽr-tīneş (*free*). Emancipated Jewish slaves; freedmen, Acts vi. 9.

Lĭb'nah (*white*). (1) An Israelite encampment, Num. xxxiii. 20, 21. (2) Levitical city in Judah, Josh. x. 29–31; 2 Kgs. xix. 8–35; 1 Chr. vi. 57.

Lĭb'nī (*whiteness*). (1) A Levite, founder of Libnites, Ex. vi. 17; Num. iii. 18–21. (2) Probably the above, 1 Chr. vi. 29.

Lĭb'ÿ-à, Ezek. xxx. 5; Acts ii. 10. The African

continent west of Egypt and contiguous to Mediterranean. *See* Lubim and Lehabim.

Līçe (*destroyers*). Constituted the third Egyptian plague, Ex. viii. 16–18; Ps. cv. 31.

Lieū-tĕn'ants (*place-holders*). Satraps or viceroys, Ez. viii. 36. Princes, Dan. iii. 2; vi. 1.

Life. Natural, Gen. iii. 17; spiritual, Rom. viii. 6; eternal, John iii. 36; Rom. vi. 23.

Līght. First gush of creation, Gen. i. 3. Frequent source of imagery, Matt. iv. 16; Luke ii. 32; John i. 7–9.

Līgn=aloes (*wood-aloes*). [ALOES.]

Līg'ūre (*lynx urine*). Possibly amber. First stone in third row of high priest's breastplate, Ex. xxviii. 19; xxxix. 12.

Līk'hī (*learned*). A Manassite, 1 Chr. vii. 19.

Lĭl'y (*pale*). Source of rich imagery, 1 Kgs. vii. 19; S. of Sol. ii. 1, 2; v. 13; Matt. vi. 28; Luke xii. 27.

Līme (*glue*). Was known and used for plaster and cement work, Deut. xxvii. 2; Isa. xxxiii. 12; Am. ii. 1.

Lĭn'en (*flax*). Used for stately robes, Gen. xli. 42; priestly vestments, Ex. xxviii. 42; Lev. vi. 10; temple veil, 2 Chr. iii. 14; choral gowns, 2 Chr. v. 12, and ordinary dress. Symbol of purity, Rev. xv. 6; of luxury, Luke xvi. 19.

Lĭn'tel (*boundary*). Support over window or door, Ex. xii. 22; 1 Kgs. vi. 31.

Lī'nus (*net*). Roman friend of Paul, 2 Tim. iv. 21.

Lī'on (*seeing*). Once found in Palestine, Judg. xiv. 5, 6; 1 Sam. xvii. 34–36; 2 Sam. xxiii. 20. Symbol of strength, Gen. xlix. 9.

Lĭt'tēr (*bed*). Covered couch or chair, carried by men or animals, Isa. lxvi. 20. "Wagons," Num. vii. 3.

Lĭz'ärd (*muscular*). Abundant in Palestine. Unclean, Lev. xi. 30.

Lŏ=ăm'mī (*not my people*). Figurative name of Hosea's son, Hos. i. 9.

Lōans. Allowed by Hebrews, but all debts cancelled in Sabbatical year, Deut. xv. 1–11. Usury not allowed, Ex. xxii. 25; Lev. xxv. 36; Deut. xv. 3–10.

Lŏck (*bar*). A bar of wood or metal for outer, and bolt for inner, doors, 1 Kgs. iv. 13; Judg. iii. 24.

Lō′cust (*leaping*). Confused original, supposably embracing the destructive insects, — locust, grasshopper, caterpillar, palmer-worm, etc. They constituted the eighth Egyptian plague, Ex. x. 1-15; Joel ii. 3-10.

Lŏd, 1 Chr. viii. 12; Ez. ii. 33. [LYDDA.]

Lō=dē′bär (*barren*). A place east of Jordan, 2 Sam. ix. 4; xvii. 27.

Lŏg. Hebrew liquid measure; about five sixths of a pint, Lev. xiv. 10-24.

Lō′ĭs (*pleasing*). Timothy's grandmother, 2 Tim. i. 5.

Looking=glass. Polished metal plate, Ex. xxxviii. 8; Job xxxvii. 18.

Lôrd (*loaf-guardian*). Jehovah, LORD, Gen. xv. 4; Ps. vii., c. Adonai, Lord, Christ, The Lord, Our Lord. Supreme ruler, and not the Saxon dignitary.

Lôrd's Dāy. First day of the week; resurrection day of Christ, Rev. i. 10. Sunday, after A. D. 321.

Lôrd's Sŭp′per. Substitute for the O. T. Paschal feast. Instituted by Christ the night before the crucifixion, as a reminder of his covenant with mankind, Matt. xxvi. 19; Mark xiv. 16; Luke xxii. 13. "Breaking of bread," Acts ii. 42; xx. 7. "Communion," 1 Cor. x. 16. "Lord's Supper," only in 1 Cor. xi. 20.

Lō=ru′ha̠-mah (*unpitied*). Hosea's daughter, Hos. i. 6.

Lŏt (*veil*). Abraham's nephew, Gen. xi. 27-31. Settled in Jordan valley, Gen. xiii. 1-13. Escaped to mountains, Gen. xix. Progenitor of Moabites and Ammonites.

Lō′tan (*hidden*). A Horite duke, Gen. xxxvi. 20-29.

Lŏth″a̠-sū′bus, 1 Esdr. ix. 44. [HASHUM.]

Lŏts, Feast of. [PURIM.]

Lŏts. Casting or drawing of, a usual way of settling questions. Possibly marked pebbles were used, in a bag or box. Canaan was allotted to the tribes of Israel, Num. xxvi. 55; Josh. xv., xix. Scapegoat so chosen, Lev. xvi. 8; priest's courses, 1 Chr. xxiv., xxv.; property divided, Matt. xxvii. 35.

Love Fĕasts. Feasts of offerings, after the community of goods ceased, Jude 12; 2 Peter ii. 13. Forbidden by Council of Laodicea, A. D. 320.

Lṳ-bĭm, 2 Chr. xii. 3; xvi. 8. [LIBYA.]

Lṳ'cas. Luke the evangelist, Phile. 24.

Lṳ'çĭ-fẽr (*light-giver*). Types the king of Babylon, Isa. xiv. 12. Popularly, Satan.

Lṳ'çĭus (*morning born*). (1) Paul's kinsman, Rom. xvi. 21. (2) A Cyrenean convert and teacher, Acts xiii. 1.

Lŭd (*strife*). Son of Shem, Gen. x. 22.

Lṳ'dĭm (*strife*). A Mizraite tribe, Gen. x. 13; Isa. lxvi. 19; Ezek. xxvii. 10.

Lṳ'hith (*board-made*). Place in Moab, Isa. xv. 5; Jer. xlviii. 5.

Lṳke (*luminous*). Evangelist and physician, Col. iv. 14; 2 Tim. iv. 11. Author of third gospel and of Acts of the Apostles.

Lṳ'nă-tĭcs (*moon-struck*). Epileptics are probably meant, Matt. iv. 24; xvii. 15.

Lŭz (*almond*). Site of Bethel, Gen. xxviii. 19; Josh. xvi. 2; Judg. i. 23.

Lўc''a-ō'nĭ-à (*wolf-land*). Wild district of Asia Minor, containing towns of Derbe, Lystra, and Iconium, Acts xiv. 6–11. Twice visited by Paul.

Lў'çĭà. A southwestern district of Asia Minor, with Myra and Patara as cities, Acts xxi. 2; xxvii. 5.

Lўd'dà (*strife*). Hebrew Lud or Lod. Now Lidd or Ludd. In Sharon plain, 9 miles east of Joppa, Acts ix. 32.

Lўd'ĭ-à (*Lydus land*). (1) A province of Asia Minor, on Mediterranean. Cities, Sardis, Thyatira, Philadelphia, 1 Macc. viii. 8. (2) Woman convert of Thyatira, Acts xvi. 14.

Lȳ-sā'nĭ-as (*that drives away sorrow*). Tetrarch of Abilene, Luke iii. 1.

Lўs'ĭas (*dissolving*). Claudius Lysias, captain of the band that rescued Paul, Acts xxi.–xxiv. 1–9. (2) Governor of southern Syria, 1 Macc. iii. 32.

Lȳ-sĭm'a-chus. (1) Translator of Esther, Esth. xi. 1. (2) Brother of Menelaus, 2 Macc. iv. 29–42.

Lўs'trà (*dissolving*). City of Lycaonia, where Paul was honored, Acts xiv. 6–18; and stoned, 19–21.

M

Mā′a-cah (*oppression*). (1) A wife of David, 2 Sam. iii. 3. Maachah, 1 Chr. iii. 2. (2) A petty kingdom, N. E. of Palestine, 2 Sam. x. 6–8. Syria-maachah, 1 Chr. xix. 6, 7.

Mā′a-chah (*oppression*). (1) Daughter of Nahor, Gen. xxii. 24. (2) A Gathite, 1 Kgs. ii. 39. (3) Wife of Rehoboam, 1 Kgs. xv. 2. (4) Concubine of Caleb, 1 Chr. ii. 48. (5) A Benjamitess, 1 Chr. vii. 15, 16. (6) Wife of Jehiel, 1 Chr. viii. 29. (7) Father of Hanan, 1 Chr. xi. 43. (8) A Simeonite, 1 Chr. xxvii. 16.

Mă-ăch′a-thī. Maachathites. People of Maacah, Deut. iii. 14 ; Josh. xii. 5.

Mă-ăd′āi (*ornament*). Son of Bani, Ez. x. 34.

Mă′′a-dī′ah. A returned priest, Neh. xii. 5. Moadiah, vs. 17.

Mă-ā′i (*merciful*). A Levite, Neh. xii. 36.

Mă-ăl′eh=ă-crăb′bim, Josh. xv. 3. Scorpion pass. [AKRABBIM.]

Mă-ā′nī, 1 Esdr. ix. 34. [BAANA.]

Mā′a-răth (*open*). Town in Judah, Josh. xv. 59.

Mā′′a-sē′iah (*work of God*). (1) Returned Levites and captive families, Ez. x. 18, 21, 22, 30 ; Neh. iii. 23 ; viii. 4, 7 ; x. 25 ; xi. 5, 7 ; xii. 41, 42. (2) Father of Zephaniah, Jer. xxi. 1. (3) Father of Zedekiah, Jer. xxix. 21. (4) A porter, 1 Chr. xv. 18–20. (5) Son of Adaiah, 2 Chr. xxiii. 1. (6) Others in 2 Chr. xxvi. 11 ; xxviii. 7 ; xxxiv. 8 ; Jer. xxxv. 4.

Mā′ath (*small*). An ancestor of Christ, Luke iii. 26.

Mā′ăz (*wrath*). Son of Ram, 1 Chr. ii. 27.

Mā′′a-zī′ah (*consolation*). Two priests, 1 Chr. xxiv. 18 ; Neh. x. 8.

Măb′dă̄-ī, 1 Esdr. ix. 34. [BENAIAH.]

Măc′a-lon, 1 Esdr. v. 21. [MICHMASH.]

Măc′că-bēes (*hammer*). The Asmonean princes who upheld the cause of Jewish independence, B. C. 166–40. The two Apocryphal books of Maccabees contain their history.

Măç″e-dō′nĭ-á (*extended*). The ancient emp.re north of Greece proper, whose greatest kings were Philip and Alexander the Great. Often visited by Paul, who made here his first European converts, Acts xvi. 9–12; xvii. 1–15; xx. 1–6.

Măch′ba̱-nāi (*stout*). A Gadite chief, 1 Chr. xii. 13.

Măch′be̱-nah (*cloak*). Person or place, 1 Chr. ii. 49.

Mā′chĭ (*decrease*). Father of the Gadite spy, Num. xiii. 15.

Mā′chĭr (*sold*). (1) Eldest son of Manasseh, Num. xxxii. 39; Josh. xvii. 1. (2) Son of Ammiel, 2 Sam. ix. 4; xvii. 27.

Mā′chĭr-ītes. Descendants of Machir, Num. xxvi. 29.

Măch′mas, 1 Macc. ix. 73. [MICHMASH.]

Măch″nă-dē′bāi (*liberal*). Son of Bani, Ez. x. 40.

Măch-pē′lah (*double*). Abraham's burial cave at Hebron, Gen. xxiii. 17–19; xxv. 9; xlix. 29–32; l. 13.

Măd′a-ī (*middle*). Son of Japheth, and progenitor of the Medes, Gen. x. 2.

Mā′dĭ-an, Acts vii. 29. [MIDIAN.]

Măd-măn′nah (*dunghill*). Town in southern Judah, near Gaza, Josh. xv. 31.

Măd′men (*dunghill*). A place in Moab, Jer. xlviii. 2.

Măd-mē′nah (*dunghill*). Town in Benjamin, Isa. x. 31.

Măd′ness. Lunacy and passionate outburst, John x. 20.

Mā′dŏn (*strife*). Ancient city of Canaan, Josh. xi. 1; xii. 19.

Măg′bish (*gathering*). Person or place, Ez. ii. 30.

Măg′da-lá (*tower*). Village on W. shore of Sea of Galilee, Matt. xv. 39. Magadan in R. V.

Măg′dĭ-el (*praise*). A duke of Edom, Gen. xxxvi. 43.

Mā′gĕd, 1 Macc. v. 36. [MAKED.]

Mā′gī (*priests*). Oriental priests and learned men.

A Median and Persian caste of royal advisers, Jer. xxxix. 3; Matt. ii. 1–11.

Măġ′ĭc (*of Magi*). The magician's art. Acting through occult agencies. Potent in Oriental religions, Ex. vii., viii. Forbidden, Lev. xix. 31; xx. 6.

Mā′gŏg (*Gog's region*). (1) Second son of Japheth, and his people, Gen. x. 2. (2) Gog's land; probably Scythia, Ezek. xxxviii. 2; xxxix. 2-6. (3) Symbolical enemies, Rev. xx. 7-9.

Mā′gôr=mĭs′sạ-bĭb (*fear everywhere*). Pashur, who imprisoned Jeremiah, Jer. xx. 1–3.

Măg′pĭ-ăsh (*moth killer*). A co-covenanter, Neh. x. 20.

Mạ-hā′lah (*sickness*). A Manassite, 1 Chr. vii. 18.

Mạ-hā′lạ-lē″el (*God's praise*). (1) Son of Cainan, Gen. v. 12-17. Maleleel, Luke iii. 37. (2) A Judahite, Neh. xi. 4.

Mā′hạ-lath (*harp*). (1) Wife of Esau, Gen. xxviii. 9. (2) Wife of Rehoboam, 2 Chr. xi. 18. (3) The tune or the instrument, Ps. liii., lxxxviii. titles.

Mā′hạ-lī (*sick*), Ex. vi. 19. [MAHLI.]

Mā″hạ-nā′ĭm (*two camps*). Place where Jacob met the angels, Gen. xxxii. 2. Afterwards a Levitical town in Gad, Josh. xxi. 38; 2 Sam. ii. 8-12.

Mā′hạ-neh=dăn (*camp of Dan*). Located as in Judg. xiii. 25; xviii. 12.

Mạ-hăr′a-ī (*swift*). One of David's captains, 2 Sam. xxiii. 28; 1 Chr. xi. 30; xxvii. 13.

Mā′hath (*grasping*). Two Kohathite Levites, 1 Chr. vi. 35; 2 Chr. xxix. 12.

Mā′hạ-vīte. Designation of one of David's captains, 1 Chr. xi. 46.

Mạ-hā′zĭ-ŏth (*visions*). Son of Heman, 1 Chr. xxv. 4, 30.

Mā′hĕr=shăl″al-hăsh′=băz (*speeding to the prey*). Name of Isaiah's son, symbolizing the Assyrian conquest of Damascus and Samaria, Isa. viii. 1-4.

Mäh′lah (*disease*). Daughter of Zelophehad, Num. xxvii. 1-11.

Mäh′lī (*sickly*). (1) A Levite, Num. iii. 20. Mahali, Ex. vi. 19. (2) Another Levite, 1 Chr. vi. 47.

Mäh′lītes. Descendants of Mahli, Num. iii. 33.

Mäh′lon (*sickly*). Ruth's first husband, Ruth i. 2–5; iv. 9, 10.

Mā′hol (*dancing*). Father of the four wise men, 1 Kgs. iv. 31.

Mā′kăz (*end*). Unidentified place, 1 Kgs. iv. 9.

Mā′kĕd. City of Gilead, 1 Macc. v. 26–36.

Măk-hē′loth (*meeting place*). A desert encampment, Num. xxxiii. 25.

Măk-kē′dah (*shepherd place*). An ancient Canaanite city, Josh. x. 10–30; xii. 16; xv. 41.

Măk′tesh (*mortar*). Denounced quarter of Jerusalem, Zeph. i. 11.

Măl′a-chī (*God's messenger*). Last of minor prophets. Nothing known of nativity or lineage. Contemporary with Nehemiah, B. C. 445–433. His book foretells the coming of Christ and John the Baptist.

Măl′cham (*their king*). (1) A Benjamite, 1 Chr. viii. 9. (2) The idol Molech, Zeph. i. 5.

Măl-chī′ah (*king*). (1) A Levite, 1 Chr. vi. 40. (2) Jeremiah's prison-keeper, Jer. xxxviii. 6. (3) Returned captives, Ez. x. 25, 31; Neh. iii. 14; viii. 4; xi. 12.

Măl′chī-el (*God's king*). An Asherite and founder of Malchielites, or Birzavith, Gen. xlvi. 17; Num. xxvi. 45; 1 Chr. vii. 31.

Măl-chī′jah (*king*). Priests and returned captives, 1 Chr. xxiv. 9; Ez. x. 25, 31; Neh. iii. 11; xii. 42.

Măl-chī′ram (*king of height*). Son of Jehoiachin, 1 Chr. iii. 18.

Măl′chī=shū′å (*king of help*). Son of Saul, 1 Chr. ix. 39. Melchishua, 1 Sam. xiv. 49.

Măl′chus (*ruling*). The one whose ear Peter cut off, Matt. xxvi. 51; Luke xxii. 50.

Må-lē′le-el, Luke iii. 37. [MAHALALEEL.]

Măl′lŏs. City in Cilicia, 2 Macc. iv. 30.

Măl′lŏ-thī (*fulness*). Chief of the 19th musical course, 1 Chr. xxv. 4, 26.

Măl′lōwş (*soft*). Jews'-mallows of the East, used for pot-herbs, Job xxx. 4.

Măl′luch (*ruling*). Levites, 1 Chr. vi. 44; Ez. x. 29. 32; Neh. x. 4; xii. 2.

Măm′mon (*riches*). A Chaldee word used by Christ, Matt. vi. 24 ; Luke xvi. 9.

Măm″nī-tâ-naī′mus. 1 Esdr. ix. 34. [MATTANIAH.]

Măm′rĕ (*strength*). The Amorite chief who gave his name to the plain where Abraham dwelt, Gen. xiv. 13–24. Hebron, Gen. xxiii. 19.

Mȧ-mū′chus, 1 Esdr. ix. 30. [MALLUCH.]

Măn. Adam, *ruddy*, Gen. i. 26. The human race, Gen. v. 2 ; viii. 21. As distinguished from woman, Deut. xxii. 5 ; 1 Sam. xvii. 33. Mortal, Isa. xiii. 14.

Măn′a-ĕn (*comforter*). A Christian teacher at Antioch, Acts xiii. 1.

Măn′a-hăth (*rest*). (1) A Horite progenitor of the Manahethites, Gen. xxxvi. 23 ; 1 Chr. ii. 52. (2) Place or person, 1 Chr. viii. 6.

Mȧ-năs′seh (*forgetting*). (1) First son of Joseph, Gen. xli. 51. The tribe divided and occupied both sides of Jordan, Josh. xvi., xvii. (2) Son and successor of Hezekiah on the throne of Judah, B. C. 698–643. Idolatrous, 2 Kgs. xxi. 1–18. Captive in Babylon ; repented ; restored, 2 Chr. xxxiii. 1–20. (3) Returned captives, Ez. x. 30, 33.

Mȧ-năs′sēs. (1) King Manasseh, Matt. i. 10. (2) Manasseh, Joseph's son, Rev. vii. 6.

Mȧ-năs′sites. Descendants of Manasseh (1), Deut. iv. 43 ; Judg. xii. 4.

Măn′drāke (*field speaker*). A narcotic plant, resembling rhubarb, bearing a yellow, aromatic fruit, Gen. xxx. 14–16 ; S. of Sol. vii. 13.

Mā′nĕh. The mina ; a variable Hebrew weight, Ezek. xlv. 12.

Măn′ger (*eating place*). Feeding crib or trough for cattle. The stall, and even the cattleyard, Luke ii. 7–16 ; xiii. 15.

Mā′nī, 1 Esdr. ix. 30. [BANI.]

Măn′nȧ (*what is this ?*). The bread substitute sent to the wandering Israelites, Ex. xvi. 14–36 ; Num. xi. 7–9 ; Deut. viii. 3 ; Josh. v. 12.

Mȧ-nō′ah (*rest*). Father of Samson, Judg. xiii. 1–23.

Măn′slāy-er. The involuntary manslayer found escape in a city of refuge, Num. xxxv. 22, 23 ; Deut. xix. 5.

Măn'tle (*hand-woven*). Blanket, Judg. iv. 18. Garment, 1 Sam. xv. 27. Sleeved wrapper, Isa. iii. 22. Chief outer garment, 1 Kgs. xix. 13-19.

Mā'och (*breast-bound*). A Gathite, 1 Sam. xxvii. 2.

Mā'on (*dwelling*). Town in Judah, Josh. xv. 55; 1 Sam. xxiii. 24, 25.

Mā'on-ītes. Mehunims, Judg. x. 12.

Mā'rä (*bitter*). Naomi so called herself, Ruth i. 20.

Mā'rah (*bitter*). The desert spring whose waters were sweetened, Ex. xv. 22-25; Num. xxxiii. 8, 9.

Măr'a-lah (*trembling*). A border of Zebulun, Josh. xix. 11.

Măr'an=ā'thả. "Our Lord cometh," 1 Cor. xvi. 22.

Măr'ble (*shining*). Any white or shining stone is meant, 1 Kgs. vii. 9-12; Esth. i. 6; Rev. xviii. 12.

Măr-chĕs'van. [BUL.]

Măr'cus, Col. iv. 10; Phile. 24; 1 Pet. v. 13. [MARK.]

Măr''dŏ-chē'us. Mordecai in Apoc.

Mǎ-rē'shah (*hill-top*). (1) A Hebronite, 1 Chr. ii. 42. (2) Lowland city of Judah, Josh. xv. 44; 2 Chr. xi. 8; xiv. 9-12.

Măr'ĭ-mŏth, 2 Esdr. i. 2. [MERAIOTH.]

Märk (*polite, shining*). John Mark, Acts xii. 12, 25; xv. 37. John, Acts xiii. 5, 13. Mark, Acts xv. 39. Convert of Peter, 1 Pet. v. 13. Companion of Paul, Col. iv. 10. Author of second Gospel, which was probably written in Rome.

Mā'roth (*bitter*). Town in Judah, Micah i. 12.

Măr'rĭảge (*husbanding*). Monogamous, Gen. ii. 18-24; vii. 13. Polygamous, Gen. iv. 19; vi. 2. Forbidden within certain degrees, Lev. xviii.; Deut. xxvii.; and with foreigners, Ex. xxxiv. 16. Monogamy re-instituted, Matt. xix. 5, 6; Mark x. 5-10.

Märs' Hill, Acts xvii. 22. [AREOPAGUS.]

Măr'se-nả (*worthy*). A Persian prince, Esth. i. 14.

Măr'thả (*lady*). Sister of Mary and Lazarus, Luke x. 38-42; John xi. 5-28.

Măr'tyr (*witness*). Matt. xviii. 16; Luke xxiv.

48. Who seals his faith with his blood, Acts xxii. 20; Rev. ii. 13 ; xvii. 6.

Mā′rȳ (*rebellion*). Greek form of Miriam. (1) The betrothed of Joseph and mother of Christ, Matt. i. 18–25 ; xii. 46 ; Mark vi. 3 ; Luke viii. 19 ; John ii. 1–5 ; xix. 26 ; Acts i. 14. (2) Wife of Cleophas, Matt. xxvii. 56, 61 ; xxviii. 1–9 ; Mark xvi. 1–8 ; Luke xxiv. 1–10. (3) Mother of John Mark, Acts xii. 12 ; Col. iv. 10. (4) Sister of Martha and Lazarus, Luke x. 41, 42 ; John xi., xii. (5) Mary Magdalene ; *i. e.*, of Magdala, Matt. xxviii. 1–10 ; Mark xvi. 1–10 ; Luke xxiv. 10 ; John xx. 1–18. (6) A Roman convert, Rom. xvi. 6.

Măs′ā-lŏth. Place in Arbela, 1 Macc. ix. 2.

Măs′chĭl. "Didactic," or "melody." Title of thirteen Psalms.

Măsh (*drawn out*). Son of Aram, Gen. x. 23. Meshech, 1 Chr. i. 17.

Mā′shal (*entreaty*). A Levitical city in Asher, 1 Chr. vi. 74. Misheal, Josh. xix. 26. Mishal, Josh. xxi. 30.

Măs′phå, 1 Macc. iii. 46. [MIZPEH.]

Măs′re-kah (*vineyard*). City in Edom, Gen. xxxvi. 36 ; 1 Chr. i. 47.

Măs′så (*gift*). Son of Ishmael, Gen. xxv. 14 ; 1 Chr. i. 30.

Măs′sah (*temptation*). Meribah ; spot of temptation, Ex. xvii. 7 ; Ps. xcv. 8, 9 ; Heb. iii. 8.

Mā̇-thu̇′sa-lå, Luke iii. 37. [METHUSELAH.]

Mā′tred (*shoving*). Mother of Mehetabel, Gen. xxxvi. 39.

Mā′trī (*rain*). A Benjamite family, 1 Sam. x. 21.

Mā′trĭx (*mother*). The womb, Ex. xiii. 12–15.

Măt′tan (*gift*). (1) A priest of Baal, 2 Kgs. xi. 18. (2) Father of Shephatiah, Jer. xxxviii. 1.

Măt′ta-nah (*gift*). A desert encampment, Num. xxi. 18, 19.

Măt″ta-nī′ah (*God's gift*). (1) Original name of Zedekiah, 2 Kgs. xxiv. 17. (2) Levites, 1 Chr. ix. 15 ; xxv. 4, 16 ; 2 Chr. xx. 14 ; xxix. 13 ; Ez. x. 26, 27, 30, 37 ; Neh. xi. 17 ; xiii. 13.

Măt′ta-thå (*God's gift*). Grandson of David, Luke iii. 31.

Măt′ta̤-thah. One who returned, Ez. x. 33.

Măt′′ta̤-thī′as (*God's gift*). (1) Two of Christ's progenitors, Luke iii. 25, 26. (2) Father of the Maccabees, 1 Macc. ii.

Măt′′te̤-nā′ī. Levites, Ez. x. 33, 37 ; Neh. xii. 19.

Măt′than. Grandfather of Joseph, Matt. i. 15.

Măt′′tha̤-nī′as, 1 Esdr. ix. 37. [MATTANIAH.]

Măt′that, Luke iii. 24, 29. [MATTHAN.]

Măt′thew (*gift of God*). Contraction of Mattathias. The Apostle and Evangelist. Levi in Luke, v. 27–29. Son of Alphæus, Mark ii. 14. Tax-collector at Capernaum when called, Matt. ix. 9. His gospel is first of N. T. Its original claimed to be the Hebrew, or Syro-Chaldaic, of Palestine. Time of writing placed at A. D. 60–66. Gist, to establish Jesus as O. T. Messiah.

Măt-thī′as (*God's gift*). Apostle allotted to fill the place of Judas, Acts i. 26.

Măt′′ti-thī′ah (*God's gift*). Levites, 1 Chr. ix. 31 ; xv. 18 ; xvi. 5 ; Ez. x. 43 ; Neh. viii. 4.

Măt′tŏck (*hoe*). A crude hoe, Isa. vii. 25.

Maul (*hammer*). Heavy wooden hammer, Prov. xxv. 18. Battle axe, Jer. li. 20.

Măz′′i-tī′as, 1 Esdr. ix. 35. [MATTITHIAH.]

Măz′za̤-rŏth. The twelve signs of the zodiac, Job xxxviii. 32.

Mĕad′ōw (*mead*). Water-plant, flag, Gen. xli. 2. Cave, Judg. xx. 33.

Mē′ah (*hundred*). Tower in Jerusalem, Neh. iii. 1 ; xii. 39.

Mĕ-ā′rah (*cave*). Unknown place, Josh. xiii. 4.

Mĕas′ṳres. Hebrew standard weights and measures provided for, Lev. xix. 35, 36 ; Deut. xxv. 13–15. Money passed by weight till era of coinage. For various weights and measures, *see* respective titles.

Mēat. In Bible sense, food of any kind, Gen. i. 29 ; Lev. ii. ; vi. 14–23 ; Matt. xv. 37 ; Luke xxiv. 41.

Mēat=ŏf′fĕr-ing. Conditions in Lev. ii. ; vi. 14–23.

Mĕ-bŭn′nāi (*building*). One of David's warriors, 2 Sam. xxiii. 27. Sibbechai, 2 Sam. xxi. 18. Sibbecai, 1 Chr. xi. 29.

Mĕch′ę-rath-īte″, 1 Chr. xi. 36. Maacathite. [MAACAH.]

Mē′dăd (*love*). A camp prophet, Num. xi. 26, 27.

Mē′dan (*strife*). A son of Abraham, Gen. xxv. 2; 1 Chr. i. 32.

Mĕd′e-bȧ (*quiet waters*). Town in Reuben, east of Dead Sea, Num. xxi. 30; Josh. xiii. 9; 1 Macc. ix. 36.

Mēdeṣ. Medians, 2 Kgs. xvii. 6.

Mē′dĭ-ȧ (*middle land*). Madai, Gen. x. 2; Media, Esth. i. 3. The country northwest of Persia and south of Caspian Sea. Held early sway in Babylon. Tributary to Assyria, B. C. 880. Independent, and conquered Babylon; next, Assyria. Empire at its height, B. C. 625. Overthrown by Persian Cyrus, B. C. 558. Medo-Persian empire overthrown by Alexander the Great, B. C. 330, Isa. xiii. 17, 18; Esth. i. 19; Dan. vi. 8–12; 1 Chr. v. 26.

Mĕd′i-çīne (*of a physician*). The science, as known in Egypt, was copied by Hebrews, Lev. xiii.-xv.; 2 Kgs. viii. 29; Prov. iii. 8; vi. 15.

Mė-gĭd′dȯ (*crowded*). A city in plain of Esdraelon, Josh. xii. 21; xvii. 11; 2 Kgs. xxiii. 29. Also the plain, or valley, itself and scene of Barak's victory over Sisera, and of Josiah's death, Judg. iv. 6–17; 2 Chr. xxxv. 20–24.

Mė-gĭd′don, Zech. xii. 11. [MEGIDDO.]

Mė-hĕt′ą-beel. Ancestor of Shemaiah, Neh. vi. 10.

Mė-hĕt′ą-bel (*God-favored*). Wife of Hadar, king of Edom, Gen. xxxvi. 39.

Mė-hī′dȧ (*famed*). His family returned, Ez. ii. 52; Neh. vii. 54.

Mē′hir (*price*). A Judahite, 1 Chr. iv. 11.

Mė-hŏl′ath-īte. Meholaite, 1 Sam. xviii. 19.

Mė-hū′ją-el (*smitten*). Son of Irad, Gen. iv. 18.

Mē′hū-man (*true*). Chamberlain of Ahasuerus, Esth. i. 10.

Mė-hū′nimṣ (*dwellings*). Maonites, 2 Chr. xxvi. 7; Ez. ii. 50.

Mē-jär′kŏn (*yellow waters*). Town in Dan, Josh. xix. 46.

Mĕk′ǫ-nah (*pedestal*). Town in Judah, Neh. xi. 28.

Mĕl″a-tī′ah (*saved*). Assistant wall-builder, Neh. iii. 7.

Mĕl′chī (*king*). Two ancestors of Christ, Luke iii. 24, 28.

Mĕl-chī′ah (*royal*). A priest, Jer. xxi. 1.

Mĕl-chī′el. Governor of Bethulia, Judith vi. 15.

Mĕl-chĭṣ′e-dĕc. N. T. form of Melchizedek, Heb. v.–vii.

Mĕl″chī-shṳ′ā, 1 Sam. xiv. 49. [MALCHISHUA.]

Mĕl-chĭz′e-dek (*king of justice*). King of Salem, and priest, Gen. xiv. 18–20. Prototype of Christ, Ps. cx. 4; Heb. v.–vii.

Mē′le-ȧ (*full*). Ancestor of Joseph, Luke iii. 31.

Mē′lech (*king*). Son of Micah, 1 Chr. ix. 41.

Mĕl′i-cū, Neh. xii. 14. [MALLUCH.]

Mĕl′i-tȧ (*honey*). The island of Malta, in Mediterranean, south of Sicily, Acts xxvii., xxviii.

Mĕl′on (*mellow apple*). Melons of Egypt prized as food, Num. xi. 5.

Mĕl′zar. Common noun — steward or tutor, Dan. i. 11, 16.

Mĕm′phis (*abode of the good*). Ancient Egyptian city, Hos. ix. 6, on west bank of Nile, near pyramids and sphinx, and 10 miles south of Cairo. Noph, Isa. xix. 13; Jer. ii. 16; Ezek. xxx. 13–16.

Mĕ-mū′can. A Persian prince, Esth. i. 14–21.

Mĕn′a-hĕm (*comforter*). Usurper of Israel's throne. Idolatrous and cruel. Reigned B. C. 772–761, 2 Kgs. xv. 14–22.

Mē′nan. Ancestor of Joseph, Luke iii. 31.

Mē′nĕ. First word of Belshazzar's warning. Entire, "Mene," he is numbered; "Tekel," he is weighed; "Upharsin," they are divided, Dan. v. 25–28.

Mĕn″e-lā′us. High priest, 2 Macc. iv. 23.

Mĕ-nĕs′the-us. Father of Apollonius, 2 Macc. iv. 21.

Mĕ-ŏn′e-nĭm (*enchanter*). Unlocated plain, Judg. ix. 37.

Mĕ-ŏn′o-thāi. A Judahite, 1 Chr. iv. 14.

Mĕph′a-ăth (*height*). Levitical town in Reuben, Josh. xiii. 18.

Mĕ-phĭb′o-shĕth (*idol breaker*). (1) A son of Saul, 2 Sam. xxi. 8. (2) Son of Jonathan, 2 Sam. iv. 4; ix. 6–13; xvi.; xix. 24–30.

Mē′rab (*increase*). Daughter of Saul, 1 Sam. xiv. 49; xviii. 17.

Mĕr′′a-ī′ah (*rebellion*). A priest, Neh. xii. 12.

Mĕ-rā′ĭoth (*rebellious*). Three priests, 1 Chr. vi. 6; Ez. vii. 3; Neh. xii. 15.

Mē′ran, Bar. iii. 23. [MEDAN.]

Mĕ-rā′rī (*bitter*). (1) Third son of Levi, and head of family of Merarites, Gen. xlvi. 11; Ex. vi. 16; Num. iii. 17; iv. 29–33; Josh. xxi. 7–30. (2) Father of Judith, Judith viii. 1.

Mĕr′′a-thā′ĭm (*double rebellion*). Symbol of Chaldea, Jer. l. 21.

Mĕr-cū′rĭ-us (*Mercury*). Name applied to Paul in Lystra, Acts xiv. 12.

Mĕr′cў Seat. Lid of the ark, Ex. xxv. 17–22; hence, covering, or atonement for sin, Heb. ix. 5.

Mē′rĕd (*rebellion*). Son of Ezra, 1 Chr. iv. 17.

Mĕr′e-mŏth (*heights*). Three priests, Ez. viii. 33; x. 36; Neh. x. 5.

Mē′rēs (*lofty*). One of Ahasuerus' wise men, Esth. i. 14.

Mĕr′ĭ-bah (*strife*). A desert encampment, where the rock was smitten, Ex. xvii. 7. Kadesh, Num. xx. 13–24.

Mĕr′ĭb=bā′al, 1 Chr. viii. 34; ix. 40. [MEPHIB-OSHETH, 2.]

Mĕ-rō′dăch (*death*). A Babylonian god, and royal surname, Jer. l. 2.

Mĕ-rō′dăch = băl′a-dăn (*Baal - worshipper*). King of Babylon, B. C. 721, Isa. xxxix. 1. Berodach-baladan, 2 Kgs. xx. 12.

Mē′rom (*heights*). The lake on Jordan above Sea of Galilee, Josh. xi. 5–7.

Mĕ-rŏn′o-thīte. Designations in 1 Chr. xxvii. 30; Neh. iii. 7.

Mē′rŏz (*refuge*). Unknown place, Judg. v. 23.

Mē′sech, Mē′shech (*drawn out*). (1) Son of Japheth, Gen. x. 2; Ezek. xxvii. 13; xxxii. 26; Ps. cxx. 5. (2) 1 Chr. i. 17. [MASH.]

Mē′shȧ (*freed*). (1) A Joktanite border, Gen. x.

30. (2) A king of Moab, 2 Kgs. iii. 4. (3) Son of Caleb, 1 Chr. ii. 42. (4) A Benjamite, 1 Chr. viii. 9.

Mē′shach (*guest*). Chaldean name of Mishael, Daniel's companion, Dan i. 6, 7 ; iii.

Mĕ-shĕl″e-mī′ah (*rewarded*). A Levite gatekeeper, 1 Chr. ix. 21 ; xxvi. 1–9.

Mĕ-shĕz′a-be-el (*delivered*). Returned captives, Neh. iii. 4 ; x. 21 ; xi. 24.

Mĕ-shĭl′le-mĭth (*repaid*). A priest, 1 Chr. ix. 12.

Mĕ-shĭl′le-mŏth (*repaid*). (1) A chief of Ephraim, 2 Chr. xxviii. 12. (2) Meshillemith, Neh. xi. 13.

Mĕ-shŭl′lam (*friend*). (1) Ancestor of Shaphan, 2 Kgs. xxii. 3. (2) Son of Zerubbabel, 1 Chr. iii. 19. (3) A Gadite, 1 Chr. v. 13. (4) Three Benjamites, 1 Chr. viii. 17 ; ix. 7, 8. (5) Eleven Levites, in Ez. and Neh.

Mĕ-shŭl′le-mĕth (*friend*). Mother of King Amon, 2 Kgs. xxi. 19.

Mĕs′o-bā-īte″. Designation of Jasiel, 1 Chr. xi. 47.

Mĕs″o-pŏ-tā′mĭ-à (*between rivers*). The country between the rivers Tigris and Euphrates, Gen. xxiv. 10 ; Deut. xxiii. 4 ; Judg. iii. 8–10 ; Acts ii. 9 ; vii. 2.

Mĕs-sī′ah (*anointed*). Applied to regularly anointed priests or kings, Lev. iv. 3, 5, 16 ; 1 Sam. ii. 10, 35 ; xii. 3–5. The Greek *kristos*, "anointed," takes its place in N. T., except in John i. 41 ; iv. 25.

Mĕs-sī′as. Greek form of Messiah, John i. 41 ; iv. 25.

Mĕt′als (*mined*). Precious and useful metals, such as gold, silver, tin, lead, copper, and iron, known to Hebrews and much used, Gen. ii. 11, 12 ; Num. xxxi. 22.

Mē-tē′rus. His family returned, 1 Esdr. v. 17.

Mē′theg=ăm′mah (*curb of the city*). A Philistine stronghold, 2 Sam. viii. 1.

Mĕ-thu′sa-el (*man of God*). Father of Lamech, Gen. iv. 18.

Mĕ-thu′se-lah (*dart - man*). Grandfather of Noah ; oldest of antediluvians. Lived 969 years, Gen. v. 21–27.

Mĕ-ū'nim, Neh. vii. 52. [MEHUNIMS.]

Mĕz'a-hăb (*gilded*). An Edomite, Gen. xxxvi. 39.

Mī'a-mĭn (*right hand*). Two who returned, Ez. x. 25; Neh. xii. 5.

Mĭb'har (*chosen*). One of David's heroes, 1 Chr. xi. 38.

Mĭb'sam (*odorous*). (1) An Ishmaelite, Gen. xxv. 13. (2) A Simeonite, 1 Chr. iv. 25.

Mĭb'zar (*fort*). A duke of Edom, Gen. xxxvi. 42.

Mī'cah (*God-like*). (1) The erratic Ephraimite whose story is told in Judg. xvii., xviii. (2) Sixth of the minor prophets. Prophesied B. C. 750–698. He foretells the destruction of Samaria and Jerusalem, and prefigures the Messiah. (3) A Reubenite, 1 Chr. v. 5. (4) Grandson of Jonathan, 1 Chr. viii. 34, 35. (5) A Levite, 1 Chr. xxiii. 20. (6) Father of Abdon, 2 Chr. xxxiv. 20.

Mī-cā'iah (*God-like*). A Samarian prophet, 1 Kgs. xxii. 8–38; 2 Chr. xviii. 7–27.

Mī'chå. Persons in 2 Sam. ix. 12; Neh. x. 11; xi. 17, 22.

Mī'chaël (*God-like*). (1) Prince of angels, Dan. x. 13; xii. 1; Rev. xii. 7. (2) Characters in Num. xiii. 13; 1 Chr. v. 13, 14; vi. 40; vii. 3; viii. 16; xii. 20; xxvii. 18; 2 Chr. xxi. 2; Ez. viii. 8.

Mī'chah, 1 Chr. xxiv. 24, 25. [MICAH, 5.]

Mī-chā'iah (*God-like*). (1) Full form of Micah in 2 Chr. xxxiv. 20. (2) Same as Micha, 1 Chr. ix. 15; Neh. xii. 35. (3) A priest, Neh. xii. 41. (4) Wife of Rehoboam and mother of Abijah, king of Judah, 2 Chr. xiii. 2. (5) A prince and teacher of the law, 2 Chr. xvii. 7. (6) Son of Gemariah, Jer. xxxvi. 11–14.

Mī'chal. Daughter of Saul and wife of David, 1 Sam. xiv. 49; xxv. 44; 2 Sam. iii. 14; vi. 23.

Mĭ-chē'as, 2 Esdr. i. 39. [MICAH.]

Mĭch'mash (*hidden*). Noted town in Benjamin, 1 Sam. xiii. 11; Isa. x. 28. Michmas, Ez. ii. 27.

Mĭch'mĕ-thah (*stony*). Border mark of Manasseh, Josh. xvii. 7.

Mĭch'rī (*precious*). A Benjamite, 1 Chr. ix. 8.

Mĭch'tam. Musical term for six Psalms.

Mĭd'din (*measures*). City in Judah, Josh. xv. 61.

Mĭd′ĭ-an (*strife*). Son of Abraham, and founder of Midianites, Gen. xxv. 2; Ex. iii. 1; Num. xxii. 4; Judg. vii. 13.

Mĭg′dal=ĕl (*tower of God*). Fenced city of Naphtali, Josh. xix. 38.

Mĭg′dal=găd (*tower of Gad*). Town in Judah, Josh. xv. 37.

Mĭg′dol (*tower*). Place in Egypt, Ex. xiv. 2; Num. xxxiii. 7, 8. Perhaps same in Jer. xliv. 1; xlvi. 14.

Mĭg′rŏn (*pinnacle*). Town near Gibeah, 1 Sam. xiv. 2; Isa. x. 28.

Mĭj′a-mĭn (*right hand*). (1) Chief of the 6th priestly course, 1 Chr. xxiv. 9. (2) Co-covenanters, Neh. x. 7.

Mĭk′loth (*staves*). (1) A Benjamite, 1 Chr. viii. 32; ix. 37, 38. (2) One of David's generals, 1 Chr. xxvii. 4.

Mĭk-nē′iah (*God-possessed*). A temple musician, 1 Chr. xv. 18–21.

Mĭl″a-lā′ĭ (*eloquent*). A priest, Neh. xii. 36.

Mĭl′cah (*queen*). (1) Wife of Nahor, Gen. xi. 29; xxiv. 15–47. (2) Daughter of Zelophehad, Num. xxvi. 33; Josh. xvii. 3.

Mĭl′com. [MOLECH.]

Mile. Roman mile in Matt. v. 41; 1618 yards.

Mī-lē′tus, Mī-lē′tum (*red*). City in Ionia, Acts xx. 15–38; 2 Tim. iv. 20.

Mĭlk, Of cows, goats, camels, and sheep a favorite Oriental food, Gen. xxxii. 15; Deut. xxxii. 14. Symbol of fertility, Josh. v. 6; Heb. v. 12.

Mĭll (*grind*). A mortar and pestle; or, two stones, upper and nether, the former turned by hand, Job xli. 24; Isa. xlvii. 1, 2; Matt. xxiv. 41. Millstones not pawnable, Deut. xxiv. 6.

Mĭl′let. Here a grass; abroad a cereal, like broom-corn, Ezek. iv. 9.

Mĭl′lō (*mound*). (1) A rampart of Jerusalem, 2 Sam. v. 9; 1 Kgs. ix. 15. (2) Where Joash was murdered, 2 Kgs. xii. 20. (3) A Shechem family, Judg. ix. 6–20.

Mī′na. [MANEH.]

Mī-nī′a-mĭn. Levites, 2 Chr. xxxi. 15; Neh. xii. 17, 41.

Mĭn'ĭs-tẽr (*assistant*). Attendant, Ex. xxiv. 13 ; Josh. i. 1 ; 1 Kgs. xix. 21 ; Ez. viii. 17. Magistrate, Rom. xiii. 6. Preacher and teacher, 1 Cor. iv. 1 ; 2 Cor. iii. 6. Celestial high priest, Heb. viii. 1–3.

Mĭn'nī. Part of Armenia, Jer. li. 27.

Mĭn'nith (*division*). An Ammonite section east of Jordan, Judg. xi. 33 ; Ezek. xxvii. 17.

Mĭn'strel (*minister*). A musician employed, or strolling, 1 Sam. x. 5 ; xvi. 16 ; 2 Kgs. iii. 15. Professional mourners, Matt. ix. 23.

Mĭnt. An aromatic herb, varieties numerous, Matt. xxiii. 23 ; Luke xi. 42.

Mĭph'kăd. A Jerusalem gate, Neh. iii. 31.

Mĭr'a-cle (*wonderful*). In scripture, a supernatural event, Num. xxii. 28 ; 1 Kgs. xvii. 6 ; Matt. ix. 18–33 ; xiv. 25.

Mĭr'ĭ-am (*rebellion*). (1) Sister of Moses and Aaron. Musician and prophetess, Ex. ii. 4–10 ; xv. 20, 21 ; Num. xii. 1–15 ; xx. 1 ; 1 Chr. vi. 3. (2) A Judahite, 1 Chr. iv. 17.

Mĭr'mà (*fraud*). A Benjamite, 1 Chr. viii. 10.

Mĭr'rôr (*wonder at*). Egyptian mirrors, which the Hebrew women affected, were highly polished metal plates, chiefly of copper, Ex. xxxviii. 8 ; Job xxxvii. 18 ; 1 Cor. xiii. 12.

Mĭs'gab (*high*). Place in Moab, Jer. xlviii. 1.

Mĭsh'a-el (*what God is*). (1) Uncle of Moses, Ex. vi. 22 ; Lev. x. 4. (2) Ezra's assistant, Neh. viii. 4. (3) Daniel's captive companion, Dan. i. 6–19 ; ii. 17.

Mĭ'shal, Mĭ'she-al (*entreaty*). Levitical town in Asher, Josh. xix. 26 ; xxi. 30.

Mĭ'sham (*fleet*). A Benjamite, 1 Chr. viii. 12.

Mĭsh'mà (*hearing*). (1) An Ishmaelite, Gen. xxv. 14. (2) A Simeonite, 1 Chr. iv. 25.

Mĭsh-măn'nah (*fatness*). A Gadite, 1 Chr. xii. 10.

Mĭsh'ra-ītes. Colonists from Kirjath-jearim, 1 Chr. ii. 53.

Mĭs'pe-rĕth. A returned captive, Neh. vii. 7.

Mĭs're-photh=mā'im (*burning waters*). Place in northern Palestine, Josh. xi. 8 ; xiii. 6.

Mīte (*little*). Half a farthing, or fifth of a cent, Mark xii. 41–44 ; Luke xxi. 1–4.

Mĭth′cah (*sweetness*). A desert encampment., Num. xxxiii. 28.

Mĭth′nīte. A designation, 1 Chr. xi. 43.

Mĭth′re-dăth (*Mithra-given*). (1) Cyrus' treasurer, Ez. i. 8. (2) Persian governor of Samaria, Ez. iv. 7.

Mĭth″rĭ-dā′tĕs, 1 Esdr. ii. 11. [MITHREDATH.]

Mī′tre (*turban*). The priestly head-dress of linen, wrapped round the head, and bearing a frontal inscription, "Holiness to the Lord," Ex. xxviii. 4, 36–39; xxix. 6; xxxix. 28–30; Lev. viii. 9; xvi. 4.

Mĭt″y̆-lē′nē (*curtailed*). Chief town of the island of Lesbos, Acts xx. 14, 15.

Mixed Multitude. Camp followers, Ex. xii. 38; Num. xi. 4; Neh. xiii. 3.

Mī′zar (*little*). Unlocated hill, Ps. xlii. 6.

Mĭz′pah, Mĭz′peh (*watch tower*). (1) Jacob's covenant heap, Gen. xxxi. 47–49. (2) Mizpeh-moab, 1 Sam. xxii. 3. (3) Hivite section in northern Palestine, Josh. xi. 3–8. (4) A city in Judah. Josh. xv. 38. (5) A city of Benjamin, Josh. xviii. 26; 1 Sam. x. 17–21; 1 Kgs. xv. 22.

Mĭz′par, Ez. ii. 2. [MISPERETH.]

Mĭz′ra-ĭm (*red soil*). Son of Ham, Gen. x. 6. The O. T. word translated Egypt, Gen. xlv. 20; Isa. xi. 11.

Mĭz′zah (*fear*). Grandson of Esau, Gen. xxxvi. 13.

Mnā′son (*remembering*). A Cyprian convert, Acts xxi. 16.

Mō′ab (*of his father*). Son of Lot by his daughter, and progenitor of the Moabites. The country lay east of the Dead Sea and south of the Arnon, Num. xxi. 13–15; xxii.; Judg. xi. 18. Though idolatrous, worshipping Chemosh, they were a strong, progressive people, holding Israel subject, Judg. iii. 12–14; but finally subdued, 15–30; 2 Sam. viii. 2; Isa. xv., xvi.; Jer. xlviii.; Ruth i., ii.

Mō′ab-īte Stōne. The celebrated stone found at Dhiban (Dibon) in Moab, in A. D. 1868, on which is engraved, in Hebrew-Phœnician, the record of Mesha, king of Moab's, rebellion against Israel, 2 Kgs. iii. 4–27.

Mō″a-dī′ah, Neh. xii. 17. [MAADIAH.]

Mŏch'mur. Brook or wady, Judith vii. 18.

Mō'din. Burial ground of the Maccabees, near Lydda, 1 Macc. xiii. 25.

Mō'eth, 1 Esdr. viii. 63. [NOADIAH.]

Mŏl'a-dah (*birth*). City in south Judah, Josh. xv. 26; xix. 2; Neh. xi. 26.

Mōle (*dirt thrower*). No ground-moles in Palestine. Chameleon or lizard in Lev. xi. 30; and rat or weasel in Isa. ii. 20.

Mō'lech (*king*). Moloch, Acts vii. 43. Milcom, 1 Kgs. xi. 5. Malcham, Zeph. i. 5. Tutelary divinity (fire-god) of the Ammonites, Lev. xviii. 21; 2 Kgs. xxiii. 10.

Mō'lī, 1 Esdr. viii. 47. [MAHLI.]

Mō'lid (*begetter*). A Judahite, 1 Chr. ii. 29.

Mō'lŏch, Acts vii. 43. [MOLECH.]

Mŏm'dis, 1 Esdr. ix. 34. [MAADAI.]

Mon'ĕy (*warning*). Gold and silver passed by weight among Hebrews, Gen. xvii. 13; xxiii. 16; though the ring tokens of Egypt may have been current, Gen. xx. 16; xxxvii. 28. Persian coined money (daric or dram) came into use after the captivity, Ez. ii. 69; Neh. vii. 70–72. The Maccabees first coined Jewish money, B. C. 140,— shekels and half shekels of gold and silver, with minor copper coins. The N. T. coins, Matt. xvii. 27; xxii. 19; x. 29; v. 26; Mark xii. 42, were Roman or Grecian.

Mon'ĕy Chān'gers. Those who made a business of supplying the annual half-shekel offering at a premium, Ex. xxx. 13–15; Matt. xxi. 12; Mark xi. 15.

Month (*moon*). Hebrew month lunar, from new moon to new moon, Num. x. 10; xxviii. 11–14. Intercalary month every three years. Months named, but usually went by number, Gen. vii. 11; 2 Kgs. xxv. 3. *See* month names in place.

Moon (*measurer*). Conjointly with the sun, appointed for signs, seasons, days, months and years. Regulator of religious festivals, Gen. i. 14–18. Worship of, forbidden, Deut. iv. 19. Used largely figuratively, Isa. xiii. 10; Matt. xxiv. 29; Mark xiii. 24.

Mō'ras-thīte. Of Moresheth, Jer. xxvi. 18; Mic. i. 1.

Môr'dę-cāi (*little*). A Benjamite captive at

court of Ahasuerus, and deliverer of Jews from plot of Haman, Esth.

Mō'reh (*teacher*). (1) First halting place of Abram in Canaan, Gen. xii. 6. (2) Hill in valley of Jezreel, Judg. vii. 1.

Mŏr'esh-eth=găth (*possession of Gath*). Place named in Mic. i. 14.

Mŏ-rī'ah (*chosen*). (1) The land in which Abraham offered up Isaac, Gen. xxii. 2. (2) Site of Solomon's temple in Jerusalem, 2 Sam. xxiv. 24; 1 Chr. xxi. 24-27; 2 Chr. iii. 1, 2.

Mŏr'tar. (1) Hollow vessel of wood or stone, in which corn was ground with a pestle, Num. xi. 8; Prov. xxvii. 22. (2) Various cementing substances used in building, as bitumen, clay, and ordinary mixture of sand and lime, Gen. xi. 3; Ex. i. 14; Lev. xiv. 42; Isa. xli. 25.

Mŏ-sē'rȧ (*bonds*). A desert encampment, Deut. x. 6.

Mŏ-sē'roth, Num. xxxiii. 30. [MOSERA.]

Mō'ṣeṣ (*drawn out*). The great leader and lawgiver of the Hebrews. Son of Amram, a Levite. Born in Egypt, about B. C. 1571. Adopted by Pharaoh's daughter, liberally educated, fled to Midian, Ex. ii. Called to lead the Exode, Ex. iii.-xix. Promulgated the law, Ex. xx.-xl.; Lev.; Num.; Deut. Died on Nebo, aged 120 years. Reputed author of Pentateuch and Job.

Mŏ-sŏl'lam, 1 Esdr. viii. 44. [MESHULLAM.]

Mŏth. Frequent scripture references to the destructiveness of this insect, Job xiii. 28; Ps. xxxix. 11; Isa. l. 9; Matt. vi. 19.

Moth'er. Held in high respect by Hebrews, Ex. xx. 12. Often used for grandmother, or remote ancestor, Gen. iii. 20; 1 Kgs. xv. 10.

Môurn'ing. Very public and demonstrative, Gen. xxiii. 2; xxxvii. 29-35. Period, seven to seventy days, Gen. l. 3; 1 Sam. xxxi. 13. Hired mourners, Eccl. xii. 5; Matt. ix. 23. Methods, weeping, tearing clothes, wearing sackcloth, sprinkling with ashes or dust, shaving head, plucking beard, fasting, laceration, etc.

Mouse (*pilferer*). Many species in Palestine, but Bible word generic, Lev. xi. 29; 1 Sam. vi. 4; Isa. lxvi. 17.

Mōw'ing. Reaping with sickle, Ps. cxxix. 7 "King's mowings," perhaps a royal right of pasturage, Am. vii. 1.

Mō'zȧ (*departing*). (1) A son of Caleb, 1 Chr. ii. 46. (2) Descendant of Saul, 1 Chr. viii. 36, 37.

Mō'zah (*departing*). City in Benjamin, Josh. xviii. 26.

Mŭl'bĕr-rў (*dark berry*). Translation disputed, 2 Sam. v. 23, 24 ; 1 Chr. xiv. 14. The bacah or balsam tree is probably meant.

Mūle. Mules not bred in Palestine, but imported, 2 Sam. xiii. 29 ; 1 Kgs. i. 33 ; 2 Chr. ix. 24. Warm springs meant in Gen. xxxvi. 24.

Mŭp'pim (*serpent*). A Benjamite, Gen. xlvi. 21. Shupham, Num. xxvi. 39.

Mûr'der (*death*). Punished with death, Ex. xxi. 12 ; Num. xxxv. 30, 31 ; but cities of refuge provided for the escape of the involuntary slayer, Ex. xxi. 13 ; Num. xxxv. 32 ; Deut. xix. 1–13.

Mûr'rain (*die*). The malignant cattle disease which constituted the fifth Egyptian plague, Ex. ix. 1–7.

Mū'shī (*deserted*). A son of Merari, Ex. vi. 19 ; Num. iii. 20.

Mū'shites. Descendants of Mushi, Num. iii. 33 ; xxvi. 58.

Mū'sĭc (*muse*). Anciently known, Gen. iv. 21 ; xxxi. 27 ; Job xxi. 12. Vocal and instrumental, reached highest perfection in temple choirs, 2 Sam. vi. 5 ; 1 Chr. xxv. Usual instruments, harp, timbrel, psalter, trumpet, flute, pipe, etc.

Mŭs'tard (*must*). The black mustard of the East grows quite large and strong, Matt. xiii. 31, 32 ; xvii. 20 ; Mark iv. 31, 32 ; Luke xvii. 6.

Mŭth=lăb'ben. Enigmatical title to Ps. ix.

Mўn'dus. Town in Caria, 1 Macc. xv. 23.

Mў'rȧ (*weeping*). Ancient seaport of Lycia, in Asia Minor, Acts xxvii. 5.

Mўrrh (*bitter*). A gum resin much prized and variously used, Ex. xxx. 23 ; Esth. ii. 12 ; Ps. xlv. 8 ; Prov. vii. 17 ; Mark xv. 23 ; John xix. 39.

Mўr'tle. A bushy evergreen, whose flowers, leaves, and berries were much used by Hebrews for perfume, ornament, and spicery, Isa. xli. 19; lv. 13; Zech. i. 8–11.

Mўs′ịȧ (*beech land*). Northwestern district of Asia Minor, Acts xvi. 7, 8.

N

Nā′am (*pleasant*). Son of Caleb, 1 Chr. iv. 15.

Nā′a-mah (*pleasing*). (1) Sister of Tubal-cain, Gen. iv. 22. (2) A wife of Solomon and mother of King Rehoboam, 1 Kgs. xiv. 21; 2 Chr. xii. 13. (3) Town in Judah, Josh. xv. 41.

Nā′a-man (*pleasantness*). (1) The leprous Syrian, cured by Elisha's orders, 2 Kgs. v. (2) Founder of the Naamites, Gen. xlvi. 21; Num. xxvi. 40.

Nā′a-math-īte″. Designation of Job's friend, Zophar, Job ii. 11.

Nā′a-mītes, Num. xxvi. 40. [NAAMAN, 2.]

Nā′a-rah (*youth*). Wife of Ashur, 1 Chr. iv. 5, 6.

Nā′a-rāi (*youthful*). One of David's warriors, 1 Chr. xi. 37. Paarai, 2 Sam. xxiii. 35.

Nā′a-răn, 1 Chr. vii. 28. [NAARATH.]

Nā′a-răth (*youthful*). A border of Ephraim, Josh. xvi. 7.

Nȧ-ăsh′on, Ex. vi. 23. [NAHSHON.]

Nȧ-ăs′son. Greek form of Nahshon, Matt. i. 4; Luke iii. 32.

Nā′a-thus. Son of Addi, 1 Esdr. ix. 31.

Nā′băl (*fool*). The Carmelite shepherd who refused food to David, 1 Sam. xxv.

Năb″a-rī′as, 1 Esdr. ix. 44. [ZECHARIAS.]

Nā′băth-ītes, 1 Macc. v. 25. [NEBAIOTH.]

Nā′bŏth (*fruits*). The vineyardist of Jezreel whom Jezebel caused to be murdered, 1 Kgs. xxi. 1–16; 2 Kgs. ix. 26.

Năb″ū-chŏ-dŏn′ŏ-sôr. Apocryphal form of Nebuchadnezzar.

Nā′chŏn (*ready*). Owner of the threshing-floor where the over-zealous Uzzah died, 2 Sam. vi. 6, 7.

Nā′chôr, Josh. xxiv. 2; Luke iii. 34. [NAHOR.]

Nā′dăb (*liberal*). (1) Son of Aaron, Ex. vi. 23; xxiv. 1. Struck dead for offering strange fire, Lev. x. 1–3. (2) Son and successor of Jeroboam on throne of Israel, B. C. 954–953. Slain by Baasha, his successor, 1 Kgs. xv. 25–31. (3) A Judahite, 1 Chr. ii. 28. (4) Uncle of Saul, 1 Chr. viii. 30.

Nă-dăb′ạ-thȧ. Place east of Jordan, 1 Macc. ix. 37.

Năg′ḡe (*shining*). Ancestor of Joseph, Luke iii. 25.

Nă′ha-lăl (*pasture*). Levitical city in Zebulun, Josh. xxi. 35.

Nă-hā′lĭ-el (*God's valley*). Israelite encampment in Ammon, Num. xxi. 19.

Nă-hăl′lăl, Josh. xix. 15. [NAHALAL.]

Nă′hạ-lŏl, Judg. i. 30. [NAHALAL.]

Nă′ham (*comforter*). Brother of Hodiah, 1 Chr. iv. 19.

Nă-hăm′ạ-nī (*compassionate*). One who returned, Neh. vii. 7.

Nă-hăr′ạ-ī (*snorer*). Joab's armor-bearer, 1 Chr. xi. 39.

Nă′ha-rī, 2 Sam. xxiii. 37. [NAHARAI.]

Nă′hăsh (*serpent*). (1) A king of Ammon, 1 Sam. xi. 1–11; 2 Sam. x. 2. (2) Father of Abigail, 2 Sam. xvii. 25.

Nă′hăth (*rest*). (1) A duke of Edom, Gen. xxxvi. 13, 17. (2) Two Levites, 1 Chr. vi. 26; 2 Chr. xxxi. 13.

Năh′bī (*secret*). The spy of Naphtali, Num. xiii. 14.

Nă′hôr (*snoring*). (1) Abraham's grandfather, Gen. xi. 22–25. (2) Abraham's brother, Gen. xi. 27–29.

Năh′shon (*enchanter*). A prince of Judah, Num. i. 7.

Nă′hum (*comforter*). Seventh of minor prophets. Probably an exile in Assyria. Approximate time of prophecy, B. C. 726–698. It relates to the fall of Nineveh. Noted for vigor and beauty.

Nă′ĭ-dus, 1 Esdr. ix. 31. [BENAIAH.]

Nāil (*hold, claw*). Nails of captives to be pared, Deut. xxi. 12. Ordinary metal nail, 1 Chr. xxii. 3; stylus, Jer. xvii. 1; stake, Isa. xxxiii. 20; tent-peg wood or metal, Ex. xxvii. 19; Judg. iv. 21, 22.

Nă′ĭn (*beauty*). A village in Galilee, now Nein, Luke vii. 11.

Nā'ioth (*dwellings*). Samuel's dwelling place and school in Ramah, 1 Sam. xix. 18–23; xx. 1.

Nă-ně'ă. A Persian goddess, 1 Macc. vi. 1–4.

Nă-ō'mī (*my delight*). Mother-in-law of Ruth, Ruth i. 2, etc.

Nā'phish (*pleasure*). Son of Ishmael, Gen. xxv. 15; 1 Chr. i. 31.

Năph'ĭ-sī, 1 Esdr. v. 31. [NEPHUSIM.]

Năph'ta-lī (*wrestling*). Fifth son of Jacob, Gen. xxx. 8. Large tribe at Sinai and Jordan, Num. i. 43; xxvi. 50. Allotment in northern Canaan, Josh. xix. 32–39. Tribe carried captive in reign of Pekah, 2 Kgs. xv. 29. For "mount Naphtali," Josh. xx. 7, read, mountains of Naphtali.

Năph'thär (*cleansing*). Naphtha, 2 Macc. i. 36.

Năph'tu-hĭm. A Mizraite (Egyptian) tribe, Gen. x. 13.

När-çĭs'sus (*narcotic*). Roman friend of Paul, Rom. xvi. 11.

Närd (*smell*). [SPIKENARD.]

Năs'băs. Nephew of Tobit, Tob. xi. 18.

Nā'sith, 1 Esdr. v. 32. [NEZIAH.]

Nā'sôr, 1 Macc. xi. 67. [HAZOR.]

Nā'than (*given*). (1) Distinguished prophet, and royal adviser and biographer of David and Solomon, 2 Sam. vii. 2–17; xii. 1–22; 1 Kgs. i. 8–45; 1 Chr. xxix. 29; 2 Chr. ix. 29. (2) A son of David, 1 Chr. iii. 5; Luke iii. 31. (3) Father of one of David's warriors, 2 Sam. xxiii. 36. (4) A returned captive, Ez. viii. 16.

Nă-thăn'a-el (*gift of God*). (1) A disciple of Christ, and native of Cana in Galilee, John i. 47–51; xxi. 2. (2) Ancestor of Judith, Judith viii. 1.

Năth''a-nī'as, 1 Esdr. ix. 34. [NATHAN.]

Nā'than=mē'lech. Chamberlain under King Josiah, 2 Kgs. xxiii. 11.

Nā'um (*comfort*). Father of Amos, Luke iii. 25.

Nāve. Hub of a wheel, 1 Kgs. vii. 33.

Nā've, Ecclus. xlvi. 1. [NUN.]

Năz'a-rēne. Inhabitant of Nazareth; Jesus so-called, Matt. ii. 23. Nazarenes, followers of Jesus, Acts xxiv. 5.

Năz'a-rĕth (*separated*). A town of Galilee, now

En-nazirah. Home of Jesus, Matt. iv. 13; Mark i. 9; Luke i. 26; iv. 16, 29; John i. 45, 46.

Năz'a-rīte (*separated*). One bound by a temporary or life vow, Num. vi. 1-21; Am. ii. 11, 12; Acts xxi. 20-26.

Nē'ah (*shaking*). A Zebulun boundary mark, Josh. xix. 13.

Nĕ-ăp'o̧-lĭs (*new city*). Seaport in northern Greece; now Kavalla, Acts xvi. 11; xx. 1, 6.

Nē'a-rī'ah (*child of God*). (1) A Judahite, 1 Chr. iii. 22. (2) A chief of Simeon, 1 Chr. iv. 42.

Nĕb'a̧-ī (*budding*). A co-covenanter, Neh. x. 19.

Nĕ-bā'jo̧th, Nĕ-bā'joth (*heights*). Son of Ishmael, Gen. xxv. 13; 1 Chr. i. 29; Isa. lx. 7.

Nĕ-băl'lat (*secret folly*). Re-peopled town of Benjamin, Neh. xi. 34.

Nē'băt (*view*). Father of King Jeroboam, 1 Kgs. xi. 26; xii. 2-15.

Nē'bo̧ (*prophet*). (1) A mountain of Moab, whence Moses viewed the promised land, Deut. xxxii. 49; xxxiv. 1. (2) A Reubenite city, Num. xxxii. 3, 38; xxxiii. 47. (3) Father of returned captives, Ez. ii. 29. (4) A Chaldean god, presiding over learning. Counterpart of the Greek Hermes, Isa. xlvi. 1; Jer. xlviii. 1.

Nĕb''u-chăd-nĕz'zar (*may Nebo protect*). King of Babylonish Empire, B. C. 605-561. Brought empire to greatest height of prosperity. Defeated Pharaoh-necho at Carchemish, Jer. xlvi. 2-26. Captured Jerusalem three different times, 2 Kgs. xxiv., xxv.; Dan. i.-iv.

Nĕb''u-chăd-rĕz'zar. Jeremiah so writes Nebuchadnezzar.

Nĕb''u-shăs'ban (*Nebo saves*). A chief of eunuchs under Nebuchadnezzar, Jer. xxxix. 13.

Nĕb''u-zär'ă-dan (*whom Nebo favors*). Chief of Nebuchadnezzar's body-guard, 2 Kgs. xxv. 8-21; Jer. xxxix. 11; xl. 1-5.

Nē'cho̧, 2 Chr. xxxv. 20. [PHARAOH-NECHO.]

Nĕ-cō'dan, 1 Esdr. v. 37. [NEKODA.]

Nĕd''a-bī'ah (*driven*). A Judahite, 1 Chr. iii. 18.

Nĕg'ī-nah. Singular of Neginoth, Ps. lxi. title.

Nĕg'ī-nŏth. Stringed musical instruments. Title to Ps. iv., vi., liv., lv., lxvii., lxxvi.; Hab. iii. 19.

Nĕ-hĕl′a̤-mīte (*dreamer*). Designation of She-maiah, Jer. xxix. 24–32.

Nē-he̤-mī′ah (*consolation*). (1) The Hebrew captive who returned, as leader of his people, to rebuild Jerusalem and administer its affairs. His book, 16th of O. T., B. C. 445–433, tells of his work. (2) Leader of returning captives, Ez. ii. 2; Neh. vii. 7. (3) An assistant wall-builder, Neh. iii. 16.

Nē′′he̤-mī′as, 1 Esdr. v. 8, 40. [NEHEMIAH.]

Nē′hĭ-lŏth (*perforated*). The flute and similar wind instruments, Ps. v. title.

Nē′hum (*comfort*). A returned captive, Neh. vii. 7.

Nĕ-hŭsh′tȧ (*brazen*). Mother of King Jehoia-chin, 2 Kgs. xxiv. 8.

Nĕ′hŭsh-tan (*little brazen thing*). Name of the preserved brazen serpent destroyed by King Heze-kiah, 2 Kgs. xviii. 4.

Nē′ĭ-el (*God-moved*). An Asherite boundary, Josh. xix. 27.

Nē′keb (*cave*). A boundary town of Naphtali, Josh. xix. 33.

Nĕ-kō′dȧ (*famous*). Two fathers of returned captive families, Ez. ii. 48, 60.

Nĕ-mū′el (*God's day*). (1) A Reubenite, Num. xxvi. 9. (2) A Simeonite, Num. xxvi. 12; Jemuel, Gen. xlvi. 10.

Nĕ-mū′el-ītes′′. Descendants of Nemuel (2), Num. xxvi. 12.

Nē′pheg (*sprout*). (1) Korah's brother, Ex. vi. 21. (2) Son of David, 2 Sam. v. 15.

Nĕph′ew (*grandson*). Grandchild or descendaːt, Job xviii. 19; Isa. xiv. 22.

Nē′phish, 1 Chr. v. 19. [NAPHISH.]

Nĕ-phĭsh′e̤-sĭm. His children returned, Neh. vii. 52.

Nĕph′ta̤-lī, Tob. i. 2–5. [NAPHTALI.]

Nĕph′tha-lĭm, Matt. iv. 13. [NAPHTALI.]

Nĕp′tha-lĭm, Rev. vii. 6. [NAPHTALI.]

Nĕph′to-ah (*opening*). A spring on boundary of Judah and Benjamin, Josh. xv. 9.

Nĕ-phū′sim, Ez. ii. 50. [NEPHISHESIM.]

Nēr (*lamp*). Grandfather of Saul, 1 Chr. viii. 33;

ix. 39. Appears as an uncle of Saul in 1 Chr. ix. 36.

Nē're-us. A Roman Christian, Rom. xvi. 15.

Nĕr'gal (*hero*). A man-lion god of Assyria, corresponding to Mars, 2 Kgs. xvii. 30.

Nĕr'gal=shă-rē'zer (*fire prince*). A prince of Babylon who released Jeremiah, Jer. xxxix. 3, 13.

Nē'rī (*lamp*). Son of Melchi, Luke iii. 27.

Nĕ-rī'ah (*light*). Father of Baruch, Jer. xxxii. 12.

Nĕ-rī'as, Bar. i. 1. [NERIAH.]

Nĕt. Used for hunting and fishing, Isa. xix. 8; Matt. xiii. 47. Style, manufacture, and method borrowed from Egyptians.

Nĕ-thăn'e-el (*gift of God*). Persons of this name in Num. i. 8; 1 Chr. ii. 14; xv. 24; xxiv. 6; xxvi. 4; 2 Chr. xvii. 7; xxxv. 9; Ez. x. 22; Neh. xii. 21, 36.

Nĕth''a-nī'ah (*God-given*). Persons in 2 Kgs. xxv. 23; 1 Chr. xxv. 2, 12; 2 Chr. xvii. 8; Jer. xxxvi. 14; xl. 8.

Nĕth'i-nĭm (*dedicated*). Assistant priests. A class, or order, associated with the temple service and wardship, 1 Chr. ix. 2; Ez. vii. 24; viii. 17–20.

Nĕ-tō'phah (*dropping*). Town near Bethlehem, Ez. ii. 22; Neh. vii. 26.

Nĕ-tŏph'a-thī. Netophathites. Dwellers in Netophah, 1 Chr. ii. 54; Neh. xii. 28.

Nĕt'tle (*sting*). The stinging nettle in Isa. xxxiv. 13; Hos. ix. 6. Supposably the prickly acanthus in Job xxx. 7; Prov. xxiv. 31; Zeph. ii. 9.

New Moon, 1 Sam. xx. 5. [MOON.]

New Tĕs'tă-ment. [BIBLE.]

New Year. [TRUMPETS, FEAST OF.]

Nĕ-zī'ah (*famed*). Returned Nethinim, Ez. ii. 54; Neh. vii. 56.

Nē'zib (*pedestal*). Lowland city of Judah, Josh. xv. 43.

Nĭb'hăz (*barker*). The Avite god, in form of a dog-headed man, introduced into Samaria, 2 Kgs. xvii. 31.

Nĭb'shăn (*sandy*). Town in wilderness portion of Judah, Josh. xv. 62.

Nĭ-cā'nor (*conqueror*). (1) A governor of Judea.

1 Macc. iii. 38. (2) One of the first seven deacons of the early church, Acts vi. 1–6.

Nĭc/′o-dē′mus (*people's victor*). The Pharisee ruler and timid convert who assisted at Christ's sepulture, John iii. 1–10; vii. 50; xix. 39.

Nĭc-o-lā′i-tanes. An heretical sect condemned in Rev. ii. 6, 15.

Nĭc′o-lăs (*people's victor*). Native of Antioch. First a Jewish and then a Christian convert. One of the first seven deacons, Acts vi. 5.

Nĭ-cŏp′o-lĭs (*city of victory*). Many ancient cities of this name. Probably the one in Epirus is meant, Tit. iii. 12.

Nī′ger (*black*). Surname of Simeon, Acts xiii. 1.

Night. The Hebrew day, from sunset to sunset, embraced the entire night, Gen. i. 5. Death, John ix. 4; sin, 1 Thess. v. 5; sorrow, sin, and death, Rev. xxi. 25; xxii. 5.

Night=hawk. An unclean bird, Lev. xi. 16; supposably the owl or night-jar.

Nīle (*dark blue*). The great river of Egypt, worshipped as a god, famous for its annual and fertilizing overflows and its many mouths. Name not mentioned in scripture, but alluded to as "the river," Gen. xli. 1; Ex. ii. 3; vii. 21; "the river of Egypt," Gen. xv. 18; "flood of Egypt," Am. viii. 8; Sihor, "black," Josh. xiii. 3; Shihor, "dark blue," 1 Chr. xiii. 5; "Nachal of Egypt," "river of Cush," etc.

Nĭm′rah (*clear*). City in Gad, east of Jordan, Num. xxxii. 3.

Nĭm′rĭm (*clear*). A stream in Moab, S. E. of Dead Sea, Isa. xv. 6; Jer. xlviii. 34.

Nĭm′rŏd (*brave*). Son of Cush. A renowned hunter, city builder, empire founder in Shinar (Babylonia), Gen. x. 8–12; 1 Chr. i. 10.

Nĭm′shī (*rescued*). Father of Jehu, 1 Kgs. xix. 16; 2 Kgs. ix. 2, 14.

Nĭn′e-veh (*dwelling of Ninus*). Capital of Assyria, on river Tigris. Founded by Asshur, Gen. x. 11. At height of its wealth and splendor during time of Jonah and Nahum, and burden of their prophecies. Taken by Medes about B. C. 750, and destroyed by combined Medes and Babylonians, B. C. 606, Jonah; Nah. i.–iii; Zeph. ii. 13. Among the ruins of Nineveh, which was supposed to embrace Nimrud and other suburbs, have been discovered many palaces and temples, and a richly sculptured obelisk whose references are to Syria and Israel.

Nĭn'e-vītes. Dwellers in Nineveh, Luke xi. 30.

Nī'san (*standard*). Abib, Ex. xiii. 4. First month of Hebrew sacred and seventh of civil year, corresponding to parts of March and April, Ex. xii. 2.

Nĭs'rŏch (*great eagle*). The eagle headed and winged Assyrian god, 2 Kgs. xix. 37; Isa. xxxvii. 38.

Nī'tre. The saltpetre of commerce. Evidently natron or washing soda is meant in Prov. xxv. 20; Jer. ii. 22.

Nō (*place*). Ancient Thebes and capital of Upper Egypt. The Diospolis of the Greeks. Situate on both banks of the Nile. Populous and splendid from B. C. 1600 to B. C. 800. Site of many imposing ruins. No-amon, "place of Amon," in marg. notes, Ezek. xxx. 14–16; Jer. xlvi. 25; Nah. iii. 8.

Nō''a-dī'ah (*met by God*). (1) A Levite, Ez. viii. 33. (2) A hostile prophetess, Neh. vi. 14.

Nō'ah (*rest*). (1) Ninth in descent from Adam, Gen. v. 28–32. Chosen to build the ark, Gen. vi. 8–22. Saved from the flood, with his three sons, Shem, Ham, and Japheth, Gen. vii., viii. Re-peopled the earth, Gen. ix., x. Died at age of 950 years. (2) A daughter of Zelophehad, Num. xxvi. 33.

Nō=ā'mon (*place of Amon*). [No.]

Nŏb (*height*). Levitical city in Benjamin, noted as scene of the massacre of the priests, 1 Sam. xxi. 1; xxii. 19–23; Neh. xi. 32.

Nō'bah (*barking*). Name given by Nobah to Kenath, Num. xxxii. 42; Judg. viii. 11.

Nŏd (*fleeing*). The land to which Cain the murderer fled, Gen. iv. 16.

Nō'dăb (*noble*). An Arab tribe, 1 Chr. v. 19.

Nō'e, N. T. and Apoc. form of Noah, Matt. xxiv. 37; Luke iii. 36.

Nō-ē'bà, 1 Esdr. v. 31. [NEKODA.]

Nō'gah (*bright*). A son of David, 1 Chr. iii. 7.

Nō'hah (*rest*). A Benjamite, 1 Chr. viii. 2.

Nŏn. Form of Nun, 1 Chr. vii. 27.

Nŏph, Isa. xix. 13; Jer. ii. 16; Ezek. xxx. 13. [MEMPHIS.]

Nō'phah (*blast*). Town in Moab, Num. xxi. 30.

Nōȝe=jĕw'elȝ. Rings worn in the nose. Still affected in the East, Isa. iii. 21.

Nŏv'ĭçe. "Newly planted." A recent convert, 1 Tim. iii. 6.

Nŭm'bĕrȝ (*distribute*). (1) Hebrews used alphabetic letters for notation. They also had preferential numbers, as "three," "seven," "ten," "seventy," etc., Gen. iv. 24; Ex. xx. 5–17; Num. vii. 13; Rev. xv. 1. (2) Fourth book of Bible and Pentateuch. Authorship ascribed to Moses. Chapters i.–x. 10 describe the departure from Sinai; x. 11–xiv. the marches to borders of Caanan; xv.–xvi. contain laws; xx.–xxxvi. describe events leading to the passage of Jordan and the conquest.

Nū-mē'nĭ-us. Jonathan's ambassador to Greece and Rome, 1 Macc. xii. 16.

Nŭn (*fish*). Father of Joshua, Ex. xxxiii. 11; 1 Chr. vii. 27.

Nûrse (*nourish*). Position of importance and honor among Hebrews, Gen. xxiv. 59; xxxv. 8; 2 Sam. iv. 4.

Nȳm'phas (*bridegroom*). A Laodicean Christian, Col. iv. 15.

O

Ōak (*strong*). Three varieties in Palestine, usually of great girth and expanse, but not noted for height, Gen. xxxv. 8; Judg. vi. 11, 19; 2 Sam. xviii. 9–14.

Ōath. Appeals to God to attest the truth of an assertion in early use, Gen. xxi. 23; xxvi. 3; Heb. vi. 16. Regulated in Ex. xx. 7; Lev. xix. 12. Forms: lifting hands, Gen. xiv. 22; placing hand under thigh, Gen. xxiv. 2; before the altar, 1 Kgs. viii. 31; laying hand on the law.

Ō''ba̸-dī'ah (*servant of God*). (1) A Judahite, 1 Chr. iii. 21. (2) A chief of Issachar, 1 Chr. vii. 3. (3) Son of Azel, 1 Chr. viii. 38. (4) A Levite, 1 Chr. ix. 16. (5) A Gadite, 1 Chr. xii. 9. (6) A court officer under Ahab, 1 Kgs. xviii. 3–16. (7) A teacher of the law, 2 Chr. xvii. 7. (8) Others, in 1 Chr. xxvii.

19; 2 Chr. xxxiv. 12; Ez. viii. 9; Neh. x. 5; xii. 25. (9) Fourth of minor prophets. Prophesied after capture of Jerusalem. His book, 31st of O. T., is a denunciation of Edom. Nothing known of his history.

Ō'bal (*naked*). Son of Joktan, Gen. x. 28. Ebal in 1 Chr. i. 22.

Ŏb'dĭ-à, 1 Esdr. v. 38. [HABAIAH.]

Ō'bed (*servant*). (1) Son of Boaz and Ruth, Ruth iv. 17; Luke iii. 32. (2) Descendant of Sheshan, 1 Chr. ii. 37, 38. (3) One of David's warriors, 1 Chr. xi. 47. (4) A temple porter, 1 Chr. xxvi. 7. (5) Father of Azariah, 2 Chr. xxiii. 1.

Ō'bed=ē'dom (*servant of Edom*). (1) He kept the ark for three months, 2 Sam. vi. 10–12; 1 Chr. xiii. 13, 14. (2) A temple treasurer, 2 Chr. xxv. 24.

Ō'beth, 1 Esdr. viii. 32. [EBED.]

Ō'bil (*camel-keeper*). David's camel-keeper, 1 Chr. xxvii. 30.

Ŏb-lā'tion (*spread out*). Act of offering. The offering itself, Lev. ii. 4.

Ō'both (*bottles*). An Israelite encampment, east of Moab, Num. xxi. 10; xxxiii. 43.

Ō'chĭ-el. 1 Esdr. i. 9. [JEIEL.]

Ŏc'ran (*disturber*). An Asherite, Num. i. 13; ii. 27.

Ŏd''a̤-när'kĕṣ. Chief of a nomad tribe, 1 Macc. ix. 66.

Ō'ded (*restoring*). (1) Father of Azariah, 2 Chr. xv. 1. (2) A Samaritan prophet, 2 Chr. xxviii. 9–11.

Ō-dŏl'lam. Greek form of Adullam, 2 Macc. xii. 38.

Ŏf'fĕr-ing (*bearing towards*). Either bloody, as of animals, or bloodless, as of vegetables. They embraced the burnt, sin, trespass, peace, and meat offerings, Lev. i.–ix.

Ŏg (*giant*). King of Bashan, last of the giant Rephaim, Num. xxi. 33; Deut. i. 4; iii. 3–13; Josh. ii. 10.

Ō'hăd (*strength*). Son of Simeon, Gen. xlvi. 10.

Ō'hel (*tent*). Son of Zerubbabel, 1 Chr. iii. 20.

Oil (*olive*). Used for preparing food, Ex. xxix. 2; anointing, 2 Sam. xiv. 2; illuminating, Matt. xxv.

1-13; in worship, Num. xviii. 12; in consecration, 1 Sam. x. 1; in medicine, Mark vi. 13; in burial, Matt. xxvi. 12. Types gladness, Ps. xcii. 10.

Oint′ment (*smear*). Highly prized, and made of perfumes in oil. For uses, *see* Oil.

Ŏl′īve. A tree resembling the apple in size and shape, bearing a plum-like fruit, prized for its oil, Gen. viii. 11; Deut. vi. 11; Job xxiv. 11. Olive wood used in the temple, 1 Kgs. vi. 23, 31-33.

Ŏl′īveş, Ŏl′i̭-vĕt. The mount of Olives, or Olivet, is the ridge east of Jerusalem, beyond the brook Kidron. So named from its olive-trees. On its slopes were Gethsemane, Bethphage and Bethany, 2 Sam. xv. 30; Zech. xiv. 4; Matt. xxi. 1; Mark xi. 1; Luke xxii. 39; John viii. 1; Acts i. 12.

Ȯ-lȳm′pas (*heavenly*). A Roman Christian, Rom. xvi. 15.

Ō-lȳm′pĭ-us. The Grecian Zeus, or Jupiter, dwelling on Olympus, 2 Macc. vi. 2.

Ŏm″a̭-ē′rus, 1 Esdr. ix. 34. [AMRAM.]

Ō′mar (*speaker*). A duke of Edom, Gen. xxxvi. 11, 15.

Ȯ-mĕg′ȧ *or* **Ȯ-mē′gȧ** (*great or long O*). Last letter of Greek alphabet, Rev. i. 8.

Ō′mẽr. A Hebrew dry measure, equal to tenth part of an ephah, Ex. xvi. 36.

Ŏm′rī (*pupil*). (1) A general under Elah, king of Israel, and eventually king, B. C. 929-918. He built Samaria and made it the capital, 1 Kgs. xvi. 16-28. (2) A Benjamite, 1 Chr. vii. 8. (3) A Judahite, 1 Chr. ix. 4. (4) A chief of Issachar, 1 Chr. xxvii. 18.

Ŏn (*strength*). (1) Grandson of Reuben, Num. xvi. 1. (2) City of Lower Egypt, Gen. xli. 45, 50. Bethshemesh or "house of the sun," Jer. xliii. 13. In Greek, Heliopolis, "city of the sun," Ezek. xxx. 17 marg. Noted for its learning, opulence, temples, shrines, monuments, sphinxes, and religious schools.

Ō′nam (*strong*). (1) Grandson of Seir, Gen. xxxvi. 23. (2) Son of Jerahmeel, 1 Chr. ii. 26.

Ō′nan (*strong*). Second son of Judah, slain for wickedness, Gen. xxxviii. 4-10; Num. xxvi. 19.

Ŏ-nĕs'ĭ-mus (*useful*). Slave of Philemon, at Colosse, in whose behalf Paul wrote the epistle to Philemon, Col. iv. 9; Phile. 10, 15.

Ŏn''e-sĭph'o-rus (*profit-bearing*). Friend of Paul at Ephesus and Rome, 2 Tim. i. 16–18; iv. 19.

Ŏ-nī'a-rē̆s. Onias and Areus, 1 Macc. xii. 19.

Ŏ-nī'as. Name of five high priests during time of Maccabees.

Ŏn'ion (*one*). The single-bulbed plant growing to perfection in the Nile valley, Num. xi. 5.

Ō'nŏ (*strong*). Town in Benjamin, 1 Chr. viii. 12.

Ō'nus, 1 Esdr. v. 22. [ONO.]

Ŏn'y̆-chȧ (*nail*). Incense ingredient; probably burnt seashell, Ex. xxx. 34.

Ō'ny̆x (*nail*). A cryptocrystalline quartz, veined and shelled, Ex. xxviii. 9–12; 1 Chr. xxix. 2.

Ō'phel (*hill*). A fortified hill in Jerusalem, 2 Chr. xxvii. 3; Neh. iii. 26; xi. 21.

Ō'phir (*fruitful*). (1) Son of Joktan, and his country in Arabia, Gen. x. 29. (2) Place whence the Hebrews drew gold, ivory, peacocks, and woods. Variously located, 1 Kgs. ix. 28; x. 11–22; xxii. 48; 1 Chr. xxix. 4; Job xxviii. 16; Ps. xlv. 9.

Ŏph'nī (*mouldy*). Town in Benjamin, Josh. xviii. 24.

Ŏph'rah (*fawn*). (1) Town in Benjamin, Josh. xviii. 23; 1 Sam. xiii. 17. (2) Native place of Gideon, Judg. vi. 11, 24. (3) Son of Meonothai, 1 Chr. iv. 14.

Ŏr'a-cle (*speaking*). In O. T. sense, the holy place whence God declared his will, 1 Kgs. vi. 5; viii. 6. Divine revelation, Acts vii. 38; Rom. iii. 2.

Ō'reb (*raven*). (1) A Midianite chief, Judg. vii. 25. (2) The rock, "raven's crag," east of Jordan, where Oreb fell, Judg. vii. 25; Isa. x. 26.

Ō'ren (*pine*). Son of Jerahmeel, 1 Chr. ii. 25.

Ŏr'gan (*instrument*). The "pipe," or any perforated wind instrument, Gen. iv. 21; Job. xxi. 12; Ps. cl. 4.

Ŏ-rī'on (*hunter*, *Orion*). The constellation, Job ix. 9; xxxviii. 31; Am. v. 8.

Ŏr'na-ments (*adornments*). Of infinite variety

among Oriental peoples, Gen. xxiv. 22 ; Isa. iii. 16–25; Jer. ii. 32 ; Ezek. xvi. 11–19.

Ŏr′nan (*active*). The Jebusite prince from whom David bought the threshing-floor on which he built the altar, 1 Chr. xxi. 15–25. [ARAUNAH.]

Ŏr′pah (*fawn*). Daughter-in-law of Naomi, Ruth i. 4–14.

Ŏr-thō′s̝ĭ-as. City of northern Phœnicia, 1 Macc. xv. 37.

Ŏ-sē′à, 2 Esdr. xiii. 40. [HOSEA.]

Ō′s̝ee. Greek form of Hosea, Rom. ix. 25.

Ŏ-shē′à. Original name of Joshua, Num. xiii. 8.

Ŏs′prăy (*ossifrage, bone-breaker*). An unclean bird ; probably the osprey or sea-eagle, Lev. xi. 13 ; Deut. xiv. 12.

Ŏs′sĭ-frăġe (*bone-breaker*). An unclean bird; the lammergeir, or bearded vulture, Lev. xi. 13 ; Deut. xiv. 12.

Ŏs′trĭch (*bird*). In Hebrew, "daughter of greediness." In Arabic and Greek "camel-bird." Largest of the bird species, Job xxxix. 13–18.

Ŏth′nĭ (*lion*). Son of Shemaiah, 1 Chr. xxvi. 7.

Ŏth′nĭ-el (*lion*). A judge of Israel, Josh. xv. 17 Judg. i. 13 ; iii. 9–11.

Ou′ches (*brooches*). Jewel settings, Ex. xxxix. 6.

Ŏv′en (*arch*). Fixed ovens, Hos. vii. 4. Portable, consisting of a large clay jar, Ex. viii. 3 ; Lev. xxvi. 26.

Owl (*howl*). An unclean bird and type of desolation. Five species found in Palestine, Lev. xi. 17 ; Deut. xiv. 16 ; Ps. cii. 6 ; Isa. xxxiv. 11–15.

Ŏx (*sprinkle*). (1) Ancestor of Judith, Judith viii. 1. (2) The male of the cow kind, and in scripture synonymous with bull. Used for plowing, Deut. xxii. 10 ; threshing, without muzzle, xxv. 4 ; draught, Num. vii. 3 ; burden, 1 Chr. xii. 40 ; beef, Deut. xiv. 4 ; sacrifices, 1 Kgs. i. 9.

Ō′zem (*strength*). (1) A brother of David, 1 Chr. ii. 15. (2) Son of Jerahmeel, 1 Chr. ii. 25.

Ŏ-zī′as. (1) Governor of Bethulia, Judith vi. 15. (2) Ancestor of Ezra, 2 Esdr. i. 2. (3) N. T. form of Uzziah, Matt. i. 8, 9.

Ŏ-zī′el. Ancestor of Judith, Judith viii. 1.

Ŏz′nĭ (*hearing*). Son of Gad, Num. xxvi. 16 ; Ezbon, Gen. xlvi. 16.

Ŏz'nītes. Descendants of Ozni, Num. xxvi. 16.

Ō-zō'rȧ, 1 Esdr. ix. 24. [SHELAMIAH.]

P

Pā'ạ-rāi (*opening*). One of David's warriors, 2 Sam. xxiii. 35; Naarai, 1 Chr. xi. 37.

Pā'dan (*table-land*), Gen. xlviii. 7. [PADAN-ARAM.]

Pā'dan=ā'ram (*table-land of Aram*). The plain region of Mesopotamia, Gen. xxiv. 10; xxv. 20; xxviii. 2–7; xxxi. 18; xxxiii. 18; xxxv. 9–26; xlvi. 15.

Pā'don (*escape*). His children returned, Ez. ii. 44.

Pā'ḡi-el (*God-allotted*). A chief of Asher, Num. i. 13; ii. 27; vii. 72, 77; x. 26.

Pā'hath=mō'ab (*ruler of Moab*). His children returned, Ez. ii. 6; viii. 4; Neh. iii. 11.

Pā'ī, 1 Chr. i. 50. [PAU.]

Pāint. Much used in East as cosmetic and beautifier, 2 Kgs. ix. 30; Jer. iv. 30. Houses, walls, beams, idols, painted, Jer. xxii. 14; Ezek. xxiii. 14. Painting as a fine art not encouraged by Hebrews.

Păl'ạçe. Royal residence, 1 Kgs. vii. 1–12; citadel, 1 Kgs. xvi. 18; fortress, 2 Kgs. xv. 25; entire royal court, Dan. i. 4; capital city, Esth. ix. 12. In N. T. any stately residence, Matt. xxvi. 3; Luke xi. 21.

Pā'lal (*judge*). An assistant wall-builder, Neh. iii. 25.

Păl''es-tī'nȧ, Păl'es-tīne (*land of sojourners*). Philistia, land of the Philistines, Ps. lx. 8; lxxxiii. 7. Palestina, Ex. xv. 14; Isa. xiv. 29, 31. Palestine, Joel iii. 4. Canaan, Gen. xii. 5; Ex. xv. 15; Holy Land, Zech. ii. 12. The indefinitely bounded region promised to Abraham, lying between the Mediterranean Sea and Jordan River and Dead Sea. It also embraced the Hebrew settlements beyond Jordan, Gen. xv. 18; xvii. 8; Num. xxiv. 2–12; Deut. i. 7.

Păl'lu (*famous*). Son of Reuben, Ex. vi. 14.

Păl'lu-ītes. Descendants of Pallu, Num. xxvi. 5.

Pälm′er=worm (*pilgrim-worm*). Canker-worm, or caterpillar, Joel i. 4; ii. 25; Amos iv. 9.

Pälm=tree (*hand-leaved*). The date-palm. Once grew luxuriantly in Palestine. Evergreen and stately, often rising to 100 feet, Ex. xv. 27; Deut. xxxiv. 3; Judg. i. 16; 1 Kgs. vi. 32; S. of Sol. vii. 7.

Păl′sy̆ (*paralysis*). Partial or total death of muscle and nerve, 1 Kgs. xiii. 4-6; Matt. iv. 24; Luke vi. 6.

Păl′tī (*deliverance*). The Benjamite spy, Num. xiii. 9.

Păl′tĭ-el (*deliverance*). A prince of Issachar, Num. xxxiv. 26.

Păl′tīte. Designation of one of David's guardsmen, 2 Sam. xxiii. 26.

Păm-phy̆l′ĭ-ȧ (*mixture of nations*). A seacoast province of Asia Minor. Its chief town was Perga, where Paul preached, Acts xiii. 13; xiv. 24; xxvii. 5.

Păn (*open*). A flat plate for baking, and a deeper vessel for holding liquids, Lev. ii. 5; vi. 21.

Păn′năg. Disputed word. Probably a place, Ezek. xxvii. 17.

Pā′per. [PAPYRUS.]

Pā′phos (*hot*). Town on island of Cyprus, visited by Paul, Acts xiii. 6-13.

Pȧ-py̆′rus. The writing-paper of the Egyptians, Greeks, and Romans, made from the papyrus plant, a rush or flag growing in Egypt, Job xl. 21.

Păr′ȧ-ble (*comparison*). Allegorical representation of something real in nature or human affairs, whence a moral is drawn. A favorite method of Oriental teaching, 2 Sam. xii. 1-4; Isa. v. 1-7. Christ spoke over 30 parables, Matt. xiii. 3-8; 24-30, 31, 32, and elsewhere in Gospels.

Păr′ȧ-dīse (*pleasure ground*). "Garden of Eden;" and, figuratively, abode of happy souls — heaven, Luke xxiii. 43; 2 Cor. xii. 4; Rev. ii. 7.

Pā′rah (*place of heifers*). City in Benjamin, Josh. xviii. 23.

Pā′ran, El=pā′ran (*places of caves*). The "desert of wandering," with Canaan on the north, desert of Sinai on the south, Etham on the west, and Arabah on the east, Gen. xxi. 14-21; Num. x. 12, 33; xii. 16; xiii. 3, 26; xxxiii. 17-36.

Pā'ran, Mount of. A mount of the Sinaitic range, Deut. xxxiii. 2; Hab. iii. 3.

Pär'bar (*suburb*). A spot between the west wall of temple at Jerusalem and the city beyond, 1 Chr. xxvi. 18.

Pärched Corn. Roasted grain, Ruth ii. 14.

Pärched Ground. Supposably the mirage frequently seen on desert tracts, Isa. xxxv. 7.

Pärch'ment (*from Pergamum*). Skin of sheep or goats prepared for writing on, 2 Tim. iv. 13.

Pär'lor (*speaking chamber*). King's audience-chamber, Judg. iii. 20-25.

Pär-măsh'tà (*stronger*). A son of Haman, Esth. ix. 9.

Pär'me-năs (*steadfast*). One of the first seven deacons, Acts vi. 5.

Pär'nach (*swift*). A Zebulunite, Num. xxxiv. 25.

Pā'rŏsh (*flea*). His children returned, Ez. ii. 3; Neh. vii. 8.

Pär-shăn'da-thà (*prayer-given*). Eldest son of Haman, Esth. ix. 7.

Pär'thĭ-anş. Jews settled in Parthia, that undefined country north of Media and Persia, Acts ii. 9.

Pär'trĭdge (*squatting*). Three varieties found in Palestine. Their flesh and eggs esteemed as food, 1 Sam. xxvi. 20; Jer. xvii. 11.

Pär'u-ah (*blooming*). Father of Solomon's commissary in Issachar, 1 Kgs. iv. 17.

Pär-vā'im (*eastern*). Unknown place whence Solomon shipped gold, 2 Chr. iii. 6.

Pā'sach (*cut off*) An Asherite, 1 Chr. vii. 33.

Păs-dăm'mim (*blood-border*). Spot of battles between Israel and Philistia, 1 Chr. xi. 13. Ephesdammim, 1 Sam. xvii. 1.

Pā-sē'ah (*lame*). (1) A Judahite, 1 Chr. iv. 12. (2) His sons returned, Ez. ii. 49.

Păsh'ŭr (*freedom*). (1) Head of a priestly family, 1 Chr. ix. 12; Neh. xi. 12; Jer. xxi. 1. (2) Priestly governor of the house of the Lord, 1 Chr. xxiv. 14; Jer. xx. i.

Păs'sion (*suffering*). Last sufferings of Christ, Acts i. 3. Kindred feelings, Acts xiv. 15; Jas. v. 17.

Păss'ō-ver (*passing over*). First of three great

Jewish feasts, instituted in honor of the "passing over" of the Hebrew households by the destroying angel, Ex. xii., xiii. 3–10; xxiii. 14–19; Lev. xxiii. 4–14. Called the "feast of unleavened bread." The Christian Passover is "The Lord's Supper," eucharist, Matt. xxvii. 62; Luke xxii. 1–20; John xix. 42.

Păs'tor (*shepherd*). Figuratively, one who keeps Christ's flocks, Eph. iv. 11.

Păt'a-ra (*trodden*). City on southwest coast of Lycia, Acts xxi. 1, 2.

Pāte (*flat*). Top of the head, Ps. vii. 16.

Pă-the̅'us, 1 Esdr. ix. 23. [PETHAHIAH.]

Păth'ros (*southern*). An ancient division of Upper Egypt occupied by the Pathrusim, Isa. xi. 11; Jer. xliv. 1–15; Ezek. xxix. 14.

Păth-rụ'sĭm, Gen. x. 14. [PATHROS.]

Păt'mos. The rocky island in the Ægean Sea, to which John was banished, Rev. i. 9.

Pā'trĭ-arch (*father*). Father of the family and chief of its descendants. The Hebrew form of government till Moses established the theocracy, Acts ii. 29; vii. 8, 9; Heb. vii. 4.

Păt'ro-băs (*paternal*). A Roman Christian, Rom. xvi. 14.

Pă-tro̅'clus. Father of Nicanor, 2 Macc. viii. 9.

Pā'u (*bleating*). Capital of Hadar, king of Edom, Gen. xxxvi. 39. Pai, 1 Chr. i. 50.

Pạul (*small*). In Hebrew, Saul. Born at Tarsus in Cilicia, of Benjamite parents, about the beginning of 1st century; a Pharisee in faith; a tent-maker by trade, Phil. iii. 5; Acts xviii. 3; xxi. 39; xxiii. 6. Studied law with Gamaliel at Jerusalem; persecuted early Christians; converted near Damascus, Acts v. 34; vii. 58; ix. 1–22. Commissioned an apostle to the Gentiles, Acts xxvi. 13–20. Carried the gospel to Asia Minor, Greece, and Rome. Author of fourteen epistles, amplifying the Christian faith. Supposably a martyr at Rome, A. D. 68.

Pāve'ment (*beaten floor*). [GABBATHA.]

Pă-vĭl'ịon (*butterfly tent*). Movable tent or dwelling. Applied to tabernacle, booth, den, etc., 1 Kgs. xx. 12; Ps. xviii. 11; xxvii. 5; Jer. xliii. 10.

Pēa′cock (*eye-feathered cock*). An import from Tarshish, 1 Kgs. x. 22; 2 Chr. ix. 21. The peacock of Job xxxix. 13 should be ostrich.

Pēarls (*little pears*). Stony secretions of the pearl-oyster. Reckoned as gems and highly prized as ornaments. Source of frequent metaphor, Matt. xiii. 45; 1 Tim. ii. 9; Rev. xvii. 4; xxi. 21. 'Pearl, in Job xxviii. 18, should be crystal.

Pĕd′a-hĕl (*saved*). A chief of Naphtali, Num. xxxiv. 28.

Pē̆-däh′zur (*rock-saved*). Father of Gamaliel, Num. i. 10.

Pĕ̆′dā′iah (*God-saved*). (1) Grandfather of King Jehoiakim, 2 Kgs. xxiii. 36. (2) Father of Zerubbabel, 1 Chr. iii. 18, 19. (3) A Manassite, 1 Chr. xxvii. 20. (4) Returned captives, Neh. iii. 25; viii. 4; xi. 7; xiii. 13.

Pē′kah (*open-eyed*). Murderer and successor of Pekahiah, king of Israel, B. C. 758–738. Conspired with Damascus against Judah, and perished in a conspiracy, 2 Kgs. xv. 25–31; xvi. ; 2 Chr. xxviii.

Pĕk″a-hī′ah (*God opens*). Son and successor of Menahem on the throne of Israel, B. C. 760–758. Murdered and succeeded by his general, Pekah, 2 Kgs. xv. 22–26.

Pē′kŏd. The Chaldeans are so called in Jer. l. 21; Ezek. xxiii. 23.

Pĕl″a-ī′ah (*distinguished*). (1) A Judahite, 1 Chr. iii. 24. (2) A co-covenanter, Neh. viii. 7; x. 10.

Pĕl″a-lī′ah (*judged*). A returned priest, Neh. xi. 12.

Pĕl″a-tī′ah (*saved*). (1) Grandson of Zerubbabel, 1 Chr. iii. 21. (2) A Simeonite warrior, 1 Chr. iv. 42. (3) A co-covenanter, Neh. x. 22. (4) One struck dead for defying Ezekiel, Ezek. xi. 1–13.

Pē′leg (*division*). Son of Eber. His family remained in Mesopotamia, Gen. x. 25; xi. 16–19.

Pē′let (*freedom*). (1) A Judahite, 1 Chr. ii. 47. (2) An adherent of David, 1 Chr. xii. 3.

Pē′leth (*freedom*). (1) Father of the rebellious On, Num. xvi. 1. (2) Son of Jonathan, 1 Chr. ii. 33.

Pē′leth-ītes (*runners*). Retainers and messengers of David, 2 Sam. viii. 18; xv. 18; xx. 7.

Pĕ-lī′as, 1 Esdr. ix. 34. [Bedeiah.]

Pĕl′ĭ-can (*axe-bill*). A voracious water-bird, large and strong-billed. The female is supplied with a pouch for supplying itself and young with water and food. Symbol of desolation. Original sometimes translated "cormorant," Lev. xi. 18; Deut. xiv. 17; Ps. cii. 6; Isa. xxxiv. 11.

Pĕl′o-nīte. Designation of two of David's warriors, 1 Chr. xi. 27, 36.

Pĕn (*feather*). Anciently, a metal graver for tracing on hard substances; the stylus, of pointed metal or bone, for writing in wax; the reed pen and hair pencil for writing on parchment and linen, Judg. v. 14; Job xix. 24; Jer. xvii. 1.

Pĕ-nī′el (*face of God*). Place beyond Jordan where Jacob wrestled with the angel, Gen. xxxii. 30. Penuel in Judg. viii. 17; 1 Kgs. xii. 25.

Pĕ-nĭn′nah (*pearl*). A wife of Elkanah, 1 Sam. 1-4.

Pĕn′nў (*cattle*). The Roman silver denarius, worth 15 to 17 cents. The Greek silver drachma was a corresponding coin, Matt. xx. 2; xxii. 19-21; Mark vi. 37; Luke xx. 24; Rev. vi. 6.

Pĕn′tȧ-teuch (*five-fold book*). Greek name for the first five O. T. books, or books of Moses. Called Torah, "the law," by Hebrews.

Pĕn′te-cŏst (*fiftieth day*). The Hebrew harvest-home festival, celebrated on fiftieth day from the Passover, or on the date of the giving of the law at Sinai, Ex. xxiii. 16; xxxiv. 22; Lev. xxiii. 15-22; Num. xxviii. In the Christian Church, Pentecost is celebrated seven weeks after Easter, to commemorate the day in Acts ii. 1-14.

Pĕ-nū′el. (1) [Peniel.] (2) A Judahite, 1 Chr. iv. 4. (3) A Benjamite, 1 Chr. viii. 25.

Pē′or (*cleft*). (1) The mountain in Moab to which Balak brought Balaam, Num. xxiii. 28; xxv. 18; xxxi. 16. (2) [Baal-peor.]

Pĕr′a-zĭm (*breach*). A figurative mountain, Isa. xxviii. 21.

Pē′resh (*dung*). Son of Machir, 1 Chr. vii. 16.

Pē′rez (*rent*). An important Judahite family, 1 Chr. xxvii. 3; Neh. xi. 4-6.

Pē′rez=ŭz′zah (*breaking of Uzzah*). Where

Uzzah died, 2 Sam. vi. 6–8. Perez-uzza, 1 Chr. xiii. 9–11.

Pĕr′fūme (*thorough-fume*). Perfumes largely used by Hebrews in religious rites and for toilet purposes, Ex. xxx. 35 ; Prov. xxvii. 9.

Pĕr′gà (*earthy*). A city of Pamphylia, Acts xiii. 13.

Pĕr′ga-mŏs (*heights*). Pergamum in R. V. A city of Mysia, in Asia Minor, celebrated for its library, which was transferred to Alexandria. Seat of one of the "seven churches," Rev. i. 11 ; ii. 12–17.

Pĕ-rī′dà (*kernels*). His children returned, Neh. vii. 57.

Pĕr′ĭz-zītes (*villagers*). Original village-dwellers in Canaan, Gen. xiii. 7 ; Josh. xvii. 15.

Pĕr-sĕp′ō-lis (*city of Persia*). Capital of Persia. Ruins very extensive, 2 Macc. ix. 2.

Pĕr′seus (*destroyer*). Last king of Macedonia ; defeated by Rome, 1 Macc. viii. 5.

Pĕr′sĭa (*land of Perses*). Originally the country around the head of the Persian Gulf ; afterwards the great empire, including all western Asia, and parts of Europe and Africa. Reached its height under Cyrus, B. C. 486–485. Conquered by Alexander, B. C. 330, Ezek. xxxviii. 5 ; 2 Chr. xxxvi. 20-23 ; Ez. i. 8.

Pĕr′sis (*Persian*). A Christian woman at Rome, Rom. xvi. 12.

Pĕ-ru′dà, Ez. ii. 55. [PERIDA.]

Pĕs′tĭ-lence (*the plague*). In Hebrew, all distempers and calamities, Ex. ix. 14 ; xi. 1 ; 1 Kgs. viii. 37.

Pē′ter (*stone, rock*). Simon, or Simeon ; son of Jonas, Matt. xvi. 17 ; Acts xv. 14. A fisherman, resident at Capernaum, Matt. viii. 14 ; called, Matt. iv. 18-20 ; name changed to Peter, John i. 42. Founder of Christian Church among the Jews, Acts ii. ; spokesman of the apostles, Acts x. ; author of two epistles ; a probable martyr at Rome. His first epistle is dated from Babylon ; his second is his valedictory. Both are advisory and exhortatory.

Pĕth′′a-hī′ah (*freed*). (1) Head of the 19th priestly course, 1 Chr. xxiv. 16. (2) Returned captives, Ez. x. 23 ; Neh. ix. 5 ; xi. 24.

Pē′thôr (*prophet*). Balaam's residence in Mesopotamia, Num. xxii. 5, Deut. xxiii. 4.

Pĕ-thū′el (*vision*). Father of Joel, Joel i. 1.

Pē′trà (*rock*). Edom. Modernly, Arabia Petræa.

Pĕ-ŭl′thāi (*wages*). Eighth son of Obed-edom, 1 Chr. xxvi. 5.

Phāi′sụr, 1 Esdr. ix. 22. [PASHUR.]

Phā′lec, Luke iii. 35. [PELEG.]

Phăl′lū, Gen. xlvi. 9. [PALLU.]

Phăl′tī (*deliverance*). The man to whom Saul gave Michal, his daughter and David's wife, 1 Sam. xxv. 44. Phaltiel, 2 Sam. iii. 15, 16.

Phăl′tĭ-el, 2 Sam. iii. 15. [PHALTI.]

Phăn-ū′el (*face of God*). Father of Anna the prophetess, Luke ii. 36.

Phăr′ạ-cim. His sons returned, 1 Esdr. v. 31.

Phā′raōh (*sun-king*). General name of Egyptian kings. Only a few are definitely named in the Bible. Different ones alluded to are, Gen. xii. 15; xli.; Ex. i. 8; v. 1; 1 Chr. iv. 18; 1 Kgs. xi. 18–22; ix. 16; 2 Kgs. xviii. 21; Pharaoh-nechoh, 2 Kgs. xxiii. 29; Pharaoh-hophra, Jer. xxxvii. 5–8.

Phā′raōh's Dạugh′ter. (1) Guardian of Moses, Ex. ii. 5–10. (2) Wife of Mered, 1 Chr. iv. 18. (3) Wife of Solomon, 1 Kgs. iii. 1.

Phā′rĕṣ, Matt. i. 3; Luke iii. 33. [PHAREZ.]

Phā′rĕz (*breach*). A Judahite, Gen. xxxviii. 29; xlvi. 12. Father of Pharzites, Num. xxvi. 20. Perez, Neh. xi. 4, 6. Phares, Matt. i. 3; Luke iii. 33.

Phăr′ĭ-see (*set apart*). A Jewish sect, strictly orthodox in religion, and politically opposed to foreign supremacy, Matt. xxiii. 23–33; Luke xviii. 9–14.

Phā′rŏsh, Ez. viii. 3. [PAROSH.]

Phăr′par (*swift*). A river of Damascus, 2 Kgs. v. 12.

Phăr′zītes. Descendants of Pharez, Num. xxvi. 20.

Phă-sē′ah, Neh. vii. 51. [PASEAH.]

Phă-sē′lis. A town on border of Lycia and Pamphylia, 1 Macc. xv. 23.

Phăs′ĭ-ron. An Arab chief, 1 Macc. ix. 66.

Phăs′să-ron, 1 Esdr. v. 25. [PASHUR.]

Phē′bĕ (*shining*). A servant of the church at Cenchrea, Rom. xvi. 1, 2.

Phĕ-nī′çĕ. (1) Acts xi. 19; xv. 3. [PHŒNICIA.] (2) Phœnix in R. V. A seaport of Crete, Acts xxvii. 12.

Phī′col (*strong*). Chief of Abimelech's army, Gen. xxi. 22; xxvi. 26.

Phĭl″a-dĕl′phĭ-à (*brotherly love*). A city of Lydia in Asia Minor, and seat of one of the seven churches of Asia, Rev. i. 11; iii. 7–13.

Phĭ-lär′chus. A cavalry leader, 2 Macc. viii. 32.

Phī-lē′mon (*friendship*). A Christian convert at Colosse in Phrygia, to whom Paul wrote an epistle during his captivity at Rome, in favor of Onesimus, Philemon's servant. Eighteenth N. T. book.

Phī-lē′tus (*amiable*). The convert whom Paul denounced for error, 2 Tim. ii. 17.

Phĭl′ĭp (*lover of horses*). (1) The apostle of Bethsaida, of whom little is known, Matt. x. 3; Mark iii. 18; Luke vi. 14; John vi. 5–9; Acts i. 13. (2) The evangelist and deacon, resident at Cæsarea, and preacher throughout Samaria, Acts vi. 5; viii. 5–13; xxi. 8–10. (3) The tetrarch. [HEROD.] (4) Husband of Herodias, Matt. xiv. 3. [HEROD.] (5) Governor of Jerusalem under Antiochus, and regent of Syria, 2 Macc. v. 22. (6) Philip V., king of Macedonia, 1 Macc. viii. 5. (7) King of Macedonia, B. C. 360–336, and father of Alexander the Great, 1 Macc. i. 1.

Phĭ-lĭp′pī (*city of Philip*). City in Macedonia, founded by Philip II., 12 miles from the port of Neapolis. Paul founded a vigorous church there, Acts xvi.; xx. 1–6.

Phĭ-lĭp′pĭ-anṣ. Dwellers in Philippi. Paul's epistle to the Christians there was written from Rome, A. D. 62 or 63. In it he sends thanks for gifts, praises their Christian walk and firmness, warns against Judaizing tendencies, and exhorts to steadfast faith.

Phĭ-lĭs′tĭà (*land of sojourners*). The plain and coast country on the southwest of Palestine, which imparted its name to Palestine, Ps. lx. 8; lxxxvii. 4; cviii. 9. [PALESTINE.]

Phĭ-lĭs'tĭneṣ (*villagers*). Dwellers in Philistia. Origin disputed, but associated with Cretans; also with the Caphtorim of Egypt, Jer. xlvii. 4; Am. ix. 7. Permanent settlers in time of Abraham, Gen. xxi. 32. Wealthy, energetic, and warlike, with many strong cities. Land not conquered by Joshua. Gaza, Ashkelon, Ashdod, Gath, and Ekron, their chief strongholds. Subdued by David, 2 Sam. v. 17–25; but became practically independent under the kings. Disappeared as a distinct people after the time of the Maccabees.

Phĭ-lŏl'ọ-gus (*learned*). A Roman Christian saluted by Paul, Rom. xvi. 15.

Phĭ-lŏs'ọ-phy̆ (*loving wisdom*). The prominent Grecian schools of philosophy in N. T. times were the Stoic and Epicurean, Acts xvii. 18. But the most formidable enemy of early Christian thought was the tendency of the learned to engraft the speculations of Eastern Gnosticism and Greek philosophy upon the evolving doctrines of Christianity, 1 Cor. i. 18–27; 1 Tim. vi. 20; Col. ii. 8, etc.

Phĭn'ẹ-es. Apocryphal form of Phinehas.

Phĭn'ẹ-has (*brazen mouth*). (1) Chief of the Korhite Levites, and high priest, Ex. vi. 25; Num. xxv. 6–15; Josh. xxii. 30–32. (2) Wicked son of Eli, 1 Sam. i. 3; ii. 34; iv. 4–19; xiv. 3. (3) A Levite, Ez. viii. 33.

Phī'son. Greek form of Pison, Ecclus. xxiv. 25.

Phlē'gon (*burning*). A Roman Christian saluted by Paul, Rom. xvi. 14.

Phœ'be. [PHEBE.]

Phœ-nī'çiạ (*land of palm-trees*). Phenicia in Acts xxi. 2. Phenice in Acts xi. 19; xv. 3. In O. T. referred to as Tyre and Sidon, or coasts of Tyre and Sidon. The small coast country north of Palestine, noted for its commercial enterprise, learning, and skill in arts. Included in the Land of Promise but never conquered, Josh. xiii. 4–6. David and Solomon employed its sailors and artisans, 2 Sam. v. 11; 1 Kgs. v.

Phœ-nī'çiạns. Dwellers in Phœnicia. In intimate commercial, political, and even religious relations with Hebrews, 1 Kgs. xvi. 31–33; xviii. 40; 1 Chr. xiv. 1; Isa. xxiii.; Ezek. xxvii. 2–8.

Phry̆g'-ĭ-ȧ (*barren*). An undefined section of

Asia Minor, out of which several Roman provinces were formed, Acts ii. 10; xvi. 6; xviii. 23.

Phŭd. Judith ii. 23. [PHUT.]

Phū′rah (*bough*).   Armor - bearer of Gideon, Judg. vii. 10, 11.

Phū′rim, Esth. xi. 1. [PURIM.]

Phŭt, Pŭt (*bow*).   Son of Ham, Gen. x. 6; 1 Chr. i. 8.   Name is rendered Libya and Libyans, people of north Africa, in Jer. xlvi. 9; Ezek. xxx. 5; xxxviii. 5.

Phū′vah (*mouth*).   Son of Issachar, Gen. xlvi. 13. Pua, Num. xxvi. 23.   Puah, 1 Chr. vii. 1.

Phў-ġĕl′lus (*fugitive*).   A Christian pervert of Asia, 2 Tim. i. 15.

Phў-lăc′te-rў (*safeguard*).   [FRONTLET.]

Pī=bē′seth (*house of Bast*).   City of Lower Egypt, on Pelusiac branch of the Nile.   Bubastis of the Greeks, noted for its temple of Bast, goddess of fire, Ezek. xxx. 17.

Pĭc′tūre (*painting*), Ezek. xxiii. 14; Prov. xxv. 11.   Sculptures, reliefs, or cornices, meant.   Movable or hanging pictures not favored by Hebrews.

Pièce (*part*).   In O. T., "pieces of gold," "pieces of silver," may well be read shekels' weight, or shekels, of gold or silver, Gen. xx. 16; 2 Kgs. v. 5.   In N. T., "pieces," Matt. xxvi. 15; xxvii. 3–9, are unknown.   In Luke xv. 8, for "pieces" read drachmas.

Pĭġ′eŏn (*chirping bird*).   [DOVE.]

Pī=ha-hī′roth (*place of sedges*).   Last Israelite encampment before crossing the Red Sea, Ex. xiv. 2, 9; Num. xxxiii. 7, 8.

Pī′late (*spear-armed*).   Pontius Pilate in Matt. xxvii. 2.   Sixth Roman procurator of Judea, A. D. 26–36.   Official residence at Cæsarea, with judicial visits to other places.   Christ was brought before him at Jerusalem for judgment.   He found no guilt, but lost his moral courage in the presence of the mob.   Eventually banished to Gaul, Luke xxiii. 1–7; John xviii. 27–40; xix.

Pĭl′dăsh (*flame*).   Son of Nahor, Gen. xxii. 22.

Pĭl′e-hå (*worship*).   A co-covenanter, Neh. x. 24.

Pĭl′lar (*pile*).   Prominent in Oriental architecture, monumental evidences, and scripture metaphor, Gen.

xxviii. 18; xxxv. 20; Ex. xiii. 21; Josh. xxiv. 26; Judg. xvi. 25-30; 1 Tim. iii. 15; Rev. iii. 12.

Pilled (*peeled*). Peeled, stripped, plundered, Gen. xxx. 37, 38; Isa. xviii. 2.

Pil'tai (*saved*). A priest, Neh. xii. 17.

Pine (*pitch*). Disputed rendering. Probably plane-tree is meant, Isa. xli. 19; lx. 13.

Pin'na-cle (*feather, edge*). Not a pinnacle, or summit, but the pinnacle, or wing, of the temple, Matt. iv. 5; Luke iv. 9.

Pi'non (*darkness*). A duke of Edom, Gen. xxxvi. 41.

Pipe. Flute. Type of perforated wind instruments, as the harp was of stringed instruments, 1 Sam. x. 5; 1 Kgs. i. 40; Isa. v. 12.

Pi'ram (*fleet*). An Amorite king, Josh. x. 3.

Pir'a-thon (*princely*). Now Ferata, six miles southwest of Shechem, Judg. xii. 15.

Pir'a-thon-īte''. Dweller in Pirathon, Judg. xii. 13, 15; 1 Chr. xxvii. 14.

Pis'gah (*hill*). The elevation, in Moab, whence Moses viewed the Promised Land, Num. xxi. 20; Deut. iii. 27; iv. 49; xxxiv. 1.

Pi-sĭd'ĭ-à (*pitchy*). A province of Asia Minor, with Antioch as its capital. Twice visited by Paul, Acts xiii. 14; xiv. 21-24.

Pi'son (*flowing*). One of the four rivers of Eden. Unlocated, Gen. ii. 11.

Pis'pah (*swelling*). An Asherite, 1 Chr. vii. 38.

Pit (*well*). Cistern or well, Gen. xxxvii. 20; grave, Ps. xxviii. 1; game-trap, Ezek. xix. 8; device, Ps. cxix. 85; Prov. xxvi. 27.

Pitch (*pine-resin*). The pitch of scripture was asphalt or bitumen, found in Dead Sea regions. Used for mortar, cement, calk, etc., Gen. vi. 14; xi. 3; Ex. ii. 3; Isa. xxxiv. 9.

Pitch'er (*goblet, wine-vessel*). A large earthen water-jar with one or two handles, Gen. xxiv. 15-20; Mark xiv. 13; Luke xxii. 10.

Pi'thom (*house of Tum*). A store-city of Egypt, built by the Israelites, Ex. i. 11.

Pi'thon (*harmless*). A son of Micah, 1 Chr. viii. 35.

Plāgue (*blow*). Pestilential disease, Lev. xiii. 2-8; xxvi. 25. Any calamitous visitation, Mark v. 29; Luke vii. 21. The judgments of God on Egypt are called plagues. They were (1) Nile changed to blood, Ex. vii. 14-25. (2) Visitation of frogs, Ex. viii. 1-15. (3) Lice, Ex. viii. 16-19. (4) Flies, Ex. viii. 20-32. (5) Murrain, Ex. ix. 1-7. (6) Boils, Ex. ix. 8-12. (7) Hail, Ex. ix. 13-35. (8) Locusts, Ex. x. 1-20. (9) Darkness, Ex. x. 21-28. (10) Smiting of the firstborn, Ex. xii. 29, 30.

Plāin (*flat*). Hebrew words so rendered have various significations. Plain, Gen. xi. 2; meadow, Judg. xi. 33; oak-grove, Gen. xiii. 18.

Plāit′ing (*folding*). Folding or pleating, as of the hair, 1 Pet. iii. 3.

Plăn′et (*wanderer*). The reference is evidently to the signs of the zodiac, as in marg. 2 Kgs. xxiii. 5.

Plăs′ter (*forming on*). Used by Hebrews as wall and stone coating, Lev. xiv. 42; Deut. xxvii. 2, 4; Dan. v. 5.

Plĕdge (*holding before*). [EARNEST.] [LOAN.]

Plē′ḷa-dēs or **Pleī′a-dēs** (*daughters of Pleione*). The "seven stars." A group of stars in the constellation Taurus, Job ix. 9; xxxviii. 31; Am. v. 8.

Plọw (*plowland*). In early times, a crude implement made of a forked stick, one branch of which was shod, or shared, with iron. Drawn by oxen, camels, and asses, Gen. xlv. 6; Deut. xxii. 10; Job i. 14.

Pŏch′e-rĕth (*beguiling*). His children returned, Ez. ii. 57; Neh. vii. 59.

Pō′ĕt-rỹ (*made up*). Hebrew literature largely poetical, and of lyrical style. Job, Psalms, Proverbs, Ecclesiastes, and Song of Solomon are distinctively poetical.

Pōll (*head*). The head, Num. iii. 47. To cut the hair, 2 Sam. xiv. 26.

Pŏl′lux. [CASTOR and POLLUX.]

Pọme′grăn-āte (*many - seeded fruit*). A low, straight - stemmed tree, native of Persia, Syria, and Arabia, bearing an orange-like fruit, Num. xiii. 23; Deut. viii. 8; S. of Sol. iv. 3; vi. 7; viii. 2.

Pŏm′mels (*knobs*). Globular ornaments on the capitals of pillars, 2 Chr. iv. 12, 13. Called "bowls" in 1 Kgs. vii. 41.

Pŏnds (*confined*). Egyptian ponds were pools left by subsidence of the Nile waters, Ex. vii. 19. Fish-ponds in Isa. xix. 10.

Pŏn'tĭ-us Pī'lạte. [PILATE.]

Pŏn'tus (*the sea*). Northeastern province of Asia Minor, bordering on the Pontus Euxinus, Euxine Sea. Empire of Mithridates, defeated by Pompey, B. C. 66. Many Jews settled there, Acts ii. 9; xviii. 2; 1 Pet. i. 1.

Pool (*hole*). Artificial reservoir for water. Very necessary in the East and sometimes built very elaborately and expensively, Eccl. ii. 6; Isa. xlii. 15.

Poor (*bare*). Poor especially cared for under Jewish dispensation, Ex. xxiii. 6; Lev. xix. 9, 10; Deut. xv. 7. Spirit continued, Luke iii. 11; xiv. 13; Acts vi. 1.

Pŏp'lär (*butterfly-leaf*). The white poplar supposed to be meant, Gen. xxx. 37; Hos. iv. 13.

Pŏr'a-thả (*favored*). A son of Haman, Esth. ix. 8.

Pōrch (*door*). In oriental architecture, veranda, colonnade, vestibule, Judg. iii. 23; 1 Chr. xxviii. 11; John x. 23. Any passage from street to inner hall, Matt. xxvi. 71.

Pŏr'çĭ-us Fĕs'tus, Acts xxiv. 27. [FESTUS.]

Pōr'terş (*gate-keepers*). Keepers of city, temple, palace, and private gates and doors. The temple had 4000 of them, in classified service, 2 Sam. xviii. 26; 2 Kgs. vii. 10; 1 Chr. xxiii. 5; xxvi. 1–19; 2 Chr. xxxi. 14.

Pŏs''ĭ-dō'nĭ-as. Nicanor's envoy to Judas, 2 Macc. xiv. 19.

Pōsts (*placed*). Runners, messengers, on foot, on horses, or on dromedaries, Esth. viii. 10–14; Job ix. 25; Jer. li. 31.

Pŏt (*drinking-vessel*). Pots of various designs, sizes, and uses. Made of clay or metal, Lev. vi. 28; 1 Sam. ii. 14; 2 Kgs. iv. 2; Jer. xxxv. 5; Ezek. iv. 9.

Pŏt'ĭ-phar (*belonging to the sun*). Captain of Pharaoh's guard, Gen. xxxvii. 36; xxxix.

Pŏ-tĭ'=phe-rah (*belonging to the sun*). A priest of On, in Egypt, and father-in-law of Joseph, Gen. xli. 45.

Pŏt'sherd (*pot-fragment*). A piece of broken pottery, Prov. xxvi. 23.

Pŏt'tage (*pot-cooked*). A thick stew of meat or vegetables, or both, Gen. xxv. 29; 2 Kgs. iv. 39.

Pŏt'ter's Field. The burial-ground for strangers, outside of Jerusalem, bought with the betrayal money, Matt. xxvii. 7. [ACELDAMA.]

Pŏt'ter-y (*pot-ware*). A very ancient art and carried to great perfection. Vessels variously moulded, and often elaborately decorated. The ceramic art furnishes many valuable contributions to ancient history, Gen. xxiv. 14; 1 Chr. iv. 23; Isa. xli. 25; Jer. xviii. 3.

Pound (*weight*). A weight; the maneh, 1 Kgs. x. 17; Ez. ii. 69; Neh. vii. 71. One sixtieth of a Grecian talent, Luke xix. 13–27.

Præ-tō'rĭ-um (*governor's headquarters*). The court, hearing-hall, and judgment-hall, of a Roman governor, wherever he might be, Matt. xxvii. 27; Mark xv. 16; John xviii. 28; Acts xxiii. 35; Phil. i. 13.

Prāy'er (*seeking favor*). Reverent petition to a divinity a universal custom. The Jews had three daily periods of prayer: 9 A. M., 12 M., 3 P. M., Ps. lv. 17; Dan. vi. 10.

Prĕṣ'ent. [GIFT.]

Prĭcks. [GOADS.]

Prĭēst (*presbyter, elder*). Representative of man in things appertaining to God. Assistants of Moses as mediator, Ex. xxiv. 5. Function of priesthood conferred on Levites, Ex. xxviii. Priests divided into regular courses, 1 Chr. xxiv. 1–19; 2 Chr. xxiii. 8; Luke i. 5.

Prĭnce (*first*). In Bible sense, patriarch, head of a family or chief of a tribe; governor or magistrate, 1 Kgs. xx. 14; satrap or ruler, Dan. vi. 1.

Prĭn″çĭ-păl'ĭ-ty. Territory of a prince. Seemingly an order of angels in Eph. i. 21; vi. 12; Col. i. 16; ii. 10.

Prĭs'cà (*ancient*), 2 Tim. iv. 19. [PRISCILLA.]

Prĭs-çĭl'là (*little Prisca*). Wife of Aquila, Acts xviii. 2, 18, 26; Rom. xvi. 3.

Prĭṣ'on (*seizing*). Ward or lock-up, Lev. xxiv. 12; Num. xv. 34; well or pit, Gen. xxxvii. 24; Jer. xxxviii. 6–11; part of a palace, 2 Chr. xvi. 10; Jer. xxxii. 2; Acts xxiii. 10, 35.

Prŏch′o-rus (*choir leader*). One of the first seven deacons, Acts vi. 5.

Prŏ-cŏn′sul (*for a consul*). A Roman official, beneath a consul, who exercised authority in a province. Appointed by the senate, Acts xiii. 7 ; xix. 38.

Prŏc′ū-râ″tor (*caring for*). A Roman provincial officer, governor, or viceroy, appointed by the emperor, Matt. xxvii. ; Acts xxiii. 24 ; xxvi. 30.

Prŏg-nŏs′tĭ-câ″tŏr (*knowing before*). Conjurer and fortune-teller, aided by the heavenly bodies, Isa. xlvii. 13.

Prŏph′et (*speaking beforehand*). Who tells the future under God's inspiration. The prophetic order embraced political, as well as spiritual, advisers and warners. The books of seventeen — four greater and thirteen lesser prophets — are comprised in the O. T. Christ is the preeminent and eternal prophet, Luke xxiv. 27, 44.

Prŏs′ė-lȳte (*come to*). A convert to the Jewish faith. "Stranger" in O. T., Deut. x. 18, 19 ; Matt. xxiii. 15 ; Acts xiii. 43.

Prŏv′ĕrb (*for a word*). Wise utterance ; enigma, Num. xxi. 27. The proverbs, collected and poetically arranged by Solomon, or by his authority, constitute the twentieth O. T. book.

Psālms (*play a stringed instrument*). In Hebrew, "Praises." The collection of one hundred and fifty lyrics which compose the nineteenth O. T. book. The liturgical hymnbook of the Hebrews, and accepted by early Christians. Authorship of seventy of them ascribed to David. The most perfect specimens of Hebrew poetry extant.

Psạl′tẽr-ȳ (*play on a stringed instrument*). A stringed instrument to accompany the voice, and supposed to resemble a guitar, 2 Sam. vi. 5 ; 2 Chr. ix. 11. The original frequently translated "viol," Isa. v. 12 ; xiv. 11.

Ptŏl″ė-mæ′us, Ptŏl′ė-my. (1) The Ptolemies were a race of Egyptian kings sprung from Ptolemy Soter, who inherited that portion of the conquests of Alexander the Great. They are supposed to be alluded to in the visions of Daniel. Ptolemy I., Soter, B. C. 323-285, Dan. xi. 5. Ptolemy II., Philadelphus, B. C. 285-247, Dan. xi. 6. Ptolemy III., Euergetes,

B. C. 247–222, Dan. xi. 7–9. Ptolemy IV., Philopator, B. C. 222–205, Dan. xi. 10–12. Ptolemy V., Epiphanes, B. C. 205–181, Dan. xi. 13–17. Ptolemy VI., Philometor, B. C. 181–146, Dan. xi. 25–30. Their kingdom fell under Rome. (2) Father of Lysimachus, Greek translator of Esther, Esth. xi. 1.

Ptŏ''le-mā'ĭs, Acts xxi. 7. [ACCHO.]

Pū'à, Num. xxvi. 23. [PHUVAH.]

Pū'ah (*mouth*). (1) Father of Tola, a judge of Israel, Judg. x. 1. (2) An Egyptian midwife, Ex. i. 15.

Pŭb'lĭ-can (*people's servant*). Gatherer of public revenue; tax-collector, abhorred by Jews, Matt. xviii. 17; Luke iii. 12, 13; xix. 2.

Pŭb'lĭ-us (*common*). Governor of the island of Melita, Acts xxviii. 7, 8.

Pū'denṣ (*modest*). A Roman Christian who saluted Timothy, 2 Tim. iv. 21.

Pū'hītes. A Judahite family, 1 Chr. ii. 53.

Pŭl (*lord*). (1) A possible African region, Isa. lxvi. 19. (2) A king of Assyria, 2 Kgs. xv. 19, 20.

Pŭlse (*pottage*). Peas, beans, lentils, etc., and, in a Hebrew sense, perhaps the cereals, Dan. i. 12–16.

Pŭn'ĭsh-ment (*pain*). Capital punishment was by hanging, 2 Sam. xxi. 6; stoning, Ex. xvii. 4; John x. 31; burning, Gen. xxxviii. 24; shooting, Ex. xix. 13; the sword, 1 Kgs. ii. 25; drowning, Matt. xviii. 6; sawing, 2 Sam. xii. 31; crucifixion. The death penalty was inflicted for parental reviling, blasphemy, adultery, rape, idolatry, perjury. Secondary punishments were generally those of retaliation, an "eye for an eye," etc., Ex. xxi. 23–25; Deut. xix. 18–21.

Pū'nītes. Descendants of Phuvah, or Pua, Num. xxvi. 23.

Pū'non (*darkness*). A desert encampment, Num. xxxiii. 42.

Pū''rĭ-fĭ-cā'tion (*cleansing*). A ritualistic form and sanitary precaution among Hebrews, Lev. xiv. 4–32; Mark vii. 3, 4; John xi. 55.

Pū'rim (*lots*). The Jewish festival commemorative of the preservation of the Jews in Persia. Celebrated yearly on 14th and 15th of the month Adar, Esth. iii. 7; ix. 20–32.

Pŭt, 1 Chr. i. 8. [PHUT.]

Pū-tē′o-lī (*sulphurous wells*). Now Pozzuoli, sea-port of Campania, on Bay of Naples, Acts xxviii. 13.

Pŭ′tĭ-el (*afflicted*). Father-in-law of Eleazar, Ex. vi. 25.

Pȳ′garg (*white-rumped*). A species of antelope, Deut. xiv. 5.

Pўr′rhus. Father of Sopater, in R. V., Acts xx. 4.

Pȳ′thon (*serpent*). Pythian Apollo, Acts xvi. 16 marg.

Q

Quāils (*quackers*). Quails of the Old World spe-cies, *Coturnix coturnix*, abound in the Arabian desert, and migrate northward, in spring, in enor-mous flocks, Ex. xvi. 13; Num. xi. 31, 32; Ps. cv. 40.

Quăr′tus (*fourth*). A Christian at Corinth, Rom. xvi. 23.

Quă-tĕr′nĭ-on (*file of four*). A Roman guard of four soldiers, two of whom watched prisoners within the door, and two watched the door outside, Acts xii. 4–10.

Quēen (*woman*). The three Hebrew words so rendered imply a queen-regnant, queen-consort, and queen-mother, with a dignity very like that of the present day, 1 Kgs. ii. 19; x. 1; xv. 13; Esth. i. 9; ii. 17; Jer. xiii. 18; xxix. 2.

Quēen of Heaven. The moon, worshipped as Astoreth or Astarte by idolatrous Hebrews, Jer. vii. 18; xliv. 17–25.

Quĭck′sănds. The Syrtis, greater and lesser. Two dangerous sandbanks or shoals off the north coast of Africa between Carthage and Cyrene, Acts xxvii. 17.

Quĭv′er (*cover*). Case or cover for arrows, Gen. xxvii. 3; Job xxxix. 23.

R

Rā′a-mah (*shaking*). Son of Cush, and father of a trading tribe on the Persian Gulf, Gen. x. 7; Ezek. xxvii. 22.

Rā′′a-mī′ah (*God's thunder*). A chief who re-turned, Neh. vii. 7. Reelaiah, Ez. ii. 2.

Rå-ăm′sēṣ, Ex. i. 11. [RAMESES.]

Răb′bah (*great*). (1) A strong Ammonite city east of Jordan; rebuilt by Ptolemy Philadelphus, B. C. 285–247, and called Philadelphia, Josh. xiii. 25; 2 Sam. xi. 1; xii. 27–29; 1 Chr. xx. 1. Rabbath-ammon, *i. e.*, Rabbath of the Ammonites, or of the children of Ammon, in Deut. iii. 11; 2 Sam. xii. 26; xvii. 27; Jer. xlix. 2; Ezek. xxi. 20. (2) Town in Judah, Josh. xv. 60.

Răb′bath=am′mŏn. [RABBAH.]

Răb′bath=mō′ab. [AR.]

Răb′bī (*my master*). A title of respect applied to Hebrew doctors and teachers. Applied also to priests, and to Christ, Matt. xxiii. 7; Mark ix. 5; John i. 38. Rabboni in John xx. 16.

Răb′bĭth (*many*). Town in Issachar, Josh. xix. 20.

Răb-bō′nĭ, John xx. 16. [RABBI.]

Răb′=măg (*chief of magi*). An important office at the court of Babylonia, Jer. xxxix. 3, 13.

Răb′sa-rĭs (*chief of eunuchs*). (1) An Assyrian general, 2 Kgs. xviii. 17. (2) A Babylonian prince, Jer. xxxix. 3, 13.

Răb′sha-keh (*cup bearer*). An Assyrian general, 2 Kgs. xviii. 17–37; xix.; Isa. xxxvi.

Rā′cå (*worthless*). A Hebrew term of contempt and reproach, Matt. v. 22.

Rāce (*rush*). As a public game, not patronized by Hebrews. A favorite game with Greeks and Romans, 1 Cor. ix. 24; Heb. xii. 1.

Rā′chăb. Greek form of Rahab, Matt. i. 5.

Rā′chăl (*trade*). A town in southern Judah. 1 Sam. xxx. 29.

Rā′chel (*ewe*). Daughter of Laban, wife of Jacob, and mother of Joseph and Benjamin, Gen. xxix.–xxxv.

Răd′da-ī (*trampling*). Brother of David, 1 Chr. ii. 14.

Rā′gaü. (1) Judith i. 5. [RAGES.] (2) Luke iii. 35. [REU.]

Rā′gēṣ. City in Media, Tob. i. 14.

Rā-gū′el (*friend of God*) (1) A priest, or prince, of Midian, Num. x. 29. Reuel in Ex. ii. 18. (2) Father-in-law of Tobias, Tob. iii. 7.

Rā′hăb (*large*). (1) The harlot of Jericho who re-

ceived the spies, and married Salmon, Josh. ii. 1–21;
vi. 17–25; Ruth iv. 21; Matt. i. 5. (2) Symbolical
term for Egypt, implying insolence and violence, Ps.
lxxxix. 10; Isa. li. 9.

Rā′hăm (*belly*). A descendant of Caleb, 1 Chr.
ii. 44.

Rā′hel, Jer. xxxi. 15. [RACHEL.]

Rain. The early rains of Palestine fall in October,
in time for seeding; the later, in April, in time for
fruits. May to October is the dry season, Deut. xi.
14; Hos. vi. 3; Joel ii. 23.

Rain′bōw. A sign of the covenant that the
earth should not again be destroyed by water, Gen.
ix. 12–17.

Rā′kem (*flower culture*). Descendant of Manasseh, 1 Chr. vii. 16.

Răk′kăth (*coast*). A fenced city in Naphtali,
Josh. xix. 35.

Răk′kŏn (*void*). Town in Dan, near Joppa, Josh.
xix. 46.

Răm (*high*). (1) A Judahite, 1 Chr. ii. 9. Aram,
Matt. i. 3, 4; Luke iii. 33. (2) Son of Jerahmeel,
1 Chr. ii. 25. (3) Kinsman of Elihu, Job xxxii. 2.

Răm (*strong*). (1) Male of the sheep, or any
ovine species, Gen. xxii. 13. (2) Battering-ram for
breaking down gates and walls, Ezek. iv. 2; xxi. 22.

Rā′mä, Matt. ii. 18. [RAMAH.]

Rā′mah (*height*). (1) City in Benjamin, near
Jerusalem, Josh. xviii. 25; 1 Kgs. xv. 17–22. Point
of departure for Jewish captives, Jer. xxxix. 8–12; xl.
1. (2) Birthplace of Samuel, 1 Sam. i. 19; vii. 17. (3)
A border place of Asher, Josh. xix. 29. (4) Town in
Naphtali, Josh. xix. 36. (5) Ramoth-gilead, 2 Kgs.
viii. 28, 29. (6) A place repeopled by returned captives, Neh. xi. 33.

Rā″math-ā′ĭm=zō′phim (*two watch-towers*).
Full form of the town in which Samuel was born,
1 Sam. i. 1. [RAMAH, 2.]

Răm′ă-them. A part of Samaria added to Judea, 1 Macc. xi. 34.

Rā′math-īte. Dweller in Ramah, 1 Chr. xxvii.
27.

Rā′math=lē′hī (*hill of the jaw bone*). Where
Samson slew the Philistines, Judg. xv. 17.

Rā′math=mĭz′peh (*watch-tower hill*). A border town of Gad, Josh. xiii. 26.

Rā′math of the South. A border place of Simeon, Josh. xix. 8 ; 1 Sam. xxx. 27.

Rȧ-mē′sĕs, Rȧ-ăm′sĕs (*sun-born*). Country and city in lower Egypt, associated with Goshen ; the city being the capital, and one of the Pharaohs' store-cities, located on the Pelusiac mouth of the Nile, Gen. xlvii. 11 ; Ex. i. 11 ; xii. 37 ; Num. xxxiii. 3, 5.

Rȧ-mī′ah (*exaltion*). One who had taken a foreign wife, Ez. x. 25.

Rā′moth (*high*). A son of Bani, Ez. x. 29.

Rā′moth=gĭl′e-ȧd (*heights of Gilead*). An ancient Amorite stronghold east of Jordan, and chief city of Gad. Both a Levitical city and city of refuge. Centre of one of Solomon's commissary districts, Deut. iv. 43 ; Josh. xx. 8 ; xxi. 38 ; 1 Kgs. iv. 13.

Răm′s Hôrns, Josh. vi. 4-20. [CORNET.]

Rā′phȧ (*tall*). (1) A Benjamite, 1 Chr. viii. 2. (2) A descendant of Saul, 1 Chr. viii. 37.

Rā′phȧ-el (*God's healer*). One of the seven holy angels, Tob. xii. 15.

Răph′ȧ-im. An ancestor of Judith, Judith viii. 1.

Rā′phŏn. A city in Gilead, 1 Macc. v. 37.

Rā′phu (*healed*). Father of the Benjamite spy, Num. xiii. 9.

Răs′sĕs. A land ravaged by Holofernes, Judith ii. 23.

Rȧ-thū′mus, 1 Esdr. ii. 16. [REHUM.]

Rā′ven (*seizer*). An unclean bird of the crow (*corvus*) family. Translation much disputed, Lev. xi. 15 ; 1 Kgs. xvii. 6 ; S. of Sol. v. 11.

Rā′zis. An elder at Jerusalem, 2 Macc. xiv. 37-46.

Rā′zor (*scraper*). Known to and much used by Hebrews. Levites shaved the entire body, Lev. xiv. 8 ; Num. vi. 9, 18 ; viii. 7 ; Judg. xiii. 5 ; Acts xviii. 18.

Rē″a-i′ȧ (*seen of God*). A Reubenite prince, 1 Chr. v. 5.

Rē″a-i′ah (*seen of God*). (1) A Judahite, 1 Chr.

iv. 2. (2) His children returned, Ez. ii. 47; Neh. vii. 50.

Rē′bȧ (*fourth*). A Midianite king slain by Israel, Num. xxxi. 8; Josh. xiii. 21.

Rĕ-bĕc′cȧ. Greek form of Rebekah, Rom. ix. 10.

Rĕ-bĕk′ah (*snare*). Wife of Isaac and mother of Jacob and Esau, Gen. xxii. 23; xxiv.–xxviii.; xlix. 31.

Rē′chăb (*horseman*). (1) Father of Jehonadab, 2 Kgs. x. 15, 23; 1 Chr. ii. 55. (2) A traitorous captain under Ishbosheth, 2 Sam. iv. 2, 5–9. (3) Father of Malchiah, an assistant wall-builder, Neh. iii. 14.

Rē′chab-ītes. Kenite or Midianite descendants of Rechab, 1 Chr. ii. 55, who became an order or sect — said to still exist near Mecca — whose tenets were abstinence from wine, tent habitations only, freedom from agricultural labor, Jer. xxxv. 2–19.

Rē′chah (*uttermost*). Place unknown, 1 Chr. iv. 12.

Rĕ-côr′der (*record keeper*). The high and responsible office of annalist and royal counselor in the Hebrew state, 2 Sam. viii. 16; xx. 24; 1 Kgs. iv. 3; 1 Chr. xviii. 15.

Rĕ-dēem′ (*buying back*). In O. T., buying back a forfeited estate. Metaphorically, freeing from bondage, Ex. vi. 6; Isa. xliii. 1. In N. T., rescuing or ransoming from sin and its consequences, Matt. xx. 28; Gal. iii. 13; 1 Pet. i. 18.

Rĕd Sēa. The arm of Gulf of Aden which separates Egypt from Arabia. "The sea," Ex. xiv. 2, 9, 16, 21, 28; xv. 1–19; Josh. xxiv. 6, 7. "Egyptian sea," Isa. xi. 15. "Sea of *Suph*," *weedy* or *reedy sea*, translated "Red Sea," Ex. x. 19; xiii. 18; xv. 4; xxiii. 31; Num. xxi. 4. In N. T., the Greek "Erythrean," or Red Sea, Acts vii. 36. At its head it separates into gulfs of Akaba and Suez, the latter of which the Israelites crossed.

Rēed (*rod*). Used generically for the tall grasses, sedges, flags, or rushes which grow in marshy soils. Applied to various uses by Hebrews, and source of frequent metaphor, 2 Kgs. xviii. 21; Job xl. 21; Isa. xix. 6; Ezek. xxix. 6; Matt. xi. 7; xii. 20; xxvii. 29.

Rē″el-ā′iah, Ez. ii. 2. [RAAMIAH.]

Rĕ-fī′ner (*who makes fine*). A worker in precious metals, Isa. i. 25; Jer. vi. 29; Mal. iii. 3.

Rĕf'uge, Cities of. The six Levitical cities set apart for the temporary escape of involuntary manslayers, Num. xxxv. 6, 11-32; Deut. xix. 7-9; Josh. xx. 2-8. [CITY.]

Rē'ḡem (*friend*). A descendant of Caleb, 1 Chr. ii. 47.

Rē'ḡem=mē'lech (*royal friend*). A messenger sent by captive Jews to inquire about the ritual, Zech. vii. 2.

Rĕ-ġĕn''ĕr-ā'tion (*begetting again*). The renovation of the world at and after the second coming of Christ, Matt. xix. 28. The new birth from the Holy Spirit, Tit. iii. 5.

Rē''ha̲-bī'ah (*enlarged*). Only son of Eliezer, 1 Chr. xxiii. 17.

Rē'hŏb (*breadth*). (1) Father of Hadadezer, king of Zobah, 2 Sam. viii. 3, 12. (2) A co-covenanter, Neh. x. 11. (3) Spot where the journey of the spies ended, Num. xiii. 21; 2 Sam. x. 8. Beth-rehob in 2 Sam. x. 6. (4) Place in Asher, Josh. xix. 28. (5) A Levitical town in Asher, Josh. xix. 30.

Rē''ho̲-bō'am (*emancipator*). Son of Solomon, 1 Kgs. xi. 43; xiv. 21, and successor to his father's throne, B. C. 975-958. During his reign the ten tribes, under Jeroboam, revolted and set up the kingdom of Israel. Shishak, of Egypt, captured Jerusalem from him, 1 Kgs. xiv. 21-31.

Rē-hō'both (*places*). (1) A city of Assyria founded by Asher or Nimrod, Gen. x. 11, 12. (2) A city on the Euphrates, home of Shaul or Saul, an early Edomite king, Gen. xxxvi. 37; 1 Chr. i. 48. (3) The third well dug by Isaac. It is located south of Beersheba, Gen. xxvi. 22.

Rē'hŭm (*merciful*). Levites and returned captives, Ez. ii. 2; iv. 8, 9, 17, 23; Neh. iii. 17; x. 25; xii. 3. Nehum in Neh. vii. 7, and Harim in xii. 15.

Rē'ī (*friendly*). A friend of David, 1 Kgs. i. 8.

Reins (*kidneys*). Once believed to be the seat of emotions; hence coupled with the heart, Ps. vii. 9; xvi. 7; Jer. xvii. 10; xx. 12.

Rē'kem (*flowered*). (1) A Midianite king slain by the Israelites, Num. xxxi. 8; Josh. xiii. 21. (2) Son of Hebron, 1 Chr. ii. 43, 44. (3) Town in Benjamin, Josh. xviii. 27.

Rĕm″a-lī′ah (*God-exalted*). Father of Pekah, king of Israel, 2 Kgs. xv. 25–37.

Rē′meth (*height*). Town in Issachar, Josh. xix. 21.

Rĕm′mon (*pomegranate*). Town in Simeon. Properly Rimmon, Josh. xix. 7.

Rĕm′mon=meth′o-är (*Remmon to Neah*). A landmark of Zebulun, Josh. xix. 13.

Rĕm′phan. An idol worshipped secretly by the Israelites in the wilderness, Acts vii. 43. Rephan in R. V. Chiun, Amos v. 26.

Rē′pha-el (*God-healed*). A Levite porter, 1 Chr. xxvi. 7.

Rē′phah (*wealth*). An Ephraimite, 1 Chr. vii. 25.

Rĕph″a-i′ah (*God-healed*). (1) Descendant of David, 1 Chr. iii. 21. (2) A Simeonite chief, 1 Chr. iv. 42. (3) Descendant of Issachar, 1 Chr. vii. 2. (4) Descendant of Saul, 1 Chr. ix. 43. Rapha in viii. 37. (5) A wall-repairer and ruler of half of Jerusalem, Neh. iii. 9.

Rĕph′a-ĭm (*giants*). (1) A giant race east of Jordan, and probably driven to the west side, Gen. xiv. 5; xv. 20. (2) "Valley of Rephaim" was a landmark of Judah, and supposably the valley stretching from Jerusalem to Bethlehem, Josh. xv. 8; 2 Sam. v. 18; Isa. xvii. 5.

Rĕph′I-dim (*rests*). Last Israelite encampment before Sinai, Ex. xvii. 1, 8–16; xix. 2.

Rē′sen (*bridle*). An Assyrian city built by Asher or Nimrod, Gen. x. 12.

Rē′sheph (*fire*). A descendant of Ephraim, 1 Chr. vii. 25.

Rĕş″ŭr-rĕc′tion (*rising again*). The rising again from the dead, Ps. xvi. 10, 11; Matt. xvi. 21; xx. 19; Acts ii. 31.

Rē′u (*friend*). Son of Peleg, Gen. xi. 18–21.

Reu′ben (*behold a son !*). Eldest son of Jacob and Leah, Gen. xxix. 32. Lost his birthright through crime, Gen. xxxv. 22; xlix. 3, 4. Tribe numerous and pastoral, and settled east of Jordan, Num. i. 20, 21; Josh. xiii. 15–23. Idolatrous, averse to war, carried captive by Assyria, Judg. v. 15, 16; 1 Chr. v. 26.

Reu'ben-ītes. Descendants of Reuben, Num. xxvi. 7; Josh. i. 12; 1 Chr. v. 26.

Reu'el (*God's friend*). (1) A son of Esau, Gen. xxxvi. 4, 10, 13, 17. (2) Ex. ii. 18. [RAGUEL.] (3) Father of Eliasaph the Gadite leader, Num. ii. 14. (4) A Benjamite, 1 Chr. ix. 8.

Reu'mah (*lofty*). Nahor's concubine, Gen. xxii. 24.

Rĕv''ĕ-lā'tion (*veil drawn back*). (1) Scripturally, revealing truth through divine agency or by supernatural means, 2 Cor. xii. 1-7. (2) Book of Revelation, or Apocalypse; last of N. T. books; written by the Apostle John, about A. D. 95-97, probably at Ephesus. It is a record of his inspired visions while a prisoner on the island of Patmos. Its aim is much disputed, but it is seemingly a prophetic panorama of church history to the end of time.

Rē'zeph (*heated stone*). An unknown place, 2 Kgs. xix. 12; Isa. xxxvii. 12.

Rĕ-zī'å (*delight*). An Asherite, 1 Chr. vii. 39.

Rē'zin (*firm*). (1) A king of Syria or Damascus, 2 Kgs. xv. 37; xvi. 5-9; Isa. vii. 1-8; viii. 6; ix. 11. (2) His descendants returned, Ez. ii. 48; Neh. vii. 50.

Rē'zon (*prince*). A Syrian who set up a petty kingdom at Damascus, 1 Kgs. xi. 23-25.

Rhē'gĭ-um (*breach*). Now Rheggio, port and capital of Calabria, southern Italy, Acts xxviii. 13.

Rhē'så (*head*). One mentioned in Christ's genealogy, Luke iii. 27.

Rhō'då (*rose*). A maid in the house of Mary, mother of John Mark, Acts xii. 12-15.

Rhōdeş (*roses*). An Ægean island, just off the coast of Asia Minor. Noted for the splendor of its capital city, Rhodes. Paul touched there, Acts xxi. 1.

Rhŏd'o-cus. A traitorous Jew, 2 Macc. xiii. 21.

Rhō'dus, 1 Macc. xv. 23. [RHODES.]

Rī'bāi (*pleader*). Father of Ittai, one of David's guard, 2 Sam. xxiii. 29; 1 Chr. xi. 31.

Rĭb'lah (*fertile*). An ancient strategic city on N. E. frontier of Canaan, and on military route from Palestine to Babylonia, Num. xxxiv. 11; 2 Kgs. xxiii. 33; xxv. 6-21; Jer. xxxix. 5-7.

Rĭd'dle (*counsel*). Oriental peoples fond of riddles. Hebrew riddles embraced proverbs, Prov. i. 6; oracles, Num. xii. 8; songs, Ps. xlix. 4; parables, Ezek. xvii. 2; intricate sentences, questions, and problems, Judg. xiv. 12-14; 1 Kgs. x. 1; 2 Chr. ix. 1; Dan. viii. 23.

Rĭm'mŏn (*pomegranate*). (1) Father of Ishbosheth's murderers, 2 Sam. iv. 2-9. (2) A Syrian deity worshipped at Damascus, 2 Kgs. v. 18. (3) Levitical city in Zebulun, 1 Chr. vi. 77. Remmon-methoar, Josh. xix. 13. (4) Town in Judah and Simeon, Josh. xv. 32. (5) A rock or fastness, now Rummon, 10 miles north of Jerusalem, to which the defeated Benjamites retreated, Judg. xx. 45, 47; xxi. 13.

Rĭm'mon=pā'rez (*pomegranates of the wrath*). A desert encampment, Num. xxxiii. 19.

Rĭng (*around*). Rings were indispensable articles of Jewish ornament. Worn on fingers, wrists, ankles, in ears and nostrils, Isa. iii. 20, 21; Luke xv. 22; Jas. ii. 2. Symbols of authority, Gen. xli. 42; Esth. iii. 10. Used as seals, Esth. iii. 12; Dan. vi. 17.

Rĭn'nah (*song*). A Judahite, 1 Chr. iv. 20.

Rĭ'phăth (*spoken*). Son of Gomer, and founder of a northern nation, Gen. x. 3; 1 Chr. i. 6.

Rĭs'sah (*ruin*). A desert encampment of the Israelites, Num. xxxiii. 21, 22.

Rĭth'mah (*bush*). A desert encampment of the Israelites, Num. xxxiii. 18, 19.

Rĭv'ĕr (*banked*). In Hebrew sense, a large flowing stream, rivulet, ravine, valley, or wady. "River of Egypt" is the Nile, Gen. xv. 18; Num. xxxiv. 5; Josh. xv. 4, 47; 1 Kgs. viii. 65; 2 Kgs. xxiv. 7. "The river" is the Euphrates, Gen. xxxi. 21; Ex. xxiii. 31.

Rĭz'pah. Concubine of Saul, and the mother who watched over the remains of her slain sons, 2 Sam. iii. 7; xxi. 8-11.

Rōad (*ride*). In Bible sense, a path or way. For "road" in 1 Sam. xxvii. 10, read "raid" or "inroad."

Rŏb'bĕr-ȳ (*breaking, riving*). Oppression, pillage, and thievery formed almost an employment among nomad tribes, Gen. xvi. 12; Judg. ii. 14; Luke x. 30; John xviii. 40.

Rọ-bō'am. Greek form of Rehoboam, Matt. i. 7.

Rŏd. Shoot or branch. Figuratively, Christ, Isa. xi. 1; root, Ps. lxxiv. 2; Jer. x. 16; support, Ps. xxiii. 4; authority, Ps. ii. 9; affliction, Job ix. 34; tithing-rod, Ezek. xx. 37.

Rōe, Rōe′bŭck (*animal*). A beautiful fleet animal, probably the roe-deer of Western Asia; but associated with antelope and gazelle, 2 Sam. ii. 18; 1 Chr. xii. 8; S. of Sol. ii. 17; viii. 14.

Rō-ḡē′lim (*fullers*). Home of Barzillai, in Gilead, 2 Sam. xvii. 27.

Rōh′gah (*clamor*). A chief of Asher, 1 Chr. vii. 34.

Rŏll (*little wheel*). The book of ancient times, consisting of long strips of linen, papyrus, or parchment written upon and wrapped on a stick, Isa. viii. 1; Ezek. ii. 9, 10.

Rō-măm′tĭ=ē′zĕr. One of Heman's fourteen sons, 1 Chr. xxv. 4, 31.

Rōme, Rō′mans. First mentioned in Bible in 1 Macc. i. 10, when Rome was pushing her conquests in Palestine and Syria. The capital, Rome, is on the Tiber, about 15 miles from the sea. Founded B. C. 752. Governed by kings till B. C. 509; then by consuls till Augustus Cæsar became emperor, B. C. 30. At the Christian era Rome was virtual mistress of the civilized world. Empire declined rapidly after removal of capital to Constantinople by Constantine, A. D. 328. Gospel early introduced among Romans, but Christians persecuted till time of Constantine. Palestine was ruled from Rome by kings, procurators, governors, or proconsuls. Paul wrote his celebrated epistle to the Romans from Corinth, about A. D. 58, to show that Jew and Gentile were alike subject to sin and in equal need of justification and sanctification.

Roof. [HOUSE.]

Room (*wide*). Frequently used in N. T. for spot, seat, place, as at table, Matt. xxiii. 6; Mark xii. 39; Luke xiv. 7; xx. 46.

Rōse (*ruddy*). Disputed translation. Some say narcissus is meant; others would simply read "flower" for "rose," S. of Sol. ii. 1; Isa. xxxv. 1.

Rŏsh (*head*). A Benjamite, Gen. xlvi. 21.

Rŏs′in (*resin*). The resin left after turpentine is distilled. But in Bible naphtha is meant, Ezek. xxvii. 17 marg.; Song of Three Children, 23.

Ru'by (*red*). A ruddy, valuable gem; but the original word is thought to mean coral or pearl, Job xxviii. 18; Prov. iii. 15.

Rue (*thick-leaved*). A shrubby, medicinal plant, cultivated in the gardens of the east. Tithable, Luke xi. 42.

Ru'fus (*red*). Son of Simon of Cyrene, Mark xv. 21. Probably the same in Rom. xvi. 13.

Ru'ha-mah (*having received mercy*). A symbolical name used in Hos. ii. 1.

Ru'mah (*high*). A place, 2 Kgs. xxiii. 36, associated with Arumah and Dumah.

Rŭsh (*reed*). [REED.]

Ruth (*beauty*). The Moabite wife of Mahlon and Boaz. The beautiful pastoral of Ruth, 8th of O. T. books, contains her life. It supplements Judges and prefaces Samuel, and traces the lineage of David. Time of writing and authorship are unknown.

Rȳe. Not an Egyptian cereal. "Spelt" is doubtless meant, it being a common Egyptian food, Ex. ix. 32; Isa. xxviii. 25. Same Hebrew word is rendered "fitches" in Ezek. iv. 9.

S

Sā"bắch-thā'nī (*hast thou forsaken me?*). An Aramaic, or Syro-Chaldaic, word, part of Christ's exclamation on the cross, Matt. xxvii. 46; Mark xv. 34. [ELI.]

Săb'a-ŏth (*hosts*). Used usually with Jehovah, — "Lord of hosts;" — hosts being comprehensive, and signifying the powers of earth and heaven, Isa. i. 9; Rom. ix. 29; Jas. v. 4.

Sā'bat (*around*). (1) His sons were returned captives, 1 Esdr. v. 34. (2) 1 Macc. xvi. 14. [SEBAT.]

Sắb'bắth (*rest*). Rest day, or seventh of the week, Gen. ii. 2, 3. Became a Mosaic institution for rest and festal occasions, Ex. xvi. 23-30; xx. 8-11; Lev. xix. 3, 30; xxiii. 3; xxv. 4-9; Deut. v. 12-15. Day for consulting prophets, 2 Kgs. iv. 23. A day of teaching and joy, Neh. viii. 1-12; Hos. ii. 11. A whole week of time is implied in Matt. xxviii. 1; Mark xvi. 1; Luke xxiv. 1; John xx. 1; Acts xx. 7;

1 Cor. xvi. 2. Among Christians, the day after the Hebrew Sabbath, or seventh-day, gradually and till fully established, became the Sabbath, or first-day, in commemoration of the resurrection of Christ. Hence, "The Lord's Day," John xx. 26; Acts xx. 6-11; 1 Cor. xvi. 2; Rev. i. 10.

Săb'băth Day's Journey. Travel on the Sabbath was limited, Ex. xvi. 29. Custom seemed to sanction 2000 paces from the walls of a city as sufficient for all needs on the day of rest, Acts i. 12.

Săb''ba-thē'us, 1 Esdr. ix. 14. [SHABBETHAI.]

Săb-băt'ĭ-cal Year. By the Mosaic code, each seventh year was sacred. The land rested, the poor were entitled to what grew, and debtors were released, Ex. xxiii. 10, 11; Lev. xxv. 2-7; Deut. xv. 1-18.

Săb-bē'us, 1 Esdr. ix. 32. [SHEMAIAH.]

Să-bē'ans. (1) Descendants of Sheba, son of Joktan, Joel iii. 8. (2) Evidently the descendants of Seba, son of Cush, Isa. xlv. 14. (3) Perhaps a third tribe, though it may be one of the two just mentioned. (4) A wrong translation in Ezek. xxiii. 42, "drunkards," in margin.

Să'bī, 1 Esdr. v. 34. [ZEBAIM.]

Săb'tă, Săb'tăh (*striking*). Third son of Cush, Gen. x. 7; 1 Chr. i. 9.

Săb'te-chă, Săb'te-chăh (*striking*). Fifth son of Cush, Gen. x. 7; 1 Chr. i. 9.

Să'car (*hire*). (1) Father of one of David's warriors, 1 Chr. xi. 35. Sharar in 2 Sam. xxiii. 33. (2) A Levite porter, 1 Chr. xxvi. 4.

Săck'bŭt (*pull and push*). A wind instrument, trombone. But in Dan. iii. 5-15, a stringed instrument of triangular shape with from four to twenty strings.

Săck'cloth (*coarse cloth*). A coarse, goat-hair cloth used for making sacks and rough garments. The latter were worn next the skin by mourners and repentants, Gen. xxxvii. 34; xlii. 25; 2 Sam. iii. 31; 1 Kgs. xxi. 27; 2 Kgs. vi. 30; Esth. iv. 1, 2; Job xvi. 15; Rev. vi. 12.

Săc'rĭ-fĭçe (*making sacred*). Propitiatory, atoning or thanksgiving offering to God. An ordained rite, Lev. xvii. 4-9; Deut. xvi. 5-19. Sacrificial offerings numerous; but chiefly, the "burnt-offering," Lev. i. 1-17; "sin-offering," and "trespass-offering," Lev. vii. 1-10; "peace-offering," Lev. vii. 11-34; the latter also a "free-will" offering. Among Christians all sacrificial offerings merged in the universal offering of Christ's body, Heb. ix., x.

Săd″a-mī′as, 2 Esdr. i. 1. [SHALLUM.]

Sā′das, 1 Esdr. v. 13. [IDDO.]

Săd′du̧-çeeṣ (*disciples of Zadok*). A Jewish sect, supposably Zadokites, 1 Kgs. i. 32-45, whose chief tenets were (1) rejection of the divinity of the Mosaic oral law and traditions; (2) rejection of the later O. T. books, but acceptance of the Mosaic teachings; (3) denial of angel and spiritual existence, and consequent immortality of the soul; (4) belief in the absolute moral freedom of man. Their hatred of Christianity was as bitter as that of the Pharisees, Matt. iii. 7; Mark xii. 18; Luke xx. 27; Acts iv. 1; v. 17; xxiii. 6-10. Though composed of men of position, the sect was never very numerous nor influential, and it disappeared from history after the first century of the Christian era.

Sā′dŏc (*just*). (1) 2 Esdr. i. 1. [ZADOK.] (2) One in the genealogy of Christ, Matt. i. 14.

Săf′fron (*yellow*). The fall crocus, much cultivated in the Orient for its perfume and medicinal properties, S. of Sol. iv. 14.

Sāint (*sanctified*). In O. T., a pious Jew, Ps. xvi. 3. In N. T., a Christian believer, Rom. i. 7; viii. 27; Heb. vi. 10.

Sā′là, Sā′lah (*sprout*). A descendant of Shem, Gen. x. 24; xi. 12-15; Luke iii. 35. Shelah in 1 Chr. i. 18, 24.

Săl′a-mis (*shaken*). A city of the island of Cyprus, visited by Paul. It was afterwards called Constantia, Acts xiii. 5. The old city was once the capital of the island and carried on a large trade in fruit, wine, flax, and copper with adjacent continents. The Jewish population was large. Its site is now traced by masses of ruins.

Să-lā′thĭ-el (*asked of God*). Son of Jechonias, 1 Chr. iii. 17; Matt. i. 12; Luke iii. 27. Shealtiel elsewhere.

Săl′cah, Săl′chah (*moving*). A city in Bashan which fell to Manasseh. Now Sulkhad, Deut. iii. 10; Josh. xii. 5; xiii. 11; 1 Chr. v. 11.

Sā′lem (*peace*). The place over which Melchizedek was king, supposably Jerusalem, Gen. xiv. 18; Ps. lxxvi. 2; Heb. vii. 1, 2.

Sā′lim (*peace*). The place near Ænon, where John baptized, John iii. 23.

Săl′la-ī (*basket-maker*). (1) A returned Benjamite, Neh. xi. 8. (2) A returned priest, Neh. xii. 20.

Săl′lu (*measured*). (1) A Benjamite, 1 Chr. ix. 7. (2) A priest, Neh. xi. 7; xii. 7.

Săl-lū′mus, 1 Esdr. ix. 25. [SHALLUM.]

Săl′mà, Săl′mŏn (*clothed*). (1) Father of Boaz and husband of Rahab, Ruth iv. 20, 21; 1 Chr. ii. 11; Matt. i. 5; Luke iii. 32. (2) One of the high hills surrounding Shechem, which afforded pasturage for Jacob's flocks, Ps. lxviii. 14. Zalmon in Judg. ix. 48.

Săl-mō′ne (*clothed*). Eastern promontory of Crete, Acts xxvii. 7.

Sā′lŏm. (1) Bar. i. 7. [SHALLUM.] (2) 1 Macc. ii. 26. [SALLU.]

Să-lō′me (*clothed*). (1) Wife of Zebedee, Mark xv. 40; xvi. 1. Mentioned indirectly in Matt. xx. 20–22; xxvii. 56. (2) The daughter of Herodias, who danced before Herod, Matt. xiv. 6; Mark vi. 22.

Salt (*sea product*). Abundant in Palestine. Used with food and sacrificial offerings, Job vi. 6; Lev. ii. 13; Num. xviii. 19; Mark ix. 49. Monument of divine displeasure, Gen. xix. 26; token of indissoluble alliance, Lev. ii. 13; Num. xviii. 19; 2 Chr. xiii. 5; used to rub new-born children, Ezek. xvi. 4; type of maintenance, Ez. iv. 14 marg.; emblem of sterility, Judg. ix. 45; Jer. xvii. 6; a manure, Luke xiv. 35; emblem of holy life and conversation, Matt. v. 13; Mark ix. 50; Col. iv. 6.

Salt, City of. Fifth of the six cities of Judah, situate in the wilderness of Judah, Josh. xv. 62.

Salt Sea. The Dead Sea. "Sea of the plain," Deut. iv. 49; 2 Kgs. xiv. 25. "Salt sea," Deut. iii. 17; Josh. iii. 16; xii. 3. "East sea," Ezek. xlvii. 18; Joel ii. 20; Zech. xiv. 8. "The sea," Ezek. xlvii. 8. "Vale of Siddim," Gen. xiv. 3. "Sodomitish sea," 1 Esdr. v. 7. Title "Dead Sea" not found among Hebrew writers, but introduced by Greek authors. Situate 16 miles E. of Jerusalem; 46 miles long by 10 wide; 1300 feet below the level of the Mediterranean; waters intensely salt; receives waters of Jordan from the north; no outlet.

Salt, Văl′ley of. Supposedly the valley, or depression, of Akabah, extending from Dead Sea to Gulf of Akabah, 2 Sam. viii. 13; 2 Kgs. xiv. 7; 1 Chr. xviii. 12; 2 Chr. xxv. 11; Ps. lx. title. But many excellent authorities limit it to a section of Edom near Petra.

Sā′lu (*weighed*). Father of Zimri, a chief of Simeon, Num. xxv. 14.

Sā′lum, 1 Esdr. v. 28. [SHALLUM.]

Săl″ū-tā′tion (*good health, greeting*). Personal salutation very formal in East. The "peace be with thee," or similar expression, was accompanied by a profound bow, kiss, embrace, or other courtesy, Gen. xix. 1; 1 Sam. xxv. 23; Matt. x. 12; Luke i. 41. Epistolary salutation took the form found in the opening and closing of the epistles, Rom. i. 7; 1 Cor. i. 3; etc.

Săl-vā′tion (*deliverance*). Temporal deliverance, Ex. xiv. 13. Spiritual deliverance, 2 Cor. vii. 10; Eph. i. 13; Heb. ii. 3.

Săm″a-rā′is. Son of Ozora, 1 Esdr. ix. 34.

Sā-mā′rǐ-à (*watch mountain*). (1) The kingdom of Samaria, synonymous with the kingdom of Israel, lay to the north of Judah. It varied in size at different times, but in general embraced the territory of the ten revolting tribes on either side of the Jordan, 1 Kgs. xiii. 32. Named from its capital, Samaria. In N. T. times, Samaria was one of the three subdivisions of Palestine, lying between Judea on the south and Galilee on the north. (2) Capital of the kingdom of Samaria or Israel, and located 30 miles north of Jerusalem. Founded by Omri, king of Israel, about B. C. 925, and called Samaria, after Shemer, from whom he bought the ground, 1 Kgs. xvi. 23, 24. It became a beautiful and strong city and remained the capital till Shalmaneser, the Assyrian, destroyed it and the empire, B. C. 721, 2 Kgs. xviii. 9–12. Herod rebuilt it and restored much of its ancient splendor, naming it Sebaste in honor of Augustus, who gave it to him. Philip preached the gospel there, Acts viii. 5–9. It is now a modest village called Sebastiyeh, which perpetuates the name Sebaste, and is noted for its many ruins, chief of which is the famous colonnade, 3000 feet in length, 100 columns of which are still standing. Respecting the city the prophecy, Mic. i. 6, has been literally fulfilled.

Să-mǎr'ĭ-tans. Inhabitants of Samaria, 2 Kgs. xvii. 29. The planting of Assyrian colonists in Samaria, 2 Kgs. xvii. 24–34, led to a strange admixture of people, language, laws, religions, and customs, and brought the name Samaritan into reproach with Jews, Matt. x. 5; John iv. 9–26; viii. 48; Acts viii. 1; ix. 31.

Săm'gär=nē'bŏ (*sword of Nebo*). A general of Nebuchadnezzar at the taking of Jerusalem, Jer. xxxix. 3.

Săm'mus, 1 Esdr. ix. 43. [SHEMA.]

Săm'lah (*raiment*). A king of Edom, Gen. xxxvi. 36, 37; 1 Chr. i. 47, 48.

Sā'mos (*height*). An island of the Grecian archipelago, off the coast of Lydia. Visited by Paul on his third tour, Acts xx. 15.

Săm''o-thrā'çĭȧ (*Thracian Samos*). An island in the northern Ægean belonging to Thrace. Visited by Paul on his first tour, Acts xvi. 11.

Sămp's̆a-mēs̟. Probably Samsun, on Black Sea coast, 1 Macc. xv. 23.

Săm'son (*sunlike*). Son of Manoah, of Dan, and judge of Israel for 20 years, Judg. xiii. 3–25. Noted for his great strength, marvellous exploits, and moral weakness. Contrary to the wishes of his parents, and to the law as laid down in Ex. xxxiv. 16, Deut. vii. 3, he married a Philistine woman of Timnath, whom he deserted on account of her treachery, Judg. xiv. Wishing to return to her, and finding her given to another, he wreaked his vengeance on the Philistines by burning their crops and slaughtering great numbers of them, Judg. xv. 1–8. He was surrounded by 3000 of his enemies, while he dwelt on the rock Etam, and surrendered to them, but burst his bands, and routed them with great slaughter, Judg. xv. 9–19. Again he was surrounded by enemies in Gaza, but escaped by carrying away the gates of the city. The secret of his strength was finally detected by Delilah, and he was imprisoned and made blind. He finally killed himself and numerous enemies by pulling down the pillars of the house in which they were feasting, Judg. xvi.

Săm′u-el (*God hath heard*). Son of Elkanah and Hannah, celebrated Hebrew prophet and last of the judges, 1 Sam. i. 19–28. Educated under Eli, 1 Sam. iii. 4–14, and became his successor in the prophetic office. His sons proved so recreant that the people demanded a king, and Samuel anointed Saul, and resigned his authority to him, 1 Sam. xii. He also anointed David, Saul's successor, 1 Sam. xvi. 13. He died at Ramah, 1 Sam. xxv. 1. The two books which bear his name, the 9th and 10th of O. T., are called also First and Second Books of Kings. They were originally one book and contain the lives of Samuel, Saul, and David. The authorship is ascribed to a period subsequent to the secession of the ten tribes, and it is clearly an authorship different from Kings, for in Kings there are many references to the law, while in Samuel there are none. In Kings the Exile is alluded to; it is not so in Samuel. The plans of the two works vary; Samuel is biographical, Kings annalistic.

Săn-băl′lat (*strong*). A Persian officer in Samaria who opposed Ezra and Nehemiah and persistently misrepresented them at court, Neh. ii. 10; iv. 1–9; xiii. 28.

Sănc′tĭ-fȳ (*to make holy*). To prepare or set apart persons or things to holy use, Ex. xiii. 2. It was in allusion to the law that Christ spoke in John xvii. 19. To establish union with Christ by faith, John xvii. 17. To exercise the graces of knowledge, such as faith, love, repentance, humility, etc., toward God and man, 2 Thess. ii. 13; 1 Pet. i. 2.

Sănc′tu-ar″ȳ (*made holy*). A holy or sanctified place, Ps. xx. 2. The secret part of the temple in which the ark of the covenant was kept, and which none but the high priest might enter, and he only once a year, on the day of solemn expiation, Lev. iv. 6. Also applied to the furniture of the holy place, Num. x. 21; to the apartment where the altar of incense, table of shewbread and holy candlestick, etc., stood, 2 Chr. xxvi. 18; to the whole tabernacle or temple, Josh. xxiv. 26; 2 Chr. xx. 8. "Sanctuary of strength," because belonging to God, Dan. xi. 31.

Any place of public worship of God, Ps. lxxiii. 17.
Heaven, Ps. cii. 19. Place of refuge, Isa. viii. 14;
Ezek. xi. 16. Land of Israel called God's sanctuary,
Ex. xv. 17. "Worldly sanctuary," one of an earthly
type, Heb. ix. 1.

Sănd (*whirling*). Abundant in the wastes of Palestine, Arabia, and Egypt. Used much figuratively.
Innumerable multitudes, Gen. xxxii. 12; abundance,
Gen. xli. 49; weight, Job vi. 3; Prov. xxvii. 3; sea
boundary, Jer. v. 22; hiding place, Ex. ii. 12; Deut.
xxxiii. 19.

Săn'dal (*board*). A sole of wood, leather, or
plaited material, bound to the foot with straps. The
shoe of the Bible. Not worn in the house nor in
holy places, Ex. iii. 5; Deut. xxv. 9; Josh. v. 15.

Săn'he-drim, Săn'he-drin (*seated together*).
The supreme council of the Jewish nation, whose
germ was in the seventy elders, Num. xi. 16, 17, and
further development in Jehoshaphat's tribunal, 2
Chr. xix. 8-11. In full power after the captivity,
and lasted till A. D. 425. The "great Sanhedrim"
was composed of 71 priests, scribes, and elders, and
presided over by the high priest. The "lesser Sanhe-
drims" were provincial courts in the towns, and
composed of 23 members appointed by the "great
Sanhedrim." The word usually appears as "council" in N. T., Matt. v. 22; Mark xiv. 55; John xi.
47; Acts iv. 5-7. The members of the Sanhedrim
embraced the three classes, priests, elders, and scribes.
After the Roman conquest it had no control of the
death power, but the confirmation and execution of
capital sentences rested with the Roman procurator.
Thus it was that while the Sanhedrim condemned
Christ for blasphemy, he was not brought under the
Roman judgment of death till accused by the Jews of
treason, Matt. xxvi. 65, 66; John xviii. 31; xix. 12.
The stoning of Stephen, Acts vii. 57-59, was either
due to mob excitement, or else illegal.

Săn-săn'nah (*branch*). A town in southern
Judah, Josh. xv. 31.

Săph (*giant*). A Philistine giant, 2 Sam. xxi. 18.
Sippai, 1 Chr. xx. 4.

Să'phat, 1 Esdr. v. 9. [SHEPHATIAH.]

Săph'ĭr (*fair*). A village addressed by Micah,
Mic. i. 11.

Săp-phī'rà (*handsome*). Wife of Ananias, and participator in his crime and punishment, Acts v. 1-10.

Săp'phīre. A light blue gem, next to the diamond in hardness, Ex. xxiv. 10. Second stone in second row of high priest's breastplate, Ex. xxviii. 18. A foundation stone of the holy Jerusalem, Rev. xxi. 19.

Sā'rà. (1) Daughter of Raguel, Tob. iii. 7. (2) Heb. xi. 11; 1 Pet. iii. 6. [SARAH.]

Sā'rah (*princess*). (1) Wife of Abraham and mother of Isaac, Gen. xi. 29; xxi. 2, 3. Name changed from Sarai to Sarah, Gen. xvii. 15, 16. At Abraham's request she passed herself off as his sister during their sojourn in Egypt, Gen. xii. 10-2u, which angered the Pharaoh and led to their banishment. Relentless toward Hagar (whom she had given to Abraham as a concubine) when she bore Ishmael, and caused her to be banished to the desert, Gen. xvi. 5-16; deceitful when Isaac was promised, Gen. xviii. 15; cruel again toward Hagar on the occasion of Isaac's weaning, causing her to be banished finally from the household, Gen. xxi. 9-21. Commended for her faith, Heb. xi. 11; and obedience, 1 Pet. iii. 6. Died at age of 127 years and buried at Machpelah, Gen. xxiii. (2) Daughter of Asher, Num. xxvi. 46.

Sā'rāi, Gen. xi. 29. [SARAH.]

Sär'a-mel (*court*). Meeting place where Simon Maccabeus was made high priest, 1 Macc. xiv. 28.

Sā'răph (*burning*). A Judahite, 1 Chr. iv. 22.

Sär-chĕd'ŏ-nus, Tob. i. 21. [ESARHADDON.]

Sär'dīne, Sär'dĭ-us (*stone of Sardis*). The sard or carnelian, a blood-red or flesh-colored stone, first in first row of high priest's breastplate, Ex. xxviii. 17; Rev. iv. 3.

Sär'dis. Capital of Lydia in Asia Minor. Once noted for beauty and wealth; now the miserable village of Sert-Kalessi, Rev. iii. 1-6. It was the residence of Crœsus, renowned for riches, and Cyrus, when he conquered it, B. C. 548, is said to have captured fabulous treasure there. Alexander captured it from the Persians, and it was again sacked and captured by Antiochus, B. C. 214. It was destroyed by an earthquake, A. D. 17, but was speedily rebuilt.

The art of wool-dyeing was discovered there. Seat of one of the seven churches of Asia, Rev. iii. 1.

Sär′dītes. Descendants of Sered, Num. xxvi. 26.

Sär′dŏ-nyx. A precious stone combining the sard and onyx varieties, whence its name, Rev. xxi. 20.

Sā′rē-à. A swift scribe, 2 Esdr. xiv. 24.

Să-rĕp′tà. Greek form of Zarephath, Luke iv. 26.

Sär′gon (*sun-prince*). An Assyrian king whom recently discovered inscriptions make the successor of Shalmaneser and father of Sennacherib, B. C. 722–705, 2 Kgs. xvii. 6; Isa. xx. 1.

Sā′rid (*survivor*). A landmark of Zebulun, Josh. xix. 10–12.

Sā′ron, Acts ix. 35. [SHARON.]

Să-rō′thie. His sons returned, 1 Esdr. v. 34.

Sär-sē′chim (*master of wardrobes*). A prince of Babylon at taking of Jerusalem, Jer. xxxix. 3.

Sā′ruch, Luke iii. 35. [SERUG.]

Sā′tăn (*adversary*). In O. T. a common noun, meaning enemy or adversary in general, 1 Sam. xxix. 4; 2 Sam. xix. 22; except in Job i. 6, 12; ii. 1; Zech. iii. 1, where the word becomes a proper noun, and spiritual representative of evil. In N. T. sense, chief of the evil spirits; great adversary of man; the devil, Matt. iv. 10; xxv. 41; Rev. xx., and elsewhere. Called also "the prince of this world;" "the wicked one;" "the tempter;" and in Rev. xii. 9, the old serpent, the devil, and Satan.

Săt′yr. A mythical creature, half man, half goat, inhabiting woods and waste places, Isa. xiii. 21; xxxiv. 14.

Saul (*wished*). (1) An early king of Edom, Gen. xxxvi. 37, 38. Shaul in 1 Chr. i. 48, 49. (2) A Benjamite, son of Kish, and first king of Israel. Anointed by Samuel; reigned B. C. 1095–1055; slain with his sons at Gilboa. His versatile career is described in 1 Sam. ix.–xxxi. He stands in Bible history for the stature, strength, and ruggedness of character so essential to judges in times of danger or necessary reform, and for the bravery, generalship and self-confidence of one called on to institute a new empire. Of boundless ambition and erratic judgment, he usurped the priestly function, and drew the reproaches of the aged prophet Samuel, who had surrendered his line in anointing him. The announcement that royalty could not be perpetuated in his family drove him to inexcusable follies, yet with the courage of youth he fought his last despairing battle with the Philistines, and finished his course on his own sword. (3) Hebrew name of Paul, Acts xiii. 9.

Săv'ạ-ran, 1 Macc. vi. 43. [AVARAN.]

Sā'vĭ-as, 1 Esdr. viii. 2. [UZZI.]

Sạw (*cutter*). Hebrew saws doubtless patterned after those of Egypt, being single-handled, with teeth inclined toward the handle, so that cutting was done by pulling. Used for sawing wood, Isa. x. 15; stone, 1 Kgs. vii. 9; torture, 2 Sam. xii. 31; 1 Chr. xx. 3; Heb. xi. 37.

Scāpe'gōat, Lev. xvi. 7-26. [GOAT.]

Scär'let (*orange-red*). A Tyrian color much prized by ancients, Ex. xxv. 4; Prov. xxxi. 21.

Sçĕp'tre (*prop*). Any rod or staff. A shepherd's crook or tithing rod, Lev. xxvii. 32; Mic. vii. 14. A symbol of royal power, Gen. xlix. 10; Num. xxiv. 17; overlaid with gold, Esth. iv. 11.

Sçē'vạ (*fitted*). An Ephesian priest, Acts xix. 14-16.

Scôr'pĭ-on (*crawler*). A venomous creature allied to the spider, but resembling the lobster. Its sting is painful and often fatal, Deut. viii. 15; 1 Kgs. xii. 11; Rev. ix. 3-10. A dangerous gift, Luke xi. 12.

Scoûrġ'ing (*thonging*). A common Hebrew punishment. The scourge was made of three lashes of leather or cord. Not more than forty stripes could be administered, Deut. xxv. 1-3; Matt. x. 17; xxiii. 34. Rods or twigs were also used, 2 Cor. xi. 25.

Scrībe (*writer*). The Hebrew scribe or writer appears to have been at first a court or military official, Ex. v. 6; Judg. v. 14; then secretary or recorder, for kings, priests, and prophets, 2 Sam. viii. 17; xx. 25; finally a secretary of state, doctor, or teacher, Ez. vii. 6. Scribes became a class or guild, copyists and expounders of the law, and through their innovations fell under the same denunciations as priests and Pharisees, Matt. xxiii. 1-33; Mark vii. 5-13; Luke v. 30.

Scrĭp (*bag*). A shepherd's bag, 1 Sam. xvii. 40. A wallet for carrying food and traveller's conveniences, Matt. x. 10; Luke x. 4.

Scrĭp'ture (*written*). By way of prëeminence, the sacred writings contained in the Old and New Testaments. [BIBLE.]

Scȳth'ĭ-an (*fierce-looking*). Name applied to the fierce, nomadic nations north of the Black and Caspian seas, Col. iii. 11.

Scȳth-ŏp'ȯ-lis (*Scythian city*). The city of Bethshean in Palestine was for a time so called because captured and held by Scythian nomads, 2 Macc. xii. 29.

Sēa. The Hebrews so designated any large body of water, whether lake, river, sea, or ocean, Gen. i. 10; Deut. xxx. 13; Job xiv. 11; Isa. xix. 5; Jer. li. 36; Ezek. xxxii. 2. (1) "Molten sea" was the immense brass laver of Solomon's temple, 1 Kgs. vii. 23–26. (2) "Sea of the Plain," Deut. iv. 49. [SALT SEA.] (3) "Great Sea," Josh. xv. 47, "uttermost sea," Deut. xi. 24, the Mediterranean, between Europe and Africa. (4) "Sea of Tiberias" [GENNESARET.] (5) "Sea of Merom." [MEROM.]

Sēal (*little mark*). Much used by ancients to authenticate documents and secure packages and doors, the impression being made in clay or wax. Seals were frequently engraved stones set in rings; Gen. xli. 42; Job xxxviii. 14: Jer. xxxii. 10; Matt. xxvii. 66.

Sē'bȧ. A son of Cush, Gen. x. 7. Mentioned as a nation or country in Ps. lxxii. 10; Isa. xliii. 3; xlv. 14, and associated with Meroe on the upper Nile.

Sē'bȧt, Shē'bȧt (*rod*). Fifth month of Jewish civil and eleventh of sacred year, corresponding to parts of February and March, Zech. i. 7.

Sĕc'a-cah (*thicket*). A city in Judah, Josh. xv. 61.

Sē'chu (*tower*). A place between Gibeah and Ramah, noted for its well, 1 Sam. xix. 22.

Sĕct (*way, school*). A party adhering to a doctrine, as the sect of Sadducees, Acts v. 17, or Pharisees, Acts xv. 5; xxvi. 5. Christians in general were for a long time called by the Jews, in a spirit of contempt, "the sect of the Nazarenes," Acts xxiv. 5. The word is also applied to a certain set of doctrines or mode of life, Acts xxiv. 14; 2 Pet. ii. 1; and to heresies proper, or perversions of Christian truth, Gal. v. 20.

Sĕ-cŭn'dus (*second*). A Thessalonian friend of Paul, Acts xx. 4.

Sĕd″ė-çī′as (1) Ancestor of Baruch, Bar. i. 1. (2) Son of King Josiah, Bar. i. 8.

Sēed (*sowed*). Seed for sowing must not be mingled, Lev. xix. 19. Children, descendants, Gen. xvii. 12; Gal. iii. 16. Pedigree, Ez. ii. 59. The male fertilizing element, Gen. xxxviii. 9.

Sēer (*who sees*). 1 Sam. ix. 9. [PROPHET.]

Sēethe (*boil*). To boil, Ex. xvi. 23.

Sē′gub (*lifted up*). (1) A son of Hiel who rebuilt Jericho, 1 Kgs. xvi. 34. (2) A Judahite, 1 Chr. ii. 21, 22.

Sē′ir (*hairy*). (1) A Horite chief, Gen. xxxvi. 21; Deut. ii. 12. (2) Land or country corresponding with valley and mountains of Arabah, stretching from the Dead Sea to the Gulf of Akaba, Gen. xiv. 6; xxxii. 3; xxxiii. 14–16. The region was first occupied by the Horites, and fell into possession of Esau and his posterity, Gen. xxxvi. 8–9. Hence Seir and Edom are sometimes spoken of as identical. The Israelites, when refused permission to march through Edom to Moab, marched round the granite ranges of Seir and entered Moab by the east and north. (3) A boundary mark of Judah, Josh. xv. 10.

Sē′ĭ-răth (*hairy*). Place to which the murderer Ehud fled, Judg. iii. 26.

Sē′là, Sē′lah (*rock*). A rock-founded city of Edom, the Petra of the Greeks, half way between the Dead Sea and Gulf of Akaba. Subdued by King Amaziah and called Joktheel, "subdued of God." Remarkable now for its ruins, among which are a rock-hewn temple and amphitheatre, 2 Kgs. xiv. 7; Isa. xvi. 1. The complete destruction and desolation of the place fulfils the prophecy of Jeremiah, Jer. xlix. 16, 17.

Sē′lah. A word of frequent occurrence in Psalms, and supposed to mean an interlude in vocal music, or a pianissimo of all parts, Ps. ix. 16; Hab. iii. 3, 9, 13.

Sē′là=hăm″mah-lē′koth (*rock of escapes*). Rocky stronghold in wilderness of Maon, where David escaped from Saul, 1 Sam. xxiii. 28.

Sē′led (*lifted up*). A Judahite, 1 Chr. ii. 30.

Sĕl″ė-mī′ah. A swift scribe, 2 Esdr. xiv. 24.

Sė-leū′çĭ-à (*city of Seleucus*). The seaport of Antioch in Syria, Acts xiii. 4. It was the port whence Paul and Barnabas started on their first missionary journey, and lay sixteen miles to the west of

Antioch. The city was founded by Seleucus Nicator about B. C. 300, and to distinguish it from other cities of the same name was frequently called "Seleucia by the sea." The harbor is now choked with sand, and the once beautiful city is but the insignificant village of Elkalusi.

Sĕ-leū′cus. The Seleuci, or Seleucidæ, sprung from Seleucus I., a general of Alexander the Great, were a line of Syrian kings, B. c. 312–65, 2 Macc. iii. 3.

Sĕm. Greek form of Shem, Luke iii. 36.

Sĕm′′a-chī′ah (*God-sustained*). A Levite porter, 1 Chr. xxvi. 7.

Sĕm′e-ī (*distinguished*). (1) 1 Esdr. ix. 33. [SHIMEI.] (2) Father of Mattathias, Luke iii. 26. Semein in R. V.

Sē′mel, Esth. xi. 2. [SHIMEI.]

Sĕ-mĕl′lĭ-us, 1 Esdr. ii. 16. [SHIMSHAI.]

Sē-nā′ah (*brambly*). His sons were returned captives, Ez. ii. 35.

Sĕn′āte (*elders*). First body, or class, of Hebrew Sanhedrim; the other two being priests and scribes, Acts v. 21.

Sē′neh (*bramble*). One of two rocks in the pass of Michmash, 1 Sam. xiv. 4, 5.

Sē′nĭr (*glistening*). Amorite name for Mount Hermon, 1 Chr. v. 23; Ezek. xxvii. 5.

Sĕn-năch′e-rĭb (*not the first-born*). Son and successor of Sargon, king of Assyria, B. c. 702–680. He extended his conquests to the Mediterranean and to Egypt, 2 Kgs. xviii. 13–37; xix. Most powerful and magnificent of eastern sovereigns, Isa. xxxvi., xxxvii. He made Nineveh his capital and adorned it with many palaces and public structures. His monuments have been found in many places, and a record of his arrival in Egypt has been unearthed close by an inscription of Rameses the Great.

Sĕ-nū′ah (*bristling*). A Benjamite, second in rule over Jerusalem after the captivity, Neh. xi. 9. Hasenuah, 1 Chr. ix. 7.

Sĕ-ō′rim (*bearded*). Head of fourth priestly course, 1 Chr. xxiv. 8.

Sē′phar (*number*). A Joktanite border in Arabia, Gen. x. 30.

Sĕph′a-răd (*severed*). Unlocated place whence

captive Jews would return to possess the cities of the south, Obad. 20.

Sĕph″ar-vā′im (*two Sipperas*). One of the two cities of Sippera in Syria, whence colonists were sent to Samaria, 2 Kgs. xvii. 24–34 ; xix. 13 ; Isa. xxxvii. 13.

Sĕph′ar-vītes. Inhabitants of Sepharvaim, 2 Kgs. xvii. 31.

Sĕp-tū′a-ġint (*seventy*). The traditional 70 or 72 translators of the Hebrew Scriptures into Greek ; but especially, the Greek version of the O. T. made by 72 learned Jews at Alexandria, at command of Ptolemy Philadelphus, about B. C. 270. The beginning of active work on this, the best known of ancient Bible translations, is fixed for the years B. C. 280–285, and it covered a long period of time, the translation of the Apocryphal books having been gradually added. It was made from Egyptian Hebrew manuscripts, and in its completed form is designated by the Roman numerals LXX. It was the version used by Hebrews in Christ's time and by the Greek Fathers and early N. T. writers, and the Latin version was made from it.

Sĕp′ŭl-chre (*ker*) (*bury*), 2 Kgs. xxiii. 16 ; Isa. xxii. 16 ; Matt. xxvii. 60 ; Mark xvi. 2 ; Luke xxiii. 53. Though the Egyptians and nearly all peoples adjacent to the Hebrews have made the name of sarcophagus familiar as a stone coffin, a chest-like tomb, often ornamented and inscribed, there seems to have been nothing akin to it in all the mention of funeral customs and burial rites in the Scriptures, if we except certain titles and inscriptions over tombs such as are mentioned in 2 Kgs. xxiii. 17. [BURIAL.] [TOMB.]

Sē′rah (*lady*). A daughter of Asher, Gen. **xlvi.** 17 ; 1 Chr. vii. 30. Sarah, Num. xxvi. 46.

Sĕr″a-ī′ah (*warrior of God*). (1) David's scribe, 2 Sam. viii. 17. Sheva, 2 Sam. xx. 25. Shisha, 1 Kgs. iv. 3. Shavsha, 1 Chr. xviii. 16. (2) A high priest, slain at Riblah, 2 Kgs. xxv. 18–21. (3) One who submitted to Gedaliah, 2 Kgs. xxv. 23. (4) A Judahite, 1 Chr. iv. 13, 14. (5) A Simeonite, 1 Chr. iv. 35. (6) A returned priest, Ez. ii. 2 ; Neh. x. 2. (7) Ancestor of Ezra, Ez. vii. 1. (8) One of the officers who arrested Jeremiah, Jer. xxxvi. 26. (9) Jeremiah's messenger to Babylon, Jer. li. 59–64.

Sĕr′a-phĭm (*burning*). An order of celestial beings, pictured in Isaiah's vision as around the throne of God, Isa. vi. 2-7.

Sē'red (*fear*). First-born of Zebulun, Gen. xlvi. 14; Num. xxvi. 26.

Sĕr'gĭ-us Paͧu'lus (*little net*). Proconsul of Cyprus at time of Paul's visit, Acts xiii. 7, 12.

Sē'ron. A Syrian general, 1 Macc. iii. 13, 23.

Sĕr'pent (*creeper*). The Hebrew original embraces the entire serpent genus. Serpents numerous and venomous in Bible lands. The word appears in Scripture under various names; adder, supposably the cerastes, Gen. xlix. 17; asp, or cobra, Deut. xxxii. 33; cockatrice, Jer. viii. 17; viper, Job xx. 16. Subtile, Gen. iii. 1; wise, Matt. x. 16; poisonous, Prov. xxiii. 32; sharp-tongued, Ps. cxl. 3; charmed, Ps. lviii. 5; emblem of wickedness, Matt. xxiii. 33; cruelty, Ps. lviii. 4; treachery, Gen. xlix. 17; the devil, Rev. xii. 9-15; fiery serpents sent as a punishment, Num. xxi. 6; sight of "brazen serpent," an antidote for poison of bite, Num. xxi. 8, 9; "fiery flying serpent," a probable allusion to dragon, Isa. xiv. 29.

Sē'rug (*branch*). Son of Reu and great-grandfather of Abraham, Gen. xi. 20-23. Saruch, Luke iii. 35.

Sĕr'vant (*server*). In a broad Bible sense, subject, assistant, person under tribute; in special sense, bondman or slave, by right of purchase, pledge for indebtedness, or indenture; which relationship was carefully guarded by Mosaic law, Lev. xxv. 39-55; Deut. xv. 12-18. [SLAVE.]

Sĕrv'ĭ-tôr (*server*). A servant, 2 Kgs. iv. 43.

Sĕth (*pay*). Third son of Adam, Gen. iv. 25; v. 3-8.

Sē'thur (*hidden*). An Asherite spy, Num. xiii. 13.

Sĕv'en. A favorite, and often symbolic, number among Hebrews, Gen. ii. 2; vii. 2; xli. 2, 3. Used as a round number, 1 Sam. ii. 5; Matt. xii. 45. Type of abundance and completeness, Gen. iv. 15, 24; Matt. xviii. 21, 22. These references, and other places, show a seventh day and seventh year sabbath and a seven times seventh year of Jubilee; also sacrificial animals limited to seven, and the golden candlesticks. Seven priests with seven trumpets surrounded Jericho for seven days, and seven times on the seventh day. In the Apocalypse we find seven churches, seven candlesticks, seven stars, seven seals, seven trumpets, seven vials, seven plagues, seven angels.

Shā′′al-ăb′bin (*place of foxes*). A boundary place of Dan, Josh. xix. 42. Shaalbim, Judg. i. 35; 1 Kgs. iv. 9.

Shā-ăl′bim. [SHAALABBIN.]

Shā-ăl′bo-nīte. One of David's heroes, so called. Place unknown, 2 Sam. xxiii. 32; 1 Chr. xi. 33.

Shā′aph (*division*). (1) A Judahite, 1 Chr. ii. 47. (2) Son of Caleb, 1 Chr. ii. 49.

Shā′′a-rā′im (*two gates*). (1) Town in Judah, 1 Sam. xvii. 52. Sharaim, Josh. xv. 36. (2) Town in Simeon, 1 Chr. iv. 31.

Shā-ăsh′găz (*lover of beauty*). Keeper of concubines in palace of Xerxes, Esth. ii. 14.

Shăb-bĕth′a-ī (*my rest*). An assistant to Ezra, Ez. x. 15; Neh. viii. 7; xi. 16.

Shăch-ī′à (*God-protected*). A Benjamite, 1 Chr. viii. 10.

Shăd′da-ī (*mighty*). *El-Shaddai*, "God Almighty." The name used by Hebrews for God, before "Jehovah" acquired its full significance, Gen. xvii. 1; Ex. vi. 3.

Shā′drach (*royal*). Chaldean name given to Hananiah, Dan. i. 7–21; ii.; iii.

Shā′gē (*erring*). Father of one of David's guard, 1 Chr. xi. 34.

Shā′′ha-rā′im (*double morning*). A Benjamite, 1 Chr. viii. 8.

Shā-hăz′i-mah (*heights*). Town in Issachar. Josh. xix. 22.

Shā′lem (*peaceful*). For "to Shalem," Gen. xxxiii. 18, read "in peace to."

Shā′lim, Land of (*land of foxes*). The wild place through which Saul passed when searching for his father's asses, 1 Sam. ix. 4.

Shăl′i-sha, Land of (*triangular*). A wild district near Mt. Ephraim through which Saul passed, in search of his father's asses, 1 Sam. ix. 4.

Shăl′le-chĕth (*thrown down*). A westward gate of the temple at Jerusalem, 1 Chr. xxvi. 16.

Shăl′lum (*revenge*). (1) Fifteenth king of Israel, B. C. 771 ; slew King Zachariah, and usurped his throne ; reigned one month ; slain and succeeded by Menahem, 2 Kgs. xv. 10–15. (2) Husband of Huldah the prophetess, 2 Kgs. xxii. 14 ; 2 Chr. xxxiv. 22. (3) A descendant of Sheshan, 1 Chr. ii. 40, 41. (4) Fourth son of Josiah king of Judah, who became King Jehoahaz, B. C. 610, and reigned for three months, 1 Chr. iii. 15 ; Jer. xxii. 11, 12 ; 2 Kgs. xxiii. 30, 31 ; 2 Chr. xxxvi. 1–4. (5) A Simeonite, 1 Chr. iv. 25. (6) A high priest, 1 Chr. vi. 12 ; Ez. vii. 2. (7) Shillem, a Naphtalite, 1 Chr. vii. 13. (8) A chief of porters, 1 Chr. ix. 17 ; Ez. ii. 42. (9) A porter, 1 Chr. ix. 19, 31. (10) An Ephraimite, 2 Chr. xxviii. 12. (11) Uncle of Jeremiah, Jer. xxxii. 7. (12) Four Levites, Ez. x. 24, 42 ; Neh. iii. 12 ; Jer. xxxv. 4.

Shăl′lun (*revenge*). A wall-repairer and governor of part of Mizpah, Neh. iii. 15.

Shăl′ma-ī (*thanks*). His children were returned captives, Ez. ii. 46.

Shăl′man, Hos. x. 14. [SHALMANESER.]

Shăl″man-ē′ṣer (*Shalman is lenient*). An Assyrian king, B. C. 727–722, who twice conquered Hoshea, king of Israel, the last time capturing his capital, Samaria, 2 Kgs. xvii. 3–6 ; xviii. 9–12.

Shā′mà (*dutiful*). One of David's guard, 1 Chr. xi. 44.

Shăm″a-ri′ah (*God-kept*). Son of King Rehoboam, 2 Chr. xi. 19.

Shăm′bleṣ (*little benches*). In general, slaughter-houses, but meat-market in 1 Cor. x. 25.

Shā′med (*destroyer*). A Benjamite, 1 Chr. viii. 12.

Shāme′fāçed-ness. Wrong writing of shame-fastness, modesty. Corrected in R. V., 1 Tim. ii. 9.

Shā′mer (*keeper*). (1) A Levite, 1 Chr. vi. 46. (2) An Asherite, 1 Chr. vii. 34. Shomer in vs. 32.

Shăm′gär (*sword*). A judge of Israel who slew 600 Philistines with an ox-goad, Judg. iii. 31 ; v. 6.

Shăm′huth (*destruction*). One of David's captains, 1 Chr. xxvii. 8.

Shā′mir (*thorn*). (1) A town in the mountains of Judah, Josh. xv. 48. (2) Residence of Tola, the judge, in Mount Ephraim, Judg. x. 1, 2. (3) Son of Michah, 1 Chr. xxiv. 24.

Shăm'mȧ (*desolation*). A chief of Asher, 1 Chr. vii. 37.

Shăm'mah (*desolation*). (1) A duke of Edom, Gen. xxxvi. 13, 17; 1 Chr. i. 37. (2) Third son of Jesse, 1 Sam. xvi. 9; xvii. 13. Called also, Shimea, Shimeah, and Shimma. (3) One of the three greatest of David's mighty men, 2 Sam. xxiii. 11–17, 33. (4) Another of David's mighty men, 2 Sam. xxiii. 25. Shammoth, 1 Chr. xi. 27. Shamhuth, 1 Chr. xxvii. 8.

Shăm'ma-ī (*desolated*). Three Judahites, 1 Chr. ii. 28, 32, 44, 45; iv. 17.

Shăm'moth, 1 Chr. xi. 27. [SHAMMAH, 4.]

Shăm-mū'ȧ, Shăm'mū-ah (*heard*). (1) The Reubenite spy, Num. xiii. 4. (2) A son of David, born in Jerusalem, 2 Sam. v. 14; 1 Chr. xiv. 4. Shimea, 1 Chr. iii. 5. (3) A Levite, Neh. xi. 17. (4) A priest representing the family of Bilgah, Neh. xii. 18.

Shăm''she-rā'ī (*hero*). A Benjamite, 1 Chr. viii. 26.

Shā'pham (*bare*). A Gadite, 1 Chr. v. 12.

Shā'phan (*rabbit*). Scribe or secretary of King Josiah, 2 Kgs. xxii. 3–14; 2 Chr. xxxiv. 8–20.

Shā'phat (*judge*). (1) The Simeonite spy, Num. xiii. 5. (2) Father of the prophet Elisha, 1 Kgs. xix. 16, 19; 2 Kgs. iii. 11; vi. 31. (3) One in the royal line of Judah, 1 Chr. iii. 22. (4) A Gadite chief, 1 Chr. v. 12. (5) A herdsman of David, 1 Chr. xxvii. 29.

Shā'pher (*bright*). A desert encampment of the Israelites, Num. xxxiii. 23.

Shär'a-ī (*set free*). A descendant of Bani, who had married a foreign wife, Ez. x. 40.

Shăr-ā'ĭm, Josh. xv. 36. [SHAARAIM.]

Shā'rär (*navel*). Father of one of David's warriors, 2 Sam. xxiii. 33. Sacar, 1 Chr. xi. 35.

Shȧ-rē'zer (*prince*). Son of Sennacherib, who helped to murder his father, 2 Kgs. xix. 37.

Shâr'on (*plain*). (1) The plain skirting the Mediterranean coast from Judah to Cæsarea. It is an extension of the " shefelah " or lowlands of Judah, and was renowned for its fertility. Called Saron in Acts ix. 35. First mentioned as Lasharon, Josh. xii. 18. David's flocks fed there, 1 Chr. xxvii. 29. Celebrated in S. of Sol. ii. 1; Isa. xxxv. 2; lxv. 10. (2) A town or district east of Jordan, and perhaps in Gilead, 1 Chr. v. 16.

Shăr'on-īte. Designation of Shitrai, one of David's herdsmen, 1 Chr. xxvii. 29.

Shâ-ru'hen (*gracious house*). A town first allotted to Judah and then to Simeon, Josh. xix. 6.

Shăsh'a-ī (*noble*). A son of Bani, who had taken a foreign wife, Ez. x. 40.

Shā'shak (*eager*). A Benjamite, 1 Chr. viii. 14, 25.

Shā'ul (*asked*). (1) A son of Simeon and founder of the Shaulites, Gen. xlvi. 10; Num. xxvi. 13. (2) A king of Edom, 1 Chr. i. 48, 49. Saul in Gen. xxxvi. 37.

Shā'ul-ītes. Descendants of Shaul, Num. xxvi. 13.

Shā'veh (*plain*). The unidentified place in Palestine mentioned as the "king's dale," Gen. xiv. 17; 2 Sam. xviii. 18.

Shā'veh Kĭr''ĭ-a-thā'im (*plain of Kiriathaim*). Spot where the Emims dwelt when smitten by Chedorlaomer, Gen. xiv. 5. It is supposably the place that afterwards belonged to Reuben, under the name of Kirjathaim, Num. xxxii. 37; Josh. xiii. 19.

Shăv'shä (*God's warrior*). Royal secretary or scribe in time of King David, 1 Chr. xviii. 16. Seraiah, 2 Sam. viii. 17. Sheva, 2 Sam. xx. 25. Shisha, 1 Kgs. iv. 3.

Shā'ving. [RAZOR.]

Shawm (*pipe*). A cornet or clarionet. Only in Prayer-book version of Ps. xcviii. 6.

Shē'al (*asking*). One who had a foreign wife, Ez. x. 29.

Shē-ăl'tĭ-el (*asked of God*). Father of Zerubbabel, Ez. iii. 2, 8; v. 2; Neh. xii. 1; Hag. i. 1, 12, 14; ii. 2, 23.

Shē''a-rī'ah (*prized of God*). A descendant of Saul, 1 Chr. viii. 38; ix. 44.

Shear'ing=house. A spot between Jezreel and Samaria where Jehu slaughtered the royal family of Judah, 2 Kgs. x. 12-14.

Shē'är=jā'shŭb (*a remnant shall return*). Symbolical name given by Isaiah to his son, Isa. vii. 3.

She'bả (*oath*). (1) Son of Bichri, a Benjamite, who revolted from David and was beheaded, 2 Sam. xx. 1-22. (2) A Gadite chief, 1 Chr. v. 13. (3) A descendant of Ham, Gen. x. 7; 1 Chr. i. 9. (4) Son of Joktan, Gen. x. 28. (5) Son of Jokshan, Gen. xxv. 3; 1 Chr. i. 32. (6) The kingdom of Sheba, whose queen visited Solomon, 1 Kgs. x. 1-13; 2 Chr. ix. 1-12. This country has been variously located in Africa, in Arabia, on the Persian Gulf, and in Arabia, on the Red Sea. The burden of authority identifies it with Yemen or Arabia Felix, on the Red Sea, and peopled by descendants of Sheba, son of Joktan. (7) A town in Simeon, Josh. xix. 2. Probably the Shema of Josh. xv. 26.

She'bah (*oath*). The famous well, or series of wells, dug by the servants of Isaac, in accordance with his compact with the Philistines. It gave name to Beersheba, Gen. xxvi. 31-33.

She'bam (*odor*). A town east of Jordan, given to Reuben and Gad, Num. xxxii. 3. [SIBMAH.]

Sheb''a-nī'ah (*grown by God*). (1) A priestly trumpeter at the bringing up of the ark, 1 Chr. xv. 24. (2) Three co-covenanters with Nehemiah, Neh. ix. 5; x. 4, 10, 12; xii. 14.

Shĕb'a-rĭm (*ruins*). Place near Ai to which the defeated Israelites were pursued, Josh. vii. 5.

Shē'băt. [SEBAT.]

Shē'ber (*breaking*). A son of Caleb, 1 Chr. ii. 48.

Shĕb'nả (*strength*). (1) Prefect of the palace under King Hezekiah, Isa. xxii. 15-25. (2) Scribe under King Hezekiah, 2 Kgs. xviii. 18, 37; xix. 2; Isa. xxxvi. 3.

Shĕb'u-el (*captive of God*). (1) A descendant of Moses, 1 Chr. xxiii. 16; xxvi. 24. Shubael, 1 Chr xxiv. 20. (2) A Levite minstrel, son of Heman, 1 Chr. xxv. 4. Shubael, 1 Chr. xxv. 20.

Shĕc''a-nī'ah (*dweller with God*). (1) A priest in time of David, 1 Chr. xxiv. 11. (2) A Levite, 2 Chr. xxxi. 15.

Shĕch''a-nī'ah (*dweller with God*). (1) A descendant of the royal line, 1 Chr. iii. 21, 22. (2) Levites and returned captives, in Ez. viii. 3, 5; x. 2; Neh. iii. 29; vi. 18; xii. 3.

She'chem (*shoulder*). (1) The Canaanite who abducted Dinah and was slain by Simeon and Levi, Gen. xxxiv. (2) An ancient and highly historic city, between mounts Ebal and Gerizim, 34 miles N. of Jerusalem. Called also Sichem, Sychem, Sychar, later Neapolis, now Nablus. Halting place of Abraham, Gen. xii. 6. A Hivite city in time of Jacob, Gen. xxxiii. 18–20; Josh. xxiv. 32. Captured by Simeon and Levi, Gen. xxxiv. Joseph buried there, Josh. xxiv. 32. Destroyed by Abimelech, Judg. ix. Rebuilt by Rehoboam, and fortified and made capital of Israel by Jeroboam, 1 Kgs. xii. 1–19, 25; 2 Chr. x. A centre of Samaritan worship after the captivity, John iv. 5, 39–42. (3) A Manassite, of Gilead, Num. xxvi. 31. (4) A Gileadite, nephew of former, 1 Chr. vii. 19.

She'chem-ites. The family of Shechem of Gilead, Num. xxvi. 31.

She-chi'nah (*dwelling-place*). The visible majesty of God, as in the "pillar of cloud" and the "glory" which covered the tabernacle and filled Solomon's temple. A word found only in the targums, Chaldaic version of Bible, and among early Christian writers. Alluded to in Luke ii. 9; John i. 14; Rom. ix. 4.

Shĕd'ĕ-ur (*light-sender*). Father of Elizur, chief of Reuben at time of exode, Num. i. 5; ii. 10; vii. 30, 35; x. 18.

Sheep. An important animal among Hebrews, and a main source of wealth. Shepherd's occupation highly respectable, Gen. iv. 2; Ex. iii. 1; 1 Sam. xvi. 11; Job xlii. 12, though odious to Egyptians. Used for sacrifices, Ex. xx. 24; xxix. 38; Lev. ix. 3; for food, 1 Sam. xxv. 18. Wool used for clothing, Lev. xiii. 47. Skins used for tabernacle coverings, Ex. xxv. 5. Paid as tribute, 2 Kgs. iii. 4. Sheep and shepherd employed much figuratively, 2 Chr. xviii. 16; Ps. cxix. 176; Matt. ix. 36; John x. 11; Heb. xiii. 20. The common sheep of Syria and Palestine was the broad-tailed variety.

Sheep'fold. Place for herding sheep, especially at night. Usually built strong to keep out wild animals, Num. xxxii. 16; 2 Sam. vii. 8; John x. 16. The fold, cote, or enclosure was also the place where the sheep were collected at shearing time, Jer. xxiii. 3; Zeph. ii. 6, which was a season of festivity, 1 Sam.

xxv. 7–11; 2 Sam. xiii. 23. Hence "shearing-house," 2 Kgs. x. 12-14.

Sheep=gate. One of the gates of Jerusalem as rebuilt by Nehemiah, Neh. iii. 1, 32; xii. 39.

Sheep=mär′ket. Should read "sheep-gate" as above, John v. 2.

She″ha-rī′ah (*Jehovah dawns*). Son of Jeroham of Benjamin, 1 Chr. viii. 26.

Shĕk′el (*weight*). A weight for weighing un-coined money, of Assyrian and Babylonian origin. There seem to have been two standards, that of the sanctuary and the king, Ex. xxx. 13; 2 Sam. xiv. 26. Both approximated half an ounce, valued in silver at about 64 cents. Later, a Hebrew silver coin, with bronze half and quarter shekels. Probably the "pieces of silver" in Matt. xxvi. 15, though the "pieces of silver" in Luke xv. 8 are clearly the Greek drachmas. The first Jewish coins were struck by Simon Maccabeus, who obtained permission to coin money from Antiochus, King of Syria. His shekel showed a vase on one side, representing a pot of manna, and on the other an almond branch with flowers, representative supposably of Aaron's rod.

She′lah (*prayer*). (1) Youngest son of Judah and founder of Shelanites, Gen. xxxviii. 5-26; Num. xxvi. 20. (2) 1 Chr. i. 18, 24. [SALAH.]

She′lan-ītes. Descendants of Shelah, Num. xxvi. 20.

Shĕl″e-mī′ah (*God repays*). (1) 1 Chr. xxvi. 14. [MESHELEMIAH.] (2) Two who married foreign wives, Ez. x. 39, 41. (3) Father of Hananiah, Neh. iii. 30. (4) A priest appointed treasurer, Neh. xiii. 13. (5) Father of Jehucal, Jer. xxxvii. 3. (6) Father of one of Jeremiah's accusers, Jer. xxxviii. 1. (7) Father of the officer who arrested Jeremiah, Jer. xxxvii. 13.

She′leph (*drawn out*). Son of Joktan, Gen. x. 26.

She′lesh (*strength*). An Asherite chief, 1 Chr. vii. 35.

Shĕl′o-mī (*my peace*). An Asherite, Num. xxxiv. 27.

Shĕl′o-mĭth (*my peace*). (1) Daughter of Dibri, of Dan, Lev. xxiv. 11. (2) Daughter of Zerubbabel, 1 Chr. iii. 19. (3) Two Levites, 1 Chr. xxiii. 9, 18. (4) A descendant of Eliezer, 1 Chr. xxvi. 25-28. (5) A returned captive, Ez. viii. 10.

Shĕl'o-mŏth, 1 Chr. xxiv. 22. [SHELOMITH, 3.]

Shĕ-lū'mĭ-el (*God's peace*). A prince of Simeon, Num. i. 6; ii. 12; vii. 36, 41; x. 19.

Shĕm (*name*). Oldest son of Noah, preserved with his father in the ark, Gen. v. 32. Blessed by Noah for his conduct, Gen. ix. 18–27. His descendants are the Hebrews, Arameans, Persians, Assyrians, and Arabians, whose languages are called Shemitic.

Shĕ'mȧ (*hearing*). (1) A Judahite, 1 Chr. ii. 43, 44. (2) A Reubenite, 1 Chr. v. 8. (3) A Benjamite chief, 1 Chr. viii. 13. (4) An assistant of Ezra, Neh. viii. 4. (5) Josh. xv. 26. [SHEBA, 7.]

Shĕ-mā'ah (*God hears*). A Benjamite whose sons joined David at Ziklag, 1 Chr. xii. 3.

Shĕm''a-ī'ah (*God hears*). (1) Prophet and chronicler in reign of Rehoboam, 1 Kgs. xii. 22; 2 Chr. xi. 2. (2) Twenty-four others, mostly priests, Levites, and returned captives, 1 Chr. iii. 22; iv. 37; v. 4; ix. 14; ix. 16; xv. 8, 11; xxiv. 6; xxvi. 4–7; 2 Chr. xxix. 14; xvii. 8; xxxi. 15; xxxv. 9; Ez. viii. 13, 16; x. 21, 31; Neh. vi. 10; x. 8; xii. 6, 18, 34, 36, 42; Jer. xxvi. 20; xxix. 24–32; xxxvi. 12.

Shĕm''a-rī'ah (*God keeps*). (1) An adherent of David at Ziklag, 1 Chr. xii. 5. (2) Two who took foreign wives, Ez. x. 32, 41.

Shĕm'e-ber (*high flight*). King of Zeboiim, Gen. xiv. 2.

Shĕ'mĕr (*guarded*). Owner of the hill which King Omri bought, and on which he built Samaria, giving it the former owner's name, 1 Kgs. xvi. 24.

Shĕ-mī'dȧ (*wise*). A son of Gilead and founder of the Shemidaites, Num. xxvi. 32; Josh. xvii. 2. Shemidah, 1 Chr. vii. 19.

Shĕ-mī'dah, 1 Chr. vii. 19. [SHEMIDA.]

Shĕ-mī'dȧ-ītes. Descendants of Shemida, Num. xxvi. 32.

Shĕm'i-nĭth (*eighth*). A musical term, variously surmised to mean the instrument, one of eight strings, the octave, the time of the piece, the part, air, pitch, or key, 1 Chr. xv. 21; Ps. vi; xii. titles.

Shĕ-mīr'a-mŏth'' (*heights of heaven*). (1) A musical Levite in time of David, 1 Chr. xv. 18, 20; xvi. 5. (2) A Levite in reign of Jehoshaphat, 2 Chr. xvii. 8.

Shĕ-mĭt′ic. The family of languages spoken by the descendants of Shem. [SHEM.]

Shĕ-mū′el (*heard of God*). (1) Representative of Simeon during the apportionment of Canaan, Num. xxxiv. 20. (2) Samuel the prophet, 1 Chr. vi. 33. (3) A chief of Issachar, 1 Chr. vii. 2.

Shĕn (*tooth*). An unknown place, 1 Sam. vii. 12.

Shĕ-nā′zar (*ivory keeper*). A descendant of David, 1 Chr. iii. 18.

Shĕ′nir, Deut. iii. 9; S. of Sol. iv. 8. [SENIR.]

Shĕ′pham (*wild*). A landmark on eastern boundary of Promised Land, Num. xxxiv. 10.

Shĕph″a-thī′ah (*God judges*). A Benjamite, 1 Chr. ix. 8.

Shĕph″a-tī′ah (*God judges*). (1) Fifth son of David, 2 Sam. iii. 4; 1 Chr. iii. 3. (2) A Benjamite warrior, 1 Chr. xii. 5. (3) A chief of Simeon, 1 Chr. xxvii. 16. (4) Son of Jehoshaphat, 2 Chr. xxi. 2. (5) Four others in Ez. ii. 4, 57; Neh. vii. 9, 59; xi. 4; Jer. xxxviii. 1–4.

Shĕp′hĕrd (*herder of sheep*). A highly honorable occupation among pastoral Hebrews, engaged in by both sexes, Gen. xxix. 6; xxx. 29-35; Ex. ii. 16-22. Often arduous and dangerous employment, Gen. xxxi. 40; 1 Sam. xvii. 34. Equipment consisted of a sheepskin mantle, a scrip or wallet, a sling and crook. He led the flock to pasture in the morning, tended them by day and folded and watched them at night, Job xxx. 1; Luke ii. 8; John x. 4. The office of sheep-master or chief shepherd was one of great trust as well as honor, 2 Kgs. iii. 4; Heb. xiii. 20; 1 Pet. v. 4. It was the shepherd's duty to count the sheep daily and to tithe them, and he was held responsible for lost ones, Gen. xxxi. 38, 39; Ex. xxii. 12, 13; Lev. xxvii. 32; Jer. xxxiii. 13. Shepherd is used figuratively for Jehovah in Ps. lxxx. 1; Jer. xxxi. 10; for kings, Ezek. xxxiv. 10; in N. T. for Christ, John x. 11; Heb. xiii. 20; 1 Pet. v. 4. It is applied also to teachers in the synagogue and to those who preside over it. Hence pastor and minister of the gospel.

Shĕ′phī (*barren*). A descendant of Seir, 1 Chr. i. 40. Shepho, Gen. xxxvi. 23.

Shĕ′phŏ, Gen. xxxvi. 23. [SHEPHI.]

Shĕ-phū′phan (*serpent*). A grandson of Benjamin, 1 Chr. viii. 5. Shupham, Num. xxvi. 39. Shuppim, 1 Chr. vii. 12, 15. Muppim, Gen. xlvi. 21.

Shē′rah (*relation*). A daughter of Ephraim, 1 Chr. vii. 24.

Shĕr″e-bī′ah (*heat of God*). A co-covenanter with Nehemiah, and assistant to Ezra, Ez. viii. 18, 24; Neh. viii. 7; ix. 4; x. 12.

Shē′resh (*root*). Son of Machir, of Manasseh, 1 Chr. vii. 16.

Shĕ-rē′zer (*fire prince*). A messenger of the people, Zech. vii. 2.

Shĕr′iff (*shire officer*). A Babylonian official, Dan. iii. 2.

Shē′shăch (*from the goddess Shach*). Symbolical name for Babylon, Jer. xxv. 26.

Shē′shāi (*princely*). A son of Anak, slain by Caleb, Num. xiii. 22; Josh. xv. 14; Judg. i. 10.

Shē′shan (*princely*). A Judahite, 1 Chr. ii. 31–35.

Shĕsh-băz′zar (*fire-worshipper*). Zerubbabel's name at the Persian court, Ez. i. 8–11.

Shĕth (*tumult*). (1) 1 Chr. i. 1. [SETH.] (2) For Sheth in Num. xxiv. 17, read "tumult," as in Jer. xlviii. 45.

Shē′thär (*star*). A Persian prince, Esth. i. 14.

Shē′thär=bŏz′na-ī (*star of splendor*). A Persian officer in Syria, Ez. v. 3, 6; vi. 6, 13.

She′vȧ. Corruption of Seraiah. (1) A son of Caleb, 1 Chr. ii. 49. (2) The scribe of David, 2 Sam. xx. 25. Shavsha, 1 Chr. xviii. 16. Shisha, 1 Kgs. iv. 3. Seraiah, 2 Sam. viii. 17.

Shew′brĕad (*showbread*). Unleavened bread baked in twelve loaves corresponding to the twelve tribes, and placed fresh every Sabbath on the golden table of the sanctuary. Eaten only by the priests, Ex. xxv. 30; Lev. xxiv. 8; 1 Sam. xxi. 1–6; Matt. xii. 3, 4. The arrangement of loaves on the table was in two rows of six loaves each. Salt and frankincense were put on each row. It was called "shewbread." "bread of the face," or "bread of the setting before," because it stood continually before the Lord. In later times it was called the "bread of ordering," 1 Chr. ix. 32 marg.; Neh. x. 33.

Shĭb′bo-lĕth (*ear of corn, stream*).   Pronounced *sib′bo-leth* by Ephraimites, and *shib′bo-leth* by Gileadites.   When the latter conquered the former, and held the fords of Jordan, they exacted the pronunciation of this word in order to distinguish friend from foe.   Any other word beginning with *sh* would have answered the same purpose, Judg. xii. 6.

Shĭb′mah (*fragrant*).   A town in Reuben, east of Jordan, Num. xxxii. 38.   Shebam, Num. xxxii. 3.   Sibmah, Josh. xiii. 19.

Shĭ′crŏn (*drunkenness*).   A boundary mark of northern Judah, Josh. xv. 11.

Shiēld (*cover*).   A defensive piece of armor, varying in size and shape, and made of skin or metal.   Worn on left arm.   Metaphorically, divine protection, Judg. v. 8 ; 1 Kgs. x. 17 ; Ps. iii. 3.

Shĭg-gā′ion (*mournful*).   A word which probably designates the character of the ode, Ps. vii. title.

Shĭ-gī′o-noth.   Plural of Shiggaion, Hab. iii. 1.

Shĭ′hŏn (*ruin*).   A town in Issachar, Josh. xix. 19.

Shĭ′hôr (*blackness*).   (1) Southern boundary of David's empire, 1 Chr. xiii. 5.   [SIHOR.]   (2) Shihor-libnath, a boundary of Asher, and probably identical with the stream called "Blue River," which empties into the Mediterranean eight miles south of Dor, Josh. xix. 26.

Shĭl′hī (*armed*).   Grandfather of King Jehoshaphat, 1 Kgs. xxii. 42 ; 2 Chr. xx. 31.

Shĭl′him (*armed*).   A city in southern Judah, Josh. xv. 32.

Shĭl′lem (*retribution*).   Son of Naphtali and founder of Shillemites, Gen. xlvi. 24 ; Num. xxvi. 49.

Shĭl′lem-ītes.   Descendants of Shillem, Num. xxvi. 49.

Shĭ-lō′ah.   The softly flowing waters of Siloam, Isa. viii. 6.

Shĭ′lōh (*peace*).   (1) A disputed rendering ; referred to a town and to the Messiah, Gen. xlix. 10 ; Isa. ix. 6.   (2) A city in Ephraim, midway between Bethel and Shechem.   Now Seilun.   Joshua's capital and site where he apportioned his conquests.

The ark remained there for three hundred years, till captured by the Philistines, Josh. xviii. 1, 8–10; Judg. xxi. 19–23. Residence of Eli and Samuel, 1 Sam. iii., and it was there that Eli received word of the capture of the ark, and died, 1 Sam. iv. The ark was not returned to Shiloh after its capture, and the tabernacle was removed to Nob and thence to Jerusalem, but the odor of sanctity clung about the venerable city for generations, and it was long a place for annual pilgrimages and religious festivals. The prophet Ahijah dwelt at Shiloh, 1 Kgs. xiv. 1–18. Jeremiah pictures Shiloh as desolate in his day, Jer. vii. 12–14; xxvi. 6–9.

Shĭ-lō′nĭ. A descendant of Shelah, Neh. xi. 5.

Shī′lo-nīte. Dweller in Shiloh, 1 Kgs. xi. 29.

Shī′lo-nītes. Members of the family of Shelah, 1 Chr. ix. 5.

Shĭl′shah (*third*). An Asherite chief, 1 Chr. vii. 37.

Shĭm′e-â (*hearing*). (1) A son of David born in Jerusalem, 1 Chr. iii. 5. (2) A Levite, 1 Chr. vi. 30. (3) Another Levite, 1 Chr. vi. 39. (4) A brother of David, called also Shammah, Shimeah, and Shimma, 1 Chr. xx. 7.

Shĭm′e-ah (*hearing*). (1) Brother of David, called also Shammah, Shimma and Shimea, 2 Sam. xxi. 21. (2) A descendant of Jehiel, founder of Gibeon, 1 Chr. viii. 32.

Shĭm′e-ăm (*hearing*), 1 Chr. ix. 38. [SHIMEAH, 2.]

Shĭm′e-ăth (*hearing*). Mother of one of the murderers of King Joash, 2 Kgs. xii. 21 ; 2 Chr. xxiv. 26.

Shĭm′e-ath-ītes″. A family of scribes, 1 Chr. ii. 55.

Shĭm′e-ī (*famed*). (1) A son of Gershon, Num. iii. 18. Shimi, Ex. vi. 17. (2) A Benjamite who cursed David, 2 Sam. xvi. 5–13 ; 1 Kgs. ii. 44–46. (3) One of David's warriors, 1 Kgs. i. 8. (4) A commissary of Solomon, 1 Kgs. iv. 18. (5) Brother of Zerubbabel, 1 Chr. iii. 19. (6) A Simeonite, 1 Chr. iv. 26, 27. (7) A Reubenite, 1 Chr. v. 4. (8) A Levite, 1 Chr. vi. 42. (9) Leader of 10th musical course, 1 Chr. xxv. 17. (10) David's vineyardist, 1 Chr. xxvii. 27. (11) Ancestor of Mordecai, Esth.

ii. 5. (12) Levites in 2 Chr. xxix. 14; xxxi. 12, 13; Ez. x. 23, 33, 38.

Shĭm'e̬-on (*hearing*). One who married a foreign wife, Ez. x. 31.

Shĭm'hī (*famed*). A Benjamite, 1 Chr. viii. 21.

Shĭ'mī, Ex. vi. 17. [SHIMEI, 1.]

Shĭm'ītes. Descendants of Shimei (1), Num. iii. 21.

Shĭm'mȧ (*hearing*) Third son of Jesse, 1 Chr. ii. 13.

Shĭ'mon (*waste*). A Judahite, 1 Chr. iv. 20.

Shĭm'rath (*watcher*). A Benjamite, 1 Chr. viii. 21.

Shĭm'rī (*vigilant*). (1) A Simeonite, 1 Chr. iv. 37. (2) Father of one of David's guard, 1 Chr. xi. 45. (3) A Levite, 2 Chr. xxix. 13.

Shĭm'rĭth (*vigilant*). A Moabitess, mother of Jehozabad, one of the murderers of King Joash, 2 Chr. xxiv. 26. Called Shomer in 2 Kgs. xii. 21.

Shĭm'rŏm, 1 Chr. vii. 1. [SHIMRON, 2.]

Shĭm'rŏn (*watch-place*). (1) An ancient Canaanite city allotted to Zebulun, Josh. xi. 1; xix. 15. (2) Fourth son of Issachar and founder of Shimronites, Gen. xlvi. 13; Num. xxvi. 24.

Shĭm'ron-ītes. Descendants of Shimron (2), Num. xxvi. 24.

Shĭm'ron=mē'ron, Josh. xii. 20. Probably complete name of Shimron (1).

Shĭm'shāi (*bright*). A scribe and Persian satrap in Judea. He, together with the chancellor, Rehum, wrote a letter to King Artaxerxes in opposition to the rebuilding of the temple by Zerubbabel, Ez. iv. 8, 9, 17, 23.

Shĭ'năb (*splendor*). A king of Admah in time of Abraham, Gen. xiv. 2.

Shĭ'năr (*two rivers*). The alluvial plain through which the Tigris and Euphrates pass, and probably inclusive of Babylon and Mesopotamia, Gen. x. 10; xi. 1-9; Isa. xi. 11; Dan. i. 2. It was the seat of the kingdom founded by Nimrod, and which reckoned among its cities, as beginnings, Babel, Erech, Accad, and Calneh, Gen. x. 9, 10. Asshur went forth from Shinar to found Nineveh, Gen. x. 11. It was in the plain in the land of Shinar that the migrating nations undertook to build the tower of Babel, and where the confusion of tongues occurred, Gen. xi. 1–9.

Ship. Ships of Scripture dependent on oars and sails for propulsion. Hebrews not sailors. The ships of Acts, xxi. 1–6; xxvii. 6–44; xxviii. 11–13, were capable of carrying many people and much freight. Primitive ships were generally coasters. They were mounted with figure-heads and had figures painted on the sides of the bow. These composed the ship's "sign," Acts xxviii. 11. Among their furnishings were under-girders, anchors shaped like those of modern times, but without flukes, sounding-lines, rudder-bands, Acts xxvii. 40. Ancient ships, being wholly or in part propelled by oars, were properly called galleys.

Shi′phi (*many*). A prince of Simeon, in time of Hezekiah, 1 Chr. iv. 37.

Shiph′mite. Probably a native of Shepham, and a designation of Zabdi, David's overseer of vineyard increase and wine cellars, 1 Chr. xxvii. 27.

Shiph′rah (*handsome*). A Hebrew midwife in Egypt, Ex. i. 15.

Shiph′tan (*judging*). Father of a prince of Ephraim, Num. xxxiv. 24.

Shi′sha (*God's strife*). Father of Solomon's scribes, 1 Kgs. iv. 3.

Shi′shak. The king of Egypt to whom Jeroboam fled, 1 Kgs. xi. 40. He invaded Judea, B. C. 969, defeated Rehoboam, and spoiled the temple, 1 Kgs. xiv 25, 26; 2 Chr. xii. 2–9. Inscriptions, reliefs, and statuary at Karnak, on the Nile, record his invasion of Palestine.

Shit′ra-i (*scribe*). Keeper of David's herds in Sharon, 1 Chr. xxvii. 29.

Shit′tah, Shit′tim (*thorny*). (1) An Asiatic tree, a species of acacia, producing a close-grained, yellowish wood used in making the sacred furniture of the tabernacle, Ex. xxv. 10–13; xxvi. 15, 26; xxvii. 1; Isa. xli. 19. (2) Last encampment of the Israelites before crossing the Jordan. Scene of the completion of the law and farewell of Moses, Num. xxv.; xxxi. 1–12; Josh. ii. 1; iii. 1. The spies were sent out from Shittim to Jericho, and there the final preparations were made for crossing the Jordan. It was also called Abel-shittim, "meadow of acacias," and was the well-watered, fertile plain stretching from the foot of the mountains of Moab to the banks of the Jordan. (3) "Valley of Shittim," Joel iii. 18, is doubtless same as Shittim (2), which was also known as Abel-shittim.

Shī′zà (*loving*). Father of a Reubenite captain, 1 Chr. xi. 42.

Shō′à (*fruitful*). An undetermined name or place, Ezek. xxiii. 23.

Shō′băb (*hostile*). (1) A son of David, 2 Sam. v. 14; 1 Chr. iii. 5; xiv. 4. (2) A son of Caleb, 1 Chr. ii. 18.

Shō′băch (*enlarging*). A Syrian general whom David defeated, 2 Sam. x. 15-18. Shophach, 1 Chr. xix. 16-18.

Shō′ba-ī (*captive*). A family of temple door-keepers who returned from captivity, Ez. ii. 42; Neh. vii. 45.

Shō′bal (*current*). (1) Second son of Seir, and a Horite duke, Gen. xxxvi. 20; 1 Chr. i. 38. (2) A son of Caleb, 1 Chr. ii. 50, 52. (3) 1 Chr. iv. 1, 2, probably same as above.

Shō′bek (*forsaken*). A co-covenanter with Nehemiah, Neh. x. 24.

Shō′bī (*captive*). An Ammonite who succored David during Absalom's rebellion, 2 Sam. xvii. 27-29.

Shō′cō, Shō′chō, Shō′choh, 2 Chr. xi. 7 xxviii. 18; 1 Sam. xvii. 1. [Socoh.]

Shoe. [Sandal.]

Shō′hăm (*onyx*). A Levite, 1 Chr. xxiv. 27.

Shō′mer (*keeper*). (1) An Asherite, 1 Chr. vii. 32. Shamer in vs. 34. (2) Mother of Jehozabad, a co-murderer of King Joash, 2 Kgs. xii. 21. Called Shimrith in 2 Chr. xxiv. 26.

Shō′phăch, 1 Chr. xix. 16-18. [Shobach.]

Shō′phan (*burrow*). A fenced city east of Jordan, which fell to Gad, Num. xxxii. 35.

Shō-shăn′nim (*lilies*). Variously construed as a melody, bridal-song, and musical instrument, Ps. xlv., lxix., lxxx., titles. In the latter, *eduth*, "testimony," is added.

Shōul'der. Baring of, signified servitude, Gen. xlix. 15; withdrawing of, denoted rebellion, Neh. ix. 29; bearing upon, meant to sustain, Isa. ix. 6; xxii. 22.

Shọv'el (*shove*). [FAN.] [WINNOW.]

Shu'à (*wealth*). Father-in-law of Judah, 1 Chr. ii. 3. Shuah in Gen. xxxviii. 2, 12.

Shu'ah (*pit*). (1) A son of Abraham, Gen. xxv. 2; 1 Chr. i. 32. (2) Brother of Chelub, 1 Chr. iv. 11. (3) Gen. xxxviii. 2, 12. [SHUA.]

Shu'al (*fox*). (1) An Asherite, 1 Chr. vii. 36. (2) An unlocated land, 1 Sam. xiii. 17.

Shu'ba-el (*God's captive*). (1) Shebuel, son of Gershon, 1 Chr. xxiv. 20. (2) Shebuel, son of Heman the singer, and leader of the thirteenth musical course, 1 Chr. xxv. 20.

Shu'ham (*well-digger*). A son of Dan, Num. xxvi. 42. Hushim, Gen. xlvi. 23.

Shu'ham-ītes. Descendants of Shuham, Num. xxvi. 42.

Shu'hīte. Designation of Bildad, one of Job's friends; associated with *Tsukhi*, an Arabic tribe, Job ii. 11.

Shu'lam-īte. One belonging to Shulem or Shunem, S. of Sol. vi. 13.

Shu'math-ītes. One of the four families of Kirjath-jearim, 1 Chr. ii. 53.

Shu'nam-īte. A native of Shunem. The nurse of David and hostess of Elisha were so called, 1 Kgs. i. 3; 2 Kgs. iv. 12.

Shu'nem (*double sleeping-place*). A city of Issachar, near Jezreel. Place where the Philistines encamped before the great battle of Gilboa; home of David's nurse and wife, Abishag; residence of the woman who entertained Elisha. Now Solam, Josh. xix. 18; 1 Sam. xxviii. 4; 2 Kgs. iv. 8.

Shu'nī (*resting*). A son of Gad, Gen. xlvi. 16.

Shu'nītes. Descendants of Shuni, Num. xxvi. 15.

Shu'pham, Num. xxvi. 39. [SHUPPIM.]

Shu'pham-ītes. Descendants of Shupham, Num. xxvi. 39.

Shŭp'pim (*serpents*). (1) Great-grandson of

Benjamin, 1 Chr. vii. 12. Shupham, Num. xxvi. 39. (2) A Levite gate-keeper, 1 Chr. xxvi. 16.

Shûr (*wall*). A desert region of Arabia, and its town, bordering on Egypt, Gen. xvi. 7; xxv. 18. "Wilderness of Etham," Num. xxxiii. 8. Inhabited by Amalekites, 1 Sam. xv. 7; xxvii. 8.

Shu′shan (*lily*). The Greek Susa, ancient capital of Elam, a province in Mesopotamia. A seat of wealth and power after the Persian conquest of Babylon. The events of Esther's history occurred there. Spot of Daniel's visions. Nehemiah commissioned there, Gen. x. 22; xiv. 1; Neh. i. 1; Esth.; Isa. xxi. 2; Jer. xlix. 34; Dan. viii. 2. The decline of this ancient city dates from its capture by Alexander the Great, or from its later conquest by Antigonus, B. C. 315. The site, nearly due east from Babylon and north of the Persian Gulf, is marked by ruins, some three miles in circumference, in the midst of which have been found the remains of the great palace of Darius, scene of the events narrated in the book of Esther.

Shu′shan=e′duth. Abbreviated form of Shoshannim-eduth, which *see*, Ps. lx. title.

Shu′thal - hītes. Descendants of Shuthelah, Num. xxvi. 35.

Shu′the-lah (*discord*). Head of the Ephraimite family of Shuthalhites, Num. xxvi. 35; 1 Chr. vii. 20, 21.

Shŭt′tle (*shooter*). This weaver's device for throwing the filling thread between the warp threads is figurative of fleeting time in Job vii. 6.

Sī′à (*assembly*). His children returned from captivity, Neh. vii. 47. Siaha, Ez. ii. 44.

Sī′a-hà, Ez. ii. 44. [SIA.]

Sĭb′be-cāi, 1 Chr. xi. 29; xxvii. 11. [SIBBECHAI.]

Sĭb′be-chāi (*weaver*). One of David's guard, and eighth captain of eighth month, 2 Sam. xxi. 18; 1 Chr. xx. 4. Sibbecai, 1 Chr. xi. 29; xxvii. 11. Mebunnai, 2 Sam. xxiii. 27.

Sĭb′bo-lĕth, Judg. xii. 6. [SHIBBOLETH.]

Sĭb′mah (*fragrant*). A fortified city of Reuben, east of Jordan, Josh. xiii. 19. Shebam, Num. xxxii. 3. Shibmah, Num. xxxii. 38. Noted for its grapes, Isa. xvi. 8, 9; Jer. xlviii. 32.

Sĭb′ra-ĭm (*twice hopeful*). A boundary mark of northern Palestine, Ezek. xlvii. 16.

Sĭ′chem, Gen. xii. 6. [SHECHEM.]

Sĭck′le (*cutter*). The reaping and mowing implement of the ancients. In its size and curvature, as represented on Egyptian monuments, it resembled the implement as known to us, Deut. xvi. 9.

Sĭç′ȳ-ŏn. A city of the Peloponnesus near the Isthmus, 1 Macc. xv. 23.

Sĭd′dim (*pitted vale*). A vale, full of slime-pits, supposably near the Dead Sea, in which the kings of the plain cities met their invaders, Gen. xiv. 1–10.

Sĭ′de (*trading*). A trading city in Pamphylia, 1 Macc. xv. 23.

Sĭ′dŏn, Gen. x. 15, 19. [ZIDON.]

Sı-dō′nĭ-anṣ. Zidonians, Deut. iii. 9 ; Josh. xiii. 4, 6 ; Judg. iii. 3 ; 1 Kgs. v. 6.

Siėġe (*sit*), Deut. xx. 19. [WAR.]

Sieve. Ancient sieves, or sifters, were crudely made of rushes, though the Gauls are credited with their manufacture from horsehair. They were used for separating the flour from the bran, or broken kernels, and what was left in the sieve was thrown back into the mill to be reground, Isa. xxx. 28.

Sĭ′hŏn (*rooting out*). An Amorite king, defeated by the Israelites, who occupied his country between the Arnon and Jabbok, Num. xxi. 21–31 ; Deut. i. 4 ; ii. 24–37 ; Josh. xiii. 15–28.

Sĭ′hôr (*blackness*). The Sihor, or Shihor, of Egypt, 1 Chr. xiii. 5 ; Isa. xxiii. 3 ; Jer. ii. 18, has ever been construed as "the Nile." But when unqualified, some Arabian ravine or wady may be meant.

Sĭ′las (*Silvanus, woody*). An eminent member of the early Christian church. Written Silvanus in Paul's epistles. Resided at Jerusalem as teacher, but accompanied Paul on his tours, and was his fellow-prisoner at Philippi. Said to have been bishop of Corinth, Acts xv. 22, 32–34, 40 ; xvii. 14 ; xviii. 5 ; 2 Cor i. 19 ; 1 Thess. i. 1.

Sĭlk (*Seric stuff*). Silk hardly known to ancient Hebrews. In Prov. xxxi. 22 ; Ezek. xvi. 10, 13, some fine linen fabric is supposed to be meant. Undoubtedly known in N. T. times, Rev. xviii. 12.

Sĭl′lȧ (*branch*). The place near which King Joash was slain, 2 Kgs. xii. 20.

Sĭ-lō′ah, Neh. iii. 15. [SILOAM.]

Sĭ-lō′am (*sent*). (1) The celebrated pool, or tank, at Jerusalem, on the south side, near the opening of the Tyrophean valley into the Kidron valley. Originally a part of the water supply of the city, Neh. iii. 15; Isa. viii. 6; John ix. 7–11. (2) An unlocated tower whose fall killed eighteen men, Luke xiii. 4. Siloam still retains its ancient name under the form of the Arabic *Silwân*. It is partly hewn from rock and partly built with masonry. A flight of steps leads down to it. It is no longer a natural spring of fresh, limpid water, but is fed from the Fountain of the Virgin through a rock tunnel over 1700 feet in length. The waters are brackish and colored, and the walls and steps in ruins.

Sĭl-vā′nus (*woody*). [SILAS.]

Sĭl′ver (*white*). Used by Hebrews from earliest times for money, vessels, and ornaments, but not in form of coins till after the captivity, Gen. xiii. 2; xxiv. 53; xliv. 2; Job xxviii. 1; Matt. xxvi. 15; Acts xix. 24. Silver supplied to Jerusalem from Arabia and Tarshish, 2 Chr. ix. 14, 21.

Sĭl′vĕr-lings (*little silvers*). Evidently bits of silver money, but whether by weight or coinage is not known, Isa. vii. 23.

Sĭ″măl-cū′e. An Arabian chief, guardian of Antiochus, son of Balas, 1 Macc. xi. 39.

Sĭm′e̦-on (*who hears*). (1) Son of Jacob and Leah, Gen. xxix. 33. For the crime in Gen. xxxiv. 25–30 his father denounced him, Gen. xlix. 5–7. His tribe was small, Num. i. 22, 23; xxvi. 14, and their inheritance a scattered portion of Canaan, Josh. xix. 1–9. (2) Son of Judah in genealogy of Christ, Luke iii. 30. (3) Simon Peter, Acts xv. 14. (4) A venerable and pious Jew who blessed the child Jesus in the temple, Luke ii. 25–35. (5) Simeon Niger, Acts xiii. 1. [NIGER.]

Sĭ′mon (*Simeon*). (1) Several distinguished Jews bore this name during the Maccabean period. (2) A native of Samaria and famous sorcerer, who professed Christ for mercenary purposes, Acts viii. 9–24. (3) Simon Peter, Matt. iv. 18. [PETER.] (4) Simon the Canaanite, or Simon Zelotes, was a member of the party of Zealots who advocated the Jewish ritual, and an apostle, Matt. x. 4. (5) Simon the brother of Jesus, Matt. xiii. 55; Mark vi. 3. (6) Simon the Pharisee, in whose house a woman anointed the feet of Jesus, Luke vii. 36-50. (7) Simon, the leper of Bethany, Matt. xxvi. 6. (8) Simon of Cyrene, who was compelled to bear Christ's cross, Matt. xxvii. 32; Mark xv. 21; Luke xxiii. 26. (9) The tanner of Joppa with whom Peter lodged, Acts ix. 43. (10) Simon the father of Judas Iscariot, John vi. 71; xiii. 2, 26.

Sĭm′rī (*alert*). A Merarite Levite in David's time, 1 Chr. xxvi. 10.

Sĭn (*clay*). (1) A city of Egypt identified with Pelusium, "town of clay or mud," on eastern mouth of Nile near the sea, Ezek. xxx. 15, 16. (2) A desert portion of Arabia between Gulf of Suez and Sinai, Ex. xvi. 1; xvii. 1; Num. xxxiii. 11, 12. It was in this wilderness that the Israelites were first fed with manna and quails. It skirts the eastern coast of the gulf for a distance of 25 miles.

Sĭn=mon′ey. Money sent from a distance to buy offerings. The surplus, if any, became a perquisite of the priest, and was called sin-money, 2 Kgs. xii. 16.

Sĭn=ŏf′fẽr-ĭng. Like the trespass-offering, the sin-offering was expiatory, but seemingly of general sins. It was presented on the great day of atonement, when one confessed the sins of the nation with his hand on the head of the scapegoat, Lev. xvi. 1-34; Num. xviii. 9.

Sī′na. Greek form of Sinai, Acts vii. 30, 38.

Sī′naī (*bushy*). The peninsula of Sinai lies between the two great arms of the Red Sea, Gulf of Akaba on the east, and Gulf of Suez on the west. This region contains the mountain system of Horeb or Sinai, on one of whose mounts, or peaks, God appeared to Moses in the burning bush, Ex. iii. 1-5, amid whose surrounding wilderness the wandering Israelites encamped, Ex. xix. 1, 2, and from whose cloud-obscured heights the law was delivered to Moses, Ex. xix. 3-25; xx.-xl.; Lev. The numbering also took place there, Num. i.-x. 1-12. The peninsula is a triangle whose base extends from the head of Suez to Akaba. This base is pierced by the plateau of Tih, the "desert of wandering," south of which are those tumultuous mountain clusters above mentioned, central among which is Mount Sinai. The coast ranges along Akaba and Suez are systematic and elevated. The region was a dependency of Egypt from earliest times, but became subject to Rome.

Sī′nim. An unidentified land mentioned in Isa. xlix. 12. Referred by some to China.

Sĭn′īte. A tribe descended from Canaan, Gen. x. 17; 1 Chr. i. 15.

Sī′ŏn (*lofty*). (1) An ancient name of Mount Hermon, Deut. iv. 48. (2) Greek form of Zion, Matt. xxi. 5; John xii. 15; Heb. xii. 22; Rev. xiv. 1.

Sĭph′moth (*fertile*). A haunt of David, while an outlaw, in South Judah, 1 Sam. xxx. 28.

Sĭp′pāi (*threshold*). Saph, the Philistine giant slain at Gezer, 1 Chr. xx. 4.

Sī′rach. Father of Jesus, writer of the Apocryphal book of Ecclesiasticus.

Sī′rah (*retreat*). The well, now *Ain Sarah*, from which Abner was called by Joab. It was near Hebron, 2 Sam. iii. 26.

Sĭr′ĭ-ŏn. Zidonian name of Mount Hermon, Deut. iii. 9; Ps. xxix. 6.

Sĭ-săm′a-ī (*famed*). A descendant of Sheshan, of Judah, 1 Chr. ii. 40.

Sĭs′e-rà (*ready for war*). (1) Captain of King Jabin's forces when defeated by Barak. Slain by Jael, Judg. iv.; v. (2) His children returned, Ez. ii. 53; Neh. vii. 55.

Sĭ-sĭn′ēs. Governor of Syria and Phœnicia under Darius, 1 Esdr. vi. 3.

Sĭt′nah (*strife*). Second of the two wells dug by Isaac in valley of Gerar, over which the herdsmen disputed, Gen. xxvi. 21.

Sī′van. Third month of Jewish sacred and ninth of civil year, beginning with the new moon of June, Esth. viii. 9.

Slāve (*Sclavonian*). Slavery came about under Hebrew institutions. (1) By poverty, when a man sold himself to cancel debt, Lev. xxv. 39; (2) by theft, when restitution could not be made, Ex. xxii. 3; (3) by parents selling their daughters as concubines, Ex. xxi. 7-11. It ended (1) when the debt

was paid; (2) on the year of Jubilee, Lev. xxv. 40;
(3) at the end of six years of service, Ex. xxi. 2;
Deut. xv. 12. This as to Hebrews. As to non-
Hebrew slaves, by far the most numerous class, they
were purchased, Lev. xxv. 45; or captured in war,
Num. xxxi. 26, 40. They were freed if ill treated,
Ex. xxi. 26, 27; to slay one was murder, Lev. xxiv.
17, 22; they were circumcised and had religious
privileges, Gen. xvii. 12, 13.

Slīme. The slime of Babel, and that of the pits
of Siddim, and the ark of Moses, was mineral pitch
or bitumen, Gen. xi. 3; xiv. 10; Ex. ii. 3.

Slĭng. The weapons of shepherds and light
troops. It consisted of leather or sinew strings with
a pouch at the end for the missile, Judg. xx. 16; 1
Sam. xvii. 40.

Smĭth (*smiter*). An artificer in iron, brass, or
other metals, Gen. iv. 22; 1 Sam. xiii. 19–22.

Smўr'nȧ (*myrrh*). A coast city of Ionia, Asia
Minor, 40 miles north of Ephesus. Mentioned in
Rev. ii. 8–11 as site of one of the seven churches of
Asia. The old city of Smyrna dates back to Theseus,
1300 years B. C. Alexander the Great built the new
city B. C. 320. It became subject to Rome and was
noted for its beauty. Christianity got an early foot-
hold there and the city sent a bishop to the council
of Nice, A. D. 325. It is still a large city of mixed
nationalities and creeds, and of considerable commercial importance.

Snāil (*snake*). In Lev. xi. 30 a lizard is meant.
In Ps. lviii. 8, the common snail, slug, or slime-snake
is meant. Snails abound in the Orient and are not
eschewed as a food.

Snōw. Only mentioned once as actually falling,
2 Sam. xxiii. 20; but of frequent poetic and meta-
phoric use, Ex. iv. 6; Num. xii. 10; 2 Kgs. v. 27;
Ps. li. 7; Isa. i. 18.

Snŭff=dĭsh'eṣ. Small dishes, made of gold, for
receiving the snuff from the tabernacle lamps, Ex.
xxv. 38.

Snŭf'fẽrṣ. Scissor-like instruments, made of
gold, for snuffing the wicks of the tabernacle lamps,
Ex. xxxvii. 23.

Sō. A king of Egypt with whom Hoshea formed
an alliance against Assyria. The discovery of this

led to the imprisonment of Hoshea, the siege and capture of Samaria, and the captivity of the ten tribes of Israel, 2 Kgs. xvii. 4, 6.

Sōap (*sap, resin*). The Hebrew word for soap implies any alkaline substance used for cleansing, Jer. ii. 22; Mal. iii. 2.

Sō'chŏ, 1 Chr. iv. 18. [Socoh.]

Sō'choh, 1 Kgs. iv. 10. [Socoh.]

Sō'coh (*brambly*). (1) A town in lowlands of Judah, Josh. xv. 35. Shocho, 2 Chr. xxviii. 18. Shoco, 2 Chr. xi. 7. Shochoh, 1 Sam. xvii. 1. (2) A town in the mountains of Judah, Josh. xv. 48.

Sō'dī (*secret*). Father of the spy from Zebulun, Num. xiii. 10.

Sŏd'om (*consuming*). Most prominent of the cities in the plain of Siddim. Destroyed by fire from heaven, Gen. x. 19; xiii. 10–13; xix. 1–29. Site of "the cities of the plain" is not known, but variously referred to the southern end, the northern end, and bottom of the Dead Sea. Sodom is often referred to in Scripture as a symbol of wickedness and warning to sinners, Deut. xxix. 23; Isa. i. 9, 10; xiii. 19; Jer. xxiii. 14; xlix. 18; Ezek. xvi. 49, 50; Matt. x. 15; xi. 23; Rev. xi. 8.

Sŏd'om-â. Greek and Vulgate form of Sodom, Rom. ix. 29.

Sŏd'om-ītes. Dwellers in Sodom, or, by figure, those who practise the abominations of Sodom, Deut. xxiii. 17; 1 Kgs. xiv. 24; xv. 12.

Sŏl'o-mon (*peaceful*). Last of David's sons by Bathsheba. Named Jedidiah, "beloved of God," by Nathan, 1 Chr. iii. 5; 2 Sam. xii. 25. Placed in Nathan's care. Secured the throne according to David's pledge, 1 Kgs. i. 13–53, and much to the consternation of Adonijah, the legal successor. Reigned forty years, b. c. 1015–975. Confirmed his father's conquests, built the palace and temple, extended commerce, contracted favorable alliances, grew famous for wisdom, raised his kingdom to great wealth, splendor, and power, mingled justice with cruelty, endorsed true and false worship, encouraged literature, and wrote largely himself, fell a prey to the sensualities of his time and position, died leaving his kingdom under the eclipse of faction and on the edge of decay, 1 Kgs. ii.–xi.; 2 Chr. i.–ix.

Sŏl'o-mon's Pools. Reservoirs erected by Solomon near Bethlehem, whence water was conveyed to the distributing pools at Jerusalem. They are still in partial use, Eccl. ii. 6.

Sŏl'o-mon's Porch. The colonnade on east side of the temple, John x. 23; Acts iii. 11; v. 12.

Sŏl'o-mon's Sĕr'vants. Returned captives, and probable descendants of a class of servants favored by Solomon, Ez. ii. 55, 58; Neh. vii. 57, 60.

Sŏl'o-mon's Sŏng. [SONG OF SOLOMON.]

Son. In Hebrew sense, any descendant however remote, Gen. xxix. 5; 2 Sam. xix. 24. Applied also to pupils, adopted persons, those of kindred faith, etc., Gen. xlviii. 5; 1 Sam. iii. 6; Acts xiii. 6.

Son of God. A term applied to the angels, Job xxxviii. 7; to Adam, Luke iii. 38; to believers, Rom. viii. 14; 2 Cor. vi. 18; but preëminently to Christ, signifying his divine origin and nature, Dan. iii. 25; Matt. xi. 27; xvi. 16; John i. 18; v. 19-26; ix. 35.

Son of Man. In a limited sense, "man," Num. xxiii. 19; Job xxv. 6; Ps. viii. 4. In a broader, higher, and perhaps more generally received Hebrew sense, "the Messiah." In the N. T. sense, where the term is used some eighty times, it means Christ in incarnate form and relation, Dan. vii. 13; Matt. ix. 6; xii. 8; xviii. 11; Mark ii. 10; John i. 51; iii. 13; vi. 53.

Sŏng of Sŏl'o-mon. "Song of Songs," or "Canticles," in Latin. Twenty-second O. T. book and last of poetic. Authorship and meaning much disputed. Some make it type conjugal love; others regard it as purely allegorical; still others as literal and descriptive of Solomon's marriage to some beautiful woman.

Sooth'say-er (*truth-sayer*). One who pretends to foretell future events, Dan. ii. 27. [DIVINATION.]

Sŏp (*sip*). Bread dipped in soup, milk, wine, sauce, or other liquid, Ruth ii. 14; John xiii. 26.

Sŏp'a-tĕr (*father saved*). A Berean companion of Paul, Acts xx. 4.

Sŏph'e-rĕth (*scribe*). His children were returned captives, Ez. ii. 55.

Sŏph''ō-nī'as. The prophet Zephaniah, 2 Esdr. i. 40.

Sôr'çêr-er (*fate-worker*). [DIVINATION.]

Sō'rek (*vine*). A valley of Philistia, where Delilah lived, Judg. xvi. 4.

Sŏ-sĭp'ạ-tĕr (*Sopater*). (1) A general of Judas Maccabeus, 2 Macc. xii. 19–24. (2) A friend of Paul; probably Sopater, Rom. xvi. 21.

Sŏs'the-nēṣ (*saviour*). (1) A ruler of the synagogue at Corinth, who was beaten by the Greeks, Acts xviii. 17. (2) Perhaps the former, after conversion, 1 Cor. i. 1.

Sŏs'trạ-tus. A Syrian general commanding in Jerusalem, 2 Macc. iv. 27.

Sō'tạ-ī (*fickle*). His children were returned captives, Ez. ii. 55; Neh. vii. 57.

Sōul. The Hebrew ideal of man was threefold: (1) The body, or material part. (2) The vital part, seat of sensations, passions, etc. (3) The sentient, thinking, or spiritual part, Gen. i. 20; ii. 7; Num. xvi. 22; 1 Thess. v. 23; Heb. iv. 12.

South Rā'moth. A place in southern Judah, bordering on the desert, and one of the resorts of David during the period of his outlawry by Saul, 1 Sam. xxx. 27.

Sow. [SWINE.]

Sōw'er, Sōw'ing. Cereal seeds were sown by hand, Ps. cxxvi. 6; Am. ix. 13; Mark iv. 3–29. In moist ground seeds were tramped in by cattle, Isa. xxxii. 20. Mixed seeds prohibited, Lev. xix. 19; Deut. xxii. 9.

Spāin. Anciently the whole peninsula of southwestern Europe, embracing Spain and Portugal; known to Greeks as Iberia and to Romans as Hispania. If identical with Tarshish, then known to Hebrews in Solomon's time; certainly to Phœnicians. Known to Paul, who contemplated a visit to it, Rom. xv. 24–28. Christianity early introduced there.

Spăn (*bind*). Distance from tip of thumb to that of little finger, when stretched apart; about nine inches. Also any small interval of space or time, 1 Sam. xvii. 4; Isa. xl. 12; Lam. ii. 20.

Spăr'row (*spurrer*). The Hebrew word signifies "twitterer" and is mostly rendered "bird" or "fowl." Though tree-sparrows abounded in Palestine, any small bird meets the sense in Ps. lxxxiv. 3; cii. 7. In N. T. the reference is directly to the sparrow species, used as a cheap food, Matt. x. 29; Luke xii. 6, 7.

Spēar (*spar*). In general, a wooden staff with a sharp metallic head. Some were light for throwing, others long and heavy for attack either by footmen or horsemen, 1 Sam. xiii. 22; xvii. 7; xxvi. 7; 2 Sam. ii. 23.

Spēar′men. Light-armed troops are evidently meant, Acts xxiii. 23.

Spĕck′led Bird, Jer. xii. 9. [HYENA.]

Spīce, Spī′çeṣ (*species*). Hardly, as with us, the entire list of aromatic vegetable substances, but rather the fragrant gums, barks, etc., of ceremonial, medicinal, and toilet value, and for embalming, Gen. xxxvii. 25; xliii. 11; S. of Sol. iv. 14; Mark xvi. 1; John xix. 39, 40.

Spī′der (*spinner*). The common spider is meant in Job viii. 14; Isa. lix. 5; but the gecko, or lizard, is probably intended in Prov. xxx. 28. The lightness and frailty of the spider's web are made emblematic of visionary hopes and wicked schemes.

Spīke′närd (*pointed leaf yielding perfume*). An ancient fragrant and costly ointment made from the spikenard plant of India, S. of Sol. i. 12; iv. 13, 14; Mark xiv. 3; John xii. 3.

Spin′ning (*spanning, drawing*). A well-known and necessary female occupation among Hebrews. The instrument — distaff and spindle — permitted of much the same drawing and twisting process as is now employed in the East, in the absence of the more modern spinning-wheel, Ex. xxxv. 25; Prov. xxxi. 19; Matt. vi. 28.

Spïr′it (*breath*). The breath, 2 Thess. ii. 8. The vital principle, Eccl. viii. 8. Elsewhere, the soul. [SOUL.] Holy Spirit, or Ghost, is the third person in the Trinity, 2 Cor. xiii. 14; Acts xv. 28. Though Holy Spirit and Holy Ghost are synonymous in meaning, preference is given to the latter form in the Scriptures, Matt. i. 18; John i. 33; Acts ii. 4; Rom. v. 5, and elsewhere, the former being used only four times.

Spôil. Plunder seized by violence, as the spoils of an army or of bandits, 1 Sam. xxx. 19-22; but in Ex. iii. 22, the sense is that of recovery without violence of unjustly taken property. David instituted very strict regulations for the division of spoils of war among his soldiers, 1 Sam. xxx. 20-25.

Sponge. Only mentioned in N. T., though probably known to ancient Hebrews, Matt. xxvii. 48; Mark xv. 36; John xix. 29.

Spouse. [MARRIAGE.]

Sprĭn′kling (*springing*). The blood of the sin-offering was sprinkled with the finger of the priest upon the mercy-seat of the inner sanctuary as an atonement for the holy place because of national uncleanness, Lev. xvi. 14-16. The "blood of sprinkling" or mediatorial blood of the new covenant, Heb. xii. 24, is made antithetical with the blood of vengeance, Gen. iv. 10.

Stā′chўs (*ear of corn*). A Roman Christian saluted by Paul, Rom. xvi. 9.

Stăc′tĕ (*drop*). An oriental gum or spice, one of the components of the holy incense, Ex. xxx. 34.

Stănd′ard. [ENSIGN.]

Stär (*strew*). All the heavenly bodies, except sun and moon, called stars by Hebrews, Gen. xv. 5; Ps. cxlvii. 4. The " star in the east," seen and followed by the " wise men," and designed to announce the birth of the Messiah, was, according to some, wholly phenomenal, and to others, natural. Stars symbolize rulers and princes, Dan. viii. 10; angels, Job xxxviii. 7; ministers, Rev. i. 16-20. Christ is "the bright and morning star," Rev. xxii. 16.

Stā′ter (*standard*). The standard gold coin of ancient Greece, worth about $4.00. Later, the silver stater, containing four drachmæ, or about sixty cents. This is thought to be the " piece of money " of Matt. xvii. 27.

Stēel. Hebrews were not acquainted with carbonized iron, or steel. Wherever the word is found in Scripture, copper is meant, Ps. xviii. 34.

Stĕph′a-năs (*crown*). One of Paul's earliest converts at Corinth, 1 Cor. i. 16; xvi. 15.

Stē′phen (*crown*). Chief of the first seven deacons, and first Christian martyr. A Greek convert of strong faith and great eloquence. Arrested and tried before the Sanhedrim, but stoned to death by an angry mob, before he had time to finish his defence.

The date of his martyrdom is fixed at about A. D. 37. It was followed by the conversion of Saul, who was present at the stoning, and a bitter persecutor of early Christians at the time, Acts vi. 5–15, vii., viii. 1–3.

Stŏcks (*sticks*). Tree-trunks, Job xiv. 8; idols, Jer. ii. 27; instruments of punishment made of beams of wood which closed over the arms or ankles, Job xiii. 27; xxxiii. 11; Jer. xx. 2; Acts xvi. 24.

Stō'ics (*porch scholars*). Members of a Grecian philosophical school, or sect, founded by Zeno, 308 B. C., who taught in the *stoa*, or porch, of the Agora at Athens. They held to a high morality, proud independence of spirit, fateful, in place of providential, superintendence, wisdom as the source of happiness, Acts xvii. 18. Paul encountered both Stoics and Epicureans at Athens, and, on being taken into Areopagus by them, delivered to them the oration in Acts xvii. 22–31.

Stom'ach-er. An article of dress worn over breast and stomach. Much affected in the 17th century; but whether that of Isa. iii. 24 was similar is not known.

Stōneş. Used for building, 1 Kgs. v. 17; Am. v. 11; memorial marks, Gen. xxviii. 18; xxxv. 14; knives, Ex. iv. 25; ballots, Rev. ii. 17. Symbols of hardness, 1 Sam. xxv. 37; of firmness, Gen. xlix. 24; Christian aggregation, 1 Pet. ii. 4–6. Precious stones highly prized by Hebrews and much used on priestly vestments and as ornaments. Twenty gems are mentioned in the Bible, Gen. ii. 12; Ex. xxviii. 9–21. India, Arabia, and Syria were the sources of gems used by Hebrews, Ezek. xxvii. 16–22.

Stō'ning. [PUNISHMENT.]

Stôrk (*vulture*). A large wading bird, plentiful in Palestine, gregarious, migratory, nesting in trees and noted for tenderness to its young. Unclean under the law, Lev. xi. 19; Deut. xiv. 18; Ps. civ. 17; Jer. viii. 7.

Strāin at a, Matt. xxiii. 24. "Strain out the," in R. V.

Strān'ger (*without*). One away from his country, Gen. xxiii. 4. One not a Jew, Ex. xx. 10. One not of Aaron's family, Num. iii. 10. One not of royal blood, Matt. xvii. 25, 26. One alienated or neglected, Ps.

lxix. 8. But, in general, any naturalized foreigner in the Jewish State, Deut. xvii. 15. Strangers, in Hebrew acceptation, were numerous in Israel, owing to the mixed multitudes which were permitted to follow the wanderers in the wilderness, to the fact that very many Canaanites remained in the land, and to the liberal regulations respecting captives taken in war.

Straw. Straw used for cattle fodder and litter, Gen. xxiv. 25; 1 Kgs. iv. 28; Isa. xi. 7; lxv. 25; in making bricks, Ex. v. 7, 16.

Sū'ah (*sweeping*). An Asherite, 1 Chr. vii. 36.

Sū'bȧ. His sons returned, 1 Esdr. v. 34.

Sŭc'coth (*tents*). (1) The place east of Jordan where Jacob built a house and booths, Gen. xxxiii. 17; Josh. xiii. 27; Judg. viii. 5-16. Between Succoth and Zarthan, in the plain of Jordan, lay the clay ground in which were cast the brazen utensils for the temple, 1 Kgs. vii. 46; 2 Chr. iv. 17. (2) First station of the Israelites after starting from Egypt, a day's journey from Rameses, Ex. xii. 37; xiii. 20; Num. xxxiii. 5, 6.

Sŭc'coth=bē'noth (*tents of daughters*). Some refer it to a Babylonian idol set up by colonists in Samaria, others to booths or tents in which the daughters of Babylon prostituted themselves in honor of their goddess, 2 Kgs. xvii. 30.

Sū'chath-ītes. A family of scribes at Jabez, 1 Chr. ii. 55.

Sŭd. River of Sura, probably Euphrates, Bar. i. 4.

Sŭk'kĭ-ĭmṣ. An African people who supported Shishak when he invaded Judah, 2 Chr. xii. 3.

Sŭn. The greater light, Gen. i. 15-18. Worshipped by idolatrous Hebrews, 2 Kgs. xxi. 3, 5; xxiii. 5; and by other nations, Job xxxi. 26, 27; Gen. xli. 45; furnishes many metaphors, Ps. lxxxiv. 11; John i. 9; Rev. i. 16.

Sûr. A place on sea-coast of Palestine, Judith ii. 28.

Sure'tȳ (*security*). Suretyship in the older sense of pledge was regulated by the Mosaic law, Gen. xliv. 32; Ex. xxii. 25, 26; Deut. xxiv. 6-17. When Solomon opened Palestine to commerce, suretyship took the forms of general law and trade, Prov. vi. 1; xi. 15; xvii. 18; xx. 16; xxii. 26. [LOANS.] [PLEDGE.]

Sṳ'sȧ, Esth. xi. 3. [SHUSHAN.]

Sụ'san-chītes. Dwellers in Shushan or Susa, Ez. iv. 9.

Sụ'sặn'nȧ (*lily*). (1) Heroine of the story of the Judgment of Daniel, as found in "The History of Susanna," one of the Apocryphal books. (2) One of the women who ministered to Christ, Luke viii. 3.

Sū'sī (*horseman*). Father of the Manassite spy, Num. xiii. 11.

Swạl'low (*throat sweller*). The common swift or swallow abounds in Palestine, and its habits, according to Bible mention, are such as we observe : building under the eaves of houses, beneath temple cornices and porticos, and in the sides of cliffs, and rapidly circling above their homes in search of their aerial food, Ps. lxxxiv. 3 ; Prov. xxvi. 2 ; Isa. xxxviii. 14 ; Jer. viii. 7.

Swạn. Swans rare in Palestine. Unclean, Lev. xi. 18 ; Deut. xiv. 16. The original seems to imply some other bird, as the ibis or water-hen.

Sweâr'ing. [OATH.]

Swĕat. The bloody sweat of the agony is known to medical science, and ascribed to violent mental emotion, Luke xxii. 44.

Swīne. The hog was pronounced unclean, Lev. xi. 7 ; Deut. xiv. 8. Priests and Arabians abstained from the meat for dietetic reasons. Swine-keeping a degrading business, Luke xv. 15 ; yet swine were kept, Matt. viii. 32. To cast "pearls before swine" was to waste truth on those who despised it, Matt. vii. 6.

Swôrd. A short, two-edged, dagger-like weapon, carried in a sheath or scabbard, and suspended to the girdle or belt, Gen. xxvii. 40 ; Judg. iii. 16 ; 2 Sam. xx. 8 ; Jer. xlvii. 6 ; Ezek. xxi. 9, 30.

Sỹc'ạ-mine, Luke xvii. 6. [SYCAMORE.]

Sỹc'ạ-mōre (*fig-mulberry*). Not our sycamore or plane-tree, but a tree of the fig species growing in Egypt and Palestine and valued for its fruit and light, soft, durable wood, 1 Kgs. x. 27 ; 1 Chr. xxvii. 28 ; Ps. lxxviii. 47 ; Luke xix. 4. Sycamine in Luke xvii. 6. Sycamore fruit grows singly or in clusters and in almost direct contact with the branches. It resembles the fig in shape, and though of acrid taste when first pulled soon becomes sweetish. Egyptian mummy-cases were made of the wood of the sycamore tree.

Sy′char, John iv. 5. [SHECHEM.]

Sy′chem, Acts vii. 16. [SHECHEM.]

Sy̅-ē′ne (*key*). A city of Egypt bordering on Ethiopia. Situated on the Nile below the first cataract, and noted for its quarries of syenite stone, Ezek. xxix. 10; xxx. 6. Syene was an important city during the reigns of the Hyksos, or Shepherd Kings, in Egypt. It is now represented by the Arab village of Aswan.

Sy̆n′a-gŏgue (*led together*). The Jewish assembly for social and religious purposes seems to have had its origin during the captivity, or to have been an outgrowth of it, Ez. viii. 15; Neh. viii. 2; ix. 1. The casual, or house, assemblages soon ran into regular congregations, with suitable buildings and stated meetings, at requisite points. These were the synagogues, often elaborate and costly, presided over by a chief, or rabbi, assisted by a council of elders, Mark v. 22, 35; Luke iv. 20; John xvi. 2; Acts xviii. 8.

Sy̆n′ty̆-chē (*fate*). A woman of the church at Philippi, Phil. iv. 2.

Sy̆r′a-cūse. A noted city on eastern coast of Sicily, where Paul spent three days on his voyage to Rome, Acts xxviii. 12.

Sy̆r′i̇-à. The Hebrew Aram. So indefinitely bounded at different times as to have been associated with Assyria (whence its name) and Babylon. More definitely the country to the north of Canaan, extending from the Tigris to the Mediterranean, and northward to the Taurus ranges. Damascus was the capital, and centre of wealth, learning, and power. Joshua subdued its petty kings, Josh. xi. 2-18; David reduced it to submission, 2 Sam. viii., x. During Solomon's reign it became independent, 1 Kgs. xi. 23-25. The earliest recorded settlers in Syria were Hittites and other Hamitic races. The Shemitic element entered it from the southeast under Abraham and Chedorlaomer. After Syria became independent it was a persistent enemy of the Jews, 1 Kgs. xv. 18-20; xx., xxii.; 2 Kgs. vi. 8-33; vii., ix. 14, 15; x. 32, 33; xiii. 3, 14-25. The attempt of the Syrian king to ally Israel with him for the overthrow of Judah led Ahaz to call in the help of Assyria, and Syria was soon merged into the great Assyrian empire. It was conquered by Alexander the

Great, B. C. 333, and finally fell to the lot of Seleucus Nicator, who made it the central province of his empire, with the capital at Antioch. The Syriac language was closely allied to the Hebrew.

Sўr′ḭ-ac. The ancient language of Syria, an Aramean dialect. In Dan. ii. 4, the word "Syriac" should read "Aramaic," the court language of Babylon at the time.

Sўr′ḭ-à=mā′ạ-chah, 1 Chr. xix. 6. [SYRIA and MAACHAH.]

Sўr′ḭ-an. Inhabitant of Syria, Gen. xxv. 20, and elsewhere.

Sӯ′rŏ=phē-nḭ′çḭan. A Phœnician at the time Phœnicia was part of the Roman province of Syria; or it may mean one of half Syrian and half Phœnician blood, Mark vii. 26.

Syr′tis, in Acts xxvii. 17, R. V. The dangerous quicksands or shallows on the African coast, southwest of Crete.

T

Tā′a-nặch (*sandy*). A Canaanite city conquered by Joshua and assigned to Levites, Josh. xii. 21; xvii. 11–18; Judg. i. 27; 1 Kgs. iv. 12. Now Taanak, 4 miles from Megiddo. Tanach, Josh. xxi. 25.

Tā′a-nặth=shī′lōh (*pass to Shiloh*). A border mark of Ephraim, Josh. xvi. 6.

Tặb′ba-ŏth (*rings*). Father of returned Nethinim, Ez. ii. 43; Neh. vii. 46.

Tặb′bath (*famous*). Where the fleeing Midianites stopped after Gideon's night attack, Judg. vii. 22.

Tā′be-al (*good God*). Father of a general under Pekah, or in Rezin's Syrian army, whom it was proposed to make king of Judah, Isa. vii. 6.

Tā′be-el (*good God*). A Persian officer in Samaria under King Artaxerxes, Ez. iv. 7.

Tặ-bĕl′lḭ-us, 1 Esdr. ii. 15. [TABEEL.]

Tặb′e-rah (*burning*). A place in the wilderness of Paran, where the Israelites encamped. It was so called because God there consumed the murmurers. The encampment remained there for a month, and the excessive eating of quail led to a pestilence, for which reason the place was called Kibroth-hattavah, or "graves of lust," Num. xi. 3, 34; Deut. ix. 22.

Tā'bĕr-ing. Beating upon the taber, tabret, or small drum. Word now obsolete, Nah. ii. 7.

Tăb'ĕr-nă-cle (*little shed or tent*). Tent of Jehovah, or movable sanctuary, which Moses was directed to erect in the wilderness, Ex. xxv. 8. Its plan, materials, and furnishings are described in Ex. xxv. 9–40; xxvi., xxvii. It could be readily taken down and set up and accompanied the Israelites during their wanderings, Ex. xl. 38. During the conquest it was stationed at Gilgal, Josh. iv. 19; ix. 6; x. 15; and at Ebal, Josh. viii. 30–35. After the conquest it was set up at Shiloh, Josh. xviii. 1, where it remained during the time of the Judges and where the ark was captured by the Philistines. 1 Sam. iv. 17, 22. Sometime after the return of the ark it was taken to Jerusalem and placed in a new tabernacle, and finally in the temple, 2 Sam. vi. 17; 1 Chr. xv. 1, but the old structure was still venerated, as long as it remained at Shiloh. It was afterwards removed to Nob, 1 Sam. xxi. 1–9, and in the reign of David to Gibeon, 1 Chr. xvi. 39; xxi. 29, where it was at the beginning of Solomon's reign. Some suppose that the tabernacle and its furniture were moved into Solomon's temple when it was completed.

Tăb'ĕr-nă-cle of Tĕs'tĭ-mŏ-nў. As the stone tables of the Ten Commandments were called the "tables of testimony," Ex. xxxi. 18; xxxii. 15; xxxiv. 29; and the ark which contained them was called the "ark of testimony," Ex. xxv. 22, so the tabernacle in which the ark was placed was called the "tabernacle of testimony," Ex. xxxviii. 21; Num. i. 50. Called also "the tabernacle of witness," in Num. xvii. 7, 8.

Tăb'ĕr-nă-cleş, Feast of. Third of the three great Hebrew feasts, celebrated from the 15th to 22d of Tisri. It commemorated the long tent life of the Israelites, and during its celebration the people dwelt in booths. Called also "feast of ingathering," Ex. xxiii. 16, because it came at end of harvest. It was closed with a holy convocation, Lev. xxiii. 36; and on Sabbatical years was similarly opened and closed, when the law was read anew, Deut. xxxi. 11–13. For law as to solemnization *see* Lev. xxiii. 34–43; Num. xxix. 12–40. Its observance is referred

to in Neh. viii. 13–18 ; Hos. xii. 9 ; Zech. xiv. 16–19 ;
John vii. 2, 37, 38.

Tăb′i̇-thȧ (*gazelle*). The Christian woman of
Joppa whom Peter raised from the dead, Acts ix.
36–42. [DORCAS.]

Tā′ble (*board*). Primitive tables were merely
leather or skins spread on the floor. After the
captivity they were slightly raised. Beds or couches
are meant in Mark vii. 4 ; writing tablet of wax in
Luke i. 63. The "tables" of Matt. xxi. 12 ; John ii.
15, were doubtless sufficiently raised to answer the
purposes of a counter for money-changing purposes.
The meaning of "serve tables" in Acts vi. 2, is that
duty which fell to the early Christian ministry of at-
tending to the gathering and distributing of food to
the poor, or of collecting and distributing the church
funds. This duty was transferred to the deacons,
Acts vi. 5, 6.

Tā′bôr (*mound*). (1) A high mountain on north
side of plain of Esdraelon ; landmark between Issachar and Zebulun, Josh. xix. 22 ; gathering place
of Barak's forces, Judg. iv. 6–14 ; scene of murder
of Gideon's brothers, Judg. viii. 18–21. (2) Levitical
town in Zebulun, 1 Chr. vi. 77. (3) "Plain of Tabor,"
1 Sam. x. 3, should read "oak of Tabor."

Tăb′ret (*little tabor*). A small drum or tambourine, without jingles ; used to accompany pipes, 1 Sam.
xviii. 6. [TIMBREL.]

Tăb′rĭ-mŏn (*Rimmon is good*). Father of Benhadad I., King of Syria in time of Asa, 1 Kgs. xv. 18.

Tăche (*tack*). Taches were hooks or clasps of
gold or copper for connecting the tabernacle curtains,
Ex. xxvi. 6, 11.

Tăch′mo̸-nīte, 2 Sam. xxiii. 8. Hachmonite, or
"son of Hachmoni."

Tăd′môr (*Tamar*, *palms*). The Palmyra of the
Greeks and Romans. A city built by Solomon in
Syria, toward the Euphrates, for the purpose of
facilitating trade with the east. Its ruins are numerous and suggestive, 1 Kgs. ix. 18 ; 2 Chr. viii. 4.
Tadmor, or Palmyra, reached the height of its splendor, wealth, and power under the celebrated Zeno-
bia, "Queen of the East," who made it the capital of
her empire. It fell a prey to the victorious Romans.
Among its notable ruins are the Temple of the Sun.

dedicated to Baal, a Street of Columns, of which 150 are still standing, and a series of magnificent tombs intended for both burial places and places of worship. The old name still exists in the form of Thadmor.

Tā'hăn (*camp*). An Ephraimite, Num. xxvi. 35; 1 Chr. vii. 25.

Tā'hăn-ītes. Descendants of Tahan, Num. xxvi. 35.

Ta-hăp'a-nēs, Jer. ii. 16. [TAHPANHES.]

Tā'hăth (*station*). (1) A desert station of the Israelites, Num. xxxiii. 26, 27. (2) A Levite, 1 Chr. vi. 24, 37. (3) Two Ephraimites, 1 Chr. vii. 20.

Täh'pan-hēs. An ancient city of Egypt on the Tanitic mouth of the Nile. Identical with the Daphne of the Greeks. A favorite resort of exiled Jews, Jer. xliii. 7–9; xliv. 1; xlvi. 14. Jeremiah was taken thither, after the murder of Gedaliah, and the Pharaoh erected a brick palace there. The children of Noph and Tahpanhes are made to type the entire population of Egypt, Jer. ii. 16.

Täh'pen-ēs. An Egyptian queen, wife of the Pharaoh who received Hadad, king of Edom, 1 Kgs. xi. 18–20.

Täh-rē'a (*cunning*). A descendant of Saul, 1 Chr. ix. 41. Tarea, 1 Chr. viii. 35.

Täh'tim=hŏd'shī. An unknown land visited by Joab during his census tour, 2 Sam. xxiv. 6.

Tāle (*number*). A reckoning by number and not by weight, Ex. v. 8.

Tăl'ent (*weight*). A Hebrew weight and denomination for money, equal to 3,000 shekels, or 93¾ pounds of silver, and varying in value from $1,550 to $2,000, Ex. xxxviii. 25; Matt. xviii. 24. The Attic, or Greek talent, was worth about $1,200; the Roman great talent, $500; the Roman small talent, $375.

Tăl'ī-thä cū'mī. Two Syro-Chaldaic words spoken by Christ, and meaning "Damsel, arise," Mark v. 41.

Tăl'māi (*brave*). (1) A son of Anak, Num. xiii. 22; Josh. xv. 14; Judg. i. 10. (2) King of Geshur and father-in-law of David, 2 Sam. iii. 3.

Tăl'mon (*captive*). A temple porter, 1 Chr. ix. 17, and father of a family of returned captives, Ez. ii. 42; Neh. vii. 45; xi. 19; xii. 25.

Tăl'mŭd (*instruction*). The body of Jewish civil and canonical law not comprised in the Pentateuch, and commonly including the *Mishna* (traditions and decisions) and *Gemara* (expositions).

Tā'mah (*mirth*). Ancestor of returned Nethinim, Neh. vii. 55. Thamah, Ez. ii. 53.

Tā'mar (*palm-tree*). (1) Widow of Er and Onan, of Judah, and mother of Pharez and Zarah, by Shelah, Gen. xxxviii. (2) Daughter of David and sister of Absalom, 2 Sam. xiii. 1–32. (3) Daughter of Absalom, wife of Uriel and mother of Maachah, queen of Abijah, 2 Sam. xiv. 27; 2 Chr. xiii. 2. (4) A frontier place in south Judah, a day's journey from Hebron, Ezek. xlvii. 19; xlviii. 28.

Tăm'mŭz (*sprout*). A Syrian idol corresponding to the Greek Adonis, Ezek. viii. 14.

Tā'năch, Josh. xxi. 25. [TAANACH.]

Tăn'hu-mĕth (*comfort*). Father of one of Gedaliah's captains, 2 Kgs. xxv. 23; Jer. xl. 8.

Tā'nis, Ezek. xxx. 14 marg. [ZOAN.]

Tăn'nĕr (*oaker*). Tanning not a reputable occupation among Hebrews. It was carried on outside of cities and towns. Peter stopped with Simon, a tanner of Joppa, Acts ix. 43.

Tā'phath (*drop*). A daughter of Solomon, 1 Kgs. iv. 11.

Tā'phŏn, 1 Macc. ix. 50. [BETH-TAPPUAH.]

Tăp'pu-ah (*apple*). (1) A descendant of Judah, 1 Chr. ii. 43. (2) A city in the plain-country of Judah, four miles N. W of Hebron, Josh. xv. 34. (3) A border place between Ephraim and Manasseh, Josh. xvi. 8; xvii. 8.

Tā'rah (*station*). A desert encampment of the Israelites, Num. xxxiii. 27.

Tăr'a-lah (*winding*). A town in Benjamin, Josh. xviii. 27.

Tā'rẹ-ȧ, 1 Chr. viii. 35. [TAHREA.]

Târeṣ (*tears*). The darnel is supposed to be meant. It grows somewhat like wheat till near ripening time, and chokes the growth of cereals, Matt. xiii. 25–30.

Tăr'gĕt (*shield*). A small shield is meant, and not a target or mark in a modern sense, 1 Sam. xvii. 6. In the margin it is called "gorget," which was a defensive piece of armor, in the days of chivalry, used to protect the joint or opening between the helmet and cuirass.

Tär'pel-ītes. , Assyrian colonists in Samaria after the captivity, Ez. iv. 9.

Tär'shish, Thär'shish (*solid, rocky*). (1) Second son of Javan, Gen. x. 4. (2) The city with which the Phœnicians traded. Associated with Tartessus in Spain, Jer. x. 9; Ezek. xxxviii. 13. (3) Another Tarshish is inferable from the statement that Solomon's ships at Ezion-geber on the Red Sea traded with Tarshish or Tharshish, 1 Kgs. ix. 26; xxii. 48; 2 Chr. ix. 21; 2 Chr. xx. 36. But many suppose that a class of ships — "ships of Tarshish," like "East India merchantmen" — is referred to rather than a port.

Tär'sus (*wing*). Chief city of Cilicia, Asia Minor, on river Cydnus, six miles from the Mediterranean. Birthplace of Paul and rival of Athens and Alexandria in literature and fine arts, Acts ix. 11, 30; xi. 25; xxi. 39; xxii. 3. At the mouth of the Cydnus were fine docks, and Tarsus had, at one time, considerable commercial importance. Some would identify it with Tarshish. It was founded by the Assyrian, Sardanapalus, and was captured by the Romans and made a free city. It is now represented by Tersons, a mean Turkish city with a fluctuating population.

Tär'tăk (*prince of darkness*). An idol introduced into Samaria by Avite colonists, and worshipped under the form of an ass, symbolizing darkness, 2 Kgs. xvii. 31.

Tär'tan. Not a proper name, but an army official, like general or commander-in-chief, 2 Kgs. xviii. 17; Isa. xx. 1.

Tăt'na-ī (*gift*). A Persian governor in Palestine, Ez. v. 3, 6; vi. 6, 13.

Tăv'ĕrns (*huts*). "Three Taverns" was a place on the Appian Way, 33 miles south of Rome, where Paul met some of his Roman brethren, Acts xxviii. 15.

Tăx'es (*touches*). First Hebrew taxes were tithes, first-fruits, redemption money, for use of the priests. Taxes amplified under the kings and became burdensome, 1 Kgs. x. 28, 29; xii. 4. Jews under heavy tribute while subject to foreign rulers, Neh. v. The tithe-tax became a poll-tax, Neh. x. 32, 33; and continued, Matt. xvii. 24. The enrollment, or census, of Luke ii. 2, and Acts v. 37, was for the purpose of Roman taxation, which was onerous, being on the head, the field-hand, the ground and the products thereof, the harbors, çity-gates, and city houses.

Tēars̨. In Ps. lvi. 8, allusion is supposed, by some, to be made to a custom of preserving the tears of mourners in a bottle and placing it in the sepulchre. Others regard the words as a bold metaphor, expressive of David's wish that God would keep in memory his many penitential tears, as the traveller stores his water, milk, or wine in leather bottles for a journey.

Tē′bah (*slaughter*). A son of Nahor, Gen. xxii. 24.

Tĕb′′a-lī′ah (*purged*). Third son of Hosah the Merarite, 1 Chr. xxvi. 11.

Tē′beth (*goodness*). Tenth month of Hebrew sacred, and fourth of civil, year; commencing with new moon in January, Esth. ii. 16.

Tĕ-hăph′ne-hes̨, Ezek. xxx. 18. [TAHPANHES.]

Tĕ-hĭn′nah (*entreaty*). Son of Eshton and founder of Ir-nahash, city of Nahash, 1 Chr. iv. 12.

Tēil=trēē (*lime-tree*). Terebinth, or oak of Palestine, Isa. vi. 13.

Tĕ-kō′à, Tĕ-kō′ah (*fort*). A town of Judah on the Hebron ridge, six miles from Bethlehem, and on the border of the wilderness, 2 Chr. xx. 20; Jer. vi. 1. Colonized by Ashur, 1 Chr. ii. 24; iv. 5; fortified by Rehoboam, 2 Chr. xi. 6. Home of the "wise woman" who interceded for Absalom, 2 Sam. xiv. 2–9. Birthplace and residence of the prophet Amos, Am. i. 1. Now Tekua.

Tĕ-kō′īte. Dweller in Tekoa, 2 Sam. xxiii. 26; 1 Chr. xi. 28; xxvii. 9; Neh. iii. 5, 27.

Tĕl=ā′bĭb (*grain-heap*). A city in Chaldea or Babylonia where captive Jews resided, Ezek. iii. 15.

Tē′lah (*strength*). An Ephraimite ancestor of Joshua, 1 Chr. vii. 25.

Tĕl′a-im (*lambs*). Place where Saul collected his forces before attacking the Amalekites, 1 Sam. xv. 4.

Te-lăs′sar, Thĕ-lā′sar (*Assyrian hill*). Place in western Mesopotamia, near Haran and Orfa, 2 Kgs. xix. 12; Isa. xxxvii. 12.

Tē′lem (*oppression*). (1) A city in extreme southern Judah, Josh. xv. 24. (2) A temple doorkeeper in time of Ezra, Ez. x. 24.

Tĕl=här′så, Tĕl=ha̤-rē′shå (*uncultivated hill*). A place in Babylonia whence captive Jews returned, Ez. ii. 59 ; Neh. vii. 61.

Tĕl=mē′lah (*salt hill*). A city mentioned with the above. Identified by some with the Thelme of Ptolemy, near the Persian Gulf, Ez. ii. 59 ; Neh. vii. 61.

Tē′må (*desert*). Ninth son of Ishmael, and name of his tribe and country. Referred to Teyma in Syria, on the caravan route from Damascus to Mecca, Gen. xxv. 15 ; 1 Chr. i. 30 ; Job vi. 19 ; Isa. xxi. 14 ; Jer. xxv. 23.

Tē′man (*desert*). Oldest son of Eliphaz, and grandson of Esau, Gen. xxxvi. 11. Also the tribe and country of Temani or Temanites, in Edom, Jer. xlix. 7 ; Ezek. xxv. 13 ; Am. i. 12 ; Obadiah 9 ; Hab. iii. 3.

Tĕm′a̤-nī, Tē′man-īte, Gen. xxxvi. 34 ; Job li. 11. [TEMAN.]

Tĕm′e̤-nī. A son of Ashur, father of Tekoa, 1 Chr. iv. 6.

Tĕm′ple. (1) Solomon's temple erected at Jerusalem on Mount Moriah. David proposed to transform the tabernacle into a permanent temple at Jerusalem, and collected much material, but its construction was forbidden by the prophet Nathan, 1 Chr. xvii. ; 2 Sam. vii. 7–29. Solomon completed the work after David's plans and with the assistance of Hiram, king of Tyre. He began to build in the fourth year of his reign, B. C. 1012, and finished and dedicated it B. C. 1005, 1 Chr. xxi., xxii., xxviii., 11–19 ; xxix. 4–7 ; 1 Kgs. vi.–viii. ; 2 Chr. iii.–vii. This costly and imposing structure, for the age, was pillaged several times during the Eastern invasions, and was finally destroyed during the last siege of Jerusalem by Nebuchadnezzar, B. C. 588. (2) The temple of Zerubbabel was begun in B. C. 534, by the returned captives under the lead of Zerubbabel and the patronage of King Cyrus of Persia. Owing to discords and direct opposition it was not completed till B. C. 515. It was much inferior to the first in cost and beauty, though one third larger in dimensions. It was partially destroyed by Antiochus Epiphanes, B. C. 163, and re-

stored by Judas Maccabeus, Ez. iii.-vi. ; 2 Macc. **x.**
1-9. (3) Herod the Great removed the decayed temple of Zerubbabel and began the erection of a new
one B. C. 17. This gorgeous and costly structure was
not completed till the time of Herod Agrippa II., A. D.
64. It was of marble, after Græco-Roman designs,
and was destroyed by the Romans under Titus, A. D.
70, thus verifying Mark xiii. 2.

Tĕmpt (*hold*). Ordinarily, the offering of an
inducement to do wrong, Matt. iv. 1-11 ; Luke iv.
13 ; but in Gen. xxii. 1 ; James i. 2, 3, a trial of one's
faith ; trial of God's patience, Ex. xvii. 2 ; 1 Cor. x.
9 ; an effort to ensnare, Matt. xvi. 1 ; xix. 3 ; xxii.
18 ; Mark x. 2 ; Luke x. 25.

Tĕnt (*stretched*). The house of nomad and pastoral peoples. It was made of strong cloth, chiefly of
goat's hair, stretched on poles, and firmly pegged to
the ground, Gen. iv. 20 ; xviii. 1 ; Judg. iv. 21 ; Isa.
xxxviii. 12.

Tē'rah (*laggard*). Father of Abraham. He was
of Ur in Chaldea, started west with his family, stopped
in Haran, and died there, aged 205 years. Through
his sons, Abraham, Nahor, and Haran, he was the ancestor of the Israelites, Ishmaelites, Midianites, Moabites, and Ammonites, Gen. xi. 27-32.

Tĕr'a-phim (*images*). Little images kept in
Eastern households for private consultation and worship. This species of idolatry or superstition was in
favor with Hebrews, though often denounced, Gen.
xxxi. 19, 34, 35 ; Judg. xviii. 17 ; 1 Sam. xv. 23; xix.
13, 16 ; 2 Kgs. xxiii. 24 ; Hos. iii. 4 ; Zech. x. 2.

Tĕr'e-binth. [TEIL-TREE.]

Tē'resh (*strict*). A eunuch of Ahasuerus, whose
plot to murder his master was discovered by Mordecai, Esth. ii. 21-23.

Tĕr'tius (*third*). Paul's scribe in writing his
Epistle to the Romans, Rom. xvi. 22.

Tĕr-tŭl'lus (*little third*). A Roman lawyer or
orator hired by the high priest and Sanhedrim to
prosecute Paul before the procurator Felix, Acts
xxiv. 1-9.

Tĕs'tá-ment (*witness*). One of the two volumes
of the Sacred Scriptures, which treat of the old and
new dispensations ; distinguished as the Old Testament, treating of revelation before the Advent of

Christ, and the New Testament, containing that made after the Advent, 2 Cor. iii. 6; Heb. ix. 15.

Tĕs'tį-mō-nў (*witness*). The entire revelation of God, Ps. cxix. 88, 99; the tables of stone, Ex. xxv. 16; the ark in which the tables were deposited, Ex. xxv. 22; the gospel of Christ, 1 Cor. i. 6; Rev. i. 2.

Tĕt'rärch (*fourth ruler*). Originally, one governing the fourth part of a country. Under Roman rule, any ruler or petty prince of the republic and empire, especially in Syria, Matt. xiv. 1; Luke iii. 1; ix. 7; Acts xiii. 1. Sometimes called king, Matt. xiv. 9; Mark vi. 14, 22.

Thăd-dæ'us (*wise*). Surname of the apostle Jude, and another form of Lebbæus, Matt. x. 3; Mark iii. 18. [JUDE.]

Thā'hăsh (*badger*). Son of Nahor, Gen. xxii. 24.

Thā'mah, Ez. ii. 53. [TAMAH.]

Thā'mar, Matt. i. 3. [TAMAR, 1.]

Thăm'mŭz. [TAMMUZ.]

Thăm'na̤-thȧ, 1 Macc. ix. 50. [TIMNATH.]

Thănk Ŏf'fer-ing. The peace offering of Lev. iii., as offered with thanksgiving in Lev. vii. 11-15.

Thā'rȧ, Luke iii. 34. [TERAH.]

Thăr'rȧ, Esth. xii. 1. [TERESH.]

Thär'shish (*rocky*). (1) 1 Kgs. x. 22; xxii. 48. [TARSHISH.] (2) A Benjamite, 1 Chr. vii. 10.

Thăs'sī. Surname of Simon, son of Mattathias, 1 Macc. ii. 3.

Thē'a̤-trē (*sight*). A place where dramatic performances are exhibited, as in Acts xix. 29; but the spectacle or performance itself in 1 Cor. iv. 9. The introduction of the theatre by Herod the Great greatly offended the Jews.

Thēbe̤s (*life of the god*). Classical name of No or No-amon, Jer. xlvi. 25; Nah. iii. 8; Ezek. xxx. 14, 16. [NO.]

Thē'bez (*prominent*). Now Tubas, a village near Shechem, and scene of Abimelech's tragic death, Judg. ix. 50-55; 2 Sam. xi. 21.

Thė-cō'ė, 1 Macc. ix. 33. [TEKOA.]

Thĕft, Thiēf. Punishment of theft was severe under the Mosaic law, as in all pastoral countries where the property was chiefly in flocks, more or less exposed to persons of felonious intent. The thief was compelled to make restitution, five-fold for a stolen ox and four-fold for a sheep. To kill a thief, caught in the act, was not a capital offence. If restitution was impossible a thief could be sold, Ex. xxii. 1–4.

Thĕ-lā'sar, 2 Kgs. xix. 12. [TELASSAR.]

Thĕ-lĕr'sas, 1 Esdr. v. 36. [TELHARSA.]

Thē'man, Bar. iii. 22. [TEMAN.]

Thĕ-ŏd'ō-tŭs (*God-given*). Envoy of Nicanor to Judas Maccabeus, 2 Macc. xiv. 19.

Thĕ-ŏph'ĭ-lŭs (*lover of God*). The unknown person, probably an official, to whom Luke addressed his Gospel and his history of the Acts of the Apostles, Luke i. 3 ; Acts i. 1.

Thē'ras, 1 Esdr. viii. 41. [AHAVA.]

Thĕs''sa-lō'nĭ-ans. People of Thessalonica, to whom Paul addressed two epistles, 13th and 14th N. T. books. The first was written at Corinth, A. D. 52 or 53, soon after the author had founded a church at Thessalonica, and upon the strength of favorable reports from Timothy. Its design was to confirm the new converts in the faith, strengthen them against persecution, correct their errors of doctrine and work, and inculcate purity of life. The second was also written from Corinth, soon after the first, and designed to correct false impressions concerning Christ's advent, and especially to place the author right before the world as an authorized apostle and teacher.

Thĕs''sa-lō-nī'cà. Ancient Thermæ, "hot springs;" now Salonika. Enlarged by Cassander and called Thessalonica after his wife, daughter of Alexander the Great. An important city of Macedonia, at the head of the Gulf of Thessalonica, or Thermæ. Paul visited it during his second tour and founded a strong church there, to whose members he wrote two epistles, Acts xvii. 1–9.

Theū'das (*God's gift*). An insurgent Jew mentioned in Gamaliel's speech before the council, Acts v. 34–39.

Thigh. Placing the hand under the thigh was a form of adjuration mentioned in Gen. xxiv. 2 ; xlvii. 29, and supposedly prevalent in patriarchal times, but only taken by inferiors, as by servants or sons, and as significant of subjection and the purpose of obedience.

Thĭm′na-thah, Josh. xix. 43. [TIMNAH.]

Thĭs′bĕ. A city in Bœotia, Tob. i. 2.

Thĭs′tle, Thôrn. No less than eighteen Hebrew words embrace the thistle, thorn, brier, and bramble species, which is prolific in Palestine, Gen. iii. 18. Figurative for desolation, Prov. xxiv. 31; Isa. v. 6; Hos. ii. 6; providential visitation, Num. xxxiii. 55; Judg. ii. 3; 2 Cor. xii. 7; hindrance, Prov. xv. 19; troubles, Prov. xxii. 5. "Crown of thorns," both punishment and derision, Matt. xxvii. 29.

Thŏm′as (*twin*). The cautious, susceptible, even doubtful, apostle, whose name, in Greek, was Didymus, "twin," Matt. x. 3; Mark iii. 18; Luke vi. 15; John xi. 16; xiv. 5, 6; xx. 24–29; Acts i. 13.

Thôrn. [THISTLE.]

Thrū′çĭà. Classic name for the country now embraced in the northern part of Turkey in Europe, 2 Macc. xii. 35.

Thrȧ-sē′us. Father of Apollonius, 2 Macc. iii. 5.

Thrēe Tăv′ẽrnş. [TAVERNS.]

Thrĕsh′ing (*thrashing*). Done anciently by treading with oxen or horses, or by drawn sleds, sometimes spiked, on earthen floors, usually on high spots of ground, Deut. xxv. 4; 1 Chr. xxi. 15–28; Isa. xxviii. 27, 28; xli. 15, 16. The flail or stick is mentioned in Ruth ii. 17.

Thrōne (*seat*). The seat of one in authority, as high priest, 1 Sam. i. 9; military chief, Jer. i. 15; but especially of a king, 2 Sam. iii. 10; 1 Kgs. ii. 12; vii. 7; x. 18–20; xxii. 10; Acts xii. 21.

Thŭm′mĭm, Ex. xxviii. 30. [URIM.]

Thŭn′der (*sound*). Rare in Palestine, hence regarded as God's displeasure, 1 Sam. xii. 17; Jehovah's voice, Job xxxvii. 2; Ps. xviii. 13; Isa. xxx. 30, 31; John xii. 29; symbol of divine power, Ex. xix. 16; 1 Sam. ii. 10; 2 Sam. xxii. 14; Isa. xxix. 6; Rev. viii. 5.

Thy″a-tī′rȧ (*burning incense*). A city of northern Lydia in Asia Minor, founded by Seleucus Nicator, much inhabited by Jews, seat of one of the seven churches of Asia, Acts xvi. 14; Rev. ii. 18–29.

Thy′ine=wood. Wood of the thyia, sandarac, or

pine variety, yielding a choice gum and hard, dark colored, fragrant wood. Indigenous to northern Africa, Rev. xviii. 12.

Ti-bē'rĭ-as. (1) Sea of, John vi. 1; xxi. 1. [GENNESARET.] (2) A town of Galilee on the west shore of Lake Gennesaret or Sea of Galilee, founded by Herod Antipas, A. D. 16–22, and named in honor of the emperor Tiberius. It seems to have imparted its name to the lake or sea. Once noted for its learning and architectural beauty, but now the miserable village of Tabariyeh, John vi. 1, 23 ; xxi. 1.

Ti-bē'rĭ-us. Tiberius Claudius Nero, second emperor of Rome, A. D. 14–37. Stepson of Augustus, a vigorous warrior, eloquent orator, and able statesman, but an indolent, despotic ruler. He is the Cæsar of Luke iii. 1 ; xx. 22–25 ; xxiii. 2 ; John xix. 12.

Tĭb'hath (*killing*). Capital of Hadadezer, king of Zobah, 1 Chr. xviii. 8. Betah, 2 Sam. viii. 8.

Tĭb'nī (*knowing*). Competitor of Omri for the throne of Israel, 1 Kgs. xvi. 21, 22.

Tī'dal (*great chief*). A chief of nomadic tribes, who joined Chedorlaomer in his attack on the cities of the plain, Gen. xiv. 1–16.

Tĭg'lath=pĭ-lē'ṣer (*Adar's son my help*). Second of the Assyrian kings in contact with Israel. He invaded Samaria, 2 Kgs. xv. 29, and a few years afterwards returned, taking many captives, 1 Chr. v. 26. King Ahaz, of Judah, became his vassal, 2 Kgs. xvi. 7–10. He reigned B. C. 747–739.

Tī'grĭs (*arrow*). Great eastern tributary of the Euphrates, rising in the Armenian mountains and flowing southeastwardly 1146 miles. Between it and the Euphrates lay Mesopotamia. In the Septuagint version it stands for Hiddekel, one of the rivers of Eden, Gen. ii. 14 ; Tob. vi. 1 ; Judith i. 6 ; Ecclus. xxiv. 25.

Tĭk'vah, Tĭk'vath (*hope*). (1) Father-in-law of Huldah the prophetess, 2 Kgs. xxii. 14 ; 2 Chr. xxxiv. 22. (2) Father of Jahaziah, Ez. x. 15.

Tīle (*cover*). A broad, thin slab of burnt clay, used as a shingle on Oriental houses, Ezek. iv. 1.

Tĭl'găth=pĭl-nē'ṣer, 1 Chr. v. 6 ; 2 Chr. xxviii. 20. [TIGLATH-PILESER.]

Tī'lon (*gift*). A Judahite, 1 Chr. iv. 20.

Ti-mæ'us (*honored*). Father of the blind Bartimæus, Mark x. 46.

Tim'brel (*bell, drum*). A Hebrew musical instrument somewhat resembling the tambourine, Ex. xv. 20; Judg. xi. 34; Ps. lxviii. 25. [TABRET.]

Tim'nà, Tim'nah (*portion*). (1) Mother of Amalek, Gen. xxxvi. 12. (2) A duke of Edom, Gen. xxxvi. 40, who gave his name to a boundary of Judah, Josh. xv. 10. (3) A mountain town of Judah, Josh. xv. 57. Thimnathah, Josh. xix. 43.

Tim'năth. (1) Gen. xxxviii. 14. [TIMNA, 2.] (2) Home of Samson's wife, Judg. xiv. 1–5.

Tim'năth=hē'rĕs, Judg. ii. 9. [TIMNATH-SERAH.]

Tim'năth=sē'rah (*fruitful portion*). A city in Ephraim given to Joshua, and his home and burial place, Josh. xix. 50; xxiv. 30. Written Timnathheres in Judg. ii. 9.

Tim'nīte. Designation of Samson's father-in-law, the Timnathite, Judg. xv. 6.

Ti'mon (*honorable*). One of the first seven deacons, Acts vi. 1–6.

Ti-mō'the-ŭs (*honoring God*). (1) An Ammonite leader defeated by Judas Maccabeus, 1 Macc. v. 6–44. (2) Acts xvi. 1; xvii. 14, etc. [TIMOTHY.]

Tim'o-thў (*honoring God*). Son of Eunice, a Jewess, by a Gentile father. Born in Derbe or Lystra, Lycaonia, Acts xvi. 1; 2 Tim. i. 5. Converted by Paul and became a close friend and valuable assistant, Rom. xvi. 21; Heb. xiii. 23. Recipient of two of Paul's epistles, 15th and 16th N. T. books. The first was written to him while at Ephesus, probably from Macedonia, and about A. D. 65. The second seems to have been written from Rome some three years later. They are called pastoral epistles, because devoted to description of church work and earnest exhortation to faithfulness.

Tin. A metal well known to ancients, Num. xxxi. 22; evidently dross in Isa. i. 25. Imported from Tarshish, Ezek. xxvii. 12.

Tiph'sah (*ford*). The Greek and Roman Thapsacus, a crossing point of the Euphrates, and eastern limit of Solomon's empire, 1 Kgs. iv. 24. Smitten by Menahem, 2 Kgs. xv. 16.

Tī'ras (*longing*). Youngest son of Japheth, and supposable progenitor of the Thracians, Gen. x. 2.

Tī'rath-ītes. Designation of a family of scribes at Jabez, 1 Chr. ii. 55.

Tīre (*attire*). A head-dress, Isa. iii. 18; Ezek. xxiv. 17, 23; but the original implies any round ornament, as a necklace, worn by persons or animals, Judg. viii. 21, 26.

Tir'ha-kah (*exalted*). A king of Ethiopia and Upper Egypt who became King Hezekiah's ally against Sennacherib, about B. C. 695, 2 Kgs. xix.; Isa. xxxvii. 9.

Tir'ha-nah (*favor*). A son of Caleb, son of Hezron, 1 Chr. ii. 48.

Tir'ī-à (*dread*). A Judahite, 1 Chr. iv. 16.

Tir'sha-thà (*governor*). Title of the governors of Judea under Persian rule, Ez. ii. 63; Neh. vii. 65, 70; viii. 9; Neh. x. 1.

Tir'zah (*pleasing*). (1) Youngest of the five daughters of Zelophehad, Num. xxvi. 33. (2) An ancient Canaanite city captured by Joshua, and which afterwards became the capital of the kingdom of Samaria, till Samaria, the new capital, was founded by King Omri. It was some 30 miles north of Jerusalem, and 5 miles east of Samaria, Josh. xii. 24; 1 Kgs. xiv. 17; xv. 21, 33; xvi. 6; 2 Kgs. xv. 14, 16; S. of Sol. vi. 4.

Tish'bīte. Elijah is so designated, 1 Kgs. xvii. 1; xxi. 17, 28; 2 Kgs. i. 3, 8; ix. 36. The place is generally referred to Thisbe in Naphtali, where Tobit lived, Tob. i. 2.

Tīs'rī. Seventh month of the Jewish sacred, and first of the civil, year, corresponding to parts of September and October. Called also Ethanim, 1 Kgs. viii. 2; 2 Chr. v. 3.

Tithe (*tenth*). One tenth of all produce of lands and herds was set apart, under the Levitical law, for the support of the Levites, and a tenth of their tenth went to the priests. There were tithe regulations among other nations, Gen. xiv. 20; xxviii. 22; Lev. xxvii. 30-33; Num. xviii. 21-32; Deut. xii. 17, 18; xiv. 22-27. The Pharisees tithed their mint, anise, cummin, and rue, Matt. xxiii. 23.

Tit'tle (*title*). Jot; iota; any minute quantity Matt. v. 18; Luke xvi. 17.

Tī'tus (*pleasant*). A distinguished Grecian who became a Christian convert and a companion of Paul in his trials and on his missionary tours, Tit. i. 4; Gal. ii. 3-5; 2 Cor. viii. 6, 16, 23. Entrusted with many important commissions, 2 Cor. xii. 18; 2 Tim. iv. 10; Tit. i. 5. Paul wrote an epistle to Titus, the 17th N. T. book, about A. D. 65, designed to instruct him in his ministerial duties in Crete, which were arduous, on account of the immorality of the people.

Tī'zīte. Designation of Joha, one of David's guardsmen. Place unknown, 1 Chr. xi. 45.

Tō'ah (*bent*). A Levite ancestor of Samuel, 1 Chr. vi. 34. Tohu, 1 Sam. i. 1.

Tŏb (*good*). A place or district beyond Jordan and between Gilead and the desert, to which Jephthah fled when banished from Gilead, Judg. xi. 3-5. Ish-tob, 2 Sam. x. 6, 8.

Tŏb=ăd″o-nī'jah (*my good God*). A Levite sent out by King Jehoshaphat to teach the law, 2 Chr. xvii. 8.

Tō-bī'ah (*God's goodness*). (1) His children returned with Zerubbabel, Ez. ii. 60; Neh. vii. 62. (2) An Ammonite servant of Sanballat who joined his master in opposing Nehemiah, Neh. ii. 10-20.

Tō-bī'as. Greek form of Tobiah and Tobijah. (1) Son of Tobit, and hero in his book, Tob. (2) Father of Hyrcanus, and a man of great prominence at Jerusalem, B. C. 187.

Tō'biē, 1 Macc. v. 13. [TOB.]

Tō-bī'jah (*God's goodness*). (1) A Levite sent out by King Jehoshaphat to teach the law, 2 Chr. xvii. 8. (2) One of the captivity in whose presence Joshua was crowned high priest, Zech. vi. 10-14.

Tō'bĭt (*goodness*). Father of Tobias, and author of Tobit, the fifth Apocryphal book. It was written in Greek, with the scene in Assyria, and is a didactic narrative of Jewish social life after the captivity.

Tō'chen (*task*). An unidentified place in Simeon, 1 Chr. iv. 32.

Tō-gär'mah (*bony*). Son of Gomer, of the family of Japheth, Gen. x. 3. His descendants became horse and mule merchants, and have been associated with the ancient Armenians, Ezek. xxvii. 14.

Tō'hu, 1 Sam. i. 1. [TOAH.]

Tō'i (*wandering*). A king of Hamath, who sent his son to congratulate David on his victory over Hadadezer, 2 Sam. viii. 9, 10. Tou, 1 Chr. xviii. 9, 10.

Tō'la (*worm*). (1) First-born of Issachar, and progenitor of the Tolaites, Gen. xlvi. 13; Num. xxvi. 23; 1 Chr. vii. 1, 2. (2) Successor of Abimelech as judge of Israel for twenty-three years, Judg. x. 1, 2.

Tō'lǎd (*generation*). A city in South Judah, called also El-tolad, 1 Chr. iv. 29.

Tō'la-ītes. Descendants of Tola, Num. xxvi. 23.

Tŏl'ba-nēṣ, 1 Esdr. ix. 25. [TELEM.]

Tōll (*tell*). The Persian taxation of conquered Judea consisted of "tribute" levied on each province and collected by the authorities thereof; "custom," which could be paid in kind; "toll," which was a cash exaction for the use of bridges, fords, and highways, Ez. iv. 13; vii. 24.

Tomb. Burial places among Hebrews were caves, recesses in rocks, natural or artificial, and walled sepulchres. [SEPULCHRE.]

Tongues. "And the whole earth was of one language, and of one speech," Gen. xi. 1. Confusion of tongues and dispersion of peoples coincident, Gen. xi. 7-9. "New tongues," Mark xvi. 17, is the first notice of a gift specially characteristic of the first outpouring of the Spirit. Ten days afterward the promise was fulfilled in the Pentecostal phenomenon, Acts ii. 1-13.

Tooth. The Jewish law of retaliation permitted the deprivation of "eye for eye, tooth for tooth," Ex. xxi. 24. The principle of this law was condemned by Christ, Matt. v. 38-42. Teeth used figuratively for the inheritable quality of sin, Ezek. xviii. 2; "cleanness of teeth" a figure for famine, Am. iv. 6; "gnashing of teeth" indicative of rage and despair, Matt. viii. 12.

Tō'păz. A variously hued gem, corresponding to the modern chrysolite, which the Hebrews obtained from Ethiopia, Job xxviii. 19, and which constituted the second stone in first row of the high priest's breastplate, Ex. xxviii. 17, and a foundation stone of the New Jerusalem, Rev. xxi. 20.

Tō′phel (*mortar*). A place east of the Dead Sea near Bozrah, Deut. i. 1.

Tō′phet, Tō′pheth (*drum, noise, place of burning*). Part of the valley of Hinnom east or south of Jerusalem. Perhaps once a pleasure garden, but afterward polluted by the abominations incident to the worship of Baal and Molech, 2 Kgs. xxiii. 10; Jer. vii. 31; xix. 13, and then turned into a dumping and burning place of the city's refuse. Hence a place of judgment, Jer. xix. 6–14. [HINNOM.]

Tôr′mah, Judg. ix. 31 marg. [ARUMAH.]

Tôr′toĭse (*twisted - foot*). A faulty rendering. The Septuagint has "land-crocodile," and doubtless one of the large lizard species is meant, Lev. xi. 29.

Tō′u, 1 Chr. xviii. i. 10. [TOI.]

Tōw. The coarser part of flax, Judg. xvi. 9.

Tow′er (*shot up*). Watch-towers, or fortified posts, were frequent on frontiers and exposed places, Gen. xxxv. 21; 2 Chr. xxvi. 10; around vineyards, Isa. xxi. 5, 8, 11; Matt. xxi. 33, and for the use of shepherds, Mic. iv. 8. "Tower of Shechem," Judg. ix. 47, evidently a citadel or stronghold. Tower of Babel [BABEL]. "Tower of Siloam," possibly an observatory, Luke xiii. 4.

Town Clĕrk. An official in Ephesus, who recorded the laws and decisions and read them in public, Acts xix. 35–41.

Trăch″ọ-nī′tis (*stony*). One of the Roman provinces into which the country north of the Jordan was divided, and generally associated with Argob, south of Damascus, Luke iii. 1.

Trănce (*going over*). The word in Num. xxiv. 4, 16, is an interjection, without a Hebrew equivalent. In Acts x. 10, xi. 5, xxii. 17, an ecstasy is implied, which carried the subject beyond the usual limits of consciousness and volition.

Trăns-fĭg″ū-rā′tion (*formed over*). The supernatural change in the appearance of Christ upon the mount — Hermon or Tabor. It served as an attestation of his Messiahship and an emblem of glorified humanity, Matt. xvii. 1–13; Mark ix. 2–13; Luke ix. 28–36.

Trĕaṣ′ûre Cĭ′tiĕṣ. The kings of Judah, and of other nations, kept their treasures in designated cities, called treasure-cities, and in special buildings called treasure-houses, Ex. i. 11; 1 Chr. xxvii. 25; Ez. v. 17.

Trĕas'ûr-ў (*place*). The place in the temple where gifts were received, 1 Chr. ix. 26; Mark xii. 41; Luke xxi. 1; John viii. 20.

Trĕnch (*cut*). In military usage, a ditch for protection, but in 1 Sam. xxvi. 5, the place where the wagons were grouped or packed.

Trĕs'păss (*passing over*). To violate the personal or property rights of another, Lev. v. 6. To violate a positive law of God, Matt. vi. 15.

Trĕs'păss Ŏf'fẽr-ĭng. This offering was closely allied to the sin offering, and in some cases offered with it as a distinct part of the same sacrifice, Lev. v. 15; xiv. 13–32.

Trībe (*division*). In a Roman sense, the third part of the empire, but with Hebrews any division of the people, especially that division which sprung from the twelve sons of Jacob, and was perpetuated in their descendants, Gen. xlviii. 5; Num. xxvi. 5–51; Josh. xiii. 7–33; xv.-xix. Of these tribes two, Ephraim and Manasseh, sprang from Joseph. Still there were only twelve partitions of conquered Canaan, for the tribe of Levi received no allotment of lands, but was diffused in cities among the other tribes and supported by them. Each tribe was headed by a prince, and each possessed considerable independence even under the monarchy. They waged war separately and among themselves, Judg. i. 2–4; 1 Chr. v. 18–22; 2 Sam. ii. 4–9; and finally ten of the tribes revolted and set up the separate kingdom of Israel, xix. 41–43; 1 Kgs. xii. For history of each tribe *see* its title.

Trĭb'ūte (*gift*). A payment made as a token of submission, or for sake of peace, or in pursuance of treaty, Gen. xlix. 15. The head-tax of half a shekel paid annually by Jews for the support of the temple service, Ex. xxx. 13.

Trĭp'ŏ-lĭs (*three cities*). The commercially linked cities of Aradus, Sidon, and Tyre, in Phœnicia, 2 Macc. xiv. 1.

Trō'ăs (*Troad*). Alexandria Troas, or in the Troad, was an important city in Mysia, Asia Minor, 6 miles south of the entrance to the Hellespont and 4 from the site of Ancient Troy. It was founded by

Alexander the Great and was for many centuries the key of commerce between Europe and Asia. Paul visited it more than once, Acts xvi. 8–11; xx. 5–10; 2 Tim. iv. 13.

Trŏ-gȳl'lĭ-um (*fruit-port*). Town and promontory on the western coast of Asia Minor, opposite Samos. Paul visited it on his third missionary tour, Acts xx. 15.

Troop, Band. These words imply small bodies of marauders in Gen. xlix. 19; 2 Sam. xxii. 30; Jer. xviii. 22; Mic. v. 1.

Trŏph'ĭ-mŭs (*fostered*). A Christian convert residing at Ephesus, and co-worker with Paul, Acts xx. 4; xxi. 29; 2 Tim. iv. 20.

Trōw (*trust*). Signifies to think or believe in, Luke xvii. 9.

Trŭm'pet (*pipe*). A wind instrument with a flaring mouth, made of horn or metal and differing but little in form and use from the cornet, Ex. xix. 16. [CORNET.]

Trŭm'pets, Feast of. The feast of the new moon which fell on the first of Tisri, Num. xxix. 1–6; Lev. xxiii. 24, 25. It was the New Year's day of the Jewish civil year, and was ushered in by the blowing of trumpets and observed by offerings.

Trȳ-phē'nà (*shining*). A Christian woman of Rome, saluted by Paul, Rom. xvi. 12.

Trȳ'phŏn (*effeminate*). Surname of Diodotus, who usurped the Syrian throne, 1 Macc. xii. 39.

Trȳ-phō'sà (*shining*). A Christian woman of Rome, saluted by Paul, Rom. xvi. 12.

Tṳ'bal (*tumult*). Fifth son of Japheth, Gen. x. 2; 1 Chr. i. 5. His descendants supposably inhabited the country between the Caspian and Euxine seas, Isa. lxvi. 19; Ezek. xxvii. 13, xxxii. 26.

Tṳ'bal=cāĭn. Son of Lamech the Cainite, by Zillah. He was instructor of artificers in brass and iron, Gen. iv. 22.

Tṳ''bĭ-ē'nī. Inhabitants of Tubion, the O. T. Tob, 2 Macc. xii. 17.

Tûr'pĕn-tīne=trēe. The terebinth, or teil-tree, Ecclus. xxiv. 16.

Tûr'tle, Tûr'tle-dove (*cooer*). The turtle embraces several species of plaintive-noted doves. Gen.

xv. 9; Ps. lxxiv. 19; Isa. lix. 11. Those who could not afford the costlier sacrifices could offer two doves or pigeons, Lev. xii. 6–8; Luke ii. 24. They were migratory, S. of Sol. ii. 12; Jer. viii. 7.

Tỹch′ĭ-cŭs (*fate*). A disciple of Paul, Acts xx. 4, and his messenger and spokesman, Eph. vi. 21, 22; Col. iv. 7, 8.

Tȳ-răn′nus (*tyrant*). A Greek rhetorician at Ephesus in whose school Paul taught for two years, Acts xix. 9.

Tȳre (*rock*). The celebrated commercial city of Phœnicia on the Mediterranean coast. It fell to the lot of Asher, but was never conquered, Josh. xix. 29. In intimate commercial relation with Hebrews, and King Hiram furnished the artificers and material for the temple and royal houses at Jerusalem, 2 Sam. v. 11; 1 Kgs. v. 1; vii. 13; ix. 11–14; 1 Chr. xiv. 1; 2 Chr. ii. 2–18. The city was denounced by the prophets, Isa. xxiii. 1–17; Jer. xxvii. 3; Ezek. xxvi. 3–21. It resisted the five-year siege of Shalmaneser and the thirteen-year siege of Nebuchadnezzar, but fell before that of Alexander. Referred to in N.T., Matt. xi. 21, 22; xv. 21; Mark vii. 24. Paul visited it, Acts xxi. 3, 4.

Tȳ′rus. Name for Tyre in O. T. prophecies and in Apocrypha.

U

Ū′cal (*power*). The prophecy of Agur is addressed to Ithiel and Ucal, Prov. xxx. 1. Some regard the names as symbolical, while others treat them as real.

Ū′el (*God's will*). One of the sons of Bani, Ez. x. 34. Juel in 1 Esdr. ix. 34.

Ŭk′năz. The name is made to stand for Kenaz in margin of 1 Chr. iv. 15.

Ū′la̤-ī (*pure water*). A river in the province of Elam, where the palace of Shushan stood, on whose banks Daniel saw the vision of the ram and the he-goat, Dan. viii. 2–16.

Ū′lam (*porch*). (1) A descendant of Manasseh, 1 Chr. vii. 16, 17. (2) Son of Eshek, a Benjamite, of the line of Saul, 1 Chr. viii. 39, 40.

Ŭl′là (*yoke*). Head of an Asherite family, 1 Chr. vii. 39.

Ŭm′mah (*community*). A city in Asher, associated with modern Alma, five miles from the Mediterranean coast, Josh. xix. 30.

Ŭn″çĭr-cŭm-çĭ′ᶻion (*not cut around*). In a Scriptural sense, Gentiles, Rom. ii. 25–29.

Ŭn-clēan′. A word which, with clean, was applied to personal and ceremonial conditions, as well as to the edibility of animals. The division of animals into clean and unclean existed before the Flood, Gen. vii. 2. Uncleanness and the processes of purification are particularly described in Lev. xi.–xv.; Num. xix. Unclean animals are specially mentioned in Lev. xi. 9–31; Deut. xiv. 3–20.

Ŭn″dẽr-gĭrd′ing. A primitive way of keeping the hull of a ship from opening by passing a cable tightly around it. The ship in which Paul sailed from Crete to Italy was undergirded, Acts xxvii. 17.

Ŭn″dẽr-sĕt′tẽrṣ. The molten projections which ornamented and supported the brazen laver in Solomon's temple, 1 Kgs. vii. 30.

Ū′nĭ-côrn (*one-horned*). A fabulous animal pictured as having one horn on its forehead and the body of a horse. The Hebrew word *re'em*, which is translated "unicorn," Num. xxiii. 22; xxiv. 8; Deut. xxxiii. 17; Job xxxix. 9; Ps. xxii. 21; xxix. 6; Isa. xxxiv. 7, does not refer to the one-horned creature of fable, but evidently to a two-horned animal, Deut. xxxiii. 17, possibly the now nearly extinct wild ox, auroch or urus of naturalists.

Ŭn′nī (*afflicted*). (1) A Levite appointed to play upon the psaltery, in the time of David, 1 Chr. xv. 18, 20. (2) Another Levite, who acted as watchman after the return from captivity, Neh. xii. 9.

U-phär′sin, Dan. v. 25–28. [MENE.]

Ū′phăz. Only in Jer. x. 9; Dan. x. 5, where it has been generally treated as an error for Ophir.

Ûr (*light, region*). (1) Place where Abraham lived with his father Terah and his wife Sarah, before they started for the land of Canaan, Gen. xi. 28, 31. Mentioned in Gen. xv. 7, as of the Chaldees, and Acts vii. 2, as in Mesopotamia. (2) Father of Eliphal, one of David's guard, 1 Chr. xi. 35. Called Ahasbai in 2 Sam. xxiii. 34.

Ŭr'bane (*of a city, polite*). Greek form of the Latin Urbanus, a Christian disciple of Paul at Rome whom he salutes in Rom. xvi. 9. Urbanus in R. V.

Ū'rī (*fire*). (1) Father of Bezaleel, one of the architects of the tabernacle, Ex. xxxi. 2; xxxv. 30; xxxviii. 22; 1 Chr. ii. 20; 2 Chr. i. 5. (2) Father of Geber, Solomon's commissary officer in the land of Gilead, 1 Kgs. iv. 19. (3) A gate-keeper of the temple in the time of Ezra, Ez. x. 24.

U-rī'ah (*light*). (1) A Hittite, 2 Sam. xi. 3, and commander of one of the thirty divisions of David's army, 2 Sam. xxiii. 39; 1 Chr. xi. 41. He was husband of the beautiful Bathsheba whom David coveted, and with whom he had committed the crime of adultery, 2 Sam. xi. 4, 5. In order to conceal his crime and procure her for a wife, he ordered Joab, commander-in-chief, to place Uriah and his forces in the hottest part of the battle with Ammon, and then to desert him, leaving him to be overwhelmed and slain by superior numbers, 2 Sam. xi. 15-17. (2) A high priest in the reign of Ahaz, Isa. viii. 2, and probably the same as Urijah in 2 Kgs. xvi. 10-16. (3) A priest of the family of Hakkoz, in time of Ezra, and head of the seventh priestly course, Ez. viii. 33; written Urijah in Neh. iii. 4, 21.

U-rī'as. (1) Matt. i. 6. [URIAH, 1.] (2) 1 Esdr. ix. 43. [URIJAH, 3.]

Ū'rī-el (*fire of God*). (1) One of the angels, 2 Esdr. iv. 1, 36. (2) A chief of the Kohathite Levites in the time of David, 1 Chr. xv. 5, 11. (3) A Kohathite Levite, son of Tahath, 1 Chr. vi. 24. (4) Father of Michaiah, or Maacha, wife of Rehoboam and mother of Abijah, 2 Chr. xiii. 2.

U-rī'jah (*light of God*). (1) A priest in the reign of Ahaz, and probably the same as Uriah (2), 2 Kgs. xvi. 10-16. (2) A priest of the family of Hakkoz or Koz, and probably same as Uriah (3), Neh. iii. 4, 21; viii. 4. (4) A prophet of Kirjath-jearim, and son of Shemaiah, who prophesied in the days of King Jehoiakim against Jerusalem and Judah according to the words of Jeremiah, and whom Jehoiakim sought to put to death. He fled to Egypt, but was pursued, caught, brought back and slain, Jer. xxvi. 20-23.

Ū'rim and Thŭm'mim (*light and perfection*). From the way these mysterious words are spoken of in Ex. xxviii. 30, and in Lev. viii. 8, compared with Ex. xxviii. 15-21, they appear to denote some material things, separate from the high priest's breastplate and its gems, and previously well known. Their purpose seems to be indicated in Num. xxvii. 21 ; 1 Sam. xxviii. 6, and, since they were connected with the ephod, in 1 Sam. xxii. 14, 15 ; xxiii. 9-12 ; xxx. 7, 8, it may be inferred they were consulted to ascertain the will of Jehovah, and that they were preserved in the bag of the high priest's breastplate to be borne "upon his heart before the Lord continually," Ex. xxviii. 30. Not in use after the captivity, Ez. ii. 63 ; Neh. vii. 65 ; Hos. iii. 4.

Ū′ṣu-rȳ (*use*). Exorbitant or unlawful interest for money loaned ; but in a Bible sense the taking of any interest at all. The law of Moses prohibited Hebrews from exacting interest of one another on loans, though not of foreigners, Lev. xxv. 36, 37 ; Deut. xxiii. 19, 20. Usury is severely denounced, Neh. v. 7, 10 ; Ps. xv. 5 ; Prov. xxviii. 8 ; Ezek. xxii. 12.

Ū′tȧ, 1 Esdr. v. 30. [AKKUB.]

Ū′tha-ī (*helpful*). (1) The son of Ammihud, of Judah, 1 Chr. ix. 4. Athaiah in Neh. xi. 4. (2) Son of Bigvai, who returned from captivity, Ez. viii. 14.

Ū′thī, 1 Esdr. viii. 40. [UTHAI, 2.]

Ŭz (*fertile*). (1) The land of Uz was Job's country, Job i. 1. It was located east or southeast of Palestine, Job i. 3 ; adjacent to the Sabeans or Chaldeans, Job i. 15, and to the Edomites, who once occupied it as conquerors, Lam. iv. 21. It is grouped with Egypt, Philistia, and Moab, Jer. xxv. 19-21. (2) The first son of Aram, son of Shem, Gen. x. 23 ; 1 Chr. i. 17. (3) Son of Nahor by Milcah, Gen. xxii. 21. Huz in A. V. and probably correct name for Uz. (4) Son of Dishan and grandson of Seir, Gen. xxxvi. 28.

Ū′za-ī (*strong*). Father of Palal, who assisted in rebuilding the walls of Jerusalem, Neh. iii. 25.

Ū′zal (*wanderer*). Sixth son of Joktan, Gen. x. 27 ; 1 Chr. i. 21. His descendants occupied the district of Yemen in Arabia and built the city of Uzal, since changed to Sana, and still the capital.

Ŭz′zȧ (*strength*). (1) The garden attached to the house of Manasseh, king of Judah. It evidently contained the family sepulchre, 2 Kgs. xxi. 18, 26. (2) A Benjamite descendant of Ehud, 1 Chr. viii. 7. (3)

One of the drivers of the cart which bore the ark from Kirjath-jearim to Jerusalem, and who was slain by the Lord for putting his hand to the cart when the oxen stumbled, 1 Chr. xiii. 7–11. Uzzah elsewhere. (4) A Merarite Levite, 1 Chr. vi. 29.

Ŭz′zah (*strength*). 2 Sam. vi. 3–8. [UzzA, 3.]

Ŭz′zen=shē′rah (*ear of Sherah*). A town built by Sherah, a daughter of Ephraim, 1 Chr. vii. 24.

Ŭz′zī (*mighty*). (1) A son of Bukki and father of Zerahiah, in the line of high priests, but never a high priest, 1 Chr. vi. 5, 6; Ez. vii. 4. (2) A son of Tola and grandson of Issachar, 1 Chr. vii. 2, 3. (3) A son of Bela, of the tribe of Benjamin, 1 Chr. vii. 7. (4) A Benjamite progenitor of several families settled in Jerusalem after the captivity, 1 Chr. ix. 8, 9. (5) A Levite, son of Bani, and overseer of the Levites at Jerusalem after the captivity, Neh. xi. 22. (6) A priest, and chief of the house of Jedaiah, in the time of the high priest Joiakim, Neh. xii. 19. (7) A priest who assisted Ezra at the dedication of the walls of Jerusalem, Neh. xii. 42.

Ŭz-zī′à (*God's strength*). Designated as the Ashterathite, one of David's guard, 1 Chr. xi. 44.

Ŭz-zī′ah (*God's strength*). (1) Son and successor of Amaziah on the throne of Judah, B. C. 810–758, 2 Chr. xxvi. 1–3. He is called Azariah in 2 Kgs. xiv. 21 and elsewhere. He was a godly king, an excellent general, and renowned city builder. But for daring to enter the temple and burn incense in violation of the law, Num. xvi. 40, xviii. 7, he was stricken with leprosy and forced to live in a separate house till he died, 2 Kgs. xv. 1–7; 2 Chr. xxvi. (2) A Kohathite Levite, son of Uriel and ancestor of Samuel, 1 Chr. vi. 24. (3) Father of Jehonathan, superintendent of David's storehouses in fields, cities, villages and castles, 1 Chr. xxvii. 25. (4) A priest of the sons of Harim, Ez. x. 21. (5) A Judahite, Neh. xi. 4.

Ŭz′zĭ-el (*God's might*). (1) Fourth son of Kohath, son of Levi, Ex. vi. 18, 22; ancestor of the Uzzielites, Lev. x. 4; and also, through Elizaphan, of the Kohathites, Num. iii. 19, 27, 30; 1 Chr. xv. 10. (2) A captain of the sons of Simeon, 1 Chr. iv. 42, 43. (3) A son of Bela and grandson of Benjamin, 1 Chr. vii. 7; (4) A son of Heman and one of the temple musicians in time of David, 1 Chr. xxv. 4. Azareel in 1 Chr. xxv. 18. (5) A descendant of Heman, 2 Chr. xxix. 14–19. (6) An assistant wall-builder, Neh. iii. 8.

Ŭz′zĭ-ĕl-ītes″. Descendants of Uzziel (1), Num. iii. 27; 1 Chr. xxvi. 23.

V

Văg′a-bŏnd (*wanderer*). In the Bible vagabond has the original meaning of fugitive or wanderer, Gen. iv. 12; Ps. cix. 10; Acts xix. 13.

Vă-jĕz′a-thå (*strong as the wind*). One of the ten sons of Haman, Esth. ix. 9.

Vāle, Văl′ley. Five Hebrew words are rendered vale or valley in the Bible, only one of which seems to imply that broad sweep of land between mountains or hills generally understood by valley. The others imply (1) a narrow ravine, gorge, or glen, Deut. xxxiv. 3, 6; (2) a wady, dry in summer but a torrent in rainy weather; (3) a plain, Josh. xi. 8, 17; xiii. 17; 2 Chr. xxxv. 22; Zech. xii 11; (4) a stretch of sloping ground, Deut. i. 7; Josh. x. 40; 1 Kgs. x. 27; 2 Chr. i. 15; Jer. xxxiii. 13.

Vă-nī′ah (*praise of God*). A son of Bani, who had married a foreign wife, Ez. x. 36.

Văsh′nĭ (*second*). Name of Samuel's oldest son, 1 Chr. vi. 28. In 1 Sam. viii. 2, Joel appears as his firstborn son.

Văsh′tĭ (*beautiful*). Wife of King Ahasuerus and queen of Persia, Esth. i. 9–22.

Văt. A large vessel for holding liquids. "Fat" in Joel ii. 24; iii. 13. [WINE-FAT.]

Veil (*carry*). The veil of Gen. xxiv. 65; xxxviii. 14; Ruth iii. 15; S. of Sol. v. 7; Isa. iii. 23, was a shawl or mantle. The veil proper was worn by Hebrew women only on special occasions, as in marriage, Gen. xxiv. 65; for ornament, S. of Sol. iv. 1, 3; for concealment as in harlotry, Gen. xxxviii. 14.

Vĕr-mĭl′ĭon (*little worm*). A bright red color much affected by Hebrews in the painting of beams, ceilings, and conspicuous objects, Jer. xxii. 14; Ezek. xxiii. 14.

Vĕtch′eṣ. A plant of the bean family. [FITCHES.]

Vī′al (*shallow cup*). In a general sense any bottle or vessel, 1 Sam. x. 1.

Vil′lage. In addition to the ordinary meaning, the unwalled suburbs of a walled town, Lev. xxv. 31.

Vīne (*wine*). A favorite Oriental plant of many varieties and cultivated from the earliest times, Gen. ix. 20; Num. xiii. 23. Subject of frequent metaphor, Deut. xxxii. 32; emblem of felicity and contentment, 1 Kgs. iv. 25; Ps. cxxviii. 3; Mic. iv. 4; rebellious Israel compared to "wild grapes," Isa. v. 2, "strange vine," Jer. ii. 21, "empty vine," Hos. x. 1; symbol of spiritual union, John xv. 1-5.

Vin′e-gär (*sharp wine*). A thin wine, Num. vi. 3; Ruth ii. 14; acid, Prov. x. 26; unpalatable, Ps. lxix. 21. The thin sour wine of the Roman soldiers was the beverage in Matt. xxvii. 48; Mark xv. 36; John xix. 29, 30.

Vīne′yärd. Vineyards were generally on hills, Isa. v. 1; Jer. xxxi. 5; Am. ix. 13; surrounded by walls or hedges to keep out boars, Ps. lxxx. 13; jackals and foxes, Num. xxii. 24; Neh. iv. 3; S. of Sol. ii. 15; Ezek. xiii. 4; Matt. xxi. 33. Towers were erected within the vineyard for watch-houses and dwellings for the vine-keeper, Isa. i. 8; v. 2; Matt. xxi. 33.

Vint′age (*taking wine away*). The vintage season a time of joy. Town people went out and lived among the vineyards in lodges and tents, Judg. ix. 27; Isa. xvi. 10; Jer. xxv. 30. Grapes were gathered in baskets, Jer. vi. 9. [WINE-PRESS.]

Vīne of Sŏd′om, Deut. xxxii. 32. A phrase used to describe the character of Israel.

Vīne′yärds, Plain of. A place east of Jordan, beyond Aroer, Judg. xi. 33. [ABEL.]

Vī′ol (*keep holiday, sacrifice*). A stringed instrument like the psaltery, Am. vi. 5. [PSALTERY.]

Vī′per (*bringing forth its young alive*). The Hebrew word implies a hissing and venomous serpent, as the common European viper or adder, the horned vipers of the *cerastes* genus, and the Indian vipers, Job xx. 16; Isa. xxx. 6; Acts xxviii. 1-6. A symbol of deceit and destruction, Matt. iii. 7; xii. 34; xxiii. 33; Luke iii. 7.

Vĭs′ion (*seeing*). An inspired dream, phantasy, or apparition, Num. xxiv. 4; Isa. vi.; Ezek. i. viii.-x.; Dan. vii., viii.; Acts xxvi. 13-19.

Vŏph'sī (*gain*). Father of Nahbi, the spy selected to represent the tribe of Naphtali, Num. xiii. 14.

Vow (*wish*). Vows were threefold, vows of devotion, abstinence, and destruction, and respecting them certain laws were laid down, Deut. xxiii. 21–23. The law in Lev. xxvii. regulated the vow of Corban, and that in Num. vi. 1–21 the Nazarite vow.

Vŭl'ture (*tearer*). A large falconoid bird, with naked head and neck, feeding mostly on carrion. The bird is pronounced unclean in Lev. xi. 14; Deut. xiv. 13; but the original implies the kite, as also in Isa. xxxiv. 15.

W

Wā'fer (*waffle*). Among Hebrews a thin cake of fine flour used in offerings. The flour was wheaten and the wafers were unleavened and anointed with oil, Ex. xvi. 31; xxix. 2, 23; Lev. ii. 4; vii. 12; viii. 26; Num. vi. 15, 19.

Wā'ġĕṣ (*pledges*). The earliest O. T. mention of wages shows that they were paid in kind and not in money, Gen. xxix. 15, 20; xxx. 28; xxxi. 7, 8, 41. Wages paid in money are mentioned in N. T., Matt. xx. 2. The Mosaic law was very strict in requiring daily payment of wages, Lev. xix. 13; Deut. xxiv. 14, 15.

Wăg'on (*mover*). Wagons of the Hebrews, like those of the ancient Egyptians, were carts, consisting of planks or at most of crude box-like bodies, supported upon axles which connected two solid wooden wheels. They were mostly drawn by oxen or kine, Num. vii. 3, 8; 1 Sam. vi. 3–14.

Wạlk (*move*). Walk has figurative use in the Bible to denote the behavior and spiritual character of a person, Ezek. xi. 20; Rom. viii. 1.

Wạll of Pär-tī'tion. The allusion in Eph. ii. 14 is to the " wall of partition " which separated the holy of holies from the holy place in Solomon's temple, 1 Kgs. vi. 31, 35.

Wạllṣ (*palisades*). Solid walls limitedly used in Oriental countries for ordinary dwellings, but at times solidly laid and strongly built for palaces and temples, and as a protection to cities. They were of various materials, palisades, clay, cemented pebbles, brick, and stone. Houses were frequently erected on the walls of cities, and towers for archers and slingers, Josh. ii. 15 ; Ps. lxii. 3 ; Isa. xxx. 13 ; Luke vi. 48.

Wạn'dĕr-ĭngs (*windings*). The wilderness wanderings of the Israelites began at Rameses, the place of rendezvous, west of the Red Sea. The time as fixed by modern Egyptologists was during the reign of the Pharaoh Menephthah, B. C. 1317, though another date, B. C. 1491, was for a long time received. After crossing into Arabia, the line of march was southerly to the wilderness of Sinai, where a long halt was made, the law given, the tabernacle built, and the people were numbered, Ex. xv. 23, 27 ; xvi.-xl. ; Lev. ; Num. i.-x. 12. From Sinai the route was northward to Kadesh near the southern border of Canaan, the time thus far consumed being two years, Num. xiii. 26. ' Here they were condemned to further wilderness wanderings for a period of thirty-eight years. This period was seemingly one devoted to nomadic existence like that of other Arabian tribes. When the time came for another move on Canaan, the route lay around the head of the Gulf of Akaba and thence eastward and northward to Moab and the Jordan crossing, Num. xxxiii. 48, 49.

Wạr (*embroil*). Primitive Hebrew weapons were clubs, arrows, slings, swords, and spears. No army divisions except those indicated by the tribes. The contests of this period often hand-to-hand and brutal, 2 Sam. i. 23 ; ii. 18 ; 1 Chr. xii. 8 ; 2 Chr. xiii. 17. Many of the modern stratagems employed, as the double attack, Gen. xiv. 15 ; ambush, Josh. viii. 12 ; false retreat, Judg. xx. 37 ; night attack, 2 Kgs. vii. 12. Sometimes battles were settled by single-handed combats, 1 Sam. xvii. ; 2 Sam. ii. 15, 16 ; 1 Chr. xi. 6. King David's army was divided into regularly disciplined and officered bands under a general-in-chief, 2 Sam. xviii. 1, 2 ; xxiii. 8–39 ; 1 Chr. xi. 25–47 ; xii., xxvii. He introduced the heavier weapons, such as catapults and battering-rams for siege-work and chariots for field-work, 2 Sam. viii. 4. Soldiers killed in action were plundered, 1 Sam. xxxi. 8 ; survivors were mutilated or killed, Judg. i. 6 ; ix. 45 ; 2 Sam. xii. 31 ; 2 Chr. xxv. 12 ; or carried into captivity, Num. xxxi. 26.

Wạrd (*watch*). A guard-room or lock-up, Gen

xl. 3; Acts xii. 10. A garrison or military post, Neh. xii. 25. A detachment of persons, guard, for any purpose, 1 Chr. ix. 23; Neh. xiii. 30.

Ward'rōbe (*watch-robe*). Place where the royal robes and priest's vestments were kept under watch or care, 2 Kgs. xxii. 14.

Wāreş. [COMMERCE.]

Wash'ing. The custom of washing hands before meals or of feet after a journey or on entering a stranger's house was not only a polite ceremony but a religious observance, Matt. xv. 2; Mark vii. 3; Luke xi. 38. After the salutation the first act of hospitality was to proffer a basin of water to the guest for washing the feet, Gen. xviii. 4; Ex. xxx. 19, 21; Judg. xix. 21; 1 Sam. xxv. 41; Luke vii. 37, 38, 44; John xiii. 5-14.

Watch (*wake*). The Hebrew night was divided into three watches, instead of hours. The first was called "the beginning of watches," beginning at sunset and lasting till ten o'clock, Lam. ii. 19: the second, the "middle watch," from ten P. M till two A. M., Judg. vii. 19; the "morning watch," from two A. M. till sunrise, Ex. xiv. 24; 1 Sam xi. 11. After the captivity the Jews gradually adopted the Greek and Roman division of the night into twelve hours of four watches; "evening," 6 to 9; "midnight," 9 to 12; "cock-crowing," 12 to 3; "morning," 3 to 6, Matt. xiv. 25; Mark xiii. 35; Luke xii. 38.

Wa'ter of Jĕal'oŭs-ў. The jealous husband brought his suspected wife before the priest, with her offering of barley meal, without oil or frankincense, in her hand. The priest took holy water in an earthen vessel in his hand and sprinkled it with the dust of the floor. Then the priest administered the oath to her. If she confessed to guilt she was compelled to drink the water, and stood accursed. If otherwise, she was allowed to go free, Num. v. 12-31.

Wa'ter of Sĕp''a-rā'tion. The preparation and use of the water of separation are described in Num. xix.

Wa'ter-spouts. The word translated "waterspouts" in Ps. xlii. 7 is rendered "gutter" in 2 Sam. v. 8.

Wāve=ŏf'fĕr-ing. The wave-offering, together

with the heave-offering, was a part of the peace-offering. The right shoulder of the victim, which was considered the choicest part, was "heaved" or held up in the sight of the Lord, and was, therefore, to be eaten only by the priests. The breast portion was "waved" before the Lord and eaten by the worshippers. On the second day of the passover feast, a sheaf of wheat and an unblemished lamb of the first year were waved, Ex. xxix. 24–27; Lev. vii. 30–34; viii. 27; ix. 21; x. 14, 15; xxiii. 10–20; Num. vi. 20; xviii. 11–18, 26–29.

Wăx. Wax in its original sense, an animal product as of bees, is frequently used in Scripture as a means of illustration, Ps. lxviii. 2; xcvii. 5; Mic. i. 4

Wēan (*accustom*). Weaning-time a festal occasion, and probably late, Gen. xxi. 8; 2 Chr. xxxi. 16.

Wĕap'onṣ. [ARMS.] [WAR.]

Wēa'ṣel. It is thought that "mole" would be a better translation, Lev. xi. 29.

Wēave. Most ancient nations knew the art of weaving. The Egyptians were skilled weavers, Gen. xli. 42. That the Hebrews brought the art along with them from bondage is clear from the fabrics manufactured in the wilderness: goat-hair covers, linen curtains, Ex. xxvi. 1–13; embroidered raiment, Ex. xxviii. 4, 39; woolen garments, Lev. xiii. 47. Though the loom is not mentioned, its various parts are, as the shuttle, beam, etc., 1 Sam. xvii. 7; 2 Kgs. xxiii. 7; 1 Chr. iv. 21; Job vii. 6; Prov. xxxi. 13, 24; Isa. xxxviii. 12.

Wĕd'ding. [MARRIAGE.]

Wĕd'ding=gär'ment. A special garment, required to be worn at marriage-suppers, seems to have been furnished by the host, Matt. xxii. 11.

Wēek. The division of time into weeks of seven days each dates from the earliest historic times among many and wide-apart nations. The Hebrew week began on our Sunday, their Sabbath being the seventh day or Saturday. The only day of their week they named was the Sabbath. The rest ran by numbers, as first, second, third, etc. Besides their week of days, Hebrews had their week of years, every seven years, and their week of seven times seven years, or year of jubilee, every fiftieth year, Gen. viii. 10; xxix. 27. The "feast of weeks" corresponded with Pentecost, Ex. xxiii. 15; xxxiv. 22; Lev. xxiii. 15-22; Num. xxviii.

Weights and Meas'ures. The standard of Hebrew weights and measures was kept in the sanctuary, Lev. xix. 35, 36. A copy of said standard was kept in the household, Deut. xxv. 13-15. The destruction of the ancient standard with the tabernacle led to the adoption of the various weights and measures of such countries as the Hebrews happened to be subject to or in commercial intercourse with. Hence the subject of Hebrew weights and measures is full of perplexity and uncertainty. *See* various weights and measures under their respective headings.

Wĕll (*boil*). Wells were of great importance in Palestine, Gen. xxiv. 11; Num. xx. 17-19; Judg. vii. 1. They were sometimes deep, John iv. 11; frequently owned in common, Gen. xxix. 2, 3; covered at times with a stone and surrounded by a low wall to protect them from drifting sand, Gen. xxix. 2-8; to stop them up an act of hostility, Gen. xxvi. 15, 16; to invade them a cause for contention, Gen. xxi. 25; water sometimes drawn by sweeps or windlasses, but generally by a bucket attached to a rope, and in some cases steps led down to them, Gen. xxi. 25-31; Judg. i. 13-15; 1 Sam. xxix. 1; emblem of blessings, Jer. ii. 13; xvii. 13.

Whāle. The Hebrew original translated "great whales" in Gen. i. 21 is used of "serpents" in Ex. vii. 9; Deut. xxxii. 33, and of the "crocodile" in Ezek. xxix. 3; xxxii. 2. In Job vii. 12; Isa. xxvii. 1, the name belongs to sea monsters. It is thought that the shark of the Mediterranean is meant in Jonah i. 17; Matt. xii. 40.

Whēat. This well-known cereal was cultivated in the East from the earliest times, Gen. xxx. 14, and grew luxuriantly and of many varieties in Egypt, Gen. xli. 22. Syria and Palestine were both fine wheat-growing countries, Ps. lxxxi. 16; cxlvii. 14; Matt. xiii. 8. Wheat-harvest denoted a well-known season, Gen. xxx. 14.

Whĭrl'wĭnd. Whirlwinds of great violence and frequency were well-known desert visitations and gave rise to many Scripture metaphors, Job xxxvii. 9; Isa. xvii. 13.

Whĭt'ed Sĕp'ŭl-chreṣ. Inasmuch as contact with the burial place was a cause of ceremonial defilement, Num. xix. 16, sepulchres were whitewashed that they might be seen and avoided, Matt. xxiii. 27.

Wĭd'ŏw (*lack*). When a married man died without children, his brother, if still living with the family, had a right under the law to marry the widow in order to preserve the family name and inheritance, Deut. xxv. 5, 6; Matt. xxii. 23-30. Other provisions of the Mosaic law show great consideration for widows, Ex. xxii. 22; Deut. xiv. 29; xvi. 11, 14; xxiv. 19-21; xxvi. 12; xxvii. 19.

Wife. [MARRIAGE.]

Wĭl'dẽr-ness (*place of wild beasts*). Like the word desert, wilderness does not necessarily imply an absolutely arid, sandy, and uninhabitable place, but an uncultivated waste, which it was possible for pastoral tribes to occupy, and with stretches of pasturage, Josh. xv. 61; Isa. xlii. 11. The wilderness of wandering in which the Israelites spent forty years, Deut. i. 1; Josh. v. 6; Neh. ix. 19, 21; Ps. lxxviii. 40-52; cvii. 4; Jer. ii. 2, was practically the great peninsula of Sinai lying between Seir, Edom, and Gulf of Akaba on the east, and Gulf of Suez and Egypt on the west. It embraced many minor divisions or wildernesses, as those of Sin or Zin, Paran, Shur, Etham, and Sinai. [WANDERINGS.]

Wĭll. The laws respecting realty rendered wills useless, but nuncupative disposition of personalty seems to be implied in 2 Sam. xvii. 23; 2 Kgs. xx. 1; Isa. xxxviii. 1.

Wĭl'lŏw. Before the captivity the willow was an emblem of joy, Lev. xxiii. 40; Job xl. 22; Isa. xliv. 4; but in allusion to the captivity, the weeping willow of Babylonia became the poetical type of sorrow, Ps. cxxxvii. 2. The "brook of willows," Isa. xv. 7, was in the land of Moab, and is called "valley of Arabians" in margin.

Wĭm'ple. In a Bible sense, a hood or veil as in Isa. iii. 22, or a mantle or shawl as in Ruth iii. 15.

Wĭnd (*blow*). Hebrews recognized the cardinal winds in their "four winds," north, south, east, west, Ezek. xxxvii. 9; Dan. viii. 8; Zech. ii. 6; Matt. xxiv. 31. The east wind injured vegetation, Gen. xli. 6; Job i. 19; Isa. xxvii. 8. The south wind brought heat, Luke xii. 55. The southwest and north winds brought clear cool weather, Job xxxvii. 9, 22; Prov.

xxv. 23. The west wind, coming from the Mediterranean, brought rain.

Wĭn′dŏw (*wind-eye*). In primitive Oriental houses the windows were simply openings upon the inner or court side of houses. But on the street or public side there were frequently latticed projections both for ventilation and sitting purposes, 2 Kgs. ix. 30 ; Judg. v. 28 ; probably the casements of Prov. vii. 6 ; S. of Sol. ii. 9.

Wīne (*drink*). The Hebrews manufactured and used wine from earliest times, Gen. ix. 20, 21 ; xix. 32 ; xxvii. 25 ; xlix. 12 ; Job i. 18 ; Prov. xxiii. 30, 31 ; Isa. v. 11. A usual drink-offering at the daily sacrifices, Ex. xxix. 40 ; at the presentation of first fruits, Lev. xxiii. 13 ; and at other offerings, Num. xv. 5. It was tithable, Deut. xviii. 4. Nazarites could not drink it during their vow, Num. vi. 3, nor priests before service, Lev. x. 9.

Wīne=făt, Wīne=prĕss. The Hebrew winefat, vat, or press, consisted of an upper and lower receptacle, the former for treading the grapes, the latter for catching the juice, Isa. lxiii. 3 ; Joel iii. 13 ; Hag. ii. 16.

Wĭn′nŏw (*wind*). The process of winnowing or winding grain was that of tossing the mixed chaff and kernels into the air, on a high, windy spot, with a fork or shovel, so that the wind could carry the chaff away. The floor on which the kernels fell was usually clean and solid, and when not so, a sheet was used to catch the grains, Isa. xxx. 24 ; xli. 16 ; Matt. iii. 12. Evening was the favorite winnowing time because the breezes were then steadiest, Ruth iii. 2.

Wĭn′tẽr. Winters in Palestine are short, lasting from December till February, S. of Sol. ii. 11.

Wĭṣ′dŏm of Jē′ṣŭs. [ECCLESIASTICUS.]

Wĭṣ′dŏm of Sŏl′o-mon. Fifth of the Apocryphal books, devoted to an exposition of wisdom in its moral, philosophic, and historic aspects.

Wīṣe Mĕn, Matt. ii. 1. [MAGI.]

Wĭst. Same as "knew," Ex. xvi. 15 ; Acts xii. 9 ; xxiii. 5.

Wĭt (*know*). To become aware, learn, know, Gen. xxiv. 21 ; Ex. ii. 4.

L

Witch (*wizard*). One who pretends to deal with evil spirits in order to work a spell on persons or their belongings; conjurer, fortune-teller, exorcist, supernatural curer of diseases, Deut. xviii. 10; 1 Sam. xxviii. 3–25. The word formerly embraced both sexes, but is now applied to women. Witches were not allowed to live, Ex. xxii. 18.

Witch'craft. The occult practices of witches and wizards, 1 Sam. xv. 23. The art, the pretender, and the person deceived were alike denounced, Lev. xx. 6; Nah. iii. 4; Gal. v. 20.

Wit'ness (*see*). Under the Mosaic law at least two witnesses were required to establish a capital charge, Num. xxxv. 30; Deut. xvii. 6, 7. False swearing forbidden, Ex. xx. 16; Lev. vi. 1–7.

Wiz'ärd (*cunning*). A male witch, Lev. xx. 27.

Wolf. Wolves of Palestine were numerous and the dread of shepherds, as they were a terrible enemy to sheep, Matt. vii. 15; x. 16; John x. 12; Acts xx. 29. A wolf typed the rapacity of Benjamin, Gen. xlix. 27; and the cruelty of Israel's oppression, Ezek. xxii. 27; and the destruction of the wicked, Jer. v. 6.

Wom'an (*wife-man*). Hebrew women cared for the household, Gen. xviii. 6; carried water, Gen. xxiv. 15; tended flocks, Gen. xxix. 6; spun, Ex. xxxv. 26; made clothes, 1 Sam. ii. 19; acted as hostess and guest on social occasions, Job i. 4; John ii. 3; xii. 2; prophesied, composed, sang, and danced, Ex. xv. 20, 21; Judg. xi. 34; xxi. 21; fêted, 1 Sam. xviii. 6, 7; held public positions, Judg. iv., v.; 2 Kgs. xxii. 14; Neh. vi. 14; Luke ii. 36; acted as workers and officials in the early Christian church, Acts xviii. 18, 26; Rom. xvi. 1.

Wool. A highly prized material for clothing among Hebrews, Lev. xiii. 47; Job xxxi. 20; Prov. xxxi. 13; Ezek. xxvii. 18; xxxiv. 3. Mixed woolen and linen fabrics forbidden, Lev. xix. 19; Deut. xxii. 11.

Word. The *logos*, or Word, in John i. 1–14; 1 John i. 1; Rev. xix. 13, stands for the Son of God, the Word incarnate.

Worm. Many Hebrew words are translated worm, all indicative of something loathsome, destructive, helpless, or insignificant, as the moth, Isa. li. 8; maggot, Job xix. 26; possibly the serpent, Mic. vii. 17. The allusion in Isa. lxvi. 24; Mark ix. 44–

48, is thought to be to he valley near Jerusalem where the refuse of the city constantly bred worms and where fires were kept burning to consume the collections. The helplessness of the worm affords the figures in Job xxv. 6; Ps. xxii. 6; Isa. xli. 14.

Worm'wood. A bitter plant found in Palestine, and often mentioned in Scripture in connection with gall to denote what is offensive and nauseous, Deut. xxix. 18; Prov. v. 4; Jer. ix. 15; xxiii. 15; Lam. iii. 15, 19; Am. v. 7.

Wor'ship-per, Acts xix. 35. The word should be temple-keeper as in marg. and in R. V.

Wŏt. "Wotteth not," Gen. xxxix. 8, means "knows not."

Wrī'tĭng. The first mention of writing in the Bible is in Ex. xvii. 14. The art among Hebrews was limited to persons of learning and position and to the class of scribes, Isa. xxix. 11, 12. [SCRIBE.] The oldest Semitic writings are the bricks and tablets of Nineveh and Babylon. The Hebrew alphabet was a development of the Phœnician, and it underwent many changes in the course of time. The record of Sinai was written on stone with the finger of God, Ex. xxxi. 18; xxxii. 15-19; xxxiv. 1-29. Later materials were wax, wood, metal, or plaster, Deut. xxvii. 2; Josh. viii. 32; Luke i. 63; and perhaps vellum, or fine parchment from skins, and linen were in early use for other than monumental writings, as they surely were at a later day, 2 Tim. iv. 13. Pliable substances, when written upon, were rolled on sticks, sealed and preserved as books, Ps. xl. 7; Isa. xxix. 11; Dan. xii. 4; Rev. v. 1. Hebrews doubtless knew the use of papyrus, 2 John 12. Rolls were generally written upon one side only, except in Ezek. ii. 9, 10; Rev. v. 1. Hebrew instruments of writing were the stylus and graver for hard materials, Ex. xxxii. 4; Job xix. 24; Ps. xlv. 1; Isa. viii. 1; Jer. viii. 8; xvii. 1; and for pliable materials, a reed pen, 2 Cor. iii. 3; 2 John 12; 3 John 13. Paul used an amanuensis, but authenticated his letters in a few lines with his own pen, 1 Cor. xvi. 21; Col. iv. 18; 2 Thess. iii. 17. Ancient ink was made of pulverized charcoal or burnt ivory in water to which gum had been added. It was carried in an ink-horn suspended to the girdle, Ezek. ix. 3, 4.

Y

Yärn. Though the art of spinning was well known to Hebrews, Ex. xxxv. 25; Prov. xxxi. 19; Matt. vi. 28, the spun product is only mentioned in 1 Kgs. x. 28; 2 Chr. i. 16, and in both these instances the word is rather significant of "band" as applied to a troop or drove of horses than to yarn.

Yēar. The Hebrew year was sacred and civil, with two beginnings. The sacred year began with the month Abib, April, the civil with the month Tisri, October. The months were lunar, twelve in number, with, of course, the necessary intercalary month *ve-adar* at the proper time, about every three years. As divided by seasons, the year was solar. There were two seasons, summer and winter, Ps. lxxiv. 17; Jer. xxxvi. 22; Am. iii. 15; Zech. xiv. 8.

Yēar of Jū′bi̧-lēe. [JUBILEE.]

Yēar, Săb-băt′ĭ-cal. [SABBATICAL.]

Yōke (*join*). This well-known means of coupling oxen for agricultural purposes was primitively laid upon the necks of the cattle, and held there by thongs which passed around their necks. A thong served also as an attachment to the cart-tongue or plow-beam. A pair of oxen yoked together were called a yoke, as to-day, 1 Sam. xi. 7; 1 Kgs. xix. 21. It would seem as if asses and mules went by pairs like oxen, Judg. xix. 10; 2 Kgs. v. 17, and even horses, camels, and chariots, Isa. xxi. 7. The word, like the Latin *jugum*, gave rise to a measurement of land, 1 Sam. xiv. 14, the amount a yoke of oxen could plow in a day. Yoke is used metaphorically for subjection, 1 Kgs xii. 4, 9-11; Isa. ix. 4; Jer. v. 5. An unusually heavy bondage was typed by "iron yoke," Deut. xxviii. 48; Jer. xxviii. 13. Removal of the yoke implied deliverance, Gen. xxvii. 40; Jer. ii. 20; Matt. xi. 29, 30. Breaking of the yoke meant repudiation of authority, Nah. i. 13.

Z

Zā′′a-nā′im (*changing*). The plain, or rather the oak, where Heber the Kenite was encamped when Sisera sought refuge in his tent, Judg. iv. 11, 17–22. It is mentioned as near Kedesh.

Zā′a-năn (*flocking-place*). A place in the lowlands of Judah, Mic. i. 11.

Zā′′a-năn′nim. A border place of Naphtali, near Kedesh, and supposed to be same as Zaanaim, Josh. xix. 33.

Zā′a-văn (*disturbed*). Son of Ezer and descendant of Seir the Horite, Gen. xxxvi. 27. Zavan in 1 Chr. i. 42.

Zā′băd (*gift*). (1) A son of Nathan, 1 Chr. ii. 36, 37, and one of David's mighty men, 1 Chr. xi. 41. (2) An Ephraimite whom the Gathites slew while on a thieving expedition, 1 Chr. vii. 21. (3) Son of Shimeath, an Ammonitess, and one of the murderers of King Joash, 2 Chr. xxiv. 25, 26. Jozachar in 2 Kgs. xii. 21. (4) Three returned captives, Ez. x. 27, 33, 43.

Zăb′′a-dā′ias, 1 Esdr. ix. 35. [ZABAD, 4.]

Zăb′′a-dē′ans. An Arab tribe smitten by Jonathan Maccabeus, 1 Macc. xii. 31.

Zăb′bāi (*limpid*). (1) One who had taken a foreign wife, Ez. x. 28. (2) Father of Baruch, one of the repairers of the walls of Jerusalem, Neh. iii. 20.

Zăb′bud (*given*). One who returned from captivity with Ezra, Ez. viii. 14.

Zăb′dī (*gift*). (1) Son of Zerah of the tribe of Judah, and ancestor of Achan, who concealed the spoils of Jericho, Josh. vii. 1, 17, 18. (2) One of the sons of Shimhi, a Benjamite, 1 Chr. viii. 19. (3) An officer who had the care of King David's wine cellars, 1 Chr. xxvii. 27. (4) Son of Asaph the minstrel, and leader of thanksgiving in prayer, Neh. xi. 17. Zaccur, Neh. xii. 35. Zichri, 1 Chr. ix. 15.

Zăb'dĭ-el (*gift of God*). (1) Father of Jasho-beam, captain of first course for the first month of David's guard, 1 Chr. xxvii. 2. (2) Overseer of a returned troop of captives, Neh. xi. 14. (3) An Arabian chieftain who put Alexander Balas to death, 1 Macc. xi. 17.

Zā'bud (*given*). A friend of Solomon and his principal officer, 1 Kgs. iv. 5.

Zăb'u-lon. Greek form of Zebulun, Matt. iv. 13; Rev. vii. 8.

Zăc'ca-ī (*pure*). His descendants, 760 in number, returned with Zerubbabel, Ez. ii. 9; Neh. vii. 14.

Zăc-chæ'us (*just*). The rich chief among publicans, resident at Jericho, who climbed a tree to see Jesus pass, was invited down, became the host of Jesus, and was converted, Luke xix. 1-10.

Zăc-chē'us. An officer under Judas Maccabeus, 2 Macc. x. 19.

Zăc'chur (*mindful*). A Simeonite of the family of Mishma, 1 Chr. iv. 26.

Zăc'cur (*mindful*). (1) Father of Shammua, the spy sent out by the tribe of Reuben, Num. xiii. 4. (2) A Merarite Levite, 1 Chr. xxiv. 27. (3) A son of Asaph the minstrel, and leader of the third musical course, 1 Chr. xxv. 2, 10; Neh. xii. 35. (4) One who assisted in rebuilding the walls of Jerusalem, Neh. iii. 2. (5) One who signed the covenant with Nehemiah, Neh. x. 12. (6) Father of Hanan, whom Nehemiah made one of his treasurers, Neh. xiii. 13.

Zăch''a-rī'ah (*remembered by Jehovah*). In better Hebrew, Zechariah. (1) Son of Jeroboam II., and his successor on the throne of Israel, 2 Kgs. xiv. 29; b. c. 773-72. He reigned only six months, 2 Kgs. xv. 8-11. (2) Father of Abi, mother of Hezekiah king of Judah, 2 Kgs. xviii. 2. Written Zechariah in 2 Chr. xxix. 1.

Zăch''a-rī'as (*remembered by Jehovah*). Greek form of Zachariah. (1) The name is borne by many priests and laymen in the books of Esdras. (2) Father of John the Baptist and husband of Elizabeth. He was a priest of the course of Abia, or Abijah, 1 Chr. xxiv. 10, and probably lived at Hebron, Luke i. 5-25, 57-80. (3) Son of Barachias, who was slain between the temple and the altar, Matt. xxiii. 35; Luke xi. 51.

Zăch'a̯-rȳ. 2 Esdr. i. 40. [ZECHARIAH, THE PROPHET.]

Zā'cher (*testimony*). A Benjamite, one of the sons of Jehiel by Maachah, 1 Chr. viii. 29, 31.

Zā'dŏk (*just*). (1) Son of Ahitub, of the line of Eleazar. He was one of the high priests in the time of David, the other being Abiathar, 2 Sam. viii. 17. He joined David at Hebron, as a chieftain of his father's house, 1 Chr. xii. 28, remained faithful to him and subsequently anointed Solomon, 1 Kgs. i. 39. (2) A priest in the reign of King Ahaziah, 1 Chr. vi. 12. (3) Father of Jerusha, wife of Uzziah and mother of Jotham king of Judah, 2 Kgs. xv. 33. (4) Son of Baana, who helped Nehemiah to repair the walls of Jerusalem, Neh. iii. 4. (5) Another assistant wall-builder, Neh. iii. 29. (6) A co-covenanter with Nehemiah, Neh. x. 21. (7) A scribe and treasurer under Nehemiah, Neh. xiii. 13.

Zā'ham (*hateful*). A son of King Rehoboam by his wife Abihail, 2 Chr. xi. 19.

Zā'ir (*little*). A vague spot or place, where King Joram overcame the Edomites, 2 Kgs. viii. 21.

Zā'laph (*hurt*). Father of Hanun who helped to repair the walls of Jerusalem, Neh. iii. 30.

Zăl'mŏn (*shade*). (1) The Ahohite who was one of David's guard, 2 Sam. xxiii. 28. Ilai in 1 Chr. xi. 29. (2) A wooded eminence near Shechem, Judg. ix. 47–49.

Zal-mō'nah (*shady*). A desert encampment of the wandering Israelites, Num. xxxiii. 41, 42.

Zal-mŭn'nȧ (*shadow*). One of two kings of Midian captured and slain by Gideon, Judg. viii. 5–21; Ps. lxxxiii. 11.

Zăm'bĭs, 1 Esdr. ix. 34. [AMARIAH.]

Zăm'brī, 1 Macc. ii. 26. [ZIMRI.]

Zā'moth, 1 Esdr. ix. 28. [ZATTU.]

Zăm-zŭm'mims̬. An Ammonite name for a race of Rephaim or giants, Deut. ii. 20.

Zȧ-nō'ah (*swamp*). (1) A town in the lowlands of Judah, ten miles southwest of Jerusalem, Josh. xv. 34; 1 Chr. iv. 18. Its inhabitants helped Nehemiah to repair the walls of Jerusalem, Neh. iii. 13; xi. 30. (2) Another town of Judah in the mountains, about ten miles southwest of Hebron, Josh. xv. 56.

Zăph'nath=pā''a-nē'ah (*revealer of secrets*). A name given by the Pharaoh to Joseph upon his promotion to a high place in the royal service, Gen. xli. 45.

Zā'phŏn (*north*). An unidentified place in Gad, Josh. xiii. 27.

Zā'rȧ (*dawn*). Zarah, a son of Judah, in genealogy of Christ, Matt. i. 3.

Zăr'a-çēs. A brother of Jehoiakim, King of Judah, 1 Esdr. i. 38.

Zā'rah (*dawn*). A son of Judah by Tamar, Gen. xxxviii. 30; xlvi. 12. Called Zerah in Num. xxvi. 20, and founder of the family of Zarhites; also Zerah in Josh. vii. 1, 18; xxii. 20; 1 Chr. ii. 4, 6; ix. 6; Neh. xi. 24. Zara in Matt. i. 3.

Zăr''a-ī'as. The name stands for Zerahiah and Zebadiah in the Apocrypha, 1 Esdr. viii.

Zā're-ah (*hornet*). Neh. xi. 29. [ZORAH, ZOREAH.]

Zā're-ath-ītes''. Dwellers in Zareah or Zorah, 1 Chr. ii. 53.

Zā'red, Num. xxi. 12. [ZERED.]

Zăr'e-phăth (*smelting-place*). The Sarepta of Luke iv. 26. A town in Phœnicia on the Mediterranean coast between Tyre and Sidon, and about seven miles from the latter. Residence of the prophet Elijah during the great drought, 1 Kgs. xvii. 8–24.

Zăr'e-tăn, Josh. iii. 16. [ZARTHAN, 2.]

Zā'reth=shā'har (*beauty of dawn*). A town in Reuben, Josh. xiii. 19.

Zăr'hītes. A branch of the tribe of Judah descended from Zerah the son of Judah, Num. xxvi. 13, 20; Josh. vii. 17; 1 Chr. xxvii. 11, 13.

Zăr'ta-nah (*cooling*). A place usually identified with Zarthan, 1 Kgs. iv. 12.

Zăr'than (*cooling*). (1) A town in the Jordan valley. Between it and Succoth was the clay-ground in which Solomon cast the utensils for the temple service. Now the mound called *Tell-sa-rem*, 1 Kgs. vii. 46. (2) The same place is doubtless meant by Zaretan, Josh. iii. 16, and by Zererath in Judg. vii. 22. (3) Supposably another name for the Zartanah of 1 Kgs. iv. 12. (4) Doubtless Zarthan (1) is meant by the Zeredathah of 2 Chr. iv. 17.

Zăth′ọ-ĕ, 1 Esdr. viii. 32. [ZATTU.]

Zăt′thu (*branch*). One who sealed the covenant with Nehemiah, Neh. x. 14.

Zăt′tu (*branch*). The children of Zattu returned from the captivity, Ez. ii. 8; x. 27; Neh. vii. 13.

Zā′van, 1 Chr. i. 42. [ZAAVAN.]

Zā′zā (*for all*). A son of Jonathan, and descendant of Judah, 1 Chr. ii. 33.

Zĕal′ŏts (*zealous*). Name of a fanatical Jewish party, strongest from A. D. 6 to 70. It was political, having for its aim the overthrow of Roman authority; and religious, seeking a Jewish theocracy over the whole earth. In Acts v. 37 it seems to have been headed by one Judas of Galilee.

Zĕb′′ạ-dī′ah (*portion of God*). (1) A son of Beriah, of Benjamin, 1 Chr. viii. 15. (2) A son of Elpaal of Benjamin, 1 Chr. viii. 17. (3) A son of Jeroham of Gedor, a Benjamite, 1 Chr. xii. 7. (4) A Korhite Levite, son of Meshelemiah, and one of the temple porters, 1 Chr. xxvi. 2. (5) A son of Asahel, brother of Joab, who succeeded his father as captain of the military course of the fourth month, 1 Chr. xxvii. 7. (6) A Levite sent out by King Jehoshaphat to teach the law to the people, 2 Chr. xvii. 8. (7) A son of Ishmael and ruler of the house of Judah in reign of King Jehoshaphat, 2 Chr. xix. 11. (8) One who returned with Ezra from the captivity, Ez. viii. 8. (9) A priest who had married a foreign wife, Ez. x. 20.

Zā′bah (*sacrifice*). One of the two Midianite kings slain by Gideon, Judg. viii. 5–21; Ps. lxxxiii. 11.

Zĕ-bā′im (*gazelles*). A disputed word, regarded as identical with Zeboim, Ez. ii. 57; Neh. vii. 59

Zĕb′ẹ-dee (*God's portion*). A fisherman of Galilee, husband of Salome, and father of the apostles James the Great and John, Matt. iv. 21; xxvii. 56; Mark i. 19, 20; xv. 40. His home is located at or near Bethsaida, and he appears to have been able to employ help in his occupation, Mark i. 20.

Zĕ̆-bī′nà (*buying*). A son of Nebo who had taken a foreign wife after the captivity, Ez. x. 43.

Zĕ̆-bō′im (*deer*). (1) One of the five cities of the plain, or circle, of Jordan, Gen. x. 19; Deut. xxix.

L 2

23; Hos. xi. 8. It is called Zeboiim in Gen. xiv. 2, 8. (2) A valley, or mountain gorge, contiguous to Michmash, 1 Sam. xiii. 18. (3) A place inhabited by Benjamites after the return from captivity, Neh. xi. 34.

Zĕ-bōi′ĭm, Gen. xiv. 2, 8. [ZEBOIM, 1.]

Zĕ-bū′dah (*given*). Wife of King Josiah and mother of King Jehoiakim, 2 Kgs. xxiii. 36.

Zē′bul (*habitation*). Ruler of the city of Shechem at the time of the contest between Abimelech and the native Canaanites, Judg. ix. 28–41.

Zĕb′u-lon-īte″, Judg. xii. 11. [ZEBULUNITES.]

Zĕb′u-lun (*dwelling*). (1) Tenth son of Jacob, and sixth and last by Leah, Gen. xxx. 20; xxxv. 23. Three sons are ascribed to him at the time of the migration to Egypt, Gen. xlvi. 14. Zebulun was one of the six tribes stationed on Ebal to pronounce the curse, Deut. xxvii. 13. The allotment of the tribe was bounded as in Josh. xix. 10–16, and in general stretched from Acre to Jordan, taking in the plain of Esdraelon. The tribe did not expel the natives in its allotment, but associated with them and fell into easy commercial intercourse with Phœnicia on the west, Judg. i. 30. It became an idolatrous tribe, 2 Chr. xxx. 10–18, and its territory was depopulated in the captivity of Israel by Tiglath-pileser, 2 Kgs. xv. 29. (2) A boundary place of Asher, Josh. xix. 27.

Zĕb′u-lun-ītes″. Descendants of Zebulun, Num. xxvi. 27.

Zĕch″a-rī′ah (*memory of God*). Son of Berechiah, Zech. i. 1; of Iddo, Ez. v. 1. Eleventh of the minor prophets and contemporary of Haggai, born in Babylon during the captivity, returned with Zerubbabel, Ez. v. 1; vi. 14. The time of his prophecies is reckoned as between B. C. 520 and 518, during the period of building the second temple, whose completion was largely due to his energies as priest and prophet. His book, 38th of O. T., is divided into two parts. Chapters i.-viii. contain hopeful visions of the restored Hebrew state, exhortations to turn to Jehovah, warnings against God's enemies. Chapters ix.-xiv. are prophetic of the future fortunes of the theocracy, the conversion of Israel, the glorification of God's kingdom and of the coming of the Messiah.

The style of the book is obscure. Many critics attribute the authorship of the second division of the book to Jeremiah. (2) A Reubenite chief, at time of the captivity by Tiglath-pileser, 1 Chr. v. 7. (3) A Korhite Levite, keeper of one of the doors of the tabernacle, 1 Chr. ix. 21. (4) A son of Jehiel, 1 Chr. ix. 37. (5) A Levite of the second order, one of the temple musicians, 1 Chr. xv. 18, 20. (6) A priest who blew the trumpet before the ark on its return, 1 Chr. xv. 24. (7) A Kohathite Levite, 1 Chr. xxiv. 25. (8) A Merarite Levite, 1 Chr. xxvi. 11. (9) A Manassite, 1 Chr. xxvii. 21. (10) A prince of Judah in reign of Jehoshaphat, 2 Chr. xvii. 7. (11) Father of Jahaziel, 2 Chr. xx. 14. (12) A son of Jehoshaphat, 2 Chr. xxi. 2. (13) Son of the high priest Jehoiada, in reign of Joash king of Judah, 2 Chr. xxiv. 20, and probably same as the Zacharias of Matt. xxiii. 35. (14) A prophet and royal counsellor in reign of Uzziah, 2 Chr. xxvi 5. (15) Father of Abijah, mother of King Hezekiah, 2 Chr. xxix. 1. (16) A member of the family of Asaph in time of Hezekiah, 2 Chr. xxix. 13. (17) A Kohathite Levite in the reign of Josiah, 2 Chr. xxxiv. 12. (18) One of the temple rulers in reign of Josiah, 2 Chr. xxxv. 8. (19) Nine priests, Levites and returned captives in Ez. viii. 3, 11, 16; x. 26; Neh. viii. 4; xi. 4, 5, 12; xii. 16, 35, 41. (20) A witness for Isaiah, Isa. viii. 2.

Ze'dăd (*hillside*). A landmark on the northern border of Canaan, Num. xxxiv. 8; Ezek. xlvii. 15.

Zĕd″ḙ-chī′as, 1 Esdr. i. 46. [ZEDEKIAH.]

Zĕd″ḙ-kī′ah (*justice of God*). (1) Last king of Judah, son of Josiah, and brother of Jehoahaz. He reigned eleven years, B. C. 598-588, 2 Kgs. xxiv. 18; 2 Chr. xxxvi. 11. He was raised to the throne by Nebuchadnezzar, who changed his name from Mattaniah to Zedekiah, 2 Kgs. xxiv. 17. In the ninth year of his reign, he revolted against Nebuchadnezzar, who thereupon completed the captivity of Judah and ended the kingdom, 2 Kgs. xxv. 1-21; 2 Chr. xxxvi. 11-21; Jer. xxi.-xxxviii.; Ezek. xvii. 15-21. (2) Son of Chenaanah, a prophet and head of the prophetic school in reign of Jehoshaphat, 1 Kgs. xxii.; 2 Chr. xviii. 10-24. (3) Son of Hananiah, and a court officer under Jehoiakim, Jer. xxxvi. 12. (4) A false prophet burnt to death by Nebuchadnezzar, Jer. xxix. 21, 22.

Zē'eb (*wolf*). A prince of Midian, slain by the Ephraimites, Judg. vii. 25; Ps. lxxxiii. 11.

Zē'eb, Wine=press of. The place where Zeeb was slain by the Ephraimites, Judg. vii. 25.

Zē'lah (*rib*). A city in Benjamin in which was located the family tomb of Kish, father of Saul, Josh. xviii. 28; 2 Sam. xxi. 14.

Zē'lek (*chasm*). An Ammonite and one of David's guard, 2 Sam. xxiii. 37; 1 Chr. xi. 39.

Zĕ-lō'phe-hăd (*firstborn*). A son of Hepher, descendant of Manasseh. The law of female inheritance was changed in favor of his daughters, Num. xxvi. 33; xxvii. 1-11; Josh. xvii. 3, 4; 1 Chr. vii. 15.

Zĕ-lō'tēs (*zealous*). A name added to that of the apostle Simon to distinguish him from Simon Peter, and to emphasize his membership of the party of Zealots, Luke vi. 15. [SIMON, 4.]

Zĕl'zah (*shade*). A place in the border of Benjamin, near which was Rachel's tomb, 1 Sam. x. 2.

Zĕm''a-rā'im (*two fleeces*). (1) A town in Benjamin, four miles north of Jericho, Josh. xviii. 22. (2) Mount Zemaraim in the mountains of Ephraim, 2 Chr. xiii. 4.

Zĕm'a-rīte. An Hamitic tribe or family descended from Canaan, Gen. x. 18; 1 Chr. i. 16.

Zĕ-mī'rā (*song*). Son of Becher, a descendant of Benjamin, 1 Chr. vii. 8.

Zē'nan (*target*). A town in the lowlands of Judah, Josh. xv. 37.

Zē'nas. A Christian lawyer whom Paul wished Titus to bring along with him, Tit. iii. 13.

Zĕph''a-nī'ah (*God's secret*). (1) Ninth in order of the twelve minor prophets. Son of Cushi and a descendant of Hezekiah. He flourished during the reign of King Josiah, B. c. 641-610. His prophecy constitutes the 36th O. T. book, and denounces Judah, Nineveh, and surrounding nations, and records many cheerful promises of gospel blessings. The style is characterized by grace, strength, and dignity. (2) Son of Maaseiah and priest in the reign of Zedekiah; Jer. xxi. 1; xxix. 25-29; xxxvii. 3; lii. 24-27. (3) A Kohathite Levite, 1 Chr. vi. 36. (4) Father of Josiah and Hen, Zech. vi. 10, 14.

Zē′phath (*watchtower*). An Amorite town in the mountains near Kadesh. Called Hormah after it was conquered by the Israelites, Judg. i. 17. [HORMAH.]

Zĕph′a-thah (*watchtower*). The valley near Mareshah in which King Asa marshalled his forces for battle against Zerah, 2 Chr. xiv. 9, 10.

Zē′phī, 1 Chr. i. 36. [ZEPHO.]

Zē′phŏ (*watchtower*). Zephi, 1 Chr. i. 36. One of the dukes of Edom, Gen. xxxvi. 11, 15.

Zē′phon (*watchman*). A son of Gad, Num. xxvi. 15. Called Ziphion in Gen. xlvi. 16.

Zē′phon-ītes. Descendants of Zephon, Num. xxvi. 15.

Zĕr (*flint*). A city in Naphtali, Josh. xix. 35.

Zē′rah (*eastern*). (1) A grandson of Esau and one of the dukes of Edom, Gen. xxxvi. 13, 17, 33; 1 Chr. i. 37, 44. (2) Num. xxvi. 20; Josh. vii. 1, 18; xxii. 20; 1 Chr. ii. 4, 6; ix. 6; Neh. xi. 24. [ZARAH.] (3) A son of Simeon and ancestor of a family of Zarhites, Num. xxvi. 13; 1 Chr. iv. 24. Called Zohar in Gen. xlvi. 10. (4) A Gershonite Levite, 1 Chr. vi. 21, 41. (5) An Ethiopian king whom Asa, king of Judah, defeated, 2 Chr. xiv. 9.

Zĕr″a-hī′ah (*rising of God*). (1) Son of Uzzi and priest of the line of Eleazar, 1 Chr. vi. 6, 51; Ez. vii. 4. (2) One whose descendants returned from captivity with Ezra, Ez. viii. 4.

Zē′red (*growth of reeds*). A brook or wady separating Moab from Edom, Deut. ii. 13, 14. Called Zared in Num. xxi. 12.

Zĕr′e-dȧ (*ambush*). Native place of Jeroboam, in the mountains of Ephraim, 1 Kgs. xi. 26.

Zē-rĕd′a-thah, 2 Chr. iv. 17. [ZARTHAN.]

Zĕr′e-rȧth, Judg. vii. 22. [ZARTHAN.]

Zē′resh. Wife of Haman, and his adviser in the conspiracy against Mordecai, Esth. v. 10-14.

Zē′reth (*bright*). A son of Ashur, founder of Tekoa, 1 Chr. iv. 7.

Zē′rī (*built*). A son of Jeduthun, a musician in the time of David, 1 Chr. xxv. 3.

Zē′rôr (*tied*). An ancestor of Kish, the father of Saul, 1 Sam. ix. 1.

Zĕ-ru'ah (*leprous*). Mother of King Jeroboam I., 1 Kgs. xi. 26.

Zĕ-rŭb'ba-bĕl (*born in Babylon*). He was of the family of David, and son of Shealtiel, Hag. i. 1, or Salathiel, Matt. i. 12, or Pedaiah, 1 Chr. iii. 19. Born at Babylon, commissioned governor of Judea by the Persian king, Cyrus, Neh. xii. 47; leader of the first colony of captives back to Jerusalem, B. C. 536, Ez. ii. 2; Neh. vii. 7; laid the foundation of the new temple, Zech. iv. 6–10; began the work of re-construction, in which he was greatly hindered by Samaritan opposition, and petty Persian intrigue; finally succeeded in completing the structure, restored the order of priests according to the institution of David, Ez. vi. 14–22; Hag. i. 12, 15; ii. 2–4. Zoro-babel in N. T., Matt. i. 12.

Zĕr''u-ī'ah (*bruised*). Sister of David and mo-ther of the three leading heroes of David's army, 1 Sam. xxvi. 6; 1 Chr. ii. 16.

Zē'tham (*olive*). A Levite, son of Laadan, 1 Chr. xxiii. 8; xxvi. 22.

Zē'than (*olive*). A son of Bilhan, of Benjamin, 1 Chr. vii. 10.

Zē'thär (*star*). One of the seven chamberlains of King Ahasuerus, Esth. i. 10.

Zī'á (*moving*). A Gadite, Chr. v. 13.

Zī'bà (*statue*). A steward of Saul, and tiller of the lands of Saul which David restored to Mephibo-sheth, 2 Sam. ix. 2–13; xvi. 1–4; xix. 17–29.

Zĭb'ę-on (*robber*). A Horite and son of Seir, Gen. xxxvi. 2, 24, 29; 1 Chr. i. 38, 40.

Zĭb'ī-à (*deer*). A Benjamite, 1 Chr. viii. 9.

Zĭb'ī-ah (*deer*). Mother of King Jehoash or Joash, 2 Kgs. xii. 1; 2 Chr. xxiv. 1.

Zĭch'rī (*remembered*). (1) A son of Izhar, son of Kohath, Ex. vi. 21. (2) A Benjamite of the sons of Shimhi, 1 Chr. viii. 19. (3) A Benjamite of the sons of Shashak, 1 Chr. viii. 23. (4) A Benjamite of the sons of Jeroham, 1 Chr. viii. 27. (5) A son of Asaph the musician, 1 Chr. ix. 15. Zabdi, Neh. xi. 17; Zaccur, Neh. xii. 35. (6) Son of Eliezer, a descendant of Moses, 1 Chr. xxvi. 25. (7) Father of Eliezer, a ruler of Reuben in reign cf David, 1 Chr. xxvii. 16. (8) Father of Amasiah, a captain of 200,000 men of valor under King Jehoshaphat, 2 Chr. xvii. 16. (9) Father of Elishaphat, a captain of hundreds under Jehoiada, 2 Chr. xxiii. 1. (10) A mighty man of Ephraim in the army of Pekah, 2 Chr. xxviii. 7. (11) A Benjamite, father of Joel, overseer of Jerusalem after the captivity, Neh. xi. 9. (12) Priest of the family of Abijah, Neh. xii. 17.

Zĭd′dim (*steeps*). A fenced city of Naphtali, Josh. xix. 35.

Zĭ′dŏn (*fishing*). The Sidon of Gen. x. 15, 19, the N. T., and Apocrypha. An ancient and wealthy commercial city of Phœnicia on the Mediterranean coast, twenty miles north of Tyre. It was a limit of the allotment of Asher, but was never conquered, Judg. i. 31; x. 12; xviii. 7, 28. The Zidonians assisted in building the temple, 1 Kgs. v. 6; 1 Chr. xxii. 4; Ezek. xxvii. 8. Israel imported her idolatries, 1 Kgs. xi. 5, 33; 2 Kgs. xxiii. 13. Paul's ship touched at Sidon, Acts xxvii. 3.

Zĭ-dō′nĭ-anṣ. Dwellers in Zidon, Judg. x. 12.

Zĭf (*bloom*). Second month of Hebrew sacred and eighth of the civil year, corresponding to parts of April and May, 1 Kgs. vi. 1.

Zĭ′hȧ (*dried*). (1) His children returned from captivity, Ez. ii. 43; Neh. vii. 46. (2) A ruler of the Nethinims in Ophel, Neh. xi. 21.

Zĭk′lăg (*flowing, winding*). A city in southern Judah, Josh. xv. 31, afterwards assigned to Simeon, Josh. xix. 5. It became of great historic importance as the rendezvous of David when outlawed by Ṣaul, and was then, or had just been, in the hands of the Philistines, 1 Sam. xxx. 1, 14, 26; 2 Sam. i. 1; iv. 10; 1 Chr. iv. 30; xii. 1-20.

Zĭl′lah (*shadow*). One of the wives of Lamech and mother of Tubal-cain, Gen. iv. 19, 22, 23.

Zĭl′pah (*dropping*). A Syrian woman who became Jacob's concubine and the mother of Gad and Asher, Gen. xxix. 24; xxx. 9-13; xxxv. 26; xxxvii. 2; xlvi. 18.

Zĭl′thāi (*shadow*). (1) A Benjamite of the sons of Shimhi, 1 Chr. viii. 20. (2) A Manassite captain who deserted to David at Ziklag, 1 Chr. xii. 20.

Zĭm′mah (*wickedness*). (1) A Gershonite Levite, son of Jahath, 1 Chr. vi. 20. (2) Another Gershonite

Levite, 1 Chr. vi. 42. (3) A Levite and father of Joah, 2 Chr. xxix. 12.

Zĭm'răn (*sung*). A son of Abraham by Keturah, Gen. xxv. 2; 1 Chr. i. 32.

Zĭm'rī (*sung*). (1) Son of Salu, a prince of Simeon slain by Phinehas, Num. xxv. 6-15. (2) Captain of half the chariots under Elah king of Israel. He smote his master in Tirsah, and reigned in his stead for a period of seven days, B. C. 929, 1 Kgs. xvi. 8-18. (3) A son of Zerah, of Judah, 1 Chr. ii. 6. Zabdi in Josh. vii. 1, 17, 18. (4) Son of Jehoadah and a descendant of Saul, 1 Chr. viii. 36; ix. 42. (5) An obscure name mentioned in Jer. xxv. 25.

Zĭn (*shrub*). That part of the Arabian wilderness or desert lying south of Palestine, adjacent to Judah, and bounded on the east by the Dead Sea and valley of Arabah; Num. xiii. 21, 26; xx. 1; xxvii. 14; xxxiii. 36; xxxiv. 3; Josh. xv. 1-3.

Zī'nà (*fruitful*). The second son of Shimei the Gershonite, 1 Chr. xxiii. 10. Zizah in vs. 11.

Zī'ŏn (*mount, sunny*). Zion or Sion in its literal and restricted sense was the celebrated mount in Jerusalem, the highest and southernmost or southwesternmost of the city. It was the original hill of the Jebusites, Josh. xv. 63. After David became king, he captured it, "the stronghold of Zion," from the Jebusites, dwelt in the fort there, and greatly enlarged and strengthened its fortifications, calling it "the city of David," 2 Sam. v. 6-9; 1 Chr. xi. 5-8. Despite David's prestige the name of Zion still clung to it, 1 Kgs. viii. 1; 2 Kgs. xix. 21, 31; 2 Chr. v. 2. The O. T. poets and prophets exalted the word Zion by frequent use and gave it a sacred turn, so that in time it came to type a sacred capital, Ps. ii. 6; holy place, Ps. lxxxvii. 2; cxlix. 2; Isa. xxx. 19; God's chosen people, Ps. li. 18; lxxxvii. 5; the Christian church, Heb. xii. 22; the heavenly city, Rev. xiv. 1.

Zī'or (*little*). A town in the mountains of Judah, Josh. xv. 54.

Zĭph (*that flows*). (1) An unidentified place in South Judah, Josh. xv. 24. (2) A town in the mountains of Judah, Josh. xv. 55. It was in the wilderness, or wastes, of Ziph that David hid himself when pursued by Saul, 1 Sam. xxiii. 14, 15, 24; xxvi. 2. (3) Son of Jehaleleel, of Judah, 1 Chr. iv. 16.

Zĭ'phah. A brother of the above, 1 Chr. iv. 16.

Zĭph'imş. Dwellers in Ziph, Ps. liv. title.

Zĭph'ītes. Dwellers in Ziph, 1 Sam. xxiii. 19.

Zĭph'ĭ-on, Gen. xlvi. 16. [ZEPHON.]

Zĭph'rŏn (*perfume*). A northern boundary of the promised land, Num. xxxiv. 9.

Zĭp'por (*little bird*). Father of Balak, king of Moab, Num. xxii. 2, 4, 10, 16 ; xxiii. 18.

Zĭp-pō'rah. A daughter of Reuel or Jethro, whom Moses married, Ex. ii. 16–22 ; iv. 25 ; xviii. 2–4.

Zĭth'rī (*protected*). A Kohathite Levite, son of Uzziel, Ex. vi. 22.

Zĭz (*cliff*). The cliff or pass of Ziz was that by which the Moabites and Ammonites came up from the shores of the Dead Sea to give battle to King Jehoshaphat's forces, 2 Chr. xx. 16.

Zī'zā (*plenty*). (1) A son of Shiphi and a prince of Simeon in the reign of Hezekiah, 1 Chr. iv. 37. (2) A son of King Rehoboam, 2 Chr. xi. 20.

Zī'zah (*plenty*), 1 Chr. xxiii. 11. [ZINA.]

Zō'an (*departure*). An ancient city of Lower Egypt, the Tanis of the Greeks and the San of modern times. It occupied a highly strategic position on the east side of the Tanitic branch of the Nile, and was built seven years before the very ancient city of Hebron, Num. xiii. 22. Isaiah mentions the " princes of Zoan," Isa. xix. 11–13 ; xxx. 4, and Ezekiel foretells its fate by fire, Ezek. xxx. 14.

Zō'ar (*little*). One of the most ancient cities of Canaan, mentioned as in the " plain of Jordan " and in connection with Sodom and Gomorrah, Gen. xiii. 10. It was originally called Bela, Gen. xiv. 2, 8. It was spared from the fiery destruction which came upon Sodom and the other cities of the plain, Gen. xix. 20–23. Isaiah and Jeremiah speak of Zoar as in the land of Moab, Isa. xv. 5 ; Jer. xlviii. 34.

Zō'bā, Zō'bah (*encampment*). That portion of Syria which formed a separate empire in the time of Saul, David, and Solomon. It lay to the northeast of Palestine and probably extended to the Euphrates. Though ruled by petty kings at first, it became united and strong and engaged in frequent wars with Israel, 1 Sam. xiv. 47 ; 2 Sam. viii. 3–8 ; x. 6–19 ; 1

Chr. xviii. 3–8 ; xix. 6. Hamath became the capital of Zobah, and it was captured by Solomon, 2 Chr. viii. 3.

Zō-bē′bah (*slothful*). A Judahite, 1 Chr. iv. 8.

Zō′har (*white*). (1) Father of Ephron, from whom Abraham bought the field of Machpelah, Gen. xxiii. 8; xxv. 9. (2) A son of Simeon, Gen. xlvi. 10 ; Ex. vi. 15. Zerah in 1 Chr. iv. 24.

Zō′he-lĕth (*serpent*). A stone or rock by En-rogel, where Adonijah slew "sheep, oxen, and fat cattle," 1 Kgs. i. 9.

Zō′heth. A Judahite, 1 Chr. iv. 20.

Zō′phah (*viol*). An Asherite, 1 Chr. vii. 35, 36.

Zō′phāi (*honeycomb*). A Kohathite Levite, 1 Chr. vi. 26. Written Zuph in vs. 35.

Zō′phar (*little bird*). A Naamathite, and one of the three friends of Job, Job ii. 11.

Zō′phim (*watchmen*). The field on the top of Pisgah to which Balak conducted Balaam for sacrifices, Num. xxiii. 14.

Zō′rah (*hornet*). A town in the lowlands of Judah, afterwards assigned to Dan, Josh. xix. 41. Written Zoreah in Josh. xv. 33, and Zareah in Neh. xi. 29. Residence of Manoah and burial place of his son Samson, Judg. xiii. 2, 24, 25 ; xvi. 31.

Zō′rath-ītes. Inhabitants of Zorah ; but the designation seems to be limited to the family of Judah descended from Shobal, 1 Chr. iv. 2.

Zō′re-ah, Josh. xv. 33. [ZORAH.]

Zō′rītes. Descendants of Salma of Judah, and probably dwellers in Zorah, 1 Chr. ii. 54.

Zŏ-rŏb′a-bĕl. Greek form of Zerubbabel, which *see*, Matt. i. 12, 13 ; Luke iii. 27.

Zū′ar (*little*). Father of Nethaneel, chief of Issachar, Num. i. 8 ; ii. 5 ; vii. 18, 23 ; x. 15.

Zŭph (*honeycomb*). (1) The land reached by Saul while in search of his father's asses, 1 Sam. ix. 5. It was there he met Samuel the prophet, 1 Sam. ix. 6–15. (2) A Kohathite Levite, and ancestor of Elkanah and Samuel, 1 Sam. i. 1 ; 1 Chr. vi. 35. Called Zophai in 1 Chr. vi. 26.

Zûr (*rock*). (1) A Midianite king slain by the Israel ites, Num. xxv. 15 ; xxxi. 8. (2) Son of Jehiel, foun der of Gibeon, 1 Chr. viii. 30 ; ix. 36.

Zŭ′rĭ-el. (*God my rock*). Son of Abihail, and a chief of the Merarite Levites, Num. iii. 35.

Zū′′rĭ-shăd′da-ī (*the Almighty my rock*). Father of Shelumiel, chief of the tribe of Simeon at the exodus, Num. i. 6; ii. 12; vii. 36; x. 19.

Zū′zims. An Ammonite name for one of the races of giants, Gen. xiv. 5.

CURIOUS FACTS AND INTERESTING INFORMATION ABOUT THE BIBLE.

The 66 Books or sub-divisions comprising the Old and New Testaments contain:

1,189 Chapters,
31,093 Verses,
773,692 Words,
3,586,489 Letters.

The Shortest Verse in the Bible is the 35th in the 11th Chapter of St. John.

The Longest Verse in the Bible is the 9th in the 8th Chapter of Esther.

The Middle Verse in the Bible is the 8th in the 118th Chapter of Psalms.

The 21st Verse of the 7th Chapter of Ezra contains all the letters of the Alphabet except "j."

The 8th, 15th, 21st and 31st Verses of the 107th Psalm are alike.

Every Verse in the 136th Psalm has the same ending.

The Longest Chapter is the 119th Psalm.

The Shortest Chapter is the 117th Psalm.

The word "Lord" occurs 7736 times in the Old and New Testaments.

The word "God" occurs 4370 times in the Old and New Testaments.

The words "Boy" and "Boys" are mentioned 3 times as follows: Gen. 25. 27; Joel 3. 3; Zech. 8. 5.

The words "Girl" and "Girls" are mentioned 2 times as follows: Joel 3. 3; Zech. 8. 5.

The name of "God" is not mentioned in the Book of Esther, or in the Song of Solomon (A. V.).

The 19th Chapter of II. Kings and the 37th Chapter of Isaiah are practically alike.

The Hart.

Wild Boar.

Absalom's Pillar. (*See* p. 9.)

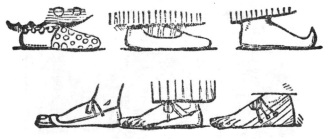

Sandals. (*See* p. 248.)

High Priest. (*See* Aaronites.)

Embroidered Robe.

Armlet.

Cuirass.

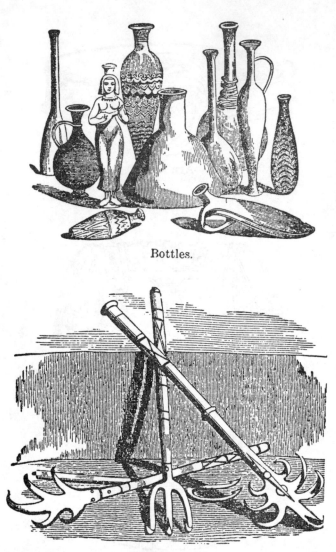

Bottles.

Flesh-hooks.

Carpenter Shop, Nazareth. (*See* p. 69.)

Coin of Macedonia.

Potter at Work. (*See* p. 228.)